In the second edition of the well-received *Research in Social Work*, the authors have updated their exposition of how research perspectives and methods can contribute to professional knowledge and practice. Among the additions are a chapter on naturalistic research design, and sections on research utilization, the use of research tools in assessment and a history of research in the profession. New material on qualitative methodology and process research has also been added. Combining stimulus and tools for the inexperienced investigator with more sophisticated methods of interest to more experienced researchers, *Research in Social Work* has something to offer all members of the profession who believe in the development of scientific but practical social work.

William J. Reid, Professor at the School of Social Welfare, the University at Albany, State University of New York, received his doctorate from Columbia University. He is the author of *Task-Centered Casework*, *Task-Centered Practice* (both with Laura Epstein), *The Task-Centered System*, and *Family Problem Solving*, in addition to numerous articles on social work practice and research methods. Until her death, **Audrey D. Smith** was an Associate Professor at the same school and an active participant in the revision of this widely-used work.

RESEARCH IN SOCIAL WORK

Second Edition

WILLIAM J. REID
AUDREY D. SMITH

RESEARCH IN SOCIAL WORK

SECOND EDITION

COLUMBIA UNIVERSITY PRESS
New York

LIBRARY OF CONGRESS CATALOGING-IN-PUBLICATION DATA

Reid, William James, 1928–
Research in social work / William J. Reid and Audrey D. Smith.—
2nd ed.
p.   cm.
Bibliography: p.
Includes index.
ISBN 0-231-06420-9
1. Social service—Research.   I. Smith, Audrey D.   II. Title.
HV11.R387 1989
361'.0072—dc19   88-31666
                                                           CIP

COLUMBIA UNIVERSITY PRESS
New York   Guildford, Surrey
Copyright © 1989 Columbia University Press

Book design by Ken Venezio

Audrey Smith, my co-author and wife, and I began the revision of this book in 1986. Shortly after work was commenced she became terminally ill; she died the following year. This edition is dedicated to her memory.

CONTENTS

PREFACE

A number of considerations often taken up in the preface, such as the purposes and plan of the book and how it may be used by different readers, are set forth in the initial chapter. But some important features of the book either did not fit into that presentation or bear restatement.

The book has been written for use by social work students and practitioners. With that purpose in mind we have tried to present research methodology as an instrument of professional social work practice. Thus the book begins, not with an introduction to research, but rather with a conception of social work. Our choice of research methods and our treatment of them have been guided by views of what social work is about and how research can best serve the interests of the profession. Accordingly, considerable attention is given to experimental strategies, as a central means of developing and testing social work interventions, to assessment of problems and needs, to measurement of the characteristics and outcomes of social work intervention, and to the research uses of social agency information systems. As these topics suggest, there is an overarching concern with evaluation research, so much so that we saw little point in devoting a chapter to that subject per se. If research is to be used to full advantage to advance the goals of social work, the profession needs to develop a climate in which both doing and consuming research are normal professional activities. By this we do not mean that all social workers should necessarily do research or that all practice should be based on the results of research, but rather that an ability to carry out studies at some level and a facility in using scientifically based knowledge should be an integral part of the skills that social workers have and use.

Several features of the book represent attempts to foster the development of such a climate. We try to provide stimulus and tools for carrying out modest studies—for example, through single case and exploratory experiments. More advanced methodology is presented to facilitate more complex studies and generally as a resource in the utilization of the kind of sophisticated research that is increasingly appearing in print.

An attempt is made to lay the basis for giving research a more persuasive and influential role in social work. In developing this theme we set forth a scientific framework for practice and examine applications of research concepts and techniques to the practice arena. We also argue that more use can be made of "softer" studies if their limitations are properly evaluated, particularly when one considers that the yield of such studies may often be considerably "harder" than knowledge based on practice wisdom or untested theory. In developing this argument a good deal of space is given to discussion of the nature of social work knowledge—to the epistemology of social work in effect. The discussion is not out of place in a book about research in a practice profession. In fact, the knowledge issues examined are, we think, fundamental in any consideration of research utilization.

Two innovations on a more technical level merit comment. We introduce a multi-dimensional framework for classification of research design (chapter 4). The framework, we hope, provides a clearer, more comprehensive and more accurate approach to design typology than conventional conceptions. In this respect we have been encouraged by the apparent ease with which this conception has been absorbed by the several classes of students who used drafts of the book as a research text. In our treatment of quantitative analysis, we briefly present and comment on several complex multivariate techniques such as multiple regression, factor analysis, and analysis of covariance. Our intent is to give readers a user's orientation to these methods since they are being used increasingly in research reported in social work journals. We realize that we may convey a less than satisfactory understanding of these methods even for consumer purposes, but assume that such a partial comprehension may be of value and perhaps preferable to total ignorance.

In the preface to the first edition, we expressed our gratitude to the many persons who facilitated our efforts to create a book about research in social work. Without their help the present edition would not have been possible.

I would like again to acknowledge the contributions off the following: Claudia Coulton, Elsie Pinkston, and Fred Seidl who read and commented on drafts of the manuscript; Rebecca Friedman, who co-authored a chapter; John Moore, presently Director of Columbia University Press, who stimulated the idea for the book and facilitated our work on it; and finally Stuart A. Kirk, who as our Dean created an optimal environment for work on both editions. Work on this edition was assisted immeasurably by colleagues and students who used the book and who provided suggestions on how it could be improved. Special thanks are due to Martin Bloom, Inger P. Davis, Anne E. Fortune, Susan Sherman, and Lynn Videka-Sherman.

For his tangible and intangible administrative support, throughout my work on the second edition, I am indebted to Richard Edwards, who served as Associate Dean and then acting Dean, School of Social Welfare, Nelson A. Rockefeller College of Public Affairs and Policy, University at Albany, State University of New York. Louise Waller, executive editor at Columbia University Press, provided valuable help during the final phase of this work. The conscientious editorial services of June Morier were most appreciated as well as the able assistance of my secretary, Jean D'Alessandro.

How does the present edition differ from the first? In addition to the usual updating of examples and references, rewriting for greater clarity, and correction of errors, several topics have been introduced or considerably expanded. Added material includes a new chapter on naturalistic designs, a discussion of research utilization, a more extensive exposition of qualitative methodology, a review of recent developments in the study of intervention processes and a brief history of social work research. To make room for these expansions certain cuts were made. Extended examples of outcome instruments were eliminated as well as the final chapter. These and other cuts involved material not seen to be integral to the book.

PART ONE

THE INTERFACE OF SOCIAL WORK
AND RESEARCH

CHAPTER 1

SOCIAL WORK AND RESEARCH

Since its beginnings, social work has attempted to develop a scientific base for its practice. This goal has remained an enduring ideal even though progress toward it has been modest. Despite growing research output during the past half century from the social sciences and the helping professions, a solid empirical foundation for social work practice has yet to be formed. Moreover, a good deal of the potentially relevant research produced has not been effectively used.

Research is only beginning to shed light on the complexities of the personal and social problems with which social workers are concerned; just as recent is the contribution of science to the testing and development of methods of effecting change in these problems. In their search for relevant knowledge, social workers have usually found the fragmentary, qualified, and often contradictory offerings of research studies of little practical help. Since research has not yet proved terribly useful, it is little wonder that front-line practitioners have traditionally turned to their own personal experience, to their supervisors, and to untested knowledge for guidance. Given this tradition, it is not surprising that research results of possible utility have not been put to work.

Although it may be true, as someone once said, that "social work is an art based on a science yet to be invented," the ideal of achieving a scientifically based practice persists. It does so, we think, because social workers sense the inadequacy of their knowledge base and of the helping methods derived from it. Science extends the hope of better knowledge and of more effective practice. Although this hope may not be realized to any substantial extent for some time to come, it provides a powerful incentive for the profession to keep trying. Its efforts in this direction are being shaped by the growing awareness that the benefits of science will be obtained in small degrees and that progress will be painfully slow. Within this long-range perspective the modest progress made in the cause of a scientifically based social work and recent signs that the cause may be gaining momentum provide encouragement.

PURPOSES OF BOOK

This book is designed to further that cause. We begin with a basic question: "How can the scientific method be best used to improve social work practice?" From that starting point two directions are pursued: One is to articulate research strategies and methods geared to specific knowledge needs of the profession—for example, to set forth ways of studying the problems, interventions, and outcomes central to the concerns of social work. The other direction is to explicate how a scientific point of view and particular research approaches can be used to enhance the performance of social work practitioners. In this second context, the scientific method is used, not to build durable knowledge as a base for practice, but rather to strengthen the carrying out of practice itself. The spelling out of these two directions is our principal task.

The book is designed as an introductory text for student and practicing social workers who presumably will make use of research in a variety of ways. A good number of our readers, we hope, will have occasion to conduct or participate in knowledge-building research. Although no introductory book about research methods can be expected to provide complete blueprints for even simple studies, we expect that this volume will present readers with an orientation and basic tools that will facilitate their own investigations. We recognize that doing research is not a common activity either for social work students or practitioners, but as the profession's emphasis on research increases, their involvement can be expected to grow. Moreover, it will grow more rapidly if stimulated and facilitated by instructional materials that present the how-to of research. We hope the present volume will serve that function. With that goal in mind, we have given particular emphasis to research designs and methods that students and practitioners can implement. Also with that goal in mind, we use the term *researcher* to denote, not a specialty, but rather a role, one that can be assumed by any social work student or professional who undertakes a study.

Whether or not they become involved in studies, our readers, with few exceptions we expect, will be engaged in some form of social work practice. The stress we give to the use of research concepts and method in the practice of social work should make the volume, or at least portions of it, worth reading to those who wish to explore ways of employing scientific thinking and procedures in their practice.

All social workers need to be able to comprehend and evaluate research products as a basis for intelligent use of scientific work in the field. This volume attempts to meet that need in part through a presentation of the strategies and methods used in conducting research. To be sure, readers unfamiliar with research can be taught skills of research "consumership" in a direct way. How to translate research language and to assess research reports can be presented and illustrated with actual studies (Tripodi. Fellin, and Meyer 1983). While such approaches have considerable value, they do not appear to be sufficient in themselves to serve as a basis for informed research consumership. To be understood properly, research needs to be understood on its own terms—as a set of problem-solving *activities*. Some knowledge of the nature of these activities and how they are organized is essential if their products are to be properly comprehended and assessed. If our intent were to train scientists ignorant of social work practice to be intelligent consumers of practice products, we would hardly limit our efforts to training them how to read and understand reports of cases or projects. We would wish to expose them to descriptions of the practice inputs that lead to the products, since practice, like research, has to be understood on *its* terms—again as a set of problem-solving activities.

Moreover, research consumership in social work practice involves more than readers' extracting and using knowledge produced by researchers. In many situations, researcher consumers—in the roles of program administrators and planners, for example—are also in a position to influence, or even to requisition, the research they are to use. Consumership at this level almost demands some knowledge of what researchers can and cannot be expected to do with a given problem.

Thus we do not see a volume that presents research as a set of methods as antithetical to the objectives of consumership. We assume that some portions of the volume—the sections on complex group experimental designs or multivariate analysis, for example—will be of value for most readers as consumers rather than as doers of research and have shaped them accordingly. On the other hand, we make no claim that our volume will provide the full complement of skills in research consumption necessary for social work practitioners to have in order to keep abreast of scientific developments in their fields of interest. No one volume can do this. Like other basic books about research in social work, ours provides only some of the tools needed for this task.

A CONCEPTION OF SOCIAL WORK

As we have said, we examine research methods from the standpoint of what social work requires. These requirements, as we see them, need then to be made clear at the outset. The great diversity of activities that might be considered social work makes it virtually impossible to define the profession in a succinct, discriminating, yet comprehensive manner. We attempt to bypass complex definitional issues by marking out a fairly broad domain in which most (though perhaps not all) social work falls. We then indicate what we see as the research priorities within this domain, priorities that guide our presentation of research strategies and methods.

In brief, our concern is with social work that in one way or another is directed at bringing about change in human systems. How such systems function and change, what problems they encounter, how professional intervention can help them work better, are the "master questions" to which our research methods are addressed. The remainder of the chapter is devoted to articulating the meaning and significance of these general statements.

Human Systems

The individual is the fundamental human system and, traditionally in social work, the most important. From the individual one moves up the scale of abstraction to more complex levels of social organization: to families, small groups, formal organizations, communities, states, and so on. With some exceptions, each higher level incorporates systems at lower levels. Thus communities include groups, which in turn are made up of individuals. A system begins to assume significance in practice when it is treated as a whole. Thus one can work with individuals in a community without considering the community as a whole, or one can define the needs of a community without reference to needs of particular individuals.

Social workers relate to these various systems in various ways. Any system may be viewed as an object of change, a client, or a resource to be used in bringing change about. In addition, one type of system—the formal organization—serves as the employer of all but a small minority of social workers.

Change Targets, Clients, and At-risk Populations

A "change target" or simply "target" is a generic term to describe the object of the social worker's efforts in work with human systems. A target can usually be defined as a particular problem, such as social isolation in an individual or delinquency in a community, a goal (to reduce conflict in a family) but may also be used in a general, unspecified way to refer to the system the practitioner hopes to affect—for example, an individual, group, or organization.

For the most part, the social worker's efforts to effect change are carried out on the behalf of clients. The word client is variously defined and used in social work, often with lack of clarity. In the strictist sense of the term, a client contracts with a social worker to perform certain services (Perlman 1957; Pincus and Minahan 1973; Garvin and Seabury 1984), but the term may also be used to denote individuals who, not always out of choice, are the objects of the social worker's attention ("involuntary clients"). A client may be any social system, in fact, the term "client system" is often used. A group or even a community may be regarded as a client.

In both social work practice and research, interest extends beyond current clients to groups from which clients are drawn or for which services may need to be developed. These groups, such as the frail elderly, the terminally ill, or troubled youth, are commonly referred to as "at-risk" populations.

Intervention

The social worker's efforts to bring about change in human systems are customarily referred to as "interventions." Intervention in social work may be defined more precisely in relation to two aspects: the system that constitutes the target of change and the system that is being worked with to bring the change about.

Systems as Media and Targets   The social system worked with may be the same as the system defined as the target of change, as in the case of work with an individual client to bring about changes in the client's functioning, or the two systems may differ; for example, the system worked with may be a formed group but the group may be formed for the purpose of helping individual members with their own problems. By juxtaposing these two aspects of intervention in relation to the social system—that is, the social system as target of change and as medium of work—it is possible to depict some of the variety and complexity of social work intervention. The grid in table 1.1 is an attempt to do this. Examples are provided to illustrate the types of intervention that can occur in various cells. The examples were selected (and deliberately varied in regard to level of abstraction) to provide a sense of the scope and variety of social work intervention.

The distinction made in the grid between a system as a medium of work and as a target of change merits further clarification. A system becomes a medium of work when the practitioner is in contact with it and is relating to it as a system—for example, when the practitioner is faced with a family in an interview or spends a day in conferences with representatives of a community. In such situations, the practitioner is usually interested in affecting the system she is working with but may wish to do so for tactical reasons and not to bring out any significant or enduring change in aspects of the system.*
In operational terms, a system becomes a target when some measure of change in its functioning, problems, or other attributes would be regarded as a measure of outcome to define the practitioner's success in a practice situation. Thus, in the example used for cell 3 (advising teacher how to set up token economy . . .), the practitioner would attempt to help the teacher do something different in her classroom itself. Success in the case would, at least in theory, be measured by a change in the occurrence of disruptive behavior in the classroom (and not by the teacher's acquisition of skills in classroom management).

As noted, a particular client system can be simultaneously the target of change and the medium of work. The cells on the diagonal of the grid (1, 8, 15, and so on) provide for such cases as well as for those involving different systems of the same type—for example, working with one organization to change another. A given case may utilize any number of cells. A practitioner may work with an organization to obtain housing for a client family (cell 20) and also work with the family as a whole to bring about change in one of its members (cell 7).

---

*Throughout this book we use the pronoun "she" for professionals, "he" for clients and other persons.

TABLE 1.1

Social Work Intervention in Relation to Social Systems

	System as Target of Change					
System as Medium of Work	Individual	Family	Small Group	Organization[a]	Neighborhood or Community	Class[b]
Individual	1	2	3	4	5	6
Family	7	8	9	10	11	12
Small group	13	14	15	16	17	18
Organization[a]	19	20	21	22	23	24
Neighborhood or community	25	26	27	28	29	30
Class[b]	31	32	33	34	35	36

[a] Includes sets of organizations.

[b] A class is a collective of persons who share common interests but who lack a well-defined group structure— for example, handicapped persons in a community.

Number of Cell	Selected Intervention Examples
1	Counseling interviews with client concerning personal problem
3	Advising teacher how to set up token economy to control disruptive behavior in her classroom
5	Securing funds from individual donors for a community center
8	Family therapy
13	Treatment of individuals through formed groups
14	Psychoeducational workshop for families with psychotic members
15	Street gang work
16	Conducting sensitivity groups to improve morale in an organization
19	Meeting with hospital personnel to obtain in-home care for patient
24	Work with a group of health and welfare organizations to coordinate services for the frail elderly
26	Meetings with neighborhood residents to improve climate for minority families
34	An effort to organize migrant farm workers to take action to secure more equitable treatment from local welfare department

Levels of Intervention The social system customarily worked with has been used in social work to define different levels of social work intervention. In recent years the designation *clinical social worker* has been used as a generic term for practitioners who work with small units—individuals, families, and small groups. Social workers whose medium is larger units, such as organizations, neighborhoods, and communities, assume roles such as administrators, community organizers, planners, and policy analysts. Expressions such as "micro" and "macro" practice are sometimes used to distinguish between work with smaller as opposed to larger systems. Practitioners whose work customarily involves both smaller and larger systems are considered to be generalists—for example, the practitioner whose focus may shift from helping a particular family obtain resources due it from an organization to helping residents of a neighborhood obtain their fair share of resources from the organization. There is probably an increasing tendency for social workers to engage in some mixture of roles, e.g., for administrators to carry caseloads and for clinical workers to be involved in some administrative and community organization activities.

Program and Case   The terms *program* and *case* have long been integral parts of the vocabulary of social work intervention, although changes in their meanings have taken place in recent years. As we use the term, a program refers broadly to intervention structured in relation to some particular type of method, target, or auspice. Thus we may refer to an assertiveness training program, a program or services for youth, or the program of a family agency. The term can be used to describe intervention of any scope—from work with a single client to a national undertaking. The latter point becomes particularly important in relation to program evaluation, which traditionally has been thought of as applying to programs of substantial scope. However, a practitioner who applies a program to a single client and studies its effects is also doing a form of program evaluation. (Briar and Blythe 1985).

Until recent years, the term *case* was used almost exclusively in social work to denote an individual client or client family, and the derivative term *casework* was applied to intervention at this level. With the development of generic approaches to social work, a broader conception of case has emerged (Hartman 1974). A case may still refer to an individual or family, of course, but may also be used to designate larger systems that may become the focus of intervention. Thus, if a hospital floor consitutes the unit of attention in a social worker's intervention efforts, it can be thought of as a case (Meyer 1979).

The extension of the concept of *program* downward to encompass single applications and of *case* upward to encompass larger systems serves a unifying purpose in social work. With these terms so defined, one can more readily link together activities, including research, of varying scope at different levels of human organization.

Roles and Skills   The actual processes of social work intervention have been described in terms of different roles and skills, (Simon and Aigner 1985; Sheafor and Landon 1987; Landon and Fiet 1987). Roles of group leader, family therapist, service broker, advocate, mediator, community organizer are among those that can be discerned from table 1.1. Although some of these roles may be used at only one level of practice, others appear across-the-board. For example, a social worker may advocate for an individual client or for a community group. Widely used skills include assessing, communicating, interviewing, analyzing, problem solving, planning, contracting, evaluating, and terminating. While all these and other activities occur in all forms of social work, their characteristics are shaped by the purposes and contexts of the type of practice they are applied to. Thus, at the micro level, communication techniques may be used largely to influence individual and family systems in clinical contexts.

At the macro level communication assumes a different purpose when used to influence community leaders in a social planning context. Still, generic skills, such as empathic listening, can be identified. One challenge is to separate generic from specific characteristics of communicative and other skills in social work practice. Another is to identify aspects of those skills that are distinctive of social work practice, as opposed to their use in other professional and occupational contexts.

IMPLICATIONS FOR RESEARCH METHODOLOGY

The foregoing conception of social work comprises, in our judgment, the core activities of the profession. It does not deal with questions about how these activities may differ from those of other human service professions, although perhaps the major distinguishing feature of social work is summed up by the grid itself. No other helping profession works with or attempts to affect such a wide range of human systems (Reid 1977).

To operate within this broad domain, social work uses knowledge from a wide variety of sources. Most of the knowledge yielded by the social sciences and other helping professions has some degree of relevance to the purposes of social work, and as a result the research methods used to generate such knowledge are equally relevant.

Our concern in this book, however, is with knowledge that social work itself needs to generate to inform its practice and the means of generating that knowledge. At its center lies knowledge to guide the activities of social workers in their efforts to bring about change—intervention knowledge, to use Fischer's (1978) term. Its essence is knowledge of which interventions are effective agents of change for which targets. But this knowledge in turn must be based on "assessment knowledge," knowledge of the targets themselves and the nature and functioning of the human systems that give rise to them. Whereas social work must of necessity obtain much of its knowledge of human systems from other disciplines, it must have its own capacity to develop this knowledge, particularly those elements that may inform intervention strategies. Thus, in developing a program to provide in-home services to the elderly in a community, a community planner might conduct a needs assessment study. A study of the stresses experienced by divorcing couples might be needed as a basis for constructing a divorce counseling model.

What is relevant to intervention and assessment knowledge is defined, not by the phenomena studied, but rather by the purposes of the study. As Fanshel (1980) suggests, investigations of the coping strengths of people who "live on the edge of disaster" but manage to survive should be of considerable interest to social workers (p. 9). But the interest would be sparked by what in the studies might add to our perspectives on intervention and assessment. We cannot help people use their strengths if our knowledge is limited to their weaknesses.

Whether they do or consume research, social workers need to have familiarity with a broad range of social research methods; nevertheless, a certain priorty within this range can be suggested. Research methods concerned with the study, testing, evaluation, and development of social work intervention should, we think, be given a first-order priority. This priority would call for emphasis on methods that would enable researchers to try out interventions under experimental conditions, to measure the characteristics and outcomes of these interventions, and to investigate human systems as a means of expanding intervention and assessment knowledge. The book is guided by this priority and in a large measure articulates it.

The scope of social work intervention, encompassing as it does virtually all levels of social organization, poses a particular challenge to any attempt to set forth the essential methodology of social work research. The challenge arises because study of systems at different levels and of intervention in relation to them calls for different emphases in research methods. Detailed treatment of all these varying emphases would require a work of encyclopedic proportions.

Our solution has been to focus on research methodology relevant to work with smaller social systems, individuals, families, and face-to-face groups. Our rationale for this decision is twofold. First, the bulk of social work activity occurs at this level. For example, according to the most recent data available (1982) over sixty percent of the employed members of the National Association of Social Workers (NASW) were reported to be in direct-service positions, which largely involve work with "micro systems" (Hopps and Pinderhughes 1987). The next largest groups, over a quarter of the members, were in administration, management, and supervision, but presumably a large portion of these social workers are connected to programs devoted primarily to providing direct services. A second reason is that we are more familiar with research methods used at the micro-systems level than at higher levels.

At the same time, through illustrations and other means, we attempt to present basic research methods in a way that would make them of interest to readers with a generalist orientation to social work. We also consider research strategies and procedures relevant to intervention at the macro level. Although they are taken up in less detail, at least beginnings that can be built upon by readers and instructors are provided.

Plan For Book

The book is divided into three parts. Part 1 (the present chapter and the next) provides a conception of social work and its relation to research. The contributions of research to social work are explored in some detail (chapter 2). An effort is made to specify the ingredients of scientifically based or empirical practice and to examine developments and issues that are a part of emerging interrelationships between research and practice. In part 2 the fundamentals of research methods are presented in a series of chapters that follow a conventional format: problem formulation (3), design (4, 5, 6, 7), sampling (8), measurement (9), data collection (10), and analysis (11). These methods are related to the framework and priorities set forth in this chapter. That is, our interest is centered on how research methodology can be used to help social work enhance the range and effectiveness of its interventions. This focus is pursued in part 3 in respect to aspects of data collection and measurement of particular interest to social work researchers and practitioners. How research can contribute to three essential tasks of the profession—assessment, evaluation of service outcome, and delineation of service characteristics—is taken up, respectively, in chapters 12, 13, and 14.

CHAPTER 2

THE CONTRIBUTION OF RESEARCH

How can science contribute to the diverse and multifaceted activities of social work? Social work practitioners and researchers have struggled with answers to this question since the beginnings of the profession. Although our own response to this question is in effect nothing less than this book itself, we indicate here what we see as the main components of the contribution of science to social work.

EMPIRICAL PRACTICE

At a fundamental level, science can provide a framework for practice activities. Practitioners who take a "scientific attitude" toward their work might be expected to gather systematic and accurate data about their clients' problems, to be cautious in making inferences from the data, to try to resolve discrepancies in evidence through further inquiry, to make use of relevant research to increase their understanding of their cases, and so on.

At this level of generality there is little disagreement in social work that practice should be scientifically based. Issues are likely to arise, however, at the level of specific application. This is to be expected. There are differing views about what constitutes "good" science. Even when there is accord on that point, there may be conflict about the appropriateness or extent of application of a given scientific dictum to a practice situation. How precise do practice data need to be? How much inference is it reasonable to use in interpreting them? What combination of empirical support from available research and from the case at hand is required before one can confidently apply a hypothesis to the case? What obligation do service practitioners or planners have to know to use relevant research in their work? To what extent should the demands of science be permitted to interfere with service require-ments? How much weight should be given to "practice wisdom" or untested theory as a base for practice and program decisions? These are examples of the host of difficult questions that arise when an attempt is made to bring a scientific perspective to the realities of social work practice.

One's conception of scientifically based or empirical practice depends, of course, on how such questions are answered. At this point our own concep-tions of this form of practice can be outlined only in general terms and perhaps can be best presented by suggesting how an empirical practitioner, as we see her, approaches her work.

First of all, she relies primarily on an *empirical language* as a means of depicting intervention targets and processes. That is, she uses a language clearly tied to empirical referents. Key terms can be spelled out or made operational in the form of specific indicators that can be observed and adequately measured. The indicators might be in the form of descriptions of behavior, or if concepts refer to internal processes, such as a client's self-image, the indicators might take the form of the client's statements or responses on a test. In any case, they are concrete pieces of evidence that can be communicated with sufficient clarity so that others can make their own assessment of them.

For example, if a couple complained that their communication was poor, the practitioner would try to help her clients define their poor communica-tion in terms of specific behaviors and occurrences, such as giving one another ambiguous messages, withholding information, and the like and would try to specify these indicators through even more concrete referents. What characterizes an ambiguous message? What kinds of information are withheld? The indicators might be quantified through counts of frequencies or ratings of intensity, although quantification of this kind, while often desirable, is not seen as an essential requirement of empirical practice.

Reliance on empirical language does not, of course, preclude the use of abstract concepts; without them one can hardly speak of either professional or scientific knowledge. But unfortunately most abstractions used in social work have neither precise nor commonly accepted meanings. This fact can be appreciated when we reflect on possible definitions of concepts commonly used by social work practitioners—concepts such as community power struc-ture, group cohesion, family balance, goal displacement, emotional neglect, permanency planning, ego strength, support, empathy, and advocacy. In empirical practice, abstractions of the kind just illustrated are assumed to convey only minimal information unless pinned to observable referents in the situation at hand. Thus, if a practitioner referred to a child as an "underachiever," she might specify this description by referring to a discrepancy between his scores on a scholastic aptitude test and his academic performance as measured by his grades. If a client is described as using the "defense of denial" to avoid recognizing his hostility, one should be able to specify responses that could be reliably classified as hostile as well as instances of the denial of the hostile import of these responses.

In addition to relying on empirical language, a scientifically based practitioner makes use, whenever possible, of *well-explicated practice models*. In any intervention approach there are hypothesized connections between the practitioner's interventions and change in the target of intervention. If the practitioner does X, then the client's functioning is likely to improve, a problem is likely to be alleviated, or some other desired change will probably occur. This statement is, of course, an oversimplification of typically more complex formulations that may make assumptions about the characteristics or actions of clients and others or factors relating to situational circumstances —for example, if the practitioner does X with Y type of client, then the client is likely to respond in Z manner, leading to a certain kind of change. By integrating diverse elements—targets, interventions, change, and so forth —into a coherent whole, such statements provide the theoretical structure of an intervention approach.

In well-explicated practice models, these connections are set forth in clear and specific terms so that it should be possible to obtain evidence that each link of the chain connects to another to produce a desired result. To the extent that such knowledge can be obtained, it becomes possible to demonstrate the effects of the approach with greater certainty and, perhaps of greater importance, to make specific improvements to increase its effectiveness or efficiency.

Examples of well-explicated models may be found in different types of social skill training programs (see, for example, LeCroy and Rose 1986). The absence of a skill, such as assertiveness, is identified; specific techniques— instruction, modeling, role play, coaching, and so on—are used to help the client learn the skill; and his performance of it is tested in simulated social situations. It becomes possible to trace clearly the process by which the skill is learned. As a result, weaknesses in the model can be identified and corrected through study of its operations. By contrast, processes of change may not be so readily discernible in an approach described only as "providing a nurturing relationship as a means of helping the client develop greater confidence in his own capacities." Such an approach may have great value, but, lacking better explication, the processes by which it achieves its effects would be difficult to sort out or study in a systematic way. Its operations would constitute a "black box." It may be impossible to secure evidence on what leads to what and hence to bring about improvements based on scientific knowledge. To bring the approach within an empirical practice framework, one would need to spell out its concepts and processes. What are the ingredients of a nurturing relationship? By what means specifically can it be provided, how does it affect clients, and how can we detect these effects?

Following principles set forth by Mullen (1983), practitioners can develop their own well-explicated personal practice models in which diverse methods can be combined and adapted. Or such methods can be put together within the kind of framework for eclectic practice devised by Fischer (1978). And, as suggested, most practice approaches can be made more explicit. This characteristic of empirical practice, as well as others, can be thought of as a matter of degree and can be advanced by degrees.

A third characteristic of a scientifically based approach to social work is the relative stress placed on *research-based knowledge and technology* as a means of informing and molding practice activities. In her attempts to identify and understand the target of intervention and to devise an intervention plan, the empirical practitioner would make use of a range of knowledge but in so doing would give priority to relevant knowledge supported by research findings, if such were available. She would consider untested knowledge but would regard it with skepticism. She would avoid wholesale application of belief systems that lack empirical support. Even if the knowledge were backed by research findings, it would be applied tentatively to the practice situation at hand and tested within that situation. The most that would be expected from available knowledge would be hypotheses that would need to be evaluated in the light of the realities of immediate concern to the practitioner. This is so because very little of the research-based knowledge that social workers use can be cast in the form of laws. At best, such knowledge states what is true for most situations. The practitioner needs to determine if the situation she is dealing with is one of the exceptions.

If such ad hoc testing is needed in any event, why should priority be given to research-supported knowledge? The priority can be justified on grounds that research support increases the probability that the knowledge in question does hold for the particular case. If there is evidence that a generalization has been found to be true in cases similar to the one at hand, one can posit that it is likely to be true in the present case. To accept this hypothesis, the practitioner may need to obtain only a small amount of confirming evidence from the case itself.

Suppose our practitioner is referred a child who has suddenly refused to go to school. She learns that this is the first time the child has had such a problem and that the child had missed two days of school the previous week because of illness and had failed a recent examination. There is research-supported knowledge suggesting that a child with these characteristics has a particular type of school phobia—one apt to occur in anxious children who are afraid of failure because of having missed school (Kennedy 1965). If parents are able to return the child to school at once, the phobia is usually short-lived and does not return. The practitioner may entertain a strong hypothesis that the child's behavior fits the general picture of this type of school phobia and may attempt to help the parents return the child to school. If the child responds as predicted, then the practitioner has confirmatory evidence that her hypothesis is correct. If the child does not, then the practitioner might abandon this premise and search for another. It is also evident that ad hoc tests of hypotheses can be accomplished more effectively with research-based knowledge than with other kinds since the former knowledge is expressed in researchable form; that is, concepts have been put in operational terms, measurement approaches have been worked out, and so on. While it is then true that each practice situation constitutes, for the empirical practitioner, a miniature study, the study is more likely to bear fruit if based on results of prior research.

Similarly, the practitioner gives priority to practice technology whose effectiveness has been demonstrated through research. In considering what intervention methods to employ, the practitioner gives weight to those that have been tested and those that appear to be the more promising in terms of the evidence revealed by the tests. But again, application is carried forward by means of further testing in the immediate practice situation.

However much priority is given to it, research-based knowledge can provide only a limited amount of guidance to practitioners. In their attempts to make sense out of the complexities of practical situations, practitioners must continually deal with knowledge and information that cannot be readily connected to a research base. But in so doing they can nevertheless employ the kind of logic that characterizes scientific work. Another attribute then of the type of practitioner we have been discussing is her use of *scientific reasoning* to order phenomena encountered in practice—for example, to construct explanations for problems, for processes of change, and for the role of intervention in bringing change about.

One facet of scientific reasoning—formulating and testing hypotheses derived from research-based knowledge—has already been described. More generally, the same process of testing generalizations against data obtained in the situation at hand is used in applications of all forms of knowledge. Such deductive reasoning is combined with inductive approaches, in which one attempts to form generalizations from the particulars of a situation. Whether using inductive or deductive modes of reasoning, the practitioner is concerned about the quality of her data and is cautious in making inferences about them. Moreover, she searches for alternative sources of explanation and does not limit herself to any one set of theoretical formulations. In considering alternative theoretical explanations, she favors the one that can account for the data at hand in the most parsimonious fashion.

For example, if faced with a client who is depressed for no apparent reason, the practitioner attempts to obtain data that might bear upon the causes of his depression and may consider a variety of possible theories to formulate an explanation. There may be some evidence to suggest that the client is harboring a good deal of resentment against his mother; other evidence may suggest that he has suffered a blow to his self-image at work. There may be indications that his wife is particularly attentive when he complains of feeling blue. There are hints that he has begun to question the meaningfulness of goals that were always important to him. Let us suppose —we can almost assert—that each piece of data points in different theoretical directions, none of which has convincing empirical support. Following a scientific mode of analysis, the practitioner would not form a hasty explanation on the basis of preconceived beliefs about the validity of a particular theory but would rather obtain further data in relation to different theoretical possibilities. She would form a tentative explanation on the basis of what best seemed to account for the data obtained, an explanation that might well be altered in the light of new evidence. Suppose further that the client's depression lifted during subsequent treatment. She would not necessarily assume that the remission was caused by her intervention or that it proved the correctness of her explanation of his problem. She would evaluate these possibilities in relation to other possible explanations that might be suggested by the data of the case.

In applying research-based knowledge and technology and in using scientific reasoning, the practitioner, as we have noted, engages in forms of research activity—such as data collection and hypothesis testing. More generally, a scientifically based approach can be characterized by *its use of research methods as an integral part* of practice (Ivanoff, Blythe, and Briar 1987). In addition to gathering data to test hypotheses in practice situations, practitioners may use research instruments for assessing intervention targets or providing feedback on the immediate consequences of interventions. They may also conduct evaluative studies of single cases or of ongoing programs to improve practice operations. In other words, research is employed as a tool for gathering systematic knowledge about activities in the "here and now."

The last two mentioned characteristics of empirical practice pertain to use of research products and methods within practice situations. These applications draw upon fundamental contributions of research to social work practice, even though it may not be scientifically based in our definition. The full scope of these contributions will now be examined.

BUILDING KNOWLEDGE AND TECHNOLOGY

Whether or not practice is scientifically based in the sense described, science can contribute to practice through generating knowledge and technology relevant to its purposes. (As we argue, however, this contribution can be augmented considerably if practice is done within a scientific framework.)

By knowledge we mean generalizations about phenomena supported by evidence. Technology, as we use the term, applies to the means—practice methods, principles, and so on—that social workers use to achieve their objectives. Although knowledge and technology in social work may look alike—for example, both may be expressed in print—they are fundamentally different. In a knowledge statement we assert that something is true; the assertion can be tested and evaluated in the light of evidence obtained. A statement of technology, on the other hand, can be cast into the form of directives or guidelines for action. Such a statement asserts nothing about the nature of phenomena; rather, it prescribes ways of changing them. Technology makes no truth claims, only claims for utility and effectiveness. We accept knowledge if it is true, technology if it works.

A principal function of knowledge in social work is to inform technology. Thus, knowledge of human problems is used as a basis for developing methods to alleviate them. Conversely, a good deal of knowledge is about technology, as illustrated by assertions about how particular methods may work with particular types of clients. Since these assertions are subject to verification, they qualify as statements of knowledge, or presumed knowledge. The extent to which they are verified will, of course, influence decisions about the technologies in question.

When we refer to the contribution of research to *building* knowledge and technology, we have in mind products that have value beyond an immediate situation, that are preserved—normally through the written word—and disseminated. (One cannot build if one's efforts leave no permanent results.) It is true that a good deal of knowledge and technology is created to solve immediate problems and is not preserved; for example, one may develop ideas and methods unique to the case at hand. Because the research designed to generate these specific and impermanent forms of knowledge and technology has a rather different character, it is considered separately at a later point.

Knowledge Building

Examining first the role of research in knowledge building, we are immediately struck by the considerable breadth of knowledge relevant to the purposes of social work. Such knowledge covers a vast domain, including most of the output of the social sciences; selected knowledge from related practice fields such as psychiatry, education, and law; and, of course, knowledge produced by social work itself. Considering the huge and steadily growing body of literature from these sources, one might conclude (some have) that social work has at its disposal more knowledge than it can use. A closer look suggests otherwise. To be sure, a great deal of knowledge exists, but most of it does not prove to be remarkably useful in social work practice. What seems to be most needed is discriminating and validated knowledge concerning the nature and causes of target problems and the dynamics of social systems that create (or resolve problems) and, more than anything else, knowledge of what interventions produce which effects for which problems. Unfortunately, knowledge of this kind is sorely lacking.

Certainly much has been written and spoken about these subjects, but the knowledge yield from this verbal harvest is distressingly low. For generalizations to form useful knowledge, they need to have sufficient breadth to apply to a range of circumstances and yet be specific enough to reduce uncertainty; above all, they need to be backed by adequate evidence.

The central contribution of research to knowledge building in social work is to provide empirical evidence for generalizations. This objective may be achieved through studies that create or suggest generalizations supported by data or through studies that bring evidence to bear on generalizations derived from theory, practice wisdom, or other sources. In some cases, scientific study may buttress these generalizations, or in other cases it will qualify them; in still others it will reveal no support for the beliefs in question. In all these cases research is contributing to knowledge building, even if its contribution takes the form of invalidating false assertions masquerading as knowledge.

The processes by which research builds knowledge are dealt with in greater detail in subsequent chapters, which consider the central role of theory in the organization of knowledge and inquiry (chapter 3) and the particular functions of research in knowledge building (chapter 4). And in a large sense the remainder of this book is an explication of this process. At this beginning stage, we address ourselves to some fundamental questions concerning the function of knowledge in social work and the place of research in its development.

In a profession such as social work the purpose of building knowledge is to improve practice. To be useful, generalizations must be applied to particular practice situations, whether in the form of the problem of a single client or the needs of a community. Few generalizations are true of all situations. Most are made on the assumption that there is some probability they will hold in a given situation. Thus, if we assert that unemployment among youth tends to produce criminal activity, we could expect this generalization to have some likelihood of holding (being true) for a particular community. What such a probability might be is usually unknown but is assumed—if the generalization is used as knowledge—to be high enough to influence practice decisions. In the final analysis this usually means only that the probability that a given generalization will hold is assumed to be greater than the probability assigned to some alternative generalization. Operating in the face of considerable uncertainty as most social work practitioners must do, what is taken to be knowledge may be the most probable of some range of plausible alternative generalizations.

Even when the most probable generalization is selected, there is no guarantee that its application will be advantageous. The generalization may be, as most are, overinclusive. We may wish to know what consequences result from relocation of a client of a particular age, in a particular set of circumstances, but we have knowledge about consequences of relocating aged people in general. Even if made to order, the generalization may not hold because the situation in question turns out to be an exception to the general rule. Our efforts to build knowledge are aimed largely at producing discriminating generalizations with a fairly high probability of being true when applied to particular situations. Research contributes to this objective by forming and testing presumed generalizations or hypotheses and by generating evidence that bears upon the "probable truth" of these and other generalizations. Research does not prove anything "for sure"; rather, it provides evidence suggesting that some things are more likely to be true than others.

From the perspective of empirical practice, preferred knowledge is that backed by the strongest evidence, assumed to be evidence generated by research. This knowledge may be questionable by the usual standards of science, but it may be better—more likely to be true—than available alternatives. This argument becomes more persuasive, we think, when some of these alternatives are considered.

First of all, many, perhaps most, generalizations applicable to social work contain at best only a modest amount of potentially useful content. Truisms are common. "Alcoholism creates problems in family relations." While such statements may not be challenged, they hardly provide much enlightenment to practitioners. At about the same level in respect to knowledge value are vague or obscure generalizations—statements that contain abstract terms whose meanings are not clear and are not explicated. Little knowledge is conveyed since what is being asserted is not apparent. Also frequently encountered are statements suggesting that certain phenomena or relations may possibly occur. "Borderline clients may make infantile demands." While such statements may in fact be true, they do not provide the practitioner with much guidance; in other words, they do little to reduce uncertainty. They inform practitioners about possibilities to watch for and may prove stimulating to the less informed but do little beyond that. There are important differences, we think, between being alerted or stimulated and having knowledge about how things are and what to do about them.

Statements that assert probable truths are, of course, a different matter. (People receiving public assistance are likely to be motivated to obtain decent jobs.) In fact, probabilistic statements of truth—those that assert that X will be found in most situations—are about the best that can be expected.

Unfortunately, many such generalizations offer only the promise of useful knowledge. Upon analysis they turn out to be not tested knowledge but rather what might be better called "unsubstantiated expertise." We have reference here to statements that would be useful, if true, but their truth is not apparent and substantiating evidence is lacking. This is not to say that unsubstantiated expert opinion is necessarily wrong, but simply that it should be treated with skepticism, regardless of the qualifications of the expert or her sources of information. In social work, much of this expert opinion is presumably based on practice experience—in fact, the term *practice wisdom* has been devised to describe it. Because practice wisdom has evolved to meet the knowledge needs of practitioners, it is generally highly relevant to practice, and since it is presumably based on the realities of practice, it seems to provide some assurance of validity.

The empirical foundations of practice wisdom are often difficult to discern or evaluate, however, since they are seldom articulated. Some assertions may be backed by a considerable amount of carefully evaluated evidence sifted from practice experience; others may be based on biased impressions of unrepresentative examples. A common source of error is the development of questionable generalizations based on a few situations that seem to conform to some pattern. These generalizations may then be presented as knowledge and thereby create the expectation that what has been asserted is true. The originators of the generalizations and others using them may then look for additional confirming examples. Given this kind of expectancy, confirming examples are likely to be discovered, and examples that do not fit are likely to be overlooked or perhaps interpreted as if they were confirming. Through these processes of biased observation and interpretation, the original general-izations may appear to "hold up" in practice applications and thus begin to assume the status of "tested"' knowledge.

Against this backdrop, generalizations for which some research evidence can be produced become more attractive. If the probing of a piece of practice wisdom reveals that it is based on some possibly biased impressions of a few cases, then a generalization grounded in a sizable number of cases systemat-ically studied may prove to offer a better basis for practice decisions, even though the research may be scarcely definitive.

This is not to say that knowledge presumably derived from research should be accepted with any less degree of skepticism or caution than practice wisdom. Research evidence can prove just as illusory as evidence gained from practice.

As subsequent chapters document, social work research is vulnerable to error from many sources. Most instruments provide at best crude and partial measures of complex social phenomena. The validity of data is inevitably threatened by two layers of human bias. At the level of data collection, the biases of subjects and their immediate observers may give false impressions of events under study. At the level of data analysis, interpretation, and reporting, biases of investigators may shape ambiguous findings in hoped-for directions.

What is more, generalizations presumably based on research often do considerable violence to the data that presumably support them. Intervention effects may be claimed on the basis of studies in which other plausible causes of problem change cannot be ruled out. Factors affecting social systems may be given dynamic (causal) interpretations on the basis of poorly controlled correlational evidence. In what are probably the most frequent sins of all, generalizations may be unreasonably extended beyond the limits of available research findings or may ignore contradictory evidence.

Despite all this, knowledge produced by research retains crucial advantages over unsubstantiated expertise. Research builds knowledge over unsubstantiated expertise. Research builds knowledge through processes that are both self-corrective and cumulative. As experience is gathered, more effective methodologies evolve. As a body of research grows, convergences in findings do appear, and studies fraught with error fall to one side. Moreover, the shortcomings of research-based knowledge are more readily identified. If a statement claims some universal truth on the basis of a few equivocal studies of the legendary college sophomore, diligent readers are at least given the opportunity to search out the evidence and to form their own judgment about it.

Our conception of the contribution of research to knowledge building in social work contains an apparent paradox. On the one hand, we have argued that the role of research in producing "verified propositions" is largely illusory and should be minimized. On the other, we have suggested that priority be given to research-based knowledge. The paradox is resolved by a simple notion: that all knowledge should be evaluated against a common standard of evidence and that knowledge backed by the best evidence should be preferred. As a rule, research produces evidence that is of a better grade and more open to critical assessment than other sources do.

Research evidence should be given the same hard look as any kind of evidence, but it should be looked at from the same vantage point from which other evidence is regarded. Thus one should not dismiss the evidence yielded by research because it fails to meet some absolute standard of scientific acceptability and at the same time embrace beliefs for which far less credible evidence exists.

If this position is accepted, then greater practical value can be placed on research that is highly relevant to the interests of practitioners but that may lack rigor in design and measurement—research that has sometimes been dismissed as "merely exploratory," "impressionistic," or "soft." A study may be so characterized yet still make a useful contribution to the pool of knowledge used by practitioners, since it may deliver knowledge as good as can be obtained by other means or offer some knowledge where none exists. For purposes of the present discussion we include qualitative studies in this type of research, although, as we shall argue subsequently (chapter 4), qualitative methodology is based on its own premises and need not be (though often is) regarded as inferior to quantitative methodology.

We are not arguing for a shift from more rigorous research that may be of less immediate relevance to less rigorous investigations of pressing practice issues. We need more of both, particularly studies that are highly rigorous and relevant. Rather, we are arguing that studies of "low quality" by classical scientific standards be mined for useful knowledge rather than disregarded. Proper mining is, of course, the key. One must be able to distinguish between illumination and error, not an easy task in a study that may be fraught with the latter. But this is a task that social workers need to perfect in their quest for knowledge from whatever source.

To put the foregoing arguments into a realistic perspective, we must recognize that practitioners acquire knowledge from many sources. In fact, research and expert opinion are only contributions to a larger fund of "personal" knowledge that practitioners acquire from firsthand experience "on the job." As Rein (1981) contends, much of this knowledge is situation specific and involves knowing particular configurations of setting, problems, clients, interventions, and so on. At a practical level, the question becomes, how can research harden and expand these funds of knowledge? The task is not simple, since few research-based generalizations may fit the particulars of the situations practitioners face. Still, an empirical orientation toward practice, the evaluation of practice wisdom and research against a common standard of evidence, and the active use of research at all levels of rigor should help further the process.

Contributions to Technology

Traditionally the contribution of research to constructing practice technology has occurred indirectly—and not very systematically—through its knowledge-building function. In this tradition, research produces knowledge that then is to be used to guide the development of practice methods. There is a marked division of labor between researchers who conduct studies and managers or practitioners ("program people") who, it is hoped, make use of them. Whatever impact research has on practice is made through reports that must be read, digested, and applied by those with practice responsibilities.

Perennial problems inherent in applying research to the improvement of services have been addressed in recent years by two quite different kinds of efforts. One has to do with the utilization by service providers of conventional forms of research evaluation and practice-related research; the other concerns new uses of research in the development of service models.

Utilization Social work researchers have long bemoaned the apparent lack of proper utilization of their work by program managers and practitioners. "Our studies are ignored, or misused," researchers complain; to which program people may reply, "Your studies are likely to be off-target, incomprehensible, out of date, or otherwise uninformative." In an effort to move beyond the sterile acrimony of such disputes, researchers have increasingly turned their attention to the study of the utilization process itself.

Early uses of the notion of utilization in service research contexts assumed a straightforward decision-making model in which the utilizer applied research findings to decisions about services. In studies of utilization it became apparent this kind of "instrumental" utilization did not occur frequently and was perhaps overshadowed by a more amorphous but pervasive type which has been referred to as "conceptual utilization" (Rich 1977). In conceptual utilization, findings are not directly acted upon but rather are added to the storehouse of contextual information possessed by the decision maker, which may include knowledge from many other sources. The findings may exercise an indirect and delayed influence through complex information processing in which their influence may be impossible to trace. It has been also noted that findings may be used as ammunition to advance a particular point of view, a type of utilization that has been termed "persuasive" (Rich 1977).

In an effort to provide some grounding and unity to these diverse ideas, Leviton and Hughes (1981) have developed a "bottom line criterion" for defining utilization. Regardless of type of utilization "there must be evidence that in the absence of the research information, those engaged in policy or program activities would have thought or acted differently" (p. 527). Thus to be considered utilized, findings must have a traceable impact, although the impact may be limited to changes in beliefs or attitudes.

These formulations help clarify two central issues in the utilization of effectiveness research in agency contexts. One of these issues has concerned the low rate of instrumental utilization and the failure to develop proved means of facilitating this kind of utilization. A second issue concerns difficulties in sorting out the complexities of conceptual utilization and in constructing models to understand and study it. These issues can be combined if we view utilization as essentially "conceptual," at least in respect to a domain as intricate as research in service processes and effectiveness. One can legitimately view virtually all utilization of service research data by program managers and practitioners in terms of complex cognitive and organizational processes in which the data constitutes one of a variety of inputs. Research information is joined with such other considerations as the staff's own impressions of effectiveness, informal case reports, general knowledge, available alternatives, and cost factors. This process may produce new insight but, as Weiss and Bucuvalas (1980) document, seldom produces a clear-cut decision. Rather what is learned may affect program people in a collective decision-making process that is responsive to an even wider range of considerations.

Strategies for enabling service providers to become better utilizers have emphasized closer working relationships between providers and researchers. As utilization studies have suggested, agency staff members are more likely to use research that relates to immediate problems, is concerned with the effectiveness of program elements rather than overall effectiveness, and fits with their own fund of knowledge (Leviton and Hughes 1980; McNeece, DiNitto, and Johnson 1983). Such findings support Patton's (1978) approach for "utilization-oriented" evaluations, in which studies are geared to specific utilization decisions. Other proposals have called for training managers in utilization skills (Rapp 1984; Pauley and Cohen 1984) and at least one training model has been tested with encouraging results (Pauley and Cohen 1984).

As more is learned about utilization processes, it is hoped that better utilization strategies and techniques can be devised. Meanwhile, the idea of conceptual utilization provides a way of understanding the intricacies of these processes and also helps identify important kinds of utilization that have heretofore been neglected. Research may have more impact than researchers assume, though often not in the manner intended.

Research and Development; Developmental Research In recent years we have seen the emergence of a quite different strategy for applying research to the improvement of social work services: the use of research to develop service approaches. In one form this strategy has taken, available research is used as a basis for designing a service model, which is then tested, evaluated, and disseminated. This strategy, referred to as *social research and development* (social R&D), makes use of concepts and methods of industrial research and development (Rothman 1980). Another form, *developmental research*, makes use of research as well as practice experience and other sources of knowledge in a continuous process of designing, testing, and modifying a service model (Thomas 1984, 1978; Briar 1980; Reid 1987). Developmental research, which has been used more widely in social work and has perhaps a broader range of application, will be examined more closely.

Developmental research in social work is designed to devise and build practice models. Its main product is not a report but rather a service approach, as set forth in descriptions of procedures to be used in practice. Studies are not done by research specialists in the hope they may be used by practitioners; rather, they are performed by persons who function as both researchers and model developers. These practitioner-researchers in effect use their own research in the development of practice models.

A preliminary practice model may be devised from existing research, theory, clinical trial and error, or other sources. The model, or elements of it, is subjected to a series of tests in which data are collected on the operations of the model and its apparent outcomes. Data from each test are used to revise the model prior to subsequent testing; in this way, the model can be progressively improved in the light of research data. Different (and not necessarily mutually exclusive) patterns may be followed. In a "constructive" strategy (Kazdin 1986), one begins by testing and perfecting a single practice method. Methods may be developed and tested separately; those proving effective may then be combined. Or one may use a "dismantling" strategy (Kazdin 1986), that is, begin with a package of interventions and, through subsequent varying and testing components, attempt to replace those that do not contribute to the effectiveness of the package and to maximize the role of those that do. Development may take the form of testing a model with different, and perhaps progressively more challenging, targets. The starting point may be a laboratory analog of an intervention. The analog is first developed and tested under highly controlled conditions and then applied to actual practice situations.

Since its purpose is to create new and superior practice technologies, a developmental research strategy offers a direct route between research activity and improvement of service. The self-corrective powers of research can be used in a systematic and efficient way in the process of model construction. Research designs and instruments for model testing can be progressively developed to provide an optimum fit to the requirements of the model. Some intransigent obstacles to research utilization are bypassed. To use the fruits of research and development, it is not necessary for practitioners to absorb and apply research reports; rather, they can apply the products resulting from the research. This evolving strategy seems to be a major step forward. Thomas (1978) puts the point more strongly, "Developmental research may be the single most appropriate model of research for social work because it consists of methods directed explicitly toward the analysis, development, and evaluation of the very technical means by which social work objectives are achieved" (p. 470).

There is evidence that a successful beginning has been made in using a developmental research strategy in social work. In the great majority of recent (post-1972) controlled group experiments in social work, the interventions tested were developed by the experimenters themselves, a pattern not often seen in earlier social work experiments. And most of these recent experiments have yielded positive results (Reid and Hanrahan 1982; Rubin 1985). An excellent example of developmental research in social work is provided by the efforts of Sheldon Rose and his associates to devise and test methods of social skills training (see for example Rose 1975; Berger and Rose 1977; Toseland and Rose 1978; LeCroy and Rose 1986).

Although developmental research approaches need to be vigorously pursued, they are themselves at an inchoate stage of development. Little is known or has been articulated about the best types of project designs to employ at different stages of model development, how these designs can be best sequenced, and how study results can be best used to inform model development.

Moreover, developmental research can help create service models but cannot ensure that they will be used at all or used appropriately in service programs. For this reason, it makes sense to conceive of research, development, and utilization strategies. This expansion of the term highlights the importance of utilization but does nothing, of course, to solve utilization problems. Although it is fashionable to use the vocabulary of engineers in referring to service models produced by research and development as "products," these products are usually not apparatuses that can be put to work with proper instructions. They consist rather of complicated, often incomplete and overgeneral, guidelines for practitioners to use. Proper use may require substantial traning and changes in accustomed work habits and practice beliefs, all of which may encounter agency and staff resistance. Unlike an apparatus, practice models can be readily picked apart by users who may incorporate some elements (usually after refashioning them somewhat) into their own practice and junk the rest.

As a result of these (and other) obstacles, the "dissemination" of service models of proved effectiveness into an ongoing program provides no assurance whatsoever about the effectiveness of the model (or parts of it) that may be used in the program. In fact, it does not even provide assurance that the methods will be used at all. The challenge is particularly great when the attempt is made to transplant practice models cultivated under the protected conditions of special projects into the turbulent climates of ongoing agency programs.

SUPPORT FOR OPERATIONS

In building knowledge and technology, science leaves a permanent product in such forms as a report, an article, or set of guidelines for practice. Through the accumulation of products, a body of research-based knowledge and technology can be built. A different function for scientific methods obtains when these methods are used to support immediate practice operations. Here the goal is not to add to a general body of knowledge and technology but rather to get a job done. Research is applied in whatever way it can best serve this goal; a lasting product is not necessary; if obtained at all, it is regarded as a secondary benefit. In such situations research can be said to serve an "operational function."

This type of research activity, sometimes referred to as operations research, has been most frequently identified in social work in relation to the management of organizations. Thus an agency executive may do a time study as a basis for reaching a decision about the most efficient use of staff or may use data from the agency's information system to determine costs of a particular program. But the notion of operations research can be readily extended to social work practice in other contexts. As part of a social action undertaking a community worker may conduct an on-the-spot survey of attitudes of neighborhood residents toward an impending highway construction program that would affect the neighborhood. A group worker might obtain sociometric measures of attraction among group members. A school social worker who is trying to help a child improve his classroom behavior might do an observational study of the child in different classrooms. In the last three examples the practitioners were using research methods in a way similar to the administrator in the first example—to collect systematic data as a means of guiding job performance. In short, all were engaged in operations research, as we define it.

Just as it is difficult to draw clear lines around scientifically based practice, it may be hard to make distinctions between operations research and other forms of practice activity. It is relatively easy to separate research from other things when the research takes the form of a full-scale project. It is another matter when reference is made to the use of particular research methods within the context of practice. For example, where does one draw the line between the careful observation that any good practitioner might make of a child's behavior and the kind of observation that might be regarded as a research method? The answer to questions of this kind lies, we think, in the extent of systematization that characterizes an activity. A quick glance may be quite informative but would be hardly called research; on the other hand, the observation of carefully defined behavior across randomly selected observational periods might well be designated as use of a research method. The distinction is clearly one of degree rather than kind and thus may not always be clear-cut. Certainly when use is made in practice of methods of data collection, measurment, and the like, of the kind that are employed in full-scale research undertakings, one can reasonably say that operations research is occurring.

The distinction between research that builds knowledge and technology and research that supports operations also merits comment. While some research activities clearly express one function or the other, a good deal of research in social work may serve both functions. A program evaluation may be undertaken to improve an agency's service, but the results of the evaluation may be published and thus add to general knowledge of the program evaluated. Developmental research can produce technology for general use and at the same time can bring about immediate changes in agency operations. Because our interest is in clarifying the different contributions or functions of research rather than in classifying particular research activities, this overlap presents no severe problem. When terms such as "operations research" or "knowledge-building research" are used, reference is to activities that are predominantly one or the other.

In keeping with the focus of this book, our interest in operations research is centered on its contribution to social work intervention. This contribution can be largely expressed in terms of three key functions: assessment of intervention targets, feedback concerning intervention efforts, and accountability.

At the assessment stage, research methods are used to collect data on needs, problems, and other characteristics of client systems or populations for which service may be planned. Surveys of community problems and needs for the purpose of program planning have had a long history in social work. Recent developments at this level have included refinements in methods of needs assessment (chapter 12) and the use of available computerized data on client and community characteristics. Of more recent origin has been use of research methods in assessment in clinical social work. Although methods that might have been used for this purpose, such as standardized diagnostic instruments, have long been available, it was assumed that the practitioner could obtain more meaningful data more quickly through the clinical interview. Moreover, the use of tests, structured observations, and the like, was seen as impeding the formation of a therapeutic relationship. Finally, social workers were likely to view themselves as lacking expertise in this area; testing was regarded as the special province of clinical psychologists. While these traditions live on, clinical social workers are increasingly using a growing variety of systematic data collection methods in the assessment process. This trend has been stimulated by the development of a number of standardized instruments that are simple and quick to administer and score (Levitt and Reid 1981; Edlesen 1985; Toseland and Reid 1985; Ivanoff *et al.* 1986). Some, in fact, have been designed for use by social workers. (See, for example, Hudson 1982.) The influence of the behavioral movement has resulted in greater use of methods such as direct observation of client behavior in natural settings, systematic client self-recording, and analysis of communication among family members.

When research methods are used to facilitate assessment, the practitioner hopes to obtain data that will help inform decisions about intervention and that would not otherwise be obtained. At the present state of the art, these criteria are perhaps more readily met when the target is a large complex social system, such as a community, than when it is a smaller system such as an individual or family. The requirements of rational planning for a program to serve the recreational needs of teenagers in a community would almost dictate a survey of need, either of the adolescents themselves or of informed members of the community. A practitioner with a client who can talk of little else except his depression may learn nothing more about the problem from administering the Beck Depression Inventory (Beck 1967). But clinical situations are not always this clear-cut. Even self-report instruments, particularly in the case of families or other multiple client systems, can often reveal important data that may not surface in a clinical interview.

The feedback function of operations research provides social workers with data that may be used to modify their interventions in a desired direction. Whether carried out in a single case or as a large-scale program, interventions are directed toward goals. How well the interventions in the case, program, and so forth, are meeting goals set for them is always a matter of concern. Feedback is a means of providing information about performance in relation to goals (Buckley 1967). In the context of social work intervention, feedback consists primarily of information about what has been done, its costs, and apparent outcomes. Data of this kind can be used to steer the intervention effort in desired directions.

Thus a program or elements of it may be evaluated through means such as reviews of case records, questionnaires from clients, or analysis of statistics on program inputs and costs. Increasingly, such data are being routinely collected and stored in computerized information systems that facilitate rapid retrieval and analysis (Rapp 1984; Mutschler and Cnaan 1985; Schoech 1987). Operations research at this level may range from a full-scale program support to pinpointed data collection and analysis concerning a specific program facet—for example, the discharge rates of children from foster care (Finch and Fanshel 1985).

For the line practitioner, systematic data may serve comparable functions in helping to steer intervention in a single case or in helping the practitioner through a series of single case evaluations to form judgments about which interventions work best for her in given kinds of case situations. The methodology of single-case research has been suggested as a means of carrying out this function (Bloom and Fischer 1982; chapter 6). Aggregating single case studies can provide agencies with a base for program evaluation (Briar and Blythe 1985).

Although beginnings have been made, the use of research to provide feedback on intervention has not yet been incorporated as an established part of social work practice. There are several reasons why this is so. Good quality data may be costly to obtain and process and, if obtained, may not be used. The data may lack relevance to immediate program decisions, may not be in a form that decision makers can readily comprehend, and may not be ready when decisions need to be made. Or the data may run counter to strongly held convictions. The amount of potentially useful information provided by research operations far exceeds the amount actually used. And unless they are utilized, operations research data fail to provide a feedback function.

Although new forms of single-case methodology have provided the direct-service practitioner with tools to guide her interventions and shape her practice, their use is not yet widespread. Lack of staff training in this methodology, pressures of high work loads, and the lack of paradigms for its application to nonbehavioral forms of practice have been among the obstacles impeding the use of methods of the single-case study as a feedback mechanism. However, elements of this methodology may be used with some frequency by practitioners who have been trained to use it (Richey, Blythe, and Berlin 1987).

Operations research performs an accountability function by providing data that can be used to determine the extent to which intervention efforts meet certain standards in their implementation and achievement. This function may make use of much the same kind of data that may be acquired in the process of obtaining feedback on programs or cases, but it shapes such data to a different purpose. The purpose is not to modify an intervention effort but rather to delineate what was done and what was accomplished. This information can then be used by supervisors, administrators, funding sources, or others who bear some responsibility for the effort in their appraisals of its merit, utility, compliance to agreed-upon terms, and the like. The immediate question is not "How can we do a better job?" but rather "Is the job we are doing good enough?"

Whereas the same research operations may yield data that may satisfy both feedback and accountability purposes, this is not always the case. Thus certain kinds of data may be useful in assessing the feasibility of a program in its early stages and in modifying the program accordingly but might be too preliminary for purposes of accountability. Conversely, it may be necessary to obtain certain data on types and numbers of clients served, on overall program expenditures, and on impact that might not be helpful for purposes of feedback—in fact, it may have been already decided not to continue the program—but that might be necessary to give a proper accounting to a funding body.

Accountability is receiving increasing emphasis in social agencies (Sarri 1982). Funds for social programs have tightened and skepticism about their accomplishments has grown. Also, public agencies, more and more, are purchasing services from the voluntary sector rather than providing them directly (Poertner and Rapp 1985). Demands for data on what is being done and how well have become more insistent. These demands have resulted in an increasing flow of accountability data to funding agencies.

The contributions of science to practice, which have thus far been considered more of less in isolation, are mutually reinforcing. Empirical practice creates a demand for knowledge and technology informed by research; moreover, such practice requires the use of operations research as a means of realizing its scientific promises. Practitioners who operate within an empirical framework are more likely not only to use research but also to know how to use it. By the same token, since empirical practice trades in readily measurable concepts, explicit methods, and specific effects, it facilitates knowledge-building inquiry and use of research methods in operational contexts.

Historical Perspective

These functions have been present and evolving since the beginnings of the profession. A brief historical overview will help put them in perspective.

A *scientific orientation* to social work was articulated in the late nineteenth century in the scientific philanthropy movement. The aim was to make the giving of relief to the poor a scientific endeavor. Science could provide the necessary understanding of pauperism, and the scientific method could be used for systematic study and treatment of individual cases.

The subsequent evolution of this perspective can be most clearly traced in casework, whose practice, supervision, and management accounted for the bulk of professional activity in social work. In *Social Diagnosis*, Mary Richmond (1917) set forth the first major statement of the principles and methods of casework. In her formulation, a social diagnosis was brought about through scientific problem solving. Facts were gathered to serve as the basis for hypotheses which were then to be tested by obtaining relevant evidence. Although the psychoanalytic movement that began in the next decade introduced radically new theories and interventions for casework, it too was the product of nineteenth century science. Although diagnosis became more psychiatric than social in the next several decades, the paradigm of study, diagnosis, and treatment following presumed scientific principles remained intact. Florence Hollis, a leading advocate of psychoanalytically-oriented casework, expressed this continuity: "Casework is a scientific art. Certainly since the days of Mary Richmond we have been committed to objective examination of the facts of each case. We draw inferences from those facts, we diagnose, we view the individual against a frame of reference which is itself the product of informal research. We constantly alert ourselves to sources of error" (1963:13).

More recently, alternative conceptions of a scientific orientation have emerged. Behavioral social work has placed greater emphasis upon measurable constructs and phenomena. Ecological social work, following the ideas of the biologist René Dubos (1965), has shifted the center of attention from the defects of the individual to "systems in mutual interaction" (Germain 1970:29). In casework, as well as in social work generally, the issue has not been one of a scientific versus a nonscientific orientation as a framework for practice. The issue has been rather the kind of scientific model to follow. A contemporary expression of this issue is discussed in chapter 4.

The role of research in building knowledge for practice also had its roots in the scientific philanthropy movement. Energies were first directed to identifying the causes of social problems—poverty, delinquency, and so on. Early studies were by today's standards naive and primitive, but they expressed the beginning of a continuing need to establish a scientific knowledge base for social work. The early leaders of the profession hoped that social work might follow the example of medicine and engineering in drawing its knowledge from basic sciences. For social work, the logical knowledge base seemed to lie in the social sciences, with ancillary sources in related helping disciplines.

Again, the process of evolution can be most clearly seen in casework. In 1929, the Report of the Milford Conference suggested the following as a base for casework: biology, economics, law, medicine, psychiatry, sociology and statistics (*Social Casework: Generic and Specific*, 1974). To this group Maurice Karpf (1931) added anthropology, education, and social psychology in one of the first major works concerned with the scientific base of social work.

Despite projections of a diversified knowledge base, one discipline, psychiatry, emerged as the dominant intellectual source for casework. Not only did one school of psychiatry—psychoanalysis—provide most of this knowledge but also molded much professional practice into a form of personal therapy.

The knowledge base of casework began to become more diverse in the fifties when the increasing scientific output of the social sciences and the helping disciplines began to have an impact. This diversification was stimulated by criticisms of the scientific credibility of psychoanalytic knowledge as well as by a growing awareness of its lack of fit to the kind of interpersonal and social problems of concern to social work. It is noteworthy that the diversity in the scientific base of casework, or direct practice to use a more inclusive and contemporary term, was realized only as practice itself became more diversified with the advent of behavioral, cognitive, family systems, ecological, and other intervention models that began to appear in the fifties and sixties. Other kinds of knowledge began to be utilized when views about the purposes and methods of practice themselves began to diversify.

Another kind of development in the scientific base of the profession has been an increased emphasis on intervention knowledge (Fischer 1978) or knowledge of the processes and effects of given intervention strategies with given types of clients or problems. Although the drive to investigate the nature of social work practice and its effects had early beginnings, it did not begin to develop momentum until the late forties. Attempts were made to study processes of client change through content analysis of process recordings (Dollard and Mowrer 1947) and to scale client movement (Hunt 1948). Efforts at classification of casework methods began to appear (Austin 1948; Hollis 1949). The spotlight, however, fell on a series of controlled experiments designed to test the effectiveness of different types of direct social work practice. (For reviews of these studies, see Mullen and Dumpson 1972; Fischer 1973; Wood 1978.) Unfortunately, most of these studies failed to provide convincing evidence that the methods tested were in fact effective, thus producing little in the way of positive intervention knowledge. With the development of new forms of practice and improvements in research design, experiments more recently, as noted earlier, have provided support for the effectiveness of a variety of social work interventions for a range of types of clients and problems (Reid and Hanrahan 1982; Rubin 1985).

Despite progress on this and other fronts, knowledge underlying direct practice in social work has hardly amounted to the scientific base that has been hoped for (and whose existence has been often asserted). Still apropos are the observations of Briar and Miller (1971:84) who described the underpinnings of casework as "a proliferation of bits and pieces of 'hard' and 'soft' knowledge—fragmented and disjointed."

These words could as well be applied to the knowledge foundations of the "macro" level of social work practice, such as community work, administration, and social action. Throughout its history, macro social work has made use of the social sciences as sources of knowledge but research-based knowledge relevant to practice at this level has been slow to accumulate and is probably even less substantial than that available for direct or micro practice. At all levels of social work an unforeseen development has been the tendency of practice itself to outdistance its knowledge base. New forms and areas of practice have emerged at a more rapid pace than research that might inform them. Rather than leading innovation, as is commonly the case in medicine and engineering, research in social work has tended to follow it, often at a good distance.

Thus, a hundred years of effort to construct a base of scientific knowledge for the profession has fallen far short of the enthusiastic hopes of the pioneers. There is now a greater appreciation of the reality that research-based knowledge can be only a part, albeit an important one, of a vast network of information that informs practice. Newer research strategies, such as developmental research and social R&D, offer hope of forging more direct and solid links between research and practice.

Action or operations research in social work found its earliest major expression in the survey movement, which began in earnest in the 1900s. The movement was spurred by increasing urban problems in poverty, housing, working conditions, child care, and so on, and took place in a progressive political climate. There was little doubt about the intent of the surveys. As Zimbalist has said "the social survey movement was first and foremost a means of publicizing the needs of the community in as compelling a manner as possible, so as to galvanize the populace into taking remedial action. Facts were gathered and analyzed as a means to this end" (1955:70). Following the monumental Pittsburg survey in 1908, the movement spread rapidly throughout the country, leading to countless applications of this method. The leading social work journal of the time, *Charities and Commons*, was in fact renamed *Survey*, an indicator of how much the movement had penetrated the intellectual life of the field.

Although the survey movement was oversold by enthusiastic advocates, did not achieve its claims as an instrument of reform, and within two decades was no longer a major force, it did lead to some instances of social change and served to focus attention on the ills of urbanization. Moreover, it was the predecessor of most contemporary forms of the needs assessment study (chapter 12). Other forms of operations research, including program evaluation, statistical reporting of services, and index construction were all in evidence at the beginning of the century.

As these examples suggest, social work has a long tradition of using research procedures and data to inform and guide its programs and activities. Although this use of research does not produce scientific knowledge (in the sense of a body of verified propositions), it has enlightened practice decisions and may be as important to professional practice as knowledge-building investigations. Also, as the examples suggest, most applications have occurred at the level of macro social work. In the past two decades, however, research procedures and tools, such as systematic observation and standardized tests, have been used increasingly at the level of direct practice with individuals, families, and groups—a development stimulated by (but not confined) to the behavioral movement in social work.

PART TWO

THE FUNDAMENTALS OF RESEARCH
IN SOCIAL WORK CONTEXTS

CHAPTER 3

GENERATION OF INQUIRY

All research is directed by some form of inquiry. In the most obvious case, questions are posed and data collected to answer them. The role of inquiry is less obvious when research is conducted to test a hypothesis; a study may begin, not with a question, but rather with a prediction, and data are obtained to determine if the prediction holds for a given situation. Yet hypothesis testing proves to be another form of inquiry. Researchers want to find out if their hypotheses will hold. If they knew for sure that they did (or did not), there would be no reason to test them.

Inquiry is also fundamental to social work practice. Before intervening or during the processes of intervention, a practitioner's actions are guided by answers to a stream of questions. What is my client like? What is the problem? What progress is being made? What effects are my interventions having? What data can I collect to determine if a piece of theory applies in my case? It is not surprising that various studies have indicated that some form of "exploration" is the dominant practitioner activity of individualized social work practice (Fortune 1981). At a more general level, inquiry stimulates the knowledge-building efforts of social work practitioners and scholars, who make use of a variety of sources of data, research among them. They seek answers to an endless variety of questions. What differentiates parents who abuse their children from those who do not? What are the risks in relocating the frail elderly? How effective is group home treatment for juvenile offenders?

It is our contention that the first stage of inquiry in social work—determining what it is one wishes to learn—can be profitably viewed within a common framework, regardless of the subsequent form the inquiry may take.

That is, the researcher interested in conducting a study, a service practitioner who wishes to learn more about her client, or an administrator who wishes to determine what is known about the effectiveness of a particular service, must go through much the same intellectual process. Aspects of this process have been delineated for inquiry that has purely scientific objectives. By combining these aspects with considerations important to social work, it is possible to develop a framework that will prove useful in pursuing a variety of forms of inquiry, from formal studies to knowledge-gathering efforts in practice contexts. This chapter is devoted primarily to that objective but also takes up more technical aspects of problem formulation used in knowledge-building research.

THEORY

In a practice profession such as social work, inquiry has its roots in the need to generate knowledge to inform practice, whether that knowledge only guides efforts in an immediate situation or is added to the pool available to the field as a whole. But to be useful for this purpose, knowledge must be organized into coherent systems of ideas or theories. Knowledge may be thought of as providing the raw material from which theories are made.

An example will perhaps make this distinction clearer, as well as provide an introduction to our conception of theory. It has been found that clients want more advice than social workers usually provide (Reid and Shapiro 1969; Davis 1975; Ewalt and Kutz 1976). There is also research evidence to suggest that clients are more likely to react negatively than positively to social workers' advice at the time it is offered (Davis 1975). Moreover, it is a common observation of social workers that clients frequently do not follow the advice they are given. Let us assume that these observations constitute pieces of knowledge. As disparate pieces their value would be limited—in fact, they seem contradictory. They become more useful when organized into a system of ideas or theory. In the present case it was theorized that clients want advice, usually more than they are given (even though they may not agree with it or may not use it), because advice seems to stimulate their own thinking about alternative actions that they might take to lessen their difficulties (Reid and Shapiro 1969; Davis 1975).

As the example has shown, theory attempts to organize knowledge into thought systems by which reality can be better understood. Although the example illustrates the essential difference between knowledge and theory and how theory may be formed from knowledge, it does not give the sense of a fully developed theory. One might attempt to build such a theory, however, by incorporating additional pieces of knowledge about the giving and taking of advice in social work practice. For example, knowledge that lower-class clients show greater preference for advice than middle-class clients do (Goldstein 1973) would need to be accounted for in the construction of the theory, as well as the fact that some pieces of advice are indeed acted on (Davis 1975). One would also soon wish to make distinctions between different types of advice and advice giving and the attempt to identify different consequences stemming from use of each.

As the example makes clear, theory is not the opposite of "fact," contrary to the popular distinction. Rather, theory organizes fact or knowledge into systems. It is true, however, that theory may contain hypotheses that have not yet been tested or verified. Such hypotheses may be derived (inferred) from knowledge incorporated in the theory or may be added to provide a more coherent system of explanation.

In Print and in Use

Nor is the theory limited to the printed page. Scratch any social worker and you will find a theoretician. Her own theoretical perspectives about people and practice may be informed by theories in print (or formal theories) but are put together in her own way with many modifications and additions growing out of her own professional and personal experience.

In a practice profession, as Argyris and Schön (1974) observe, it is the theory in use that counts. Our ultimate interest is not in what is contained in print but in what is used in the field. If we pay more attention to the former, it is largely because it is more accessible to scrutiny. In a similar vein Kaplan (1964) has noted the differences between the "reconstructed logic" one finds in textbooks on scientific method and logic in use that characterizes the problem solving of scientists.

Theory in use is an almost inevitable concomitant of any kind of social work activity, whether one is serving a client or formulating a research problem. A practitioner's interview with a person who has made a suicidal gesture may be guided by her theory that such actions are likely to be prompted by a desire to make someone feel guilty; the practitioner is then likely to construct a more elaborate "theory of the case" to explain her client's behavior. A researcher may combine elements of sociological and psychological theories in an effort to develop a set of hypotheses concerning factors associated with attempts of youngsters to run away from an institution.

Definitional and Explanatory Functions

In general we can say that a theory is a system of concepts and hypotheses that attempt to define, explain, and predict phenomena. As a *system* of concepts and hypotheses, a theory, as we have seen, organizes units of knowledge. It provides connective tissue that unites disparate elements of what is presumed to be true. This organization of knowledge serves functions that are essential to practitioners' efforts to comprehend and influence the realities with which they must deal.

At a basic level, theory provides a coherent way of defining and ordering complex events. In performing this "definitional" function, theory presents sets of concepts and terms that enable the practitioner to comprehend and describe aspects of reality that otherwise might be difficult to order or that might escape attention altogether. Thus Watzlawick, Beavin, and Jackson (1967), communication theorists, develop the notion that any interpersonal communication has both a "content" and "relationship" aspect—that is, it "not only conveys information, but . . . at the same time it imposes behavior" (p. 51). If a wife unexpectedly announces to her husband that they are going to the Smiths' for dinner on Friday, her message has "content" (concerning plans for Friday) but also reflects on their relationship (that she appears to assume a controlling position in social matters). These concepts help us examine communication processes in a systematic way and, more specifically, alert us to less obvious, but vital, facets of those processes (the relationship aspects). It is clear, however, that the function of theory here is definitional—no hypotheses that might explain or predict communication are contained in the distinction.

Theory becomes potentially more useful if it can produce hypotheses that explain or predict events. In a preceding example a theory was developed containing a hypothesis that explained why clients might seek advice but not use it. Explanatory or causal hypotheses are at the heart of theories that practitioners find most valuable, since such hypotheses provide the "whys" of problems and behavior and the rationale for intervention. The thoughtful practitioner intervenes in a particular way because she has reason to suppose that the intervention will be effective. The "reason to suppose" is derived from a causal hypothesis existing in some form of theoretical structure. Thus, a practitioner who points out to the client the consequences of his behavior is being guided by a hypothesis that such awareness will have an impact on the client's behavior, a hypothesis related to others in a theory of intervention.

To say that a theory has an explanatory function says nothing about its actual power to explain. A theory is explanatory to the extent it contains causal hypotheses. Whether or not those hypotheses prove to be correct is another matter. While one may refer to the validity of a theory, it is perhaps more accurate to assess a theory in relation to its capacity to generate hypotheses that are confirmed when tested. In these terms a good theory is one that generates valid hypotheses.

Most explanatory theories that social workers use are rich in causal hypotheses, but relatively few of these hypotheses have been rigorously tested and, of those that have, even fewer have been consistently supported. In fact, with some of these theories—psychoanalytic theory is a prime example—it proved difficult even to extract hypotheses amenable to empirical testing.

Practice Theory

Of central interest to the profession is social work practice theory, which consists of hypotheses that guide the social worker's diagnostic and intervention activities. There are, of course, numerous practice theories in social work relating to different types of practice (such as with families, groups, and communities) or to different theoretical orientations (psychodynamic, behavioral, and so on). Despite their variation, practice theories are similar in function. At their core are explanatory hypotheses that predict that certain kind of changes in certain kinds of targets will result from certain kinds of interventions.

As can be surmised, practice theory organizes the knowledge base that underlies the practice principles, methods, models—in short, the practice technology—that social workers use. Thus, the hypothesis that use of a combination of verbal limit setting and emphatic response in a therapeutic interview with an acting-out child will enhance the child's participation in the interview (Broxmeyer 1978) serves as the base for a practice principle or method that can be used in interviews with such children. Note that practice theory serves as a base for technology but that practice theory and technology are not the same. In essence, practice theory says, "If X is done, Y will follow"; technology tells us "do X to achieve Y." As we move from theory to technology, we introduce desirable goals or values that convert "what we expect to happen" into "how to bring about what we want to happen." The distinction is parallel to that between knowledge and technology (chapter 2).

Practice theory, then, occupies a pivotal role in social work. To be used in professional activities, theories from other domains need to be translated into practice theory, which in turn can be translated into practice technology. From the hypothesis that A will lead to B (that verbal limit setting and emphatic response will increase a child's participation in an interview), one must construct principles and methods that state in effect "do A to achieve B." (To increase the child's participation in the interview, the practitioner should both set verbal limits and respond emphatically.)

The development of practice theory should command, we think, a first-order priority in social work research. There needs to be greater emphasis on the study of the impact of different kinds of interventions on different kinds of problems and populations. The development of theories in other domains, such as theories of human behavior and social organization, should be left largely to social scientists. The concern of social workers should be to apply such theories to social work problems. By the same token, study of social work practice should be conducted not simply to test bits of technology, although that is important, but also to inform a practice theory that may be helpful in identifying methods with a wide range of effective application.

THEORY AND THE INCEPTION OF INQUIRY

Theory provides the matrix for the formulation of the questions and hypotheses that guide systematic inquiry. The generative role of theory is most obvious when hypotheses to be tested are derived from a body of existing theory. It is less obvious, but still crucial, when inquiry arises from unknowns encountered in practice. For example, in one study in which the authors participated (Garvin, Smith, and Reid 1978), there was interest in determining if a monetary incentive ($30 a month) offered welfare recipients for participation in a federal work-training program (the Work Incentive Program) was accomplishing its stated purpose of attracting recipients into the program. Various specific questions were posed for study. Did the recipients perceive the payment as an inducement to participate? Did they think it was adequate? Would they have participated without it? And so on. Although these questions seem very practical, and were, they were suggested by an informal theory of how the monetary incentive could be expected to operate.

It was theorized that welfare recipients would be influenced to participate in the program because of the incentive; if so, they would need to know about the incentive prior to the program and to view it as extra money that would result from the program. Further, other possible incentives, such as prospects of obtaining a better job, must not be so powerful as to nullify the effect of the "bonus" in the recipient's decision about entering the program. Thus a network of concepts and explanatory hypotheses—that is, the theory under-lying this aspect of the program—could (and did) stimulate questions about the supposed incentive payment.

Since the theory in such instances may be only informal and also implicit, questions might seem to arise "naturally"; the role of theory may be over-looked. It is important, however, that the theoretical structures that include questions of interest be explicated. If this is done, the formulation of inquiry can be evaluated in a more systematic and thorough manner; in particular, important questions that might otherwise be overlooked can often be brought to light.

Formulating Hypotheses and Questions

Systematic inquiry begins with a hypothesis to be tested or question to be answered. We consider hypotheses first and in greater detail, since the principles of hypothesis construction incorporate most of those pertaining to question formulation.

Hypotheses A hypothesis is a conjecture about reality. It is a statement that one has reason to believe is true but for which adequate evidence is lacking.

Social work practitioners engage continually in hypothesis formulation in their day-to-day work. A program planner predicts (hypothesizes) that at least a quarter of the elderly citizens in his community would utilize a minibus service. A practitioner in a residential treatment center (hypothesizes) that periodic expressions of aggression among members of her therapeutic group are related to flareups of overt conflict among center staff. Hypothesis for-mulation involves the same process in practice as it does in research studies. The chief difference is that these processes are usually carried out more deliberately in the latter. These examples illustrate two forms that a hypoth-esis can take. In the first example, a certain value is predicted for a single factor or variable—the proportion of elderly clients who would use a service.

In the second example, the hypothesis asserts a relation between variables—the occurrence of conflict among staff members and aggression expressed by members of a therapeutic group. The distinction can be made clearer if one thinks of the number of variables that would need to be measured to test the hypothesis. In the first case, data would need to be obtained on the proportion of elderly citizens using the minibus service. In the second case, it would be necessary to obtain data on the occurrence of both staff conflict and expressions of aggression within the group and then to relate the two sets of data.

Since most hypotheses are concerned with relations among different aspects of phenomena, hypotheses containing one variable are not common. In fact, some research methodologists (Kerlinger 1985) require that at least two variables be present before a statement is considered to be a hypothesis. Although the notion of a single-variable hypothesis may strike some researchers as akin to the sound of one hand clapping, the notion does have value. Many predictions assume this form and do so legitimately. Because of their greater importance and complexity, hypotheses expressing relations between two or more variables (relational hypotheses) occupy the focus of our attention.

A relational hypothesis can state one of several types of relations between variables. As Ripple (1960) has pointed out, a hypothesis may assert that two variables are simply associated in some manner, without indicating which is the cause of the other; or it may state a causal relationship between the variables. That is, it is possible to assert that there is a degree of covariation between marital conflict and child abuse, without claiming that one is the cause of the other: or the relationship could be put in causal terms—that marital conflict contributes to child abuse. Since relational hypotheses tend to originate in explanatory theory (or in explanatory theorizing), most are initially stated in causal terms.

Although one can state at a theoretical level that X is the cause of Y, the hypothesis actually tested must necessarily be limited to a statement of relation between X and Y. This is so because one can only demonstrate empirically that a degree of relation can occur between variables. Attribution of one as the cause of the other can be made only through a process of inference involving, among other things, the elimination of other variables as possible causes.

Thus inquiry might begin with interest in testing the causal hypothesis that prolonged periods of separation from their mothers will have damaging psychological effects on infants. In reworking this hypothesis for an actual test, an investigator might predict a significant degree of association between length of separation (or occurrences of separation) and "psychological damage" measured in some way. If an association were found, the investigator might then argue that maternal separation was the cause of the damage. In support of her argument she would need to demonstrate among other things that some prior factor, such as the economic status of the mother, was not responsible for both separation and damage.

Causal hypotheses may also lead to predictions in which one group is compared to another. In the preceding example, one might have compared a group of mothers who did not separate from their infants with another group who did. The prediction would then be that the children of the former mothers would show less psychological damage than the children of the latter. Although expressed in the form of differences between groups, the hypothesis still asserts that maternal separation is related to psychological damage.

Relational hypotheses, then, come down to "hypotheses of association" and "hypotheses of difference," as Black and Champion (1976) have put it, though both types of hypothesis can be thought of as different sides of the same coin. Thus, two-variable relational hypotheses can be expressed in sentences that are variations of the following:

(a) X will be positively associated with Y
(The level of practitioner empathy will be positively correlated with client satisfaction with treatment.)
(b) Group A will differ from Group B in respect to Y
(The clients of "high empathy" practitioners will be more satisfied with treatment than clients of "low empathy" practitioners.)

Hypotheses predicting change in a single group over time is basically a variation of (b) above—the hypothesis of difference format. For example, in their study of the acquisition and use of verbal interview skills by graduate social work students, Kopp and Butterfield hypothesized after training that "students would: (1) decrease their use of close-ended questions; (2) increase the use of exploratory skills; and (3) increase their use of self-understanding skills" (1985:70). In other words, the group at Time 1 will differ from itself at Time 2 in respect to skill acquisition.

Hypotheses may, of course, incorporate more than two variables. A researcher may predict that some combination of factors may be associated with Y. For example, in a study of factors predictive of change in drinking behavior of alcoholics treated in a social work program, Finlay (1977) formulated the following hypothesis:

Marked change in drinking behavior is more likely when, in the first interview, problem drinkers

- Are in a crisis state—that is, they manifest a high level of concern about their drinking.
- Acknowledge considerable dependence on alcohol or loss of control of their drinking.
- Identify their drinking as a problem to be solved.
- State their intention to substantially modify their drinking behavior.

Although more difficult to develop and more demanding to test, multivariate hypotheses of this kind are more reflective of the interrelationships that usually characterize social phenomena than hypotheses that examine only two variables at a time.

Various attempts have been made to identify criteria of "good" hypotheses. (See, for example, Goode and Hatt 1952; Black and Champion 1976.) The criterion most consistently identified is, in one form or another, the criterion of testability—that is, a hypothesis should be stated in terms indicating how an empirical test could be conducted. The language of the hypothesis should be translatable into research operations; one should be able to develop empirical or operational definitions for the terms of the hypothesis and it should be clear that a decision to accept or reject the hypothesis can be made on the basis of data obtained.

Hypotheses may fall short on the testability criterion for a variety of reasons. Two of the more common will be considered. Application of the criterion may reveal that a "hypothesis" is really a statement of a practice principle or a point of view that cannot be accepted or rejected through an empirical test. Consider, for example, the assertion that "use of indigenous workers as counselors is an essential component of effective delinquency prevention programs in low-income inner-city areas." Although one might study the contribution of indigenous workers to such programs, it is not possible to develop a way of testing for their "essentialness." What is essential, needed, desirable, and so forth, are in themselves questions of judgment or value that cannot be decided by data.

If a hypothesis contains terms that are too ambiguous or value ladened, it may be hard to develop adequate empirical or operational definitions. Thus it may be hypothesized that marriages between partners at the same level of maturity will be more stable than marriages in which partners are at different levels of emotional maturity. Whereas acceptable empirical referents might be found for "stability," they may be difficult to identify for "emotional maturity" because of the multiple meanings and value connotations of that term. As Black and Champion (1976) observe, hypotheses may be evaluated "in terms of the amount of information they provide about phenomena" (p. 139). In the present example, the hypothesis provides so little real information that it is difficult to proceed with the specification of terms.

A second criterion for evaluating a hypothesis concerns the likelihood of its being confirmed when tested. To be worth testing, a hypothesis should have, as Ripple (1960) has observed, an uncertain outcome. If an outcome is reasonably certain, there is little point in proceeding with a test; it might be said that the hypothesis lacks interest. An uninteresting hypothesis in this sense is one that is sure to be either accepted or rejected. One should, however, be reluctant to dismiss a hypothesis as "self-evident" simply because it seems to be testing what is thought of as "common knowledge." The literature of social work and the social sciences is replete with examples of hypotheses that seemed like "sure things" but for which confirming evidence could not be found.

The problem of the "fail-safe" hypothesis is more likely to occur in quasi-tautological statements, in which variables to be related are by definition overlapping. Suppose, for example, it is hypothesized that in bureaucratically organized social agencies there will be greater conflict among staff over formal division of labor than in social agencies that are not bureaucratically organized. Suppose, further, that among indicators used to identify bureaucratic organizations one finds the "extent of formal division of labor." Support for the hypothesis as stated could be expected since bureaucratically organized agencies would have, by definition, greater division of labor and have greater opportunity for conflict. Sometimes the overlap between variables may not become apparent until methods measuring them are examined. A predicted correlation between depression and "a self-critical orientation" may be a foregone conclusion if tests of both variables include similar items.

Tautologies may then (as may practice principles) masquerade as hypotheses. With obvious tautologies, the question is not of the statement's not being testable but of its not being a hypothesis. On occasion we have encountered variations of the hypothesis that "reinforcement will increase X behavior." Since reinforcement turns out to be defined in such instances (and generally) as an addition to the environment that will increase the rate of behavior, such statements are totally circular, assert nothing, and hence are really not hypotheses at all. A good way of making this determination is, however, to treat them as if they were and then ascertain if in fact they make assertions that can be disproved.

At the other end of the spectrum are hypotheses that are almost certain to fail. This determination may not be easy to make, however, since one needs to know something about the phenomena to be studied, the proposed method of testing, and the fate of similar hypotheses that have been tested in a similar manner. Moreover, one should be reluctant to dismiss a hypothesis because it goes against the grain of what appears to be obvious. If any generalization can be made about "unconfirmable" hypotheses, it is perhaps that they attribute more potency to presumed causative factors (independent variables) than can be determined in light of competing sources of variation and measurement error. In social work such hypotheses are frequently proposed for small-scale correlational studies in which some isolated client or service characteristic is predicted to be associated with case "outcome," often crudely defined and measured. For example, suppose an association was predicted between minor differences in practitioner experience levels and a gross measure of client improvement in a sample of twenty cases. Although such a difference might conceivably have an effect on the practitioners' effectiveness, there is little likelihood that it would be revealed in the study in view of other factors that might affect improvement, the imprecision of measurement of client change, and lack of evidence from prior research that practitioner experience is a potent variable.

Questions   Often, if not usually, in social work research not enough is known about phenomena to be studied to justify the formulation of hypotheses, or convincing theory about the supposed relations among variables may be lacking. What is more, there may not even be sufficient knowledge to identify and define relevant variables. Before hypotheses can be formed and tested, there may be need to describe phenomena of interest, to locate promising variables and to explore relations among them. Although inquiry may progress from studies organized around questions to more definitive, hypothesis-testing research, this progression does not always occur. The immediate objects of inquiry may be in perpetual flux as, for example, the programs of many agencies are. Descriptive research guided by questions may be then the ultimate form of inquiry in many contexts.

Like hypotheses, questions may be concerned with a single variable or with the relationship among two or more. Thus a program planner may ask "What proportion of discharged patients will remain in our aftercare program for the first year after discharge?" Her interest is in a single variable—the proportion of discharged patients. (When inquiry is focused on one variable at a time, it generally takes the form of questions since it is usually difficult to predict the values that may be found for that single variable). Or the planner might combine this variable with another in a question such as, "What patient characteristics are associated with continuance (up to one year) in the aftercare program?" Or, more specifically, "Are patients who live with family members more likely to remain than patients who live alone?" As can be seen, the first of these relational questions could not be restated in the form of a meaningful hypothesis, since the range of possible characteristics that might be associated with continuance is not specified. The second question could be recast as a hypothesis, if there were any reason to suppose that the continuance rate would be higher in one group than the other.

The criteria presented earlier for good hypotheses may be applied to questions. A good research question is one that can be answered by collecting data and is one whose answer cannot be foreseen prior to the collection of the data. Nevertheless, because they may be used to organize inquiry about relatively unknown phenomena, questions may be couched in terms that cannot be precisely defined at the outset. As we shall see, this "open" definition of terms may be all that is possible at the beginning of inquiry; more precise definitions may need to wait until more is learned about the subject. Thus an investigator studying a new program might ask "What benefits do clients see in the program?" The term *benefit* may be broadly defined since the investigator may not be sure what clients will perceive as benefits. The openness of the initial definition may be carried through to "open-ended" questions asked of clients. Thus, clients might be asked to cite what they saw as benefits they received from the program. In some forms of inquiry initial questions serve as points of entry into a subject, with recognition that the questions may be radically altered or replaced by more interesting questions as inquiry proceeds. For example, a participant observation study of hospital attendants' attitudes toward closed-ward patients may begin with a general question that asks in effect what these attitudes are; as the investigator gathers knowledge about these attitudes, the initial question may give rise to a series of more specific questions about their attitudes toward different kinds of patients, how their attitudes are affected by different kinds of behavior, and so on.

Hypotheses versus Questions When there is opportunity for choice about whether to pursue inquiry through questions or hypotheses, what considerations might help one decide which to use? When a relationship between two or more variables can be predicted on theoretical grounds, stating the relationship in the form of a hypothesis has certain advantages. The confirmation of a hypothesis that predicts a relationship provides stronger evidence for the existence of the relationship than answering a question about its existence in the affirmative.

For this reason, a predicted relationship needs to pass a less stringent statistical test when inferential statistics are used to evaluate the role of chance factors in producing an observed relationship. Although the logic of this decision making is taken up subsequently (chapter 11), we can note at this point that stating a relationship as a hypothesis has the practical advantage of requiring less proof to establish its existence. Moreover, the confirmation of a hypothesis drawn from a theory increases the probability that other hypotheses in the theory are confirmable, since the hypothesis is part of a network of assertions related to a common pool of knowledge. Hence the successful test of a hypothesis derived from theory has greater implications for a system of ideas than answering research questions. Finally, a study organized around hypotheses generally has a more definitive structure than one organized around questions. Hypotheses provide a bounded framework for inquiry since the study is concentrated on tests of relatively specific relationships; as in a clearly drawn contract the scope of work is well demarcated at the outset. While these considerations may also apply to such specific questions as "Is X greater than Y?," they do not not open queries such as "What are the characteristics of X?" It is often difficult to know when an open question has been satisfactorily answered or even how it may be best answered. As a consequence, the more open the question, the more difficult it may be to focus and limit inquiry.

The full advantages of hypothesis testing can be reaped, however, only when the investigator can make use of a theory that yields hypotheses with a good chance of being confirmed or hypotheses that are generally believed to be true. In the first instance, a successful test can advance knowledge building by providing direct empirical support for a relationship between variables and indirect support for a theory. In the second instance, a test can raise doubts about a set of accepted but questionable beliefs and thus stimulate a search for something better.

But when these conditions do not obtain, the special advantages offered by hypothesis testing may be lost. In fact, concentrating on the test of specific hypotheses may be dysfunctional when relevant theory is poorly developed or when little is known about the area under investigation. Since hypotheses narrow the focus of inquiry, it is possible that, without adequate theory or knowledge as a guide, the investigator may "look in the wrong place" or at least overlook aspects of greater interest.

EXPLICATION OF THE PROBLEM

Research problems consist of sentences that assert hypotheses to be tested or pose questions to be answered. These sentences contain terms that usually can be understood in many different ways. The particular meanings given these terms in the investigation at hand need to be made clear.

Levels of Explication

The process of explication moves down a "ladder of abstraction" (Bernard Phillips 1985). Terms first need to be understood at an abstract level, as part of the theory or system of ideas to which the problem is related. Explications at this level are variously referred to as "nominal," constitutive," or "theoretical" definitions. Sometimes terms are expressly defined. Thus, in their study of the effects of skill training on burnout, Corcoran and Bryce write: "Simply defined burnout is the loss of motivation for creative involvement with one's client population and/or organizational setting" (1983:72). In other instances, terms are clarified in the course of presenting the theoretical framework pertaining to the problem.

Whereas precise nominal definitions may be desirable, precision in initial definitions of terms is not always possible. A certain amount of openness is not only inevitable but is preferable to premature closure. At the beginning of an investigation, the researcher may not have the necessary knowledge to be exacting in her definitions, and it may turn out that terms can be much better defined in the light of the data obtained by the study. As Kaplan observes, definitions should be regarded as "successive" rather than fixed. "The closure that strict definition consists in is not a precondition of scientific inquiry but rather its culmination" (1964:77). This position does not justify unnecessary vagueness; rather it suggests that theoretical definitions evolve as inquiry proceeds.

With a first approximation of the general meaning of her terms in mind, the investigator pushes toward greater specificity. Terms used to define abstractions may in turn need to be spelled out. If "outcome" is said to be change in communication between parents and children, one needs to consider what is meant by "communication." The process leads to the development of the indicators that will actually be measured. At the lowest rung of the ladder, parent-child communication may be defined in terms of such specific characteristics as interruptions, disparaging remarks, approving comments, and the like. Such indicators are then used as the basis for instruments. For example, a coding scheme might be used to analyze characteristics of parent-child communication from tape-recorded samples of dialogue.

The process of moving from the abstract to the concrete and ultimately to instruments for data collection and measurement is often referred to as developing an "operational definition." This notion was originally advanced by Bridgman, a physicist, who suggested that the meaning of a concept can be best expressed by the operations used to measure it. To use the familiar example, intelligence is what an intelligence test measures. As various philosophers of science have argued (Kaplan 1964; Scriven 1969), operationalism in extreme form is probably untenable since each instrument (or even each change in measuring procedures) would demand a new concept. If intelligence is what an intelligence test measures, then we would need to have as many concepts of intelligence as we have intelligence tests.

In contemporary usage, an operational definition generally refers to the more specific indicators employed in concept measurement. Thus, if an investigator is studying practitioner productivity, she may say that "productivity was operationally defined as the number of interviews conducted by practitioners per week."

As she proceeds with spelling out or operationalizing concepts, the investigator must deal with definitions of phenomena at different levels of abstraction and must be concerned with how these levels relate to one another. Ideally one hopes to define clearly concepts contained in the research problem and to select indicators that accurately and comprehensively reflect the key meanings of those concepts. This ideal is seldom attained, however, since concepts often cannot be defined with a high degree of precision at the outset. Indicators are likely to tap only aspects of these concepts and to do so imperfectly. Moreover, the indicators selected may measure phenomena that fall outside the scope of the concept.

Suppose an investigator wishes to study aggressive behavior exhibited by children on the playground during school recess. Aggression may be theoretically defined as actions done with the apparent intent of injuring another person. The definition is obviously less than clear-cut, but some reflection will show that there is no one easy way of defining aggression. Thus, "apparent intent" is vague, but there are problems in defining aggression strictly in terms of overt behavior. A child who accidentally injures another is not seen as behaving aggressively, but a child who tries to punch a peer but misses would probably be regarded as having been aggressive. Further dilemmas are encountered in relation to the scope of the concept. Should verbal aggression be included? The investigator may wish to do so since insults that may hurt a person psychologically are normally seen as aggressive acts, even though it may be difficult to define verbal aggression with any degree of precision. The chances are that whatever definitions were formed would omit actions that would be considered aggressive under the circumstances. Thus, certain gestures or verbal expressions that may seem innocuous to the investigator may be interpreted by the children as aggressive acts. On the other hand, the indicators may result in classifying actions as aggressive when under the circumstances they would not be considered as such. For example, one student researcher found to her dismay that observers using her carefully worked-out descriptions of acts of physical aggression (shoving, jumping on, grabbing, and so on) were dutifully reporting as "aggressive actions" the normal behaviors of boys in a football game!

As the foregoing suggests, operational definitions may suffer from both underinclusiveness and overinclusiveness. Parts of the concept may be neglected in the indicators, but at the same time the indicators may in error cover phenomena that are not a part of the concept.

Problems of correspondence between different levels of definition are to some degree inevitable. Even though the researcher may not be able to solve them satisfactorily, she needs to be aware of their existence and consequences. A common pseudosolution is to move directly from terms to measurements, pretty much bypassing the sticky business of theoretical definitions. Although such naive operationalism may lead to convenient measures and neat data, the resulting findings are often of questionable significance. What has been measured may not add up to much that is meaningful, because problems of meaning were not adequately addressed in the formulation of the problem.

Thus far we have discussed definitions only in terms of level of abstraction. Another distinction has to do with the researcher's ability to influence the phenomena to be defined. In naturalistic studies the investigator defines phenomena as they lie; in experiments, however, she may be able (ideally, should be able) to manipulate the experimental intervention. One still proceeds from the abstract to the specific. The intervention is defined in general terms; then the specific procedures to be followed in applying the intervention are worked out. These are equivalent to the indicators or operational definition of the intervention. The validity issues previously discussed apply here as well. In one study, for example, Tolson (1977) tested the efficacy of a task-centered approach as a means of resolving specific communication problems experienced by a particular couple. The method tested, the task implementation sequence or TIS (Reid 1975a), was described in general terms. Tolson then specified the task-centered procedures she used to treat the problems. As one might expect, some of the methods prescribed in the TIS were not used in her experiment; moreover, certain of her procedures were different from those suggested by the TIS. These problems of correspondence, while not atypical, raise important questions. To what extent can the experiment be regarded as a test of the TIS? To what extent can her experimental results (which indicated that the procedures used were effective in the case) be viewed as providing support for the efficacy of the set of methods?

Variables

The creation of variables is a part of the process of putting terms into operational form. As the name implies, a variable is an entity expected to vary or to take on different values in the investigation. These values may be either quantitative (that is, in the form of numbers) or qualitative (that is, in the form of attributes). Age is a variable commonly expressed in quantitative form. Sex, as a variable, inevitably takes on two qualitative values: male and female.

As a step in problem explication, the creation of variables isolates the specific factors that will be investigated and indicates how they will be measured. Variables provide the means of capturing the variation in phenomena that provide the major focus of research. When the terms of the problem are clear-cut, variables can be derived directly from them (sex and age are examples). When the terms need definition, variables may be drawn from whatever indicators are developed. A complex concept, such as "outcome," may produce a large array of separate variables, perhaps in the form of scales to measure different aspects of change in clients and their family members. Not all key terms of the research problem yield variables, however. Some terms refer to constants, factors that do not vary in the study. For example, suppose a problem states the following hypothesis: "Among the frail elderly, residential mobility (including moves from homes to institutions) will be associated with the rate of survival." "Residential mobility" and "rate of survival" would yield variables, but "the frail elderly" would be a constant since only this group of older people is to be studied in the problem as stated. It might be decided during the study, however, to treat "the frail elderly" as a variable; if so, different degrees of frailty would need to be distinguished.

Since explanation is a major goal of research, it is customary to classify variables according to their function in explanatory chains. *Independent* variables are presumed causative factors, as "residential mobility" in the cited example, factors to be explained or presumed effects are referred to as *dependent variables*, since their variation is presumably dependent on the influence of an independent variable. "Survival rate" in the preceding example would be the dependent variable. An *antecedent variable* operates prior in time to both independent and dependent variables. An antecedent variable becomes of particular interest if it may be able to explain the relation between the independent and dependent variables. Residential mobility might indeed be correlated with survival rate, but both mobility and survival might be explained by an antecedent variable—health. The sicker frail elderly might move more for health reasons (particularly from home to institution), which in turn might be responsible for their lower survival rate. Sometimes the relation between an independent and dependent variable is influenced by a variable that occurs between them in time—*intervening variable*. Residential mobility may be found to have less impact on survival if the move is to a group foster home than to an institution. In other words, the type of move as an intervening variable may alter the relation between mobility and survival.

The classification of variables is generally useful in attempts to order events relevant to social work practice, whether or not one is attempting to develop a formal research problem. The variables in the preceding example might be fruitfully analyzed in the manner suggested by a planner as well as a researcher. More generally, in thinking about social problems, we hypothesize that certain factors (independent variables) produce certain effects (dependent variables) on the lives of our clients. In evaluating these presumed causative factors, we search for antecedent variables. Broken homes may be related to delinquency, but does the one-parent family per se make the difference or is it the fact that low socioeconomic status breeds both broken homes and delinquency? In developing these causal chains, we are alert to intervening variables, an important class of which are social work services. The connection here between research and practice thinking is in fact captured by our use of the term *intervention* to describe these services. The social worker "intervenes" to affect the relation between problem-causing factors and their untoward consequences for clients.

Implicit in the foregoing discussion is another distinction among variables: a variable can refer to either an attribute or an action. An *attribute variable*, such as a measure of socioeconomic status, is a measurement imposed on phenomena; an *active variable*, such as an experimental treatment, represents something done to affect phenomena (Kerlinger 1985). The distinction (reflected in our earlier discussion of the operational definition of experimental interventions) is particularly important in social work. Attribute variables tend to measure phenomena we wish changed or need to take into account in our change efforts. Active variables represent our means of bringing change about.

Working Statement of the Problem

To recapitulate, the explication of a problem consists of translating general into specific terms. This translation becomes the working statement of the problem. Carried to its ultimate limits, the statement would be nothing less than a description of the sampling plan, data collection procedures, instruments, and, if relevant, the intervention program. Practically speaking, one thinks of a more compact statement describing what is actually to be studied. Thus, in general form a hypothesis may be as follows: "Social work practitioners tend to view passivity as more problematic in male than in female clients." As the problem is explicated, it is decided to use as subjects social workers attending a workshop. The subjects will be randomly divided into two groups. Both groups will receive a case summary portraying a passive client. The summaries will differ in only one respect: in the summaries given one group (masculine form), the client will be described as a man; for the other group (feminine form), the client will be described as a woman. All subjects will complete an original instrument called the Perceived Maladjustment Index, designed to measure a social worker's perception of degree of maladjustment in a client. The working statement of the hypothesis in such a study might be put as follows: the social workers receiving the "masculine" form of the case summary will have a higher mean score on the Perceived Maladjustment Index than those receiving the "feminine" form.

The working statement may not appear as such in a report, though a restatement of the problem at this level may often be helpful to the reader. Even if it remains in the mind of the investigator, the working statement is of value since it provides a way of comparing the research problem in the abstract with what will actually be studied. The gap between the meanings connoted by the former and the information that can be expected from the latter is a measure of the limitations of the study—a point well illustrated by the example just given.

CHAPTER 4

DIMENSIONS OF RESEARCH DESIGN

Research design refers to the overall plan or strategy by which questions are answered or hypotheses tested. Although each study is done according to its own particular plan, it is possible to think in terms of general features or principles of design used for different purposes or representing different approaches to inquiry. Generalizations about design are useful, in fact necessary, in an exposition of research methodology, and various frameworks for viewing design in social research have been developed. In our judgment no single scheme has proved adequate to the task of capturing the multidimensional qualities of research strategy and probably none' can be devised. Operating from this premise, we consider in this chapter different dimensions used in analysis of design. From this review we attempt to develop some perspectives that may be helpful in assessing and planning research strategy.

NATURALISTIC VERSUS EXPERIMENTAL RESEARCH

A key distinction in research strategy concerns what the researcher does with the phenomena under investigation. On the one hand, she can investigate phenomena "as they lie"; that is, she can study events without trying to alter them. This approach to inquiry is commonly referred to as "naturalistic research." On the other hand, she can deliberately seek to alter phenomena and then study the effects of her manipulations—a form of research traditionally referred to as experimental. This distinction is fundamental in the world of science. Some sciences, in which events of interest cannot be affected, are primarily naturalistic; astronomy is an example. Other sciences, such as nuclear physics, are primarily experimental. Most sciences make use of both methods, often as complementary means of advancing knowledge in the same area.

The purpose of both strategies is of course to gain knowledge, and ultimately this objective is achieved in each through observations of events. The key to the difference is that in naturalistic research the observed events would have taken place anyway; in experimental research the events were made to happen in order that they could be studied.

The reason for making events happen is to gain special knowledge. Experimentation provides a powerful means of acquiring knowledge about causal relations since the experimenter can observe what happens when one factor is changed and others are held constant. Through systematic manipulations she can build up bodies of knowledge that may be impossible to acquire if events were allowed to vary in their natural complexity.

Even when experimental methods cannot be applied directly to phenomena of interest, it is often possible to apply them to facsimiles or analogs of these phenomena. Such simulations, which are probably limited only by the researcher's ingenuity and resources, certainly span a wide range in science. The causes of earthquakes have been studied through simulations of plate tectonics (movements in the earth's crust). Experimental anthropologists have sought to explain events that occurred early in the history of man through such means as sailing an ocean in a reconstruction of a primitive vessel and using technology available to ancient Egyptians to build a portion of a pyramid. More relevant to social work are experimental simulations of factors affecting human behavior. Most factors—for example, the effects of frustration, decision-making, problem-solving, even intervention processes —can be simulated for purposes of experimental study.

Since experimentation involves bringing something about, it may in addition lead to invention—a new and better way to accomplish practical objectives. Experimental research and technological innovation have a close affinity, a theme we return to subsequently (chapter 7). It is possible to be innovative without studying what happens subsequently, which we would not regard as experimentation, although the term is sometimes used in a popular sense to refer to almost any novel action. It is also possible to experiment without inventing technology—a researcher may introduce an established procedure as an experimental variable. But by providing the opportunity to combine innovation and the study of innovation, experimentation can lead to the creation and testing of new approaches—and hence to technological advances.

Although experimental research frequently makes use of devices, for example, untreated equivalent groups, to isolate causative factors, such mechanisms of experimental control are not, in our judgment, an essential characteristic of the experimental method. An experimenter may introduce and study an innovation without using control mechanisms. She may do this to learn what the innovation looks like when tried, to learn about obstacles to its implementation, ways of measuring it, or its possible effects. To experiment is to do and study what has been done; how the study is conducted simply defines the type of experiment performed.

In social work most experiments consist of the tryout and evaluation of a service approach without the benefit of control devices (Reid 1979a). In our view, they are still experiments even if they lack the controls that may be necessary for a rigorous test of the effectiveness of the approach. Experiments that incorporate adequate control devices (controlled experiments) can then be distinguished from those that do not (uncontrolled experiements) or from those whose control mechanisms may be less than adequate (partially controlled experiments). We realize that we are defining the term *experiment* more broadly than it has been employed by some research methodologists who have used "experiment" or "true experiment" to refer to designs with equivalent groups produced by random assignment. This narrower conception of the experiment was of doubtful validity to begin with and in any single case no longer reflects current usage. For example, single-case experiments do not fit at all well to this conception. What are sometimes referred to as quasi-experiments (those lacking equivalent groups) become in our lexicon uncontrolled or partially controlled experiments.

However, not all research on service is experimental. Thus, follow-up evaluations of routine services would be naturalistic research as would be a secondary analysis of intervention data if the analysis was not related to the purposes of the experiment from which the data were taken. Still some studies are difficult to classify on this dimension. For example, an innovative service may be introduced without a clear intent to study its results but an evaluation component is added later. Naturalistic or experimental? A case could be made for either designation. In such instances it may be well to avoid summary classification in favor of a description of what was actually done.

Knowledge-Building Purposes and Functions

Research is conducted to accomplish a range of purposes in building knowledge. A study may be designed to discover possible generalizations or hypotheses—an exploratory objective. It may focus on developing tools for measurement. It may seek to describe phenomena or produce explanations of relationships among variables.

Such purposes have often been used to categorize studies as "exploratory," "descriptive," and so on (Selltiz, Wrightsman, and Cook 1976; Atherton and Klemmack 1982). Although it is sometimes convenient to classify a study in terms of one main knowledge-building goal, most studies serve more than one purpose. For example, it is hard to do an exploratory study without providing some descriptive information of the phenomena investigated. Moreover, classification by purpose encounters difficulty in respect to explanation where a variety of designs can be used.

Typologies have typically handled the problem by shifting to a different basis of classification. For example, Atherton and Klemmack (1982) divide studies into "exploratory," "descriptive," "experimental," and "evaluative." While "exploratory" reflects the purpose of a study an "experiment" represents a way of conducting an investigation, thus obscuring the fact that some experiments, such as uncontrolled pilot studies, can have exploratory purposes. The difficulties are avoided if the purpose of a study is viewed as one of its attributes and if studies generally are classified, as is attempted in this chapter, in a multi-dimensional system.

It is also useful to distinguish between purpose and function. Knowledge-building "purpose" reflects what the investigator intends to produce; "function" refers more broadly to what the study produces. When the reference point is the planful activity of the researcher, it makes sense to relate to purpose in knowledge-building. However, a single-purpose study may serve a variety of functions, sometimes quite by accident. Experiments carefully designed to test an explanatory relationship may be remembered more for incidental discoveries having no connection with the purpose of the experiment. The unexpected exploratory function of research, known in science as serendipity, has been responsible for a host of discoveries including penicillin, Pavlov's conditioned reflex, REM sleep, the Rorschach test, and the Hawthorne effect (Merbaum and Lowe 1982). Moreover, a study may have different functions for different users. The investigator's purpose may have been largely descriptive but to another researcher the study's value lies in the evidence it provides for the validity of a particular attitude scale. A theorist may combine the findings along with those of other studies to form the basis of an explanatory theory. A case in point is Durkheim's use of data on suicide rates to develop his explanatory theory of suicide.

Two conclusions can be drawn from this consideration of the knowledge-building functions of research. First, we should be alert for yields from research that fall outside its purpose, whether the research be our own or someone else's. Avoidance of hard-and-fast positions on theoretical and methodological issues helps here. Second, the research we do may have value to others in ways of which we may not be aware, a notion that researchers may find comforting when the more straightforward results of their work appear to be ignored.

In what follows we shall discuss knowledge-building primarily within the broader context of function, a concept more useful for research utilization. References to purpose will be made when we have the researcher's planning processes in mind.

Exploration   Research has an exploratory purpose when it is used to gain preliminary understanding of phenomena or to stimulate the development of concepts, hypotheses, theories, and technology. Suppose that a community agency has established a new manpower program designed to provide on-the-job training and job placement services to unemployed youth. Within the first few months of operation a problem appears: many of the youths who entered the program are dropping out. The administrator wants an immediate study of the problem as a basis for taking possible corrective action and for answering questions likely to be raised at a forthcoming meeting of the agency's board. Assuming a researcher's role, the director's assistant contacts by phone a dozen youths who have recently dropped out of the program—the first twelve who were at home when she called and were willing to talk. Her brief telephone interviews are focused on eliciting the teenagers' reasons for leaving the program. As might be expected, they vary considerably, but almost half the youths mention that they were being used to carry out menial tasks at the training sites and were not being given the training they had been promised. She then calls a staff member who had visited a training site at which several of the interviewed youths had been placed. The staff member recalls that the trainees did seem to spend a lot of time just helping out. Although the data are limited in scope and subject to bias, they provide a basis for a hypothesis about reasons for the dropout problem. The hypothesis may serve as a basis for immediate action, such as some form of communication to the trainers. It also focuses further inquiry, which may be pursued through various means from collection of anecdotal data to a more elaborate study.

The example illustrates a study that served a primarily exploratory purpose.

The intent was to gain an initial look at a piece of reality and to stimulate ideas about it. At this level, research yields a sense of what is possible, rather than what is probable. But these possibilities may have generative effects. They may support other sources of evidence or may provoke new ways of construing reality.

Research done with largely exploratory purposes in mind requires, as the examples indicate, only a modest investment of resources, one commensurate with an initial look, and allows considerable flexibility in method. Samples may be selected according to which sources of data will provide the most useful information most readily, and additional sources of data may be added to pursue leads. Data collection procedures may be similarly open to improvisation. Insightful analyses of one or a few cases may take precedence over an attempt to secure uniform measurements.

This is not to say that research must necessarily be "loose" to serve exploratory goals. More systematic studies may also have such purposes (often in addition to others, as we shall see). The point is that research need not necessarily be highly systematic to achieve worthwhile exploratory objectives.

According to some methodologists, the role of exploratory research is limited to laying the groundwork for more definitive studies. Although this role is indeed important, it should not be regarded as the only one, in our judgment. The products of exploratory research can be applied to practical problems pending more definitive studies or even if such studies are not contemplated. In a profession such as social work where decisions must constantly be made in the absence of much knowledge, the results of an exploratory study can help inform action. A hypothesis based on some data may be better than one based on fiction. This argument holds only, however, if the user of exploratory research has a clear-sighted view of its limitations.

Measurement

An important by-product of most research is a contribution to ways of measuring phenomena. Moreover, some research is designed primarily to perfect measurement methodology—for example, most standardized instruments are the product of considerable methodological research. While the measurement function of research contributes to knowledge building largely in an indirect manner by providing researchers with measurement tools, this function makes a direct contribution as well. Through defining and spelling out variables for study, research can help clarify and specify key concepts within a body of knowledge. An excellent example of methodological research in social work is found in the work of Hudson and his associates to develop and validate a series of standardized instruments to measure different aspects of client functioning (Hudson 1982; Abell, Jones, and Hudson 1984). The indirect contribution of this research to knowledge has been considerable: the "Hudson scales" have been widely used in social work research. An example of a more direct contribution has been the efforts of Hollis and her associates to construct and test a scheme for classifying methods of casework with individuals and families (Hollis 1972; Hollis and Woods 1981). This methodological research produced a systematic and refined set of concepts for understanding (and communicating about) practice. Similarly, research has played a major role in developing a wide range of concepts used in the social sciences and social work—socioeconomic status, intelligence, anomie, self-concept, empathy, to name but a few.

Description

In one way or another, all research is concerned with describing phenomena. In social work this descriptive function involves primarily the delineation of characteristics of social systems, target problems, and interventions. The descriptive function of research encompasses not only delineation of phenomena in a holistic fashion (a quarter of the families in East Town are single parent) but also specification of how different parts are related (the lower the income of East Town families, the more likely they are to be single parent). In fact, the logic of this function is to break wholes down into interconnected parts, to achieve as detailed a picture as possible. Thus, in describing the clientele of a family agency, we may wish to have initial breakdowns of the clients by age, sex, level of education, ethnicity, marital status, social class, presenting problem, and referral source and then might want to determine whether the presenting problem differed by social class or whether ethnic background varied according to referral source, and so on.

Although investigation of these relations might stimulate (or even be guided by) speculations about causality, the descriptive function delivers only information about the presence of associations among factors. It does not point to causal connections. Thus, in the example given earlier, we learn that income and single-parent status are related in a particular community, but we do not know if low income was a cause or consequence of single parenthood. Regardless of its purpose, size or representativeness of sample, or sophistication of its measurement, any study can serve a descriptive function since it can provide at least some information about the characteristics of the phenomena studied. But this function can be served only if limitations of sample, measurements, and so forth, are made explicit. Otherwise the description may be misleading. If a survey designed to determine the expressed needs of older residents in a community were limited to participants in senior citizen centers, one could not reasonably claim that the results reflected an accurate description of the expressed needs of all elderly in the community, since the less social and less mobile would not be adequately represented. Nevertheless, if this limitation were recognized, descriptive information concerning the needs of the elderly who were surveyed might still be useful—for example, in planning services for the kind of residents who do participate in senior citizen centers. The descriptive function is of course served better in some studies than others. Generally the more representative the sample and the more accurate the measurement, the better the resulting description.

In social work the descriptive function of research plays an important role in developing knowledge about client needs, problems, and attitudes toward service; about the nature of services provided; and about service use. Excellent examples of primarily descriptive studies are Beck and Jones's (1973) census of cases served by family service agencies and Shyne's (1980) survey of public social services for children.

Explanation and Prediction

Probably the most esteemed function of research is its contribution to the explanation and prediction of phenomena. In social work considerable importance is attached to explanation—for example in determining the etiology of target problems, in understanding the dynamics of social systems, and in assessing the impact of different modes of intervention. At the core of such knowledge are assertions of cause-effect relations.

In a practice profession, explanation is of primary interest as a basis for prediction. We are interested in understanding causation so we can predict what is likely to happen—what kind of depressions are likely to lead to suicide, what kind of service programs are likely to have positive effects on certain types of clients. The better our capacities to predict, the more effectively we can intervene.

As we have seen, part of the descriptive function of research is to show

how different factors are associated or occur together. The explanatory function takes this process a step further by providing evidence that factors are associated in a causal fashion. If it can be shown that factor A and factor B are associated, factor A has occurred prior to factor B, and that no other prior (extraneous) factors are found to be associated with factor B, then it can be inferred that A is a cause of B. A key point in this chain of logic is that causal relations are not "proved" in a clear-cut fashion; rather, they are deduced through a process of elimination. Inferences are guided by theoretical expectations (chapter 3). We use theory to select and test those factors likely to provide alternative causal explanations. As a result, explanations offered by research always carry the qualification "as best as can be determined at this time." They are always open to the possibility that other explanatory factors, perhaps discovered by a novel theory, will be found.

Isolation of probable causative factors through elimination of other possibilities, variously called "extraneous factors," "alternative explanations," or "rival hypotheses," is achieved through processes of "control" in research design and analysis. The most clear-cut and familiar example is the "classical" experiment in which equivalent groups are formed through random assignment; one group receives some form of treatment, the other does not. Changes expected to occur as the result of the treatment are measured for each group. If the treated group changes as predicted and the other (control) group does not, and if it can be assumed that the groups differed in no other respect, then it may be concluded that the treatment was the causative agent. Note that the term *treatment* as used in discussions of experimental method refers generically to the independent or experimental variable, whatever it may be, and not simply to treatment in the clinical sense.

The same logic can be used in controlled tests limited to single cases by comparing change in a target during periods when no treatment is given with periods when treatment is applied. In both group and single-case experiments one attempts to "rule out" possible extraneous factors by holding them more or less constant while treatment is introduced. In group experiments a control group is used to demonstrate the changes that might be expected to occur as a result of maturation, ordinary environmental influences, or other factors that might be expected to operate in the absence of treatment; the experimental group has presumably been exposed to these factors plus the addition only of treatment. Thus any margin of difference in change between the two groups can be attributed to treatment. In the single-case experiment the case serves as its "own control"; one uses control "periods" in the case (when treatment is withheld) to determine the effects of extraneous factors. Change that appears when treatment is added is ascribed to the effects of the treatment on the assumption that the extraneous factors will continue to operate as before. The implementation of this logic in the context of experimental design will be considered in detail in the following two chapters.

Control of extraneous variation through use of equivalent groups and "own control" devices is not possible in naturalistic research. In such research one must deal with a complex web of associations among variables as they naturally occur. It may be difficult to determine which variables occur prior to others or to isolate any one factor as a cause of another. A naturalistic study may reveal that adolescents exposed to harsh parental discipline are, as hypothesized, more likely to engage in antisocial behavior in the community than those whose parents are moderate in discipline. But the investigator may be hard put to conclude that parental discipline provides an explanation of the behavior of the children. It may be that the antisocial behavior of some of the children, perhaps the result of peer group influences, may have preceded and, in fact, may have caused the parental discipline patterns observed in the study. In other words, it may not be possible to determine clearly the time order of the variables, and the flow of influence between variables may be in a direction quite the reverse from theoretical expectations.

Even when the time order of variables may be determined, other variables may provide competing explanations for a relationship. To take another example, a researcher may find that young boys whose fathers are absent from the home because of marital separation or divorce have a poorer self-concept than boys whose fathers are present. Although one might reasonably assume that the self-concept of the child was not a cause of the father's leaving, it does not follow that the fathers' absence affected their sons' self-concepts. Thus the presence of prior marital conflict in the home may have caused both the parental separation and a lowering of the boys' self-concepts. Or socioeconomic circumstances may provide an explanation of both phenomena. Compared to middle-class boys, lower-class boys may be more likely to lose their fathers and, given their more deprived socioeconomic circumstances, may be more likely to have a poorer self-concept.

If so, boys lacking fathers in the home would differ from boys whose fathers are present in respects other than the presence or absence of the father. A study might find that father-absent boys would indeed have poorer self-images but also that they would more likely come from families with a history of marital conflict and be lower class. It may not be possible to determine which of these variables are actually affecting self-concept and, more important, other influential factors may not have been identified.

The logic of controlled experimentation illuminates the problem. In a controlled experimental test, one would begin with a group of families randomly assigned to either an experimental or control group. In the experimental group, fathers would leave home (the experimental treatment); in the control group, they would stay put! If the self-concept of the experimental boys showed a greater worsening than those of the control boys, the fathers' absence could be regarded as a causative variable. Obviously an experiment that would so disrupt family life and threaten the mental health of children would never be done, but it forces us to think of what might be required to mine explanations from variables found to be associated in naturalistic research. What is needed is to eliminate possible confounding differences between groups being compared—in other words, to control extraneous variation.

There are several ways to tackle this problem in naturalistic research. All reflect the logic of controlled experimentation.

One means of reducing extraneous variation is through restrictive sampling. If socioeconomic differences are thought to affect self-concept, a study may be confined to middle-class boys. By this means father-absent and father-present boys are made equivalent in respect to social class. But increasing the homogeneity of the group studied limits the researcher's ability to generalize from the sample and makes it more difficult to obtain a sample of adequate size.

A second means of controlling an extraneous variable is to incorporate it as part of the study. Instead of restricting the sample to middle-class, father-absent and father-present boys, one could add a sample of lower-class boys so divided. Through this means, one obtains a more diversified sample and can study possible effects of social class as well as father absence on self-concept. At the same time, one can isolate and hence control for (through statistical techniques discussed later) the influence of social class on the dependent variable.

An alternative, which constitutes a third form of control, is to use some form of matching. Thus, if one wished to control for social class and age, one would build up a sample through selecting pairs of boys. Each pair would differ only in the father-whereabouts variable but would be alike in respect to class and age. Although matching of this kind provides more precise control over extraneous variables than the second method, usually the researcher can match on only a very small number of variables. Possibly decisive variables remain uncontrolled.

A fourth method of control for extraneous variation relies on statistical techniques that can be used in conjunction with the sampling and matching methods considered earlier or can be applied entirely *post hoc*. Suppose a predicted difference in self-concept is found between father-present and father-absent boys but the father-absent boys are more likely to be lower class, a variable that appears to be associated with self-concept. Although a variety of analytic methods can be used to control for extraneous variation (chapter 10), the basic principle can be seen in tables 4.1 and 4.2.

If the study had not identified social class as a possible extraneous variable, the data would have shown a moderately strong relation between presence of the father and the self-concept rating (table 4.1). When social class, a presumably antecedent variable, is introduced into the analysis of the same

TABLE 4.1
Self-Concept Ratings for 92 Boys by Presence of Father in Home (hypothetical data)

Self-Concept Ratings	Father Present	Father Absent
Good	23	22
Poor	14	33
Total	37	55

TABLE 4.2
Self-Concept Ratings for 92 Boys by Social Class and Presence of Father in Home

	Social Class			
	Lower		Middle	
Self-Concept Rating	Father Present	Father Absent	Father Present	Father Absent
Good	3	10	20	12
Poor	9	30	5	3
Total	12	40	25	15

data (table 4.2), we see that a different picture emerges. Lower-class boys are much more likely to have a poor self-concept than middle-class boys, but in neither stratum does self-concept appear to be affected by the presence or absence of the father. The statistical control in effect holds social class "constant" (or eliminates it as a source of variation) in the test of the relation between the father's presence and self-concept. When this is done, the apparent relation disappears. It can be seen as an artifact of having more lower-class than middle-class boys in the sample. As the data lie, social class then emerges as a more promising explanatory variable. If social class had made no difference, both sides of table 4.2 would have mirrored the apparent relationship between the father's presence and self-concept found in table 4.1. In that case, the original relationship could be said to hold controlling for social class. Like sampling and matching techniques, statistical controls can never be used with any certainty that all possible relevant variables have been taken into account. Moreover, the simultaneous control of more than one variable—for example, to control for boys who are *both* of a particular class and age—requires samples of large size.

As can be seen, each of these methods of ruling out extraneous variation in naturalistic "explanatory" studies attempts to perform the function of random assignment or "own control" comparisons in experimental research, that is, to make the subjects being compared as equivalent as possible on variables other than the presumed explanatory variable. As has been shown, none of these methods can, practically speaking, exhaust the range of possible variables that may provide plausible alternatives.

Moreover, these methods are limited in another important respect. Certain variables may be so inextricably linked with the presumed explanatory variable that they cannot be extracted through such methods of control. To return to our example, history of prior marital conflict was identified earlier as a possible rival to presence of the fathers in explaining variation in self-concept. But some reflection will reveal that control of such a variable in a naturalistic study would be extremely difficult since one would need to have samples of boys exposed to the same degree and kind of prior marital conflict. In some cases the parents would have separated and in other cases not. But does not a parental separation in itself suggest that the prior marital conflict had been of a different order than it would be for cases in which parents remained together? The question is difficult to answer in the negative. If so, then father-absent boys inevitably differ from father-present boys in respect to a critical variable that would explain differences in self-concept. Such fusion of variables, sometimes labeled self-selection (chapter 7), introduces an irreducible amount of uncertainty into any naturalistic study that attempts to isolate explanatory variables, regardless of the type and sophistication of the controls used.

Efforts to control for extraneous variation through design and analysis can be strengthened by what Krathwohl refers to as "explanation credibility" (1985:79). According to Krathwohl, an explanation gains in credibility if it is based on well-accepted knowledge and is predicted in advance. Further, the more precise and detailed the prediction, the more the case for a valid explanation is enhanced, assuming, of course, that the prediction is confirmed. To continue with our example, suppose there was a substantial amount of evidence showing that the absence of the father was associated with poor self-concept in boys, and further, that this evidence led to a prediction of a strong positive correlation between the boy's self-concept and the amount of contact boys had with fathers absent from the home. If this hypothesis were confirmed, the investigator would need less in the way of design and statistical controls in order to claim a causal relationship. A well substantiated theory that permits the researcher to call her shots, is a potent ally in developing explanations from data. (See also chapter 6.) Two cautions need to be kept in mind, however. One needs to examine the credentials of the "well-substantiated theory" critically, since it may be based on studies that repeat the same flaws. Second, the confirmation of even a fairly precise prediction does not offer definitive proof of the theory that gave rise to it. Another theory may be found to explain the relationship.

Although the difficulties inherent in achieving explanation through naturalistic research are formidable, attempts to do so can still be justified. To reiterate a basic theme in this book, knowledge in social work becomes gradually "hardened" through accretions of modest findings. Possible cause-and-effect relationships that hold when a number of variables are controlled gain some probability of providing valid explanations, even though we may regard them as best guesses and in need of further testing. Accumulations of evidence possibly built up over a number of naturalistic studies in which most plausible rival hypotheses have been controlled, can lead to persuasive evidence of cause-and-effect relations. For example, few now question the causal connection between cigarette smoking and lung cancer, a relation established almost entirely on a base of naturalistic studies.

Even controlled experiments seldom, however, provide perfect control over alternative explanations. Moreover, it is difficult to generalize from experiments to other situations given the inordinate amount of variation present in social phenomena and their tendency to change over time. While in theory variation and change can be addressed through repeated experimentation, cost limits and other practical constraints pose severe limitations on the amount of experimentation possible. Finally, experimentation cannot be applied at all to many questions.

Whether explanation is attempted through naturalistic or experimental methods, the traditional mode of attack in science has been to try to isolate one or at best a few independent variables as the cause of a solitary dependent variable or to view causation as proceeding in a single direction—from independent to dependent variables. As systems theorists have argued and as common sense suggests, this explanatory model is inadequate for many social phenomena, particularly those in which variables are likely to have reciprocal effects on one another (Buckley 1967; Watzlawick, Beavin, and Jackson 1967). Interactions within social systems such as families, organizations, or communities provide the most obvious examples. Thus parental discipline and the behavior of children clearly affect one another, often in an escalating series of exchanges. Moreover, there may be simultaneous interactions among numerous variables within social systems or impinging on these systems from their environments. The loss of a federal grant may trigger a host of reactions within an agency, affecting staff, program, and clients. These changes in turn may result in new responses from the agency's environment.

Research methods devised for study of these phenomena cover a broad spectrum. One strategy has been to employ elaborate statistical techniques to tease out causal relationships within sets of variables. These include variations of more traditional multivariate methods such as path analysis, (Blalock 1972) as well as newer methods of sequential analysis (Cousins and Power 1986). A quite different approach has been to piece together word pictures of the operation of complex systems through participant observation and other qualitative methods. But the rigorous specification of causal patterns in social systems does not yet appear to be within the grasp of any available methodology.

In short, the scientific method cannot be expected to provide complete or certain explanations for the diverse phenomena with which social workers are concerned. It can only provide a source of evidence that certain factors may influence others in certain ways. In professional decision making, this evidence, which may be derived from both experimental and nonexperimental research, forms a part of a complex equation composed of various sources of knowledge, including an understanding of the particular characteristics of the situation at hand. Scientific knowledge may affect these equations by increasing or decreasing the probability that one factor is the cause of another under a given set of circumstances. A scientifically oriented practitioner normally gives greater weight to research evidence than to expert opinion in determining probable causes of phenomena but seldom finds that this evidence alone provides a sufficient base for decision making.

SIZE AND MAKEUP OF SAMPLE

A third basis for distinguishing among research strategies is the size and makeup of samples. Samples are composed of basic units that in social work research are generally social systems—individuals, families, organizations, communities, and so on. A study may focus on a single unit, several, or a large number. These differences have important implications for strategy.

Because the most common unit in social work research is the individual, we begin at this level. Let us contrast a study involving a single subject with one involving, say a group of twenty. The general purpose of each study may be the same, say, to learn more about the behavior of young, profoundly deaf children, but with a sample of one an investigator is likely to do a highly intensive study in which a considerable amount of data is collected about one child. In the group study less is likely to be learned about any particular child, but the investigator may uncover behavior patterns that characterize most of the children. If so, she has some basis for inferring that other deaf children will show that pattern. The single-subject investigator is more limited in her ability to generalize from her data since the child selected may have been atypical. Yet in the single case the investigator may have uncovered more to generalize about. Being able to concentrate on a single child and to mold measurements to fit the particular characteristics of that child, she may emerge with hypotheses that are more revealing and have possibly greater general significance, even if their significance is more difficult to establish.

In the foregoing illustration, a study of a single individual was compared with that of a group of individuals selected because of common characteristics; all were young, profoundly deaf children. Such a group is an example of a homogeneous group, for its members are presumably similar in respect to the variable of primary interest. The investigator is interested in learning about other ways in which the group as a whole can be characterized. Do the children express aggression in a similar manner? Are there consistent themes in the kind of reactions they evoke from their parents? While studies confined to homogeneous groups may serve useful exploratory and descriptive functions, they are fundamentally limited in one major respect: they lack comparative data. Thus descriptions of how the children behave have an inevitable inconclusive quality since it is difficult to say if such behavior distinguishes this group from other groups of children. Generalizations about a single group do not "speak for themselves." They are accompanied by implicit assumptions about the rest of the world.

The logic of this process bears a closer look because it involves an important principle of research strategy. Interpretations of research data, unlike water, tend to gravitate toward the highest level—toward establishing associations, causal if possible, between variables. In interpreting results of a study of a homogeneous group, we implicitly move in that direction. Thus if we say that our deaf children appeared to evoke certain common reactions from their parents, we are implicitly suggesting an association between the deafness of the children and certain behaviors or attitudes on the part of their parents. We say in effect deafness in children and this type of parental reaction "go together." We would not expect such a reaction with, say, normal children. The study has not, however, provided us with data on the reactions of parents to other kinds of children, data needed to provide evidence for the association inferred.

By extending this logic, we can readily see why an investigation is typically not confined to a homogeneous group but rather involves comparisons between sets of subjects. To continue our example, a researcher, if possible, would usually attempt to contrast a sample of deaf children with a sample of children without this handicap, and she would proceed in a more explicit way to relate deafness to parental reactions (among other factors) by comparing reactions of parents of both kinds of children.

What has been illustrated is the use of *multiple groups* to investigate relationships between variables. Multiple group designs are used for this purpose in both naturalistic and experimental research. In a service experiment, for example, one group of clients may receive one form of treatment; a second group may receive another; and outcomes for both groups are compared. Although the results may be expressed as differences between groups, they may be thought of as well as expressing a relation between two variables: type of treatment and outcome (see chapter 3). As can be seen, the design accomplishes somewhat the same purpose as the addition of a group of normal-hearing children in the first example; in each case, two groups differing on one variable are compared in relation to a second variable.

Our examples have been kept deliberately simple to illustrate general principles. In practice, associations between numerous pairs (or other combinations) of variables may be examined, and more than two groups may be used. When multiple groups are used, the investigator selects distinct groups of subjects according to predetermined criteria or forms groups through assigning subjects to treatment or control conditions. In short, the investigator sets out to create groups in order to compare them; she deliberately builds variation into her study.

Variation may be achieved by another means. A group may be selected that is sufficiently heterogeneous that one can reasonably expect sufficient variation to occur on independent variables of interest. Thus a researcher may be interested in doing a naturalistic study of the relation between the social worker's use of accurate empathy and change in adolescent clients. She is able to recruit a sample of twenty social workers with caseloads of adolescent clients with five cases from each worker. She assumes that there will be sufficient variation in both empathy ratings (obtained from analysis of tape recordings) and her measures of outcome to permit a study of the relationship. After her data have been collected and measurements obtained, she might well create multiple groups by dividing cases into those in which worker empathy was "high" and those in which it was "low" and compare the two sets of cases on client change. Even though she may actually use methods of analysis such as correlation, that would not require the formation of groups, she would nevertheless need to have the kind of variation that would permit her to do so. If all cases were rated at the same level of empathy, she would be able to learn nothing about the association between empathy and client change. In the example it would not have been possible to form groups of "high" and "low" empathy cases at the beginning of the study, because data for making this classification could be obtained only during the investigation.

We have thus far outlined a simple progression in sampling units—from the individual subject to a homogeneous group of subjects and then to multiple and heterogeneous groups. This progression involves considerations of both sample size and variability. As sample size is increased, the amount of attention that can be paid to study of any given subject is decreased, if the resources of the researcher are assumed to be fixed. At the same time, an increase in size enhances the potential for generalization—we say potential, for how well one can generalize from data about a set of subjects depends also (and more importantly) on the representativeness of the sample. Moreover, the larger the sample, the greater the chance that sufficient variability will occur to permit examination of relationships between variables.

In studies with larger samples the distinction between homogeneous and heterogeneous groups may be difficult to draw since sub-groups may be formed during the course of the analysis. The purpose of the study is perhaps the critical consideration. In a heterogenous group study the investigator sets out to examine the relation of independent and dependent variables and forms groups in respect to one or more independent variables—e.g., "high" versus "low" empathy practitioners—or accomplishes the equivalent through correlations. However, in homogeneous group studies, which generally serve descriptive-exploratory purposes, such variation is not critical to the purposes of the study, even though it may be examined if measurements and sample size permit.

A common pitfall is to obtain a sample one thinks is sufficiently large and heterogeneous to permit an adequate test of particular relationships, when in fact it is not. This problem is most likely to occur when sample sizes are small and when little is known about expected variability. Thus, in one instance, a student was interested in testing a hypothesis about the relationship between self-concept and assertiveness in a sample of thirty-five sixth-grade girls. Given the size and composition of her sample, there proved to be insufficient variability in self-concept (as she was able to measure it) to permit a meaningful test of the hypothesis. Some of the ways of avoiding this predicament include use of screening instruments in subject selection to obtain "high" and "lows" in a variable, pretesting of the instrument to be used, getting data from published research on its discriminative capacities, and estimating variability needed in order to show significant relationships.

These considerations also apply when the sampling unit is a larger social system. Thus a single case study might consist of a description of the decision-making processes of an organization. A heterogeneous group study could be a comparison of delinquency rates of communities varying in socioeconomic characteristics. Study of larger social systems often involves, however, more complex considerations relating to sample size and composition than a study of individuals. This is so because such larger systems, as noted in chapter 1, are in themselves made up of subsystems including individuals. For example, in a "case study" of the child care service system in a community, the investigator might elicit data from dozens of individuals in various agencies. These data might then be analyzed and even interpreted as one might in a heterogeneous group study of individuals. What would make it a case study would be an effort to use the data to make statements about a particular service system.

TIMING OF MEASUREMENT

When measurements are taken constitutes another dimension of research strategy. (We use "measurement" here in a general sense to include data collection processes.) A fundamental distinction concerns whether measurement occurs before or after the operation of the presumed causative or independent variable. If an initial measurement takes place prior in time, the study is referred to as prospective or projected; if measures are not obtained until after the independent variables have exerted their influence, the research is designated as retrospective or ex post facto. If a study lacks an explanatory purpose—for example, if it is designed primarily to describe the current state of some phenomenon, the distinction between independent and dependent variables may not occur. In that case, a third category, which we term "undifferentiated," is possible.

Let us first consider prospective and ex post facto strategies within the context of naturalistic research, where the issue of which to select is most likely to arise. Consider a study of the effects of "mothering ability"—warmth, attentiveness, and the like—on the development of infants during the first six months of life. If a prospective strategy were used, a sample of women might be obtained prior to delivery and their mothering ability measured. Whereas data on the infants might be obtained shortly after birth, data pertaining to the possible effects of mothering abilities on the infants' development would not be obtained until after these abilities had presumably had a chance to work. Using an ex post facto strategy, a researcher would obtain a sample of women who had children about six months of age; measurements of mothering abilities and the infants' developmental characteristics would be obtained at about the same time—that is, after the independent variable had supposedly exerted its effects.

Clearly the prospective strategy is preferable, if feasible. In the ex post facto case, the passage of time alone would make it difficult to obtain adequate measures of independent (and control variables) and to secure baseline data. Moreover, the action of the independent and dependent variables themselves may distort the picture. Thus, in the given example, women with poor mothering ability might be aware of their limitations or as a result of them may be having difficulty with their infants. For these or other reasons associated with their mothering ability, they may choose not to participate in the ex post facto study; these women might have agreed to be subjects in the prospective study. Some infants may have developed slowly for reasons unrelated to mothering abilities, but their retarded development may have adversely affected these abilities (a mother might react with less warmth to an unresponsive infant). Such reversals of the expected causal direction might be impossible to detect after the fact and could give false support to the hypothesis that poor mothering ability adversely affects infant development. It is difficult to reconstruct the past—to determine how one thing looked before another thing happened or to ascertain what preceded what in the time order of events.

A naturalistic study that moves forward in time largely avoids this particular set of problems but encounters others. First of all, in a prospective study one must wait for events to happen. Many natural processes work slowly, too slowly for the circumstances of some researchers, students in particular. The longer the time period that must elapse before effects can be detected, the greater the likelihood that attrition in the original sample will occur (although in ex post facto studies, the equivalent of sample loss can occur in ways that cannot be detected). Perhaps the most serious limitation, however, is in range of application. For a prospective study to be practical, one must deal in effects that are likely to occur. Many effects of concern to social work are problems, such as child abuse or running away, whose occurrence can hardly be counted on for any given sample. A prospective strategy fits well to a study of maternal behavior and infant development, for all infants develop in one way or another. It might not be at all feasible for a study of maternal contribution to "failure-to-thrive" syndrome, for an inordinately large number of mothers would need to be sampled to ensure that the problem would occur with enough frequency to permit meaningful study of its relation to maternal behavior. Finally, a prospective strategy does not rectify the limitation of a naturalistic study in respect to lack of control over extraneous variables; for example, an observed relation between mothering ability and infant development would need to be considered in the light of shared genetic factors that might explain both phenomena.

Difficult choices between prospective and ex post facto strategies are less likely to arise in the context of experimentation. A prospective approach is the standard because the researcher controls the occurrence of the independent variable. Ex post facto measurement may be used, however, in "after only" evaluations of experiments in which measurements of outcome are confined to treated groups and obtained after treatment has been completed (chapter 7).

REPETITION OF MEASUREMENT

A related dimension concerns the repetition of measurement. A variable may be measured in one, two, several, or numerous occasions as time passes. If measurement is confined to a single occasion, the study may be referred to as cross-sectional. In experiments and prospective naturalistic studies, there are normally at least two measurement points, one prior to and one following the occurrence of the independent variable. Our focus here is on longitudinal or time-series investigations in which measurements are repeated several times; further we limit our attention to naturalistic research. Use of repeated measurement in experimental contexts is taken up in the next two chapters.

Regardless of the number of occasions on which measures are taken or the terms used to describe the process, the repetition of measurement serves one fundamental purpose: to record variation of the same phenomena over time. Although data on such variation is used in conjunction with all knowledge-building functions of research, their role in respect to two functions—description and explanation—is of particular importance.

From a descriptive standpoint, knowledge of how phenomena change provides a foundation for prediction even if the causes of the change are not apparent. Thus through longitudinal research we can address a range of questions of considerable interest to social work practitioners: What kinds of troublesome behaviors are children likely to outgrow? How long does it take psychological crises to run their course? Is street crime increasing in a particular neighborhood? Answers to such questions provide data that can inform the assessment of targets and the planning of intervention. Descriptive longitudinal studies perform this function by providing data about what is likely to happen in the case or situation at hand. With this knowledge, practitioners can attempt to devise interventions that may alter a predictable course of events, or they may decide that intervention is not warranted.

Longitudinal studies can serve explanatory functions if independent variables can be identified and their presumed effects assessed over time. Such studies can be thought of as extensions of the kind of naturalistic prospective investigation considered in the preceding section: mothers and their infants in the previous example can be measured at repeated intervals over a period of a year or so. The additional measurements would help determine whether differences in mothering capacity persisted over time and, more importantly, whether apparent effects on their infants became more or less pronounced.

Because meaningful variation in most phenomena occurs at a slow pace, naturalistic research involving repeated measurements normally spans substantial periods of time, from months to years. Such studies are costly and often suffer from sample attrition. Their lengthy time spans pose feasibility problems for researchers, such as students who must complete their work within limited time periods, and require researchers to delay satisfaction of their curiosity.

Still a longitudinal study need not be so formidable as the foregoing suggests. Longitudinal studies are conducted in stages, and between stages other kinds of work can be done. Moreover, data can be analyzed and reported for each stage, and thus one can avoid the need to wait endlessly for "final" results. A good deal of longitudinal research makes use of available data. For example, the large-scale, long-term panel study of the economic practices of 5,000 families conducted at the University of Michigan (Morgan et al. 1974) has been used as the basis for a number of longitudinal investigations. Longitudinal studies done from existing data sets are quite feasible for students, for there is no need to wait for data to be collected.

For our discussion of longitudinal research, we have assumed that the same persons are studied over time, and this is generally the case. In naturalistic research these groups are often referred to as "panels"—hence, "panel study." However, certain longitudinal investigations—sometimes referred to as "trend studies—may use data drawn from a population whose composition may shift over time. Thus, a study of youth crime rates in a community over a period of several years would be based on successive waves of youths. Interpretations of these trend studies may be complicated by shifts in the population base. A youth crime rate may show an increase because of increased numbers of youth in a community or because of changes in the makeup of the youth population resulting from in-migration and other factors.

METHODOLOGICAL ORIENTATION

Our final distinction concerns differences between "quantitative" and "qualitative" strategies for investigating phenomena. This distinction sometimes refers simply to techniques of data collection and analysis. For example, qualitative analysis makes use of numbers; quantitative analysis relies on words. However, it may also stand for marked differences in conception of the scientific method and in basic approaches to conducting an investigation. Our focus will be on the second meaning of this distinction.

Quantitative methodology can be said to describe the extension to the social sciences of the methodology of the natural sciences. In the canons of this methodology the researcher's role is that of the objective observer whose involvement with phenomena being studied is limited to what is required to obtain necessary data. Studies are focused on relatively specific questions or hypotheses that ideally remain constant throughout the investigation. Data collection procedures and types of measurement are constructed in advance of the study and applied in a standardized manner. Data collectors, such as interviewers or observers, are expected to obtain only the data called for in schedules or guidelines and to avoid adding their own impressions or interpretations. Measurement is normally focused on specific variables that are, if possible, quantified through rating scales, frequency counts, and other means. Analysis proceeds by obtaining statistical breakdowns of the distribution of the variables and by using statistical methods to determine associations (or differences) between variables.

This paradigm has long been dominant in the social sciences and in social work research. The methodology presented in this book reflects that dominance.

Qualitative methodologists proceed from the premise that the methods of the natural sciences, while useful in the study of social phenomena, should not be regarded as the ideal model for all social research. In their view important, if not the most meaningful, social phenomena are best understood through a rather different approach. When executed in pure form, this strategy reveals a number of characteristics that set it apart from orthodox methodology. First of all, the researcher attempts to gain a firsthand, holistic understanding of phenomena of interest by means of a flexible strategy of problem formulation and data collection shaped as the investigation proceeds. Methods such as participant observation and unstructured interviewing are used to acquire an in-depth knowledge used to guide further study. For example, a qualitative researcher may be interested in a study of hospital emergency rooms. As any investigator about to embark upon a study, she would have certain questions in mind—perhaps concerning reasons patients came for treatment and how they were treated—but would regard a focus on a small set of specific questions premature. She would expect questions and hypotheses to emerge as she gained knowledge of this particular system. She might proceed with the study through taking the role of a patient (one kind of participant observation) or by simply sitting in the waiting room and watching what happened (another kind of participant observation). During the investigation, she might talk informally to patients or staff. Some of these conversations might take the form of unstructured interviews. Whom she talked to, or interviewed, would depend on her emerging knowledge of the situation and the questions or hypotheses it stimulated. Learning that certain patients were frequent users of the emergency services, she might hypothesize that some patients might be using the service as a clinic and pursue this hypothesis through additional collection of data from whatever patients or staff might be most informative. Stress would be placed on understanding the system from the perspectives of the actors involved rather than through imposition of the researchers' theoretical views. She would analyze her data as she acquired them, not only at the end of the study, and the results of her analysis would guide further inquiry.

As may be gathered from the example, qualitative methodology rests on the assumption that valid understanding can be gained through accumulated knowledge acquired firsthand by a single researcher. In the words of Glaser and Strauss, one puts "trust in one's own credible knowledge" (1970:294).

Lincoln and Guba expand on this principle in their conception of the "human-as-instrument" (1985:192). As these authors point out, the human being possesses unique qualities as an instrument of research, including capacity to respond to a wide range of cues, to view phenomena within a holistic perspective, while noting atypical features, to process data on the spot bringing a fund of knowledge to the task, and to test out new knowledge immediately.

Thus essential validity is accorded the researcher's understanding gained through variable methods of data collection and through the use of her own capacity for analysis and synthesis of complex events. In taking this position, qualitative methodologists assume that the researcher is able to make rigorous observations and to control the effects of her own biases on the events observed and interpretations of them. Measures of reliability in the sense of determining how well independent observers agree on the same events are usually not possible to obtain and, in view of assumptions about the validity of the researcher's knowledge, are not seen as crucial. The assumptions and methods of qualitative research lead to products that differ markedly from the products of quantitative research. Reports of qualitative research tend to be largely presentations of the researcher's accumulated knowledge of the phenomena studied with documentation in the form of examples and quotes from subjects. One usually does not find details of method, such as who was queried about what, layouts of data upon which conclusions were based, and, needless to say, much in the way of numbers.

In a comparative assessment of quantitative and qualitative methodology, one must confront a fundamental difference in the epistemological basis of the two approaches. As indicated, qualitative methodologists ascribe an essential validity to the firsthand, holistic knowledge acquired by the researcher. Quantitative methodologists, on the other hand, are basically skeptical about knowledge gained in this way, objecting to its imprecision, its vulnerability to bias, and lack of rigor in investigating causal sequences. As a result, they tend to view qualitative methodology as a form of exploratory-formulative research, useful primarily as a precursor to more definitive quantitative investigations. Rejecting this subordinate role, qualitative researchers believe that their methods are quite capable of acquiring definitive knowledge. For example, Glaser and Strauss have argued that qualitative methodology is "a strategy concerned with the discovery of substantive theory, not with the feeding of quantitative researchers" (1970:289). Further, they contend that "qualitative research is of the the the most 'adequate' and 'efficient' method for obtaining the type of information required and for contending with the difficulties of an empirical research situation."

Using such arguments, a number of writers have questioned the philosophical and methodological foundations of social work research in recent years (Ruckdeschel and Farris 1981; Rein and White 1981; Heineman Pieper 1985; Karger 1983; Haywood 1984). Although these critics have not spoken with one voice, common themes in their arguments have related to the inadequacy of paradigms commonly taught, used, and accepted by social work researchers. More specifically, conventional research methodology has been faulted for placing undue value on quantitative approaches, experimental designs, objective measurement, and statistical analysis. They have argued that social work research, as well as much social science research, has borrowed from the physical sciences methodologies often ill-suited for study of the ever-changing and elusive complexities of social phenomena. The critics see a place for "hard-science" methodology in social work but argue that it has been erroneously equated with "good science." They charge that the social work research establishment is wedded to an excessively narrow or obsolescent philosophy of science—logical empiricism as Heineman (1981, 1985) puts it. They propose instead new paradigms based on different assumptions about what constitutes valid research (Haworth 1984). These advocates appear to be calling for a more fundamental reorientation to the nature of knowledge, one that would eliminate or even revise the usual one-up position of traditional research models. However, means for putting these ideas into practice have not yet been developed in any detail (Karger 1983).

Their criticisms and proposals have been vigorously disputed (Schuerman 1983; Hudson 1982; Geismar 1982). For example, Schuerman (1983) has argued that conventional research approaches are rooted in principles that antedate and transcend these philosophical movements.

In any event, there appear to be differences that cannot be resolved by fact or argument in what one assumes to be valid knowledge and the kind of evidence needed to establish its validity. Apropos is the distinction made by the philosopher William James between "tough-minded" and "tender-minded" approaches to knowledge, as elaborated by Kogan and Shyne (1965). To assert that something is true, the tough-minded may want evidence based on quantitative and objective measures with control for alternative explanations. The tender-minded may be more willing to accept as true the unverified perceptions of a thoughtful and systematic investigator, especially if they seem to portray the complex interrelationships and nuances of the situation studied. The distinction is not limited to research. There are tough-minded and tender-minded practitioners in respect to the extent to which inferences and theoretical speculations are used as the basis for practice decisions.

Rooted as they are in different orientations to knowing, these espistomological differences can never be completely resolved. Instead, what is now being seen in social work is an expression of a philosophical dispute that is old as science.

It may be true that the knowledge gained by the qualitative researcher may be skewed by her biases, but at the same time it may reveal a richness and depth of understanding of complex situations that is simply beyond the capacity of quantitative research, no matter how rigorously and artfully applied. Firsthand involvement in data collection, a holistic viewpoint, and the gradual synthesis of data from many sources can result in a grasp of relationships that might never emerge in fragmented quantitative analysis.

Qualitative approaches have particular strengths as a means of acquiring holistic knowledge of complex social systems, including service networks, organizations, small groups, families, and the social systems of different kinds of people—for example, the worlds of the drug addict or the welfare recipient. The need for such knowledge is of unquestioned importance in social work.

Whereas qualitative methodology can often yield knowledge that cannot be obtained by quantitative methods, the converse is also true, as most qualitative methodologists would acknowledge. Control over extraneous variables, systematic measurement, precision in analysis, and the capacity to study large numbers of subjects enable quantitative researchers to acquire knowledge beyond the scope of qualitative investigations. The need for both kinds of approaches can be justified, and this seems to be what qualitative methodologists are arguing for.

Furthermore, the argument for the complementary use of these two methodologies can be carried to the level of the individual researcher. For some studies, the researcher may find that methods work better; for others, she may decide a qualitative approach may be superior. Often, she may wish to use some combination of the two within a single study.

Underlying differences in philosophical premises can be reconciled by taking the pragmatic position that it is desirable to quantify, exert experimental control, secure reliability data, and so on, when it is feasible to use these procedures and when the result in terms of knowledge gained warrants their use. For example, few qualitative metholologists would argue against the use of rigorously controlled experiment with highly quantified measures to test the effects of a specific intervention, say in a laboratory setting, if the results could be expected to yield definitive conclusions about the effectiveness of the intervention. However, when the limited range of valid application of quantitative methods is realized, a vital role for qualitative approaches emerges —not as a "second best" methodology but one that provides a better fit to a wide range of research situations.

DIMENSIONS IN COMBINATION

This chapter has presented a multidimensional conception of research strategy, one that reflects, we think, the complexity of decisions involved in study design. The dimensions identified, together with important subcomponents, are outlined here.

   I. The Researcher's Control over Phenomena Studied
      A. Experimental
         1. Field
            a. Controlled

            b. Partially Controlled
            c. Uncontrolled
        2. Laboratory
            a. Controlled
            b. Partially Controlled
            c. Uncontrolled
    B. Naturalistic
 II. Size and Composition of Sample
    A. Single Case
    B. Homogeneous Group
    C. Heterogeneous Group or Multigroup
III. Function in Relation to Type of Knowledge Produced
    A. Exploratory
    B. Measurement
    C. Descriptive
    D. Explanatory
 IV. Timing of Measurement in Relation to Occurrence of Independent Variable
    A. Ex Post Facto
    B. Prospective
    C. Undifferentiated
  V. Repetition of Measurement
    A. Single Occasion
    B. Two Occasions (Before and After)
    C. Repeated Occasions (Panel, Longitudinal, Time Series)
 VI. Methodological Orientation
    A. Quantitative
    B. Qualitative

These dimensions can be combined in various ways to generate different types of studies. Consider, for example, a field experiment involving a single case conducted for exploratory purposes using before-and-after measurement and quantitative methods. Such a configuration would be illustrated by a preliminary test of a method of intervention carried out with a client by a practitioner who obtained frequency measures of the client's behavior before and after intervention. Or consider a study with the following facets: naturalistic; homogeneous group; exploratory and descriptive; repeated occasions; qualitative. An example might be an investigation in which a researcher, as a participant observer, recorded the "induction process" experienced by a cohort of elderly persons during their first few weeks in a residential institution. (As this example illustrates, a particular facet, in this case the knowledge-building function, may yield mixed types.) A study that compared a group of children reared by alcoholic mothers with a group reared by normal mothers to determine through correlational techniques the effects of parental drinking on child development might be characterized as naturalistic, explanatory, multigroup, ex post facto, quantitative.

Although our multifaceted scheme can be used to generate types of design and to classify studies, its primary value, we think, is to present a systematic layout of possible research strategies. We hope this overview will facilitate the understanding and assessment of research, as well as research planning. For the latter purpose, the scheme provides a range of possibilities that may be useful to consider in designing a study and perhaps can suggest combinations of strategies that might not otherwise be considered.

CHAPTER 5

NATURALISTIC DESIGNS

In this chapter we shall consider some types of naturalistic designs within a social work context, types that emerge from combining dimensions in the scheme set forth in the preceding chapter. Actual or potential importance in generating social work knowledge and the feasibility of use in student research were among the considerations employed in selecting the designs.

Studies will be grouped into two major categories of knowledge-building function: exploratory-descriptive and explanatory-predictive. Within these groupings specific types, further characterized by additional dimensions, will be looked at. The chapter will also provide critiqued illustrations of a variety of naturalistic studies.

EXPLORATORY-DESCRIPTIVE

Many social work research studies combine both exploratory and descriptive functions. They aim to gain preliminary understanding, develop hypotheses, *and* also to provide descriptive data, especially in areas where little empirically based knowledge is available. Common applications include studies of characteristics of client or at-risk groups and studies of community, agency practitioner and service characteristics. Since exploratory and descriptive studies, as a rule, are neither prospective nor use repeated measures, they will be delineated by dimensions relating to size and composition of sample and to methodological orientation.

Heterogeneous Group: Quantitative Since the beginnings of the survey movement (chapter 3), a common application of studies of this type in social work has been to explore and describe the characteristics of client or at-risk populations. Although a particular population may be the target, sample size and selection usually permits some comparisons of subgroups.

For example, Goldberg, Kantrow, Kremen, and Lauter addressed a study to questions concerning the support systems of childless, elderly women. They were interested in the sources of support used by these women "to meet needs for companionship and socialization" and to cope with illness, social-psychological problems and financial need. Other questions covered differences in support provided by kin and friends and the extent the elderly women were engaged "in a mutual exchange of benefits (reciprocity) with friends and kin" (1986:104–105).

In short, an at-risk group of women was identified and a study was designed to answer basic descriptive questions about their support systems: at the same time the researchers hoped to gain preliminary understanding that could lead to hypotheses for practice and research. In-person interviews were held with 52 single, elderly, childless women 65 years and older from diverse socioeconomic backgrounds and communities in northeastern United States. As is typical in this kind of study, the interview consisted of a combination of fixed and open-ended questions derived from the basic questions of the researchers.

A number of findings were revealed. "On the whole, women in the sample had close ties and frequent contacts with families, friends, or both. Informal social support was being provided to nearly all of the women in the sample who were over 80" (p. 110). Women who shared a home with a friend or relative (over 25 percent of the sample) seemed particularly well off in respect to informal supports.

Although the findings were generally reassuring, the picture was not uniformly rosy. For instance, "more than two-fifths of the women in the sample had no younger-generation relatives to whom they felt close." As might be expected, in fact welcomed, in a study with exploratory purposes, some results were not anticipated. A number of women were living together in what might have been lesbian relationships. Unprepared for this contingency, the researchers did not investigate the possibility. Also unexpected and not provided for in the research instrument was the large number of women who had close friends and relatives in the same building—"building mates" as the authors describe them.

A major limitation of the study, as descriptive research, had to do with biases in the sample—toward women who were perhaps younger, healthier and more likely to be city dwellers than the average woman over 65. As noted earlier, such a limitation need not preclude program planning or other service initiatives that are directed at a similar population.

One of the authors' main recommendations was that "housing and living arrangements that facilitate supportive relationships should be encouraged by social policy." Although this recommendation flows typically from the findings of the study, one might say that the sample is too small and not sufficiently representative to serve as a base for such a policy initiative. Granted this, it is still useful for researchers to project the kind of policy recommendations that follow from the samples they study. By so doing, they can generate ideas and possible courses of action that have at least some empirical basis.

Homogeneous Group: Qualitative Studies of this type have a time-honored tradition in anthropology and sociology. Such classics as the *Street Corner Society* (Whyte 1981) and *Five Families* (Lewis 1959) come to mind. Basically, this kind of investigation consists of in-depth study of a homogeneous group of subjects or a single system. Use is made of such methods as semi-structured interviews and participant observation. The purpose is to provide a "thick description" (Geertz 1973; Lincoln and Guba 1985) of the complexities that characterize the objects of study.

An example is provided by Krassner's (1986) study of *curanderismo,* a form of faith healing common among Mexican-Americans. Krassner conducted in-depth interviews (from one to six hours) with five experienced practitioners of *curanderismo (curanderos).* Viewing curanderismo as a form of interpersonal therapy, Krassner asked the five practitioners questions that might be asked of any therapist—questions concerning training, how they obtained their theories of illness, and methods of diagnosis and treatment. Her report was a description of the curanderos' beliefs and practices empirically grounded with liberal quotes from the interviews and conceptualized in a way to facilitate comparison with mainstream "anglo" therapists. Thus, she was able to provide an account of how curanderos used the client's religious faith to heighten expectations that the treatment experience would be beneficial in a manner similar to mainstream therapists' use of their client's faith in the expertise of professionals. Although variations among the curanderos studied are discussed, stress is on themes that characterize them as a group.

The study is of interest to social workers for two reasons: it depicts a minority "therapy culture" that can enhance our understanding of dominant western practices; it provides insight into a helping system widely used by Mexican-Americans, often as an alternative to standard mental health services. The study also illustrates a type of design that is feasible for student research. In fact, Krassner herself completed the study as a thesis requirement for her MSW.

We think this kind of design deserves to be used more than it is—one reason for presenting it as an example. Although one must take into account its limitations, including small sample size and investigatory bias, it can be a rich source of knowledge. This is especially so when the phenomena to be studied do not lend themselves to more conventional research methods, as in the Krassner example.

Studies with Explanatory and Predictive Functions

A naturalistic study that attempts to explain or predict must first establish some form of association between variables as they naturally occur. Using means previously considered—matching, statistical control, explanation credibility, and so on—the researcher makes the case that one variable provides a possible explanation or prediction of another. The case is usually made with considerable qualification, as it should be, and of course the study may have other knowledge-building functions. Selected quantitative designs will be reviewed.

Ex Post Facto; Multigroup   A frequently used design in naturalistic research in social work and related fields is an ex post facto, multigroup comparison that attempts to identify factors responsible for a problem or characteristic. In brief, a group that has the problem or characteristic is compared with one that does not. Differences, if any, are discovered, and an attempt is made to use the differences for explanatory purposes. One can begin with groups defined by a presumed causative factor and treat differences as presumed effects, or one can start with groups identified by possible effects and treat differences as potential causes. An example of the first type of study, which Chapin (1955) has referred to as "cause-to-effect," would be a comparison of cohesive versus noncohesive communities with the hypothesis that the crime rates would differ. "Cohesiveness" would be the cause and "crime rates" the effect. The second type, or "effect-to-cause" (Chapin 1955), is illustrated by a study that compares addicted and nonaddicted children in terms of differences in family structure. Addiction of children would be the effect and family structure, the cause. In both types, the researcher must be concerned with the time order of variables, unwanted variation between groups, and the possibility of alternative explanations.

An example of one of these types of study is an effort by Weihe (1984) to investigate the impact of divorce on children. Weihe compared 62 children from divorced families with 60 children from intact families in a cause-to-effect study. The children, who ranged in age from 9 to 14, were pupils in a public school serving primarily blue-collar families. From available research and theory, three hypotheses were advanced. Essentially, it was predicted that children from divorced families would differ from intact families in the following respects: (1) "exhibit lower self-esteem"; (2) "be functioning from a more external than internal locus of control orientation"; and (3) "reflect less positive attitudes toward their parents" (p. 19). The children completed self-report instruments measuring self-esteem, attitude toward parents, and locus of control. Results were essentially as predicted and interpreted by the author as a consequence of divorce.

Although the two groups of children were similar in respect to age and sex, lack of data from parents made it difficult to assess other variables, such as socioeconomic status. That the children, as noted, came from the same school serving a working-class population provides an argument that the groups may not have differed in respect to socioeconomic status. As with the hypothetical example considered earlier, differences between the groups that may influence both divorce rate and children's self-esteem—ethnicity, for example—need to be taken into account. The possibilty of rival explanations from such sources is offset, however, by the confirmation of the three hypotheses. Two of these hypotheses, those concerning locus of control and attitudes, carry particular weight, or explanation credibility, since they reflect specific theoretical predictions relating to the effects of divorce. As the author theorized, "post-divorce children may be likely to perceive divorce as a phenomenon over which they have no control, which may reinforce in them an external orientation of control" (p. 19). The expected difference in attitude toward parents, while perhaps self-explanatory, is also keyed specifically to theory relating to post-divorce family life. Although rival hypotheses relating to antecedent factors cannot be ruled out, the credibility of the explanation provides strong support for the author's interpretation of the findings.

But can the differences be *simply* explained by divorce? The study illustrates points made earlier: it is difficult to disentangle factors that have already occurred, and the theory offered as the explanation may not be the only one that fits the findings. Children who have experienced divorce have also experienced poor marriages, and there is evidence to suggest that marital discord itself may have a deleterious effect on children. Perhaps cumulative effects of marital conflict and divorce, *and* their aftermath, account for the findings. In any case, "divorce" can be seen as a useful "marker" variable, one that points to a constellation of processes that need to be better understood. Like this study, much ex post facto research aimed at explanation may provide less than definitive evidence concerning the causal role of independent variables. It may still, however, suggest the possible causal role of those variables, thereby serving explanatory functions, and it may help to characterize populations studied, thereby serving descriptive functions. For example, if replications of the present study found that children of divorced parents were more likely than other children to have low self-esteem, that knowledge would be clinically useful even though we might not be able to pinpoint processes responsible.

As discussed in chapter 2, a key question in social work practice theory concerns the relation of client characteristics to differences in service outcomes. Although this question can be considered as a part of prospective experimental research (chapters 6 and 7), it is also frequently addressed in naturalistic studies that are conducted after services have been completed.

A good example is provided by a series of studies that have attempted to isolate factors associated with length of time children spend in foster care. The purpose of such studies is to construct "predictive" models that would help service practitioners and policy makers identify characteristics of children and their families likely to result in lengthy stays, on the one hand, or short stays on the other.

One such study was an investigation by Seaberg and Tolley (1986) of a national sample of 3,950 cases of children who had been in foster placement. Essentially, a large number of variables characterizing the children, their families, and services received by them were correlated with the number of months children spent in foster care. The statistical analytic procedures (stepwise multiple regression, chapter 11) enabled the researchers to exercise the kind of statistical control discussed in the preceding chapter. Among the strongest predictors were the child's age and race. Older black children were likely to remain longer in foster care. Children who were handicapped or abandoned were also likely to remain longer. Although these findings may not be surprising to child welfare practitioners, the analysis provides measures of the relative strengths of the factors and also reveals a range of others that one might also expect to be related, such as institutionalization of the parent or the parent's unwillingness to care for the child, that did not prove to be predictors. Moreover, some relations proved puzzling and hence interesting. While children with shorter stays were more likely to have practitioners with social work training, their practitioners were also less experienced—a combination of results that warrants further investigation. Although such studies use the language of prediction, we again need to keep in mind that they attempt to reconstruct past events—in fact, they are more properly termed "postdictive." The distinction becomes important when we try to sort out time order of the variables. For example, is there something about practitioner experience that leads to longer time in foster care or are more experienced workers given cases that are more likely to become long term?

Even with over sixty variables entered into the analysis, a number were not included, which the authors helpfully enumerate. For example, one variable not included, "judicial delay" in processing cases, could be influential if delays were more likely to affect certain populations—e.g., black children. As the authors report, all their variables account for only 40 percent of the variance in length of case (chapter 11). This leaves a lot of variation unexplained (even though the amount of explained is quite respectable in social research).

The findings of the study provide a better basis for prediction than explanation and also illustrate the distinction between these two functions. From the results we learn that occurrence of abuse prior to placement is a predictor, but not neglect. An interesting finding, but we are not sure why this should be so. To be sure, explanations come to mind, but they are not part of any theory tested by the researcher. Contrast this with the Weihe (1984) study just discussed.

A final illustrative point concerns the importance of replication in ex post facto research. As sophisticated and comprehensive as this study is, it did not include all variables that might be influential. However, the validity of certain predictor variables—for example, the age of the children—is strengthened by their identification as predictors in previous studies that used different samples of cases and different sets of variables. Consistency in findings in such research reduces the likelihood of alternative explanations as well as helping to establish their generality.

Prospective; Multiple Occasion   Another approach to explanation in naturalistic research is to study a sample prospectively through repeated measures over a period of time, a type of study that is generally referred to as "longitudinal." In respect to sample size and composition, these studies normally use mixed groups of at least moderate size. Even if the group is originally identified as homogeneous at the outset, it is expected that differentiation will occur as time progresses. The explanatory function is obtained through analysis of factors that are apparently predictions of subsequent changes.

An example of a longitudinal study with an explanatory function is provided by Ell and Haywood (1984). This social worker-physician team was interested in investigating the influences of social support, sense of personal control, and other variables in recovery from myocardial infarction (MI) or heart attack. A panel of patients who had experienced heart attacks was selected from the coronary care units of two hospitals in the Los Angeles area. Data were collected at three time points: T_1, acute hospitalization (n = 114); T_2, six months later (n = 75); and T_3, one year later (n = 60). Social data, which were collected by graduate social workers in face-to-face interviews, consisted of instruments to measure recent life change events; network resources; social support from family and others; sense of control; and personal and family functioning. Data on the patient's physical functioning were obtained from chart review. Attrition from the sample was attributed to refusals to continue participation in the study, departures from the area, and a small number (7) of deaths.

Analysis was carried out by correlating "predictors," such as severity of illness and extent of social support obtained at T_1, with outcome variables, such as personal and physical functioning, obtained at T_2. The analysis was repeated using predictors at T_2 and outcomes at T_3. Among the findings from this complex analysis were that measures of social support and personal control (especially the latter) proved to be even better predictors of personal and physical functioning than severity or prognosis of illness. Statistical controls (stepwise multiple regression, chapter 11) indicated that measured sociodemographic factors, such as age, gender, marital status, SES, and ethnicity were not significantly related to outcome. Contrary to the belief that "support exerts greater influence during the presumed higher stress period of early recovery, support variables account for equal or greater variance among T_3 outcomes" (Ell and Haywood 1984:13). In other words, the influence of support variables does not diminish over time.

In addition to securing measures of variables less influenced by recall as well as repeated measures over time, the longitudinal feature of the design strengthens hypotheses that predictor variables, such as support and personal control, did not exert influence on personal and physical functioning. In a retrospective study that would start with cardiac patients at different levels of functioning it would be more difficult to rule out self-selection or (time order of variables) as an alternative explanation. That is, because a patient is doing better, he may be more likely to elicit support or enjoy a sense of control. While the panel design does not eliminate this possibility or other alternative explanations entirely, it provides better evidence than a retrospective study. Moreover, only a longitudinal feature could lead to the important conclusion concerning the importance of support in later stages of recovery. Panel studies also serve valuable descriptive functions. Thus, in the present example, one can trace over time the progress of recovery and changes in related factors even if explanations are not discovered. In fact some of the more arresting findings from longitudinal research are of this order. Thus, in a longitudinal study of 624 children in foster care by Fanshel and Shinn (1978), numerous predictive findings were overshadowed in the judgments of the authors by one brute fact: after five years, 36 percent of children were still in foster care. In their study of male alcoholism over a 33-year period, Vaillant and Milofsky (1982) discovered that severe alcohol abuse was more likely to lead to stable abstinence than mild abuse but that some "mild" alcoholics were able to return to social drinking—findings with both explanatory and descriptive implications.

The Ell-Haywood study also illustrates some of the disadvantages of longitudinal design: the lengthy span of data collection, the cost of repeated measures, the complexity of the analysis, and the inevitable problem of sample attrition. In their study, we note that almost half the sample had been lost by the time of the last measurement. The pattern of associations among variables by the researchers might have been different if the full sample, rather than half, had been available at the end. A sample of continuers can overrepresent the subjects who are less transient, more cooperative, and better functioning. Still, despite panel attrition and other limitations, studies like the present one can provide a useful picture of the process of change over time.

Although the study uses a predictive framework, essentially the same design can be used with an explanatory purpose, either through testing theoretical hypotheses or bringing theory to bear on the interpretation of findings. For example, Gary (1985) tested eighteen hypotheses in an "explanatory survey" of a sample of 142 noninstitutionalized black men. The hypotheses centered around possible explanations of depression in this population. Like Seaberg and Tolley, Gary basically determined patterns of associations between independent variables (e.g., conflict with women, racial consciousness) and a dependent variable (scores on a depression scale).

CHAPTER 6

SINGLE CASE EXPERIMENTS

In chapter 4, we argued that experimental strategies are of particular importance in social work research because they provide a direct and powerful means of enhancing methods of social work intervention. Hence, we examine these strategies in relation to how they can contribute to the improvement of those methods. We begin with single case experiments because they provide, we think, a convenient way to present and understand basic features of experimental research, which can then be applied to more complex group undertakings. Throughout the present chapter we usually interpret the single case to mean the single client, several clients (as in across-client designs), or a family unit. Application of single case methodology to the study of larger social systems is taken up in the next chapter.

Our intent is to present the fundamentals of single case experimentation as it may be used in social work practice contexts. Writing also from a social work perspective, Bloom and Fischer (1982) consider application of this methodology by practitioner-researchers. An extensive exposition of single case experiments from the perspective of behavioral psychology may be found in Barlow and Hersen (1984).

THE CASE STUDY

The most elementary form of the single case design is the case study, to use Bloom and Fischer's (1982) term. The case study consists of collection of data on case characteristics and change, and on interventions that presumably were influential in producing change. The design is "uncontrolled" in the sense that intervention is not systematically withheld or varied so that one can observe what happens in its absence.

Although this design is severely limited in its capacity to isolate treatment effects, it is of interest for several reasons. It is the most feasible and readily applied of any design that might be used to study the effects of intervention. It can serve an important function in preliminary tests of service approaches. Although it may not be able to determine effects of intervention in a definitive way, it can be used to generate hypotheses about these effects. And, as we shall see, in some studies this design can provide strongly suggestive, if not persuasive, evidence about the accomplishments of service. Finally it makes clear the need for (and the function of) the kind of controls used in more sophisticated single case designs.

In rudimentary versions the case study requires little more than accurate and complete recording of what many practitioners routinely do: conduct an assessment of a case situation, intervene in it, record interventions, and assess progress. The evolution of these practice routines into a research design begins when the practitioner-researcher desires to learn about the effects of some type of intervention with some case situation, either for enhancing results with the case at hand or acquiring knowledge that can be applied to other cases. An additional step is the collection of sytematic data on intervention targets and methods of intervention.

Problems in Determining Effectiveness

Regardless of the precision with which targets are measured, the case study is confronted with inherent problems in determining the contribution of intervention to change. Changes in client systems that *follow* the introduction of intervention may or may not be the *result* of the intervention. We return here to the problem of isolating causative factors that we considered in the previous chapter, though we now examine this problem within the context of experimental research and more specifically within the context of single case experimental trials of social work intervention.

Within the latter context, the question becomes "What proof do we have that intervention contributed to changes observed in client systems?" It is normally hypothesized that intervention was in fact responsible for the changes; one then needs to examine rival hypotheses or alternative explanations, that is, other factors that may have brought the changes about.

For a detailed examination of alternative explanations, we draw upon the work of Campbell and his associates (Campbell and Stanley 1963; Campbell 1969; Cook and Campbell 1979) and an extension of this work by Krathwohl (1985). Using their mode of analysis, one considers types of nontreatment factors that might account for variation in measures of dependent variables. These factors are viewed as potential "threats" to the "internal validity" of an experiment, that is, threats to the hypothesis that treatment was in fact responsible for change.

One such class of factors can be encompassed by the notion of *maturation*. In the context of social work experiments, maturational factors would include the client's self-generated problem-solving actions, diminution of emotional distress occurring with the passage of time, and normal growth. A second group of factors, *history*, would comprise specific environmental events that might influence the problem state, such as a change in the client's situation or the actions of others. A third source of alternative explanation—*statistical regression*—is more difficult to grasp but is of vital importance in research on intervention. Most of the problems dealt with by social workers are likely to show variation in magnitude (frequency and severity) over time; one common pattern is for a problem to build up to a peak (or crisis), then to decline; or many problems, such as depression or forms of marital conflict, may take cyclical courses, showing peaks and valleys over time. Suppose one selects a group of these fluctuating problems at a high point of magnitude, then takes measures of their magnitude and repeats these measures at a second point of time. Almost invariably the problem magnitude scores at the point of subsequent measurement will show a decline on the average. This is so because the problems had been initially selected at points of greatest magnitude; as a group they will naturally slide downward or "regress" to some lower level because of the inherent variability of the problem. By the same token, there is a good probability that the score of any given problem in the group will show a decline in magnitude. These regression artifacts are of particular concern in research on intervention, for intervention (and hence studies of it) is likely to begin when problems are at or close to their peak level. Hence, some positive change can often be expected as a result of regression alone. Some problems are, of course, more susceptible to regression effects than others: if a problem shows little variation over time—a stabilized pattern of heavy drinking, for example—regression may not be a major source of concern.

The factors described thus far, *maturation*, *history*, and *regression*, relate to changes in problems that may occur independent of efforts to measure or treat them. Additional sources of alternative explanations are related to the measurement processes used to determine if change has occurred.

Any study of the effects of experimental variables may be subject to various types of assessment errors, making *instrumentation* a potential source of rival hypotheses. Of particular concern in research on intervention are systematic biases in measurement that may erroneously suggest that changes have occurred in response to intervention. Practitioners or researchers responsible for data collection and the clients who may provide the data usually hope that the practice methods tested will in fact prove helpful and may have a strong prior conviction that they are effective. These hopes and convictions may influence the collection and analysis of data. Consequently, in interviews, observations, or other commonly used procedures in which bias may operate, gains occurring after treatment may be exaggerated and evidence of continued problem occurrence may be overlooked. Or if assessment consists, as it often does, of a set of instruments, there may be a tendency to select out or stress measures that cast the experimental intervention in a favorable light and to downplay those that do not produce positive findings. (An instrument originally thought to be dubious may be found to have all sorts of redeeming features if it yields results that the experimenter hopes to find!) Biases that favor the experimental hypothesis, or experimental "demand" (Rosenthal 1966), may operate in all phases of a project from selection of subjects to analysis of data. Whereas instrumentation may be particularly vulnerable to these biases, the possibility of their presence elsewhere should not be overlooked.

Along with errors of *instrumentation*, one must also consider the possible effects of *testing*. That is, devices used to collect initial assessment data may themselves contribute to change or apparent change. For example, in a study of a parent-skills training program, a parent's skills before training may be tested with paper-and-pencil inventory. The items of the test may provide the parent with clues about his skill deficiencies and he may take steps to correct them. Observations of behavior may cause individuals observed, if they are aware of being observed, to alter their behavior.

The assessment of the effects of social work intervention is inevitably complicated by difficulty in defining what an intervention is. The difficulty arises from the complexity and elusiveness of helping processes. Interventions seldom come in the form of single, specific, clear-cut methods but rather take the shape of messy gestalts—like "casework," for example—that are difficult to break down or to draw lines around. Now if an intervention is defined in terms of a certain set of activities that are supposed to work in a certain way, alternative explanations can be found in other activities that may have accompanied the interventions but may not have been defined as a central part of it. For instance, focusing the client's attention on a problem, conveying expectations that help will be provided and that change will occur, or simply allowing the client to ventilate his concerns might be a part of any attempt of one person to help another with a problem. Although such nonspecific elements may be regarded as a part of professional intervention, it is usually assumed that they are not sufficient to provide clients with the help they need. Definitions of interventions generally emphasize more specific and presumably more potent elements that take the form of procedures, skills, and the like. There is considerable evidence to suggest, however, that nonspecific components—or what are sometimes referred to as placebo effects—can produce significant change (Shapiro and Morris 1978; Shapiro 1984). Accordingly, they can be regarded as a potential source of an alternative explanation. In this manner, if clients who receive "behavioral casework" show certain benefits, one hopes to demonstrate that these resulted from the special characteristics of this form of casework and not simply from having someone show interest in the client, listen to his problem, and so on. If a comparable group of clients received a form of "treatment" consisting essentially of these minimal efforts and the results were similar, one would conclude that the model of casework tested had failed to demonstrate its effectiveness in any meaningful sense.

However, the interpretation is certainly complicated in such cases by the overlap between the "placebo" and "the real thing"—both contain certain common therapeutic denominators. As Kazdin (1986) suggests, more attention needs to be paid to these common nonspecific effects in intervention research, and there is need for greater clarity about what a placebo treatment is controlling for. Meanwhile, it is probably better to avoid altogether the term placebo. Its pharmaceutical connotation of "inert" ingredients is misleading when applied to interpersonal contacts that may provide clients with interest, attention, emotional support, opportunity to ventilate their concerns, and so on.

In addition to nonspecific effects, there may be more specific interventive or quasi-interventive procedures that are not seen as part of the intervention tested. For instance, a client on a ward might be moved to another location to receive some form of treatment. This change might need to be regarded as an alternative explanation if the treatment appeared to be effective. Possible effects such as these have been referred to by Glass, Willson, and Gottman (1975) as "multiple intervention interference."

In summary, the contribution of nonspecific or excluded intervention elements—or what might be called non-specific multiple intervention effects —need to be taken into account in evaluating service effectiveness. How these effects are evaluated depends in large measure on how the intervention itself is defined.

Finally, there is the possibility that apparent change following intervention may reflect the operation of chance. Like any set of scores, outcome measures exhibit some degree of fluctuation caused by unidentifiable factors that, for want of knowledge of them, are referred to as chance or random influences. This *instability* of outcome measures must therefore be taken into account in evaluating gains associated with treatment. An outcome measure might have been taken at an "up" point in the patterns of fluctuation. (Although instability is similar in some respects to statistical regression, the source of variation in instability is chance rather than the initial measurement as is the case in regression.) As will be shown, the role of instability can be evaluated through inspection of the data and through statistical tests of significance (see what follows and chapter 11).

The sources of alternative explanation examined thus far need to be considered in any experiment. Some additional sources must be taken into account in experimental designs involving groups of clients; these sources are taken up in the chapter following.

To illustrate how alternative explanations may be identified and appraised, let us consider a study in which a school social worker is interested in learning something about the effects of a home-based incentive system (Gambrill 1977) as a means of improving in-class academic performance of underachieving children. The intervention calls for the teacher to complete a daily report card on the child's performance. The card is sent home with the child at the end of each day. The child's parents review the card and provide rewards (e.g., food treats, TV privileges) contingent upon "good" marks on the report card. The practitioner meets with the child and parent initially to explain the program and as needed thereafter. The social worker conducts a study with the next such child referred. Initial assessment data consist of grades the child received on classroom assignments during the previous week. The social worker and teacher then institute the program. The child appears to do better after the program begins. The apparent upward trend is confirmed a month later when a second assessment, based on grades for classroom assignments, reveals a marked improvement in the child's academic work.

In analyzing this example, we can readily see that intervention is not the only plausible explanation of the changes observed. The child might have been motivated to change by the referral to the social worker or may have been in the process of improving his performance in response to any number of internal or external influences (maturation). Any number of changes occurring in the classroom or at home during the experiment might have affected the child's behavior (history); more specifically, the teacher, having identified the child's behavior as problematic, might have begun to treat him differently—in ways not related to the program. Because the child may have been referred at a low point in fluctuating performance pattern, statistical regression would provide an additional possible explanation. Instrumentation error would need to be considered in relation to the type of assessment data obtained, for the teacher's own stake in a successful outcome for the case and the intervention method could well have influenced her grading of the child's academic performance following treatment. Testing effects might be discounted on grounds that an underachieving child would not learn a great deal from routine classroom assignments. (The search is for plausible alternative explanations and not for explanations that may be conceivable but not likely.) Nonspecific/multiple intervention effects could have been operative in the initial session with the child and parents; in particular, one would need to consider the possible consequences of identifying the child's classroom performance as a problem and of conveying the expectation that the proposed program would be a means of resolving it. Instability of measurement would need to be considered. Although these factors have been presented one by one, it is obvious that they can interact in various ways. For example, an improvement in the child's behavior resulting from maturation could cause the teacher and his parents to act differently toward him.

Strengthening the Design

In the cited example, and in most case studies, it is difficult to draw definitive conclusions about the effects of intervention. However, when sufficiently strengthened and when used under the right conditions, the design may provide valuable evidence on effects of intervention. Because problem variability resulting from maturation and regression is a major source of alternative explanation in research on intervention, the first step in strengthening a case study is to obtain baseline data on variations in the problem before intervention. If research considerations were paramount, the data would be obtained prospectively; that is, one would collect data on the problem through observation or other means over a period of time, perhaps as long as several weeks, before intervention. (The design would then become a basic time series design in our classification. That design will be taken up in the section following.) If we assume it is not feasible to delay intervention for such a period or to devote the time required for prospective data collection, baseline data, albeit less accurate, may be collected retrospectively in initial interviews with clients and others or from available records.

Whatever the methods used, the investigator assesses how the problem has varied prior to intervention and thus can evaluate the extent to which maturation and regression might complicate interpretation of the effects of intervention. For certain problems, it may be possible to establish that little fluctuation has occurred. Thus in the preceding example it might have been possible, through an interview with the teacher or through records, to determine that the child's classroom academic performance had been relatively stable for the past several months (since the beginning of the school year). In other cases, baseline stability can be more readily determined: a man has been unemployed for the past two years, or for the last six months a landlord has done nothing to fix a rundown apartment. Establishing the chronicity of a problem obviously "helps" an uncontrolled design since changes following intervention cannot be readily attributed to maturation or regression. If the baseline pattern reveals considerable variation in the problem or a trend toward alleviation, an uncontrolled design may provide little information about treatment effects.

Although environmental influences (history) cannot be completely controlled, the investigator can collect data on the occurrence of more obvious events that might have affected problem change. Moreover, the investigator may be able to take action to avoid the occurrence of confounding environmental events; accordingly, the parents in our example might have been asked to postpone a plan to have the child tutored until the home-based program could be tested.

As we noted in chapter 2, the capacity of research to inform practice is enhanced if the practice under consideration is well explicated. This principle can be applied to the case study. If practice events and outcomes are explicated in terms of specific, observable indicators, they can be more precisely measured. Whereas any data collection procedure can be applied in a biased manner, instruments requiring specific details are less subject to bias than those based on general impressions.

What is more, the specificity of the connections between problem intervention and change found in well-explicated approaches may help rule out effects of maturation and history. The more globally a problem is defined the broader the range of factors that may affect it. For example, there is a host of maturational and historical influences that might affect a problem as broadly defined as a mother's inability to cope with her children. If the problem is narrowed to the mother's habit of slapping her infant son when he cries, the range of such influences is narrower. The specificity and directness of the intervention also become an important consideration. If the intervention is aimed at general changes difficult to delineate and if it operates in an indirect manner and if its processes are not clearly demonstrable, then alternative explanations become more attractive or competitive. For instance, to attribute a change in the mother's slapping her son to participation in an unstructured parents' discussion group would require a chain of inferences connecting supposed values derived from the group experience—such as emotional support from other parents—to the change in question. Although a plausible explanation linking the group treatment to change can be constructed, a certain amount of speculation would be required. For this reason, that explanation may prove not much more convincing than others based on speculation about changes in the mother's motivation, family circumstances, or other factors that might not be the result of intervention.

By contrast, an intervention consisting of direct, explicit efforts to change the problem, through means such as having the mother rehearse and practice other responses when her son cries, could be more plausibly connected to the change. The link between intervention and change requires fewer assumptions; the process by which intervention may produce change is more apparent. The plausibility of the connection can, of course, be further strengthened through documentation of the intervention-change process. For example, one might be able to provide evidence that a problem changes immediately following an intervention and in a way specifically suggested by the intervention. The mother in our example might agree, in response to the practitioner's suggestion, to have one of her older children attend to the infant if she felt as if she was losing control. If it could be shown that she in fact then behaved in this manner, the case that she did so because of the intervention becomes more persuasive.

As Cook and Campbell (1979) observe, a cause may operate with such specificity that it leaves a unique "signature" in its effects. For example, the identity of a criminal may be revealed by the *modus operandi* of the crime, or characteristics of a trainee's performance may tell us who trained him. Social work may likewise assume properties of such "signed causes," as perhaps in the example just cited. In these cases, plausible alternative explanations may not arise and controls may not be necessary to rule them out in order to establish the effectiveness of the intervention.

Kazdin (1981) has cited several conditions that can be used to argue for treatment effectiveness in single case studies even if design controls are lacking: reliance on objective measurement, a problem that has followed a stable course prior to treatment, the use of continuous assessment to monitor problem change before and after treatment, the occurrence of immediate and marked effects after the intervention is introduced, and the replication of effects with multiple cases. Not all of these conditions need be present. For example, a large, dramatic effort following an intervention—a slam-bang effect, as Gilbert, Light, and Mosteller (1975) have called it—may obviate the need for objective measurement. Applications of these ideas in case studies may be found in Reid and Davis (1987) and Reid (1988).

Strengthening of the case study has been discussed at some length not only because of the wide range of application of this type of study but also because the discussion, we hope, demonstrated the thinking used in considering the possible effects of treatment in any design. Whether uncontrolled or controlled, or whether it uses single cases or groups, a study of the effects of intervention must be evaluated through careful comparison of the plausibility of hypotheses asserting that intervention is a causal agent against the plausibility of alternative hypotheses. Design controls never provide a substitute for logic and judgment.

THE BASIC TIME SERIES (AB) DESIGN

In considering ways in which the case study might be strengthened, we cited the value of baseline measurements as a means of providing some control over extraneous factors. If the researcher obtains these measures before intervention and continues to obtain them after intervention is begun, it becomes possible to obtain a continuous reading of problem occurrence or severity and to determine what happens to this reading when intervention is introduced. This *basic time series design*, as Kratochwill (1978) has termed it, is often designated by the letters AB, with the A symbolizing measurements obtained during a baseline period before intervention and the B standing for measurements taken during intervention. The design has considerable utility in its own right and serves as a foundation for understanding the more complex single case designs to be considered subsequently.

The essential features of the design can be grasped from figure 6.1, which presents the results of a hypothetical case in which modeling and coaching were used to increase the frequency of "positive messages" (expressions of approval, praise, etc.) imparted by a mother to her ten-year-old son during a series of tape-recorded interactions between them.

As the graph indicates, the design yields data on change coincident with the introduction of intervention. The pretreatment baseline helps reduce the plausibility of maturation and regression as alternative explanations but does not rule them out completely. It provides only weak control over the operation of history (contemporaneous events).

Time Series Measurement

Central to the basic time series design, as well as to more elaborate variations of single case studies, is the notion of time series measurement. As previously

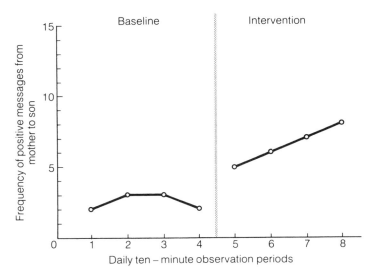

FIGURE 6.1
Illustration of basic time series design (hypothetical data)

indicated, a time series consists of repeated measurement of a given variable over time. At least three fundamental features of a time series need to be taken into account in planning studies and in analyzing their results: *variability, trend,* and *level. Variability* is the extent to which repeated measurements (data points) fluctuate over time. *Trend* refers to tendencies of the series to move either upward or downward. For instance, in figure 6.1 the graph shows an ascending trend following the beginning of intervention. *Level* describes the location of a data point on the scale used to measure the variable—in figure 6.1 there is also a noticeable change in level after the intervention is introduced.

Baselines   In planning time series experiments the researcher must consider the kind of baseline to be obtained. In general, the lengthier and less variable the baseline the better the capacity of the design to demonstrate possible effects of intervention. One must have a minimum number of repeated measurements, three at the very least, to form a time series, but the desired number depends on the variability exhibited by the target: the greater its variability, the more data points required to establish a pretreatment pattern.

Researchers have been traditionally advised to extend the baseline period until a stable pattern has been attained. There is at least one difficulty with this solution in obtaining baseline data on human subjects in social work contexts. Many problems display such erratic variability (perhaps because of the complexities of the human problems and limitation in measuring them) that baselines would need to be extended an inordinate length of time, raising practical and ethical problems. Clients or referral sources may not be willing to wait or a practitioner-researcher may not have the time. While the traditional solution may be the most desirable, all things considered, a more practical alternative is to limit the length of the baseline periods in advance of the experiment, perhaps after a brief exploration that might provide some basis for estimating the length of the baseline period needed to establish adequate baseline stability. This solution has the additional advantages of eliminating arbitrary and possibly biased decisions by the researcher about the length of the period and of enabling the researchers to plan better, particularly with clients. Barlow and Hersen (1984) make a similar point in arguing that baseline and treatment phases should ideally be of equal length in single case experiments.

In making these estimations, or more generally in making decisions about the length of baseline and intervention phases, the kind of baseline needed is relative to the potency of the intervention. Generally, the more potent interventions require less stability in baselines to show effects. This point can be appreciated by comparing the two hypothetical time series presented in figure 6.2. Although the baseline for client A is less variable that for client B, the data during the intervention phase provide more convincing evidence for an effect with the latter. The change in level for client B after intervention is begun is great enough to "override" the variability in baseline.

The same principle also applies to another kind of troublesome baseline pattern: when the baseline shows a trend toward improvement in the target. Consider the baselines in figure 6.3. Both baselines show an accelerating trend, which is, of course, fine from the standpoint of client recovery but complicates interpretation of the data. In the case of client C, it is virtually impossible to rule out the possibility of spontaneous improvement (maturation), for change during the intervention could be predicted by extrapolating the baseline trend. In the case of client D, we have a similar positive trend in baseline but a marked acceleration of the trend during the intervention period. Although the positive trend creates difficulties for any interpretation, the data for client D present a pattern more consistent with an intervention effect. (For more extended discussion of baseline issues, see Barlow and Hersen 1984; Jayaratne and Levy 1979.)

Assessing Change As the preceding discussion has suggested, it may be difficult in time series to determine if the pattern of change during the intervention period in fact differed in any meaningful way from that during the baseline period. The design implications of this question are considered at this point; methods of analysis are taken up subsequently (chapter 10).

Decisions about presence and magnitude of change in time series designs are customarily made on the basis of visual inspection ("eyeballing") of graphs or other data displays. This method works reasonably well when differences between baseline and intervention periods are relatively clear-cut (as in figure 6.1) but not so well when the data are more ambiguous, as in the examples presented in figures 6.2 and 6.3. The question of how much change is "meaningful," that is, worth considering as a possible intervention effect, is always difficult to answer in experimental research. At the very least, the investigator would like to exclude change that may occur as a result of random variation or instability. In group experiments this problem is tackled through statistical tests of significance. The interdependencies (auto-

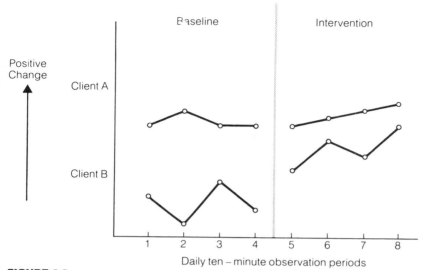

FIGURE 6.2

Contrasts in baseline stability and apparent treatment efforts (hypothetical data)

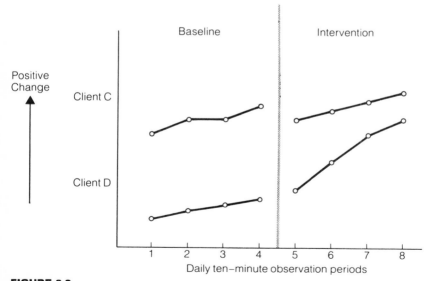

FIGURE 6.3

Ascending baselines followed by different trends during intervention (hypothetical data)

correlation) that occur in repeated measurement require special and, by no means simple, adaptations of such tests (Kazdin 1976; Kratochwill 1978).

Advocates of single case times series have argued that statistical tests, even if properly applied, have little value. If you need a test to tell you if "real" change has occurred, they say in effect, then you do not have enough change to get excited about anyway. Although there is some validity to the argument, it does not resolve the question of criteria to use in ruling out instability as an explanation of change. In planning a single case experiment then, an investigator cannot count on simple tests of significance to control for instability in the case of marginal change. A fairly large amount of change is needed to make a convincing case that random fluctuation can be discounted as a possible explanation.

Requirements To use an AB design, at least three requirements must be met. First, it must be possible to delay intervention until baseline data can be obtained. Second, the target must be so defined that variation in its characteristics—usually frequency or severity—can be measured at different points of time. Finally, it must be possible to obtain adequate measurement of these variations. These requirements are usually met in behavior modification, which introduced this design to the human services. When social work takes a nonbehavioral form but is still scientifically based (as defined in chapter 2), the design has a broad range of application. For example, it has been used to assess insight-oriented, psychosocial casework as a means of bringing about change in an adolescent girl's perception of her parents (Haynes 1977), to test empathy and limit setting in psychodynamic treatment of a child (Broxmeyer 1978), and to examine techniques based in communication theory (Nelsen 1978).

Variations

Certain variations of the AB design may be particularly useful in social work applications. As we shall see, these variations provide some additional elements of control.

In the changing criterion design (Hall 1971), the practitioner and client work toward achievement of a particular goal (criterion); once this is achieved, another is set at a higher level. Thus a child reluctant to read out loud in class may have reading two sentences out loud as a first goal, a paragraph as a second goal, and, once the second goal is achieved, then two paragraphs.

If the client moves ahead in this predicted fashion, the design can provide persuasive evidence that intervention is the influencing variable. The range of application of design is, of course, limited to cases in which performance goals can be "laddered" in the manner suggested in the example, and it may require slowing down the pace of change to demonstrate experimental control.

In a variation discussed by Barlow and Hersen (1984), an extended follow-up and "booster" treatment is employed. A usual AB design may have demonstrated that positive change occurred during treatment, but it may not have been possible to rule out alternative explanations. A follow-up, say several weeks after the termination of intervention, may reveal that some backsliding has occurred. A second brief course of treatment is made. If the client's problem again shows positive change, evidence that treatment is effective is strengthened, though placebo effects would still need to be considered. As will be seen, this variation of the AB design is based on the logic of the withdrawal-reversal design and in fact can be seen as a somewhat adventitious form of that design.

Finally, repetitions of the AB design with different subjects and in different settings can result in an accumulation of evidence of effectiveness if it can be shown that consistent results are achieved across such variations. Planned variations in different settings could be used as a control for history, and use of baselines of different lengths would provide additional control for maturation.

WITHDRAWAL-REVERSAL DESIGNS

The first of the controlled single case designs to be considered is based on the fairly simple premise that one can determine the effects of any agent if one can show that effects occur after the agent is applied but do not occur when the agent is withheld. It is the logic that is used if a person wishes to make sure that a particular appliance, and not other causes, is responsible for static in a radio. To make sure, he might turn the appliance on and off several times. If the static appears when the appliance is turned on but disappears when it is turned off, then there is little doubt that it is the cause. Similarly, if an investigator applies an intervention, withholds it, and applies it again, and change occurs (or becomes more pronounced) when the intervention is applied but vanishes (or becomes less pronounced) as soon as it is withheld, the intervention may be logically regarded as a cause of this change.

Within this family of designs, perhaps the one of greatest utility in social work is the *ABAB.* (We use here the conventional symbols introduced earlier in the chapter.) A pretreatment baseline *(A)* is taken of a problem occurrence; an intervention is administered *(B)*; the original intervention is stopped for a period *(A)* and then reinstated *(B).* Although we refer to designs of this type as "withdrawal-reversal," a distinction can be made between designs in which treatment is simply withdrawn and those in which it is reversed. In withdrawal designs, intervention is simply suspended and reinstated. In reversal designs, intervention is not simply withheld but rather an active effort is made to restore the target condition.

A reversal design is illustrated in a study reported by Pinkston and Herbert-Jackson (1975). It was hypothesized that a mother's displays of affection were reinforcing her son's irrelevant and bizarre verbalizations. Intervention consisted of having the mother react to such verbalizations by "freezing" (giving the child a blank look) and by having her respond with "warm attention" following appropriate verbalization. When this program was instituted, the child's rate of inappropriate verbalization showed a decrease. During the reversal phase, "the mother was instructed to give [her son] love and affection following irrelevant verbalization" (p. 50). When this was done, the rate of inappropriate verbalization began to increase. The intervention program was reapplied and the rate again declined. Although the reversal design can provide strong evidence on the effectiveness of a method, it may be difficult to do for practical and ethical reasons.

To illustrate an experiment using withdrawal only (and also the point that controlled single case research need not be complex or costly), we have selected a modest study completed by a practitioner (Andreoni 1980) in a children's institution. Andreoni was interested in helping a sixteen-year-old boy, George, improve his personal hygiene (which George and staff agreed needed to be improved). A target problem—infrequency of showering—was identified. Baseline data on frequency of showering were collected over a three-week period. Intervention consisted of rewards (extension of curfew) contingent upon showering. The intervention was introduced, withdrawn, and reintroduced with the following results (figure 6.4). Although more data points would have been desirable, the results suggest that the intervention was effective in resolving the target problem.

The basic principle of the withdrawal-reversal design can be used to generate a variety of strategies for study of intervention in the single case.

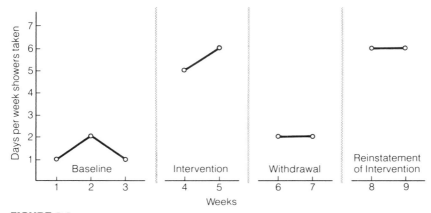

FIGURE 6.4
Use of withdrawal design to assess effects of intervention on problem of infrequent showering   (*Source:* Andreoni 1980)

Only a few variations are considered here. Others can be found in Barlow and Hersen 1984; and Bloom and Fischer 1982.

To determine if changes can be maintained with decreasing amounts or intensity of intervention, an $ABABB^1B^2$—— design can be used. The intervention is "faded out" incrementally $(B^1B^2$——$)$ while continued measurements are obtained. Accordingly, after the effectiveness of the reward program in Andreoni's study had been demonstrated through an $ABAB$ experiment, the amount of extra curfew time might have been progressively decreased.

To study the comparative effects of two intervention methods, an ABA-CA—— design can be used. Variations of this design may be used to test the relative effectiveness of different components of complex intervention packages; each component or method making up the package can be tested in turn.

The basic withdrawal-reversal design *(ABAB)* generally provides good control over maturation, history, and regression because it is usually unlikely that these sources would produce an ebb and flow of change coincident with the use and suspension of intervention. Changes associated with intervention are unlikely to be the result of testing if change can be reversed and reinstated while continuing measurements are taken.

Despite its powerful controls, the withdrawal-reversal design presents certain limitations as a strategy for testing the effects of intervention. Its most serious drawback is its limited range of application. To use it, one must have an intervention whose effects will not persist after it is withdrawn or can be readily undone. Often this criterion cannot be met; in fact, we usually hope for the opposite. For example, forms of intervention designed to bring about changes through cognitive methods are expected to have effects that are persistent and irreversible. One does not expect insight or altered beliefs to vanish when treatment stops. Even interventions that rely on manipulation of environmental contingencies to produce results may leave effects that are difficult to undo—the reason perhaps why researchers are advised to "reverse early."

THE MULTIPLE BASELINE DESIGN

In the reversal-withdrawal design, control over extraneous variations was achieved by *interruption*—for example, by turning intervention "on and off." In the multiple baseline design, one attempts to attain this control through *replication*, that is, through repeating the same intervention across different targets to determine if change consistently follows the introduction of the intervention. Control is further strengthened by successively increasing the length of the baseline for each target before introducing the intervention. By so staggering the inception of the intervention, one attempts to rule out the possibility that change might simply coincide with intervention but actually result from maturation, history, or other extraneous factors. In other words, by staggering the inception of intervention across a series of targets, a researcher can demonstrate that change occurs only when intervention is introduced and hence is the result of the intervention. The pattern could theoretically, of course, be produced by a series of coincidences, but such an explanation begins to sound implausible when the investigator has been able to call her shots repeatedly.

The strategy is illustrated by figure 6.5. The targets, which could be behaviors, problems, situations, or clients, are monitored over time with intervention introduced successively in each. When the targets consist of clients, the design, technically speaking, is no longer a single case experiment though it is convenient to present it within this general category of design.

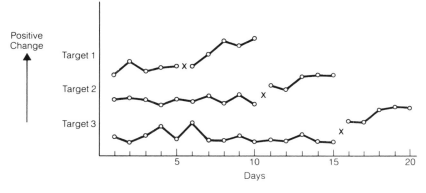

X = beginning of intervention

FIGURE 6.5
Illustration of general form of multiple baseline design: the targets can stand for different clients or for different problems or situations involving the same client

Across-Clients Multiple Baseline

Because its utility in social work is perhaps greater than other multiple baseline designs, the across-clients design is considered first and in greater detail. We begin with a review of basic procedures and considerations involved in this design.

A set of clients as closely matched as possible is selected. Usually one wishes to have clients who share the same type of problem and are similar in respect to other important characteristics, such as age, that might influence the characteristics of the intervention. With a similar group of clients it is possible to design an intervention program expressly suited for clients of a particular type. Additionally, baselines are more likely to be similar, and this makes it easier to detect changes associated with treatment and to generalize about a set of similar clients. Precision matching is not essential, however, for equivalence among clients is not assumed. Differences in initial characteristics among clients are presumably controlled by determining patterns of change within each client over time. The crucial comparison involves differences in these *patterns*, differences that are presumably a function of *when* intervention is introduced.

Baseline data on a target behavior or problem are obtained for each client, and intervention is introduced in staggered fashion. It is expected that each time series will show systematic improvement over its own baseline only after intervention is introduced.

The design is nicely illustrated by an experiment conducted by Blackman, Gehle, and Pinkston (1979) in a home for the aged. The purpose of the study was to test methods of improving the self-feeding abilities of elderly, senile residents. Observational data were collected on three residents meeting study criteria during baseline periods. The data consisted of recording inappropriate eating behavior, such as using utensils by the wrong end. Individualized training and maintenance programs designed to help the subjects learn more appropriate eating behavior were introduced sequentially, both at lunch and dinner. The design and results used at one of these meal times are presented in figure 6.6.

As can be seen, the maintenance program used during dinner appeared to be effective in reducing inappropriate eating behavior. (The more intensive training program was used during lunch.) Effectiveness can be inferred from the dramatic change in level of problem frequency that occurs immediately after the program is introduced with each client.

The length of the baseline periods and the timing of the inception of intervention are affected by certain requirements of the multiple baseline design. Because the baselines must be staggered, their lengths are progressively increased—an argument for keeping the initial baseline as short as possible and for limiting their duration in advance of the study. The length of the second and subsequent baselines is also a function of the time required to produce an intervention effect. Hence, if the initial baseline runs for a ten-day period, the second for twenty days, and the third for thirty days, the intervention must show a change over baseline within a ten-day period—a point illustrated by figures 6.5 and 6.6.

In discussion of the multiple baseline design so far, we have used three targets as a norm. This figure is somewhat arbitrary, although it is frequently suggested as a minimum number to provide evidence on the effectiveness of intervention (Barlow and Hersen 1984). Whereas a larger number of clients may be advantageous, a practical problem unique to this design is encountered as the sample size increases. Because each client added has to wait progressively longer, the last client in a set of, say, five clients may be required to spend a rather lengthy period of time in baseline, possibly too long if the client is anxious to receive help.

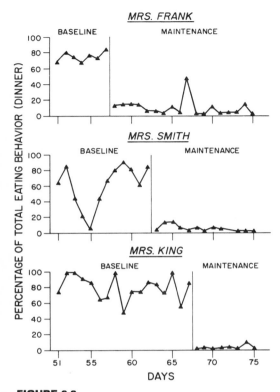

FIGURE 6.6
Daily rates of inappropriate eating behavior as a percentage of total intervals
of eating behavior recorded during dinner   (*Source:* Blackman, Gehle and
Pinkston 1979:23)

As in any service experiment, the size of the client sample needed to
demonstrate an intervention effect depends on the strength of the intervention. The "rule of three" used in multiple baseline designs seems to be based
on the assumption that if a change in the target follows the introduction of
treatment that many times, then the case for a treatment effect becomes
"persuasive." This assumption may be reasonable if the pattern of change
conforms to the ideal expected results presented in figure 6.5 and 6.6. These
results are not, however, always obtained. A typical outcome might be that
the expected pattern (probably in a more ambiguous form) would be found
for two clients but not the third. The findings would no longer be so

convincing. In social work, most interventions are not so potent as to produce dramatic effects in an unbroken succession of cases. Consequently, more than three cases is usually desirable for this reason, although as noted, there may be practical problems in expanding the number beyond this limit. One solution is to have more than one client for each baseline condition. In this design, six clients can be treated within the baseline period that would be normally consumed by three. It is not necessary to use pairs, or even to be consistent about the number of clients bunched together. Clients are paired only in relation to length of baseline; otherwise they are treated independently. The design is an improvement over the three-client multiple baseline, for it can yield a greater amount of evidence on effects of intervention. It is not as strong as six baselines each of varied length would be.

The across-clients design has a broad range of application in tests of social work intervention. It can be used with "non-reversible" methods. Clients can be treated in a holistic manner; that is, one does not need to concentrate on one problem or situation at a time. For these reasons, it may be more suitable than other controlled single case designs for studies of the effects of nonbehavioral forms of social work practice.

Generally, the across-clients design can be used to evaluate any intervention amenable to testing through an AB design, whose requirements were discussed earlier. The only additional constraint imposed by the across-clients design is that the treatment to be tested must be able to generate measurable effects rather quickly; otherwise, the waiting (or baseline) period for the last client to be treated might become excessively long. Many varieties of social work intervention could meet this requirement. For those that can, multiple baseline designs may be applied and not necessarily with the methodology used in behavioral research.

Suppose, for example, that one wished to test the effectiveness of a weekend marathon group that uses methods of Gestalt therapy as means of treating depression. Three depressed clients are selected as a sample and their levels of depression are measured by means of a standardized test. The first client waits a week, is measured again, enters a group, and is measured a third time, immediately after the experience. This procedure is repeated for the remaining clients with the exception that the second client waits two weeks before having the group experience and the third client, three weeks. Each client then enters treatment at different points with his own baseline. If the depression score of each shows improvement over this baseline during the weekend marathon, one has evidence that the group treatment produced the change, since it would be otherwise difficult to explain the coincidence between the group experience and the lessening of depression. The design could be strengthened by introducing brief "placebo" sessions of friendly listening between baseline tests, and each client could, of course, be followed up after the group experience to obtain data on the durability of change. If evidence on the effectiveness of intervention appeared to be inconclusive from this three-client test, or if one were not content with a sample this small, one or more replications with additional sets of clients could be done.

Across-Problems Multiple Baseline

In the across-problems design the researcher tests the efficacy of an intervention method with different problems of the same client system. In other respects the design is equivalent in structure to the across-clients multiple baseline; that is, baselines are taken on different problems and the timing of intervention is staggered across the set of problems.

The principal advantage of this design over its across-clients counterpart is that an experiment requires only one client, rather than several concomitantly. Clients do not need to be kept waiting lengthy periods in baseline conditions before service is started.

Certain prices are paid for this advantage. A single client system provides less basis for generalization than several. The interdependency that usually exists among different problems in the same client is almost always a matter of concern. Treatment of one problem is likely to affect another, or spontaneous recovery may occur in all problems simultaneously. If all problems show positive change at the same time, one cannot determine whether treatment or extraneous factors were responsible. If carry-over effects are to be avoided, the intervention must be problem specific. Behavioral treatment meets this criterion better than most other modalities that social workers use, but any approach that permits highly focused work on specific problems can conceivably be tested through this type of design.

An imaginative application of an across-problems design in social work may be found in a study by Tolson (1977). Tolson was interested in testing the efficacy of a package of task-centered interventions—the Task Implementation Sequence (TIS)—as a means of alleviating communication problems between marital pairs. Tolson and a client couple, Mr. and Mrs. T, selected three problems that appeared to be interfering in the clients' ability to communicate with one another. Although the clients' major concerns were focused on other issues in the marriage, they agreed to work on these problems, in part because they were helped to see that the problems constituted obstacles to their resolution of other difficulties. It was also agreed that treatment of the communication problems—the experiment proper—would be followed by work on other aspects of their marriage. Table 6.1 (excerpted from the report of the study) presents the structure of the experiment, the problems selected, and findings concerning the effectiveness of the TIS.

As can be seen, the study deals with three problems, with the husband and wife's contributions to each problem separately analyzed. On the whole, the data suggest that the TIS was effective although interpretation is complicated by an apparent carryover effect. Note that the marked decrease in "interrupting speeches" during the second week, presumably as the result of intervention, is matched by an increase in monopolizing (lengthy) speeches during the same week, while this problem was still in a baseline condition. The two

TABLE 6.1

Changes in Three Communication Problems, Mr. and Mrs. T.

Phase	Weeks	Condition	Mr. T.	Mrs. T.	Combined
Percentages of Interrupting Speeches, Mr. and Mrs. T.					
I	1	Baseline	67	47	57
II	2	Treatment	26*	30*	28*
III	3,4	Follow-up	23	35	29
IV	5,6,7	Follow-up	17	29	25
V	30	Follow-up	20	28	24
Percentages of Monopolizing Speeches					
I	1	Baseline	4	3	4
II	2	Baseline	9	13	11
III	3,4	Treatment	4*	8*	6*
IV	5,6,7	Follow-up	4	10	7
V	30	Follow-up	13	9	11
Percentages of Speeches Containing Topic Shifts					
I	1	Baseline	49	52	50
II	2	Baseline	34	34	34
III	3,4	Baseline	36	53	45
IV	5,6,7	Treatment	28*	47*	31*
V	30	Follow-up	21	30	26

Source: Tolson (1977).

* Point at which TIS was applied.

problems are obviously intertwined. As interruptions are brought under control, there might be greater opportunity for monologues to occur. An unusual aspect of this carryover effect is that it affected the yet-to-be treated problem adversely, although subsequent treatment of that problem (weeks 3 and 4) apparently reversed these effects to some extent (without increasing the rate of interrupting). As the study well illustrates, carryover effects need not be fatal; and they can, as Jayaratne and Levy (1979) observe, add to understanding about the interrelationship among problems.

The study illustrates some additional points. Data on problem change (derived from analysis of tape recordings of the couple's communication, highly summarized in the table) reveal a pattern of change associated with treatment, all of which suggests that a large number of repeated measurements is not essential to this design. The study involves two clients instead of one, a feature particularly germane to applications of the design in social work where problems are frequently shared by more than one person. One notes here that having measurements on two persons helps establish the pattern of change and reduces the need for repeated measurements. Finally, the study shows how research and clinical purposes can be combined in a single case. An experiment generated by the practitioner's research interests but also of benefit to the clients was followed by a course of marital treatment oriented to the clients' priorities.

Across-Situations Design

In the across-situations multiple baseline, the researcher is concerned with separate locations of a problem within a single client system. A child's problem of aggressive behavior may be expressed in the classroom, in play with peers, and at home. Separate problem baselines are taken for each situation, and the inception of intervention is staggered across situations. The limitations parallel those cited for the across-problems design. A problem that occurs in different situations is required; treatment of the problem and resulting change need to be situation specific, the design has a better fit with behavioral treatment than other forms, and so on. It does, however, provide a means of using a controlled design with a single client and single problem.

GENERALIZATION (EXTERNAL VALIDITY)

Thus far in this chapter we have paid particular attention to the "control" features or internal validity of a design—the capacity of the design to isolate the effects of the experimental intervention by controlling for extraneous variables. We now take up a contrasting aspect—the extent to which a research design offers a basis for generalization. This aspect, which Campbell and Stanley (1963) refer to as the "external validity" of an experiment, is taken up for single case experiments as a whole. As in our discussion of internal validity, we introduce some basic ideas that are later applied to group experiments.

In social work experiments, two questions are at issue in generalization. One question asks in effect, "Will the interventions tested produce similar results in other situations?" The interventions may have worked in a given experiment, but will they work well if applied to other clients, used by other practitioners, and in a nonexperimental context? Questions of this kind, which of course can never be completely answered, are the classical ones posed in thinking about generalization (Campbell and Stanley 1963; Kratochwill 1978; Krathwohl 1985). They may be thought of as relating to the "reproducibility" aspects of generalization. As important as this aspect is, it leaves out a dimension of particular importance in a practice profession: the pragmatic aspects of applying an intervention. "Are the results worth reproducing?" is the question here. An intervention may be reproducible, but it may also be difficult and costly to deliver and its payoff may not be commensurate with the difficulties and costs. These might be called the "pragmatic" aspects of generalization.

In considering the reproducibility of results, our starting point is a unique event involving particular targets, interventions, research methodology, and so on. Whereas any such facet or combination of them may limit generalization, it is most productive to focus on the interventions tested as they relate to other facets.

If so, we might first consider limitations resulting from the selection of clients on whom the intervention was tested. To what extent can they be considered representative of some larger group of clients with whom the intervention might be used?

As noted earlier (chapter 4), a single case study can provide little assurance about representativeness of this kind. (In this discussion, we continue to use "single case" or "single client" to include across-clients designs. Because they involve several clients, these designs usually provide a slightly better basis for generalization than the "pure" single client study.) But generalizability is often further limited by the nature of case selection: the case(s) treated may be particularly well suited to the intervention. These selection tendencies may operate in a fairly subtle fashion, often in ways not reflected in descriptions of cases treated. Although this phenomenon may occur in any intervention experiment, it is likely to be more of a problem in the single case study. In a group experiment, selectivity is usually constrained by the need to obtain a sufficient number of cases. In a single case study the investigator may be selective not only in choice of client but also about the case she chooses to report. Consequently, we may be presented with the one case in which the intervention worked best; less successful cases may be buried in the experimenter's files. Further, in a single case design, the researcher can model her interventions to suit the particular characteristics of the case. This plasticity is an advantage in achieving effects in the case (internal validity) but may create a rather idiosyncratic mesh between case requirements and the interventions used, one hard to generalize about.

However, the single case design does have one special strength in respect to generalization: one can generalize from a base of a considerable amount of detailed knowledge about the case studied. Generalization from group experiments must inevitably be based on averages of one kind or another, which may mask specific relationships between certain target and treatment variables. For example, in a group experiment, ten children may be treated for a school phobia. All may recover except one who gets worse. In a group design, one cannot say if that particular child would have become worse anyway or was made worse by the intervention, since the effects of the intervention are not tested on a case-by-case basis. They are, of course, in a single case design. If the child was affected by a particular type of school phobia that was made worse by the intervention, this important fact would be more likely to come to light in a single case study. In this sort of situation, not uncommon in clinical practice, a series of single case studies might provide a basis for discriminating generalizations; for example, the intervention works well with type X phobia but may aggravate type Y.

Interventions tested in social work experiments usually consist of complex packages of methods, and usually the relative contribution of different components to the results is not clear. Hence, one needs to generalize in terms of the intervention as a whole rather than to select parts of it, unless, of course, the roles of different elements have been isolated by means of complex designs. Characteristics of practitioners and more generally the setting of the experiment must also be taken into account. The experience and skill of the practitioner, caseload size, the quality of supervision, and the cooperativeness of agency staff are among the more specific factors that may limit generalizations. In the single case study, as Jayaratne and Levy (1979) point out, special consideration must be given to the knowledge and experience that a practitioner-researcher may accrue in the course of her efforts to perfect methods of treating a particular type of case. Her accumulated expertise, which may not be exportable, may have been decisive in the success of her methods. A similar issue arises in attempts to disseminate the methods of celebrated "super practitioners" who by all accounts are remarkably successful but whose methods defy emulation because they may be so much a part of the practitioner's special knowledge or personal qualities.

Whether they express it as the Heisenberg principle or Hawthorne effect, researchers are very much aware of the influence of their experiments on the phenomena they study. One must always be alert to the possibility that the effectiveness of an intervention may be attributable in part to the procedures used to study it. Observing a child in order to collect baseline data on his behavior may give him a clue that his behavior is amiss, which may make him more receptive to the subsequent intervention—an example of what Campbell and Stanley called "the reactive or interactive effect of testing" (1963:175). Note that testing is not directly responsible for a change in outcome measures, as is the case when testing is a source of extraneous variation or threat to internal validity; it is rather that testing increases the potency of the intervention. Hence, the intervention may not produce the same effects when it is used in the absence of prior measurement.

Being a part of an experiment may affect the practitioner or client in additional ways. The practitioner may put forth extra effort because of her commitment to the method and her desire to demonstrate its effectiveness. The client may be stimulated by the worker's enthusiasm or may try harder because he is a focus of study. Such "reactive effects of experimental arrangements" (Campbell and Stanley 1963) may then produce an extra impact that may vanish when the intervention is used under ordinary practice conditions. A similar phenomenon has been noted in trials of new methods outside of research contexts. For example, Malan (1963) once observed that therapists appear to achieve their best success with short-term methods when they first use them—when perhaps they are "fired up" by their initial enthusiasm for a novel approach.

These limits on generalization, which apply to all experiments but with greater force to the single case design, may seem so restrictive that one might be tempted not to peer at all beyond the confines of a particular study. Our intent has been, not to discourage generalization but rather to make clear what needs to be taken into account in the process. To strike a more positive note, we should like to rephrase a point made in chapter 2: any set of valid findings affects to some extent the probability weights we use in appraising the tenableness of general propositions. If we can learn some truth about a slice of reality, even a single case, our knowledge of the world is increased.

There are other reasons why generalization from limited evidence need not be a fool's mission. The findings of an experiment may be consistent with findings from other studies—that is, grounds for generalization may already exist. In the context of operations research, we may need to generalize very far. A practitioner-researcher may wish only to determine if a method is effective for the type of clients she has in her own caseload, or to reduce generalization almost to a vanishing point, she may be simply interested in determining if a particular intervention is working with a particular client.

The pragmatic aspects of generalization, to which we now turn, involve for the most part two related considerations: feasibility and cost-effectiveness. Feasibility problems arise if the intervention would be difficult to implement on a broader scale. For example, it may run counter to the norms of practitioners, require apparatus not usually available, or demand that staff perform tasks that might interfere with other responsibilities. Cost-effectiveness considerations are always relevant to generalization, though they may not be identified as such, and are always difficult to assess. Although in the strict sense cost-effectiveness usually refers to the comparative monetary costs of alternative means of achieving a given goal or effect (Masters, Garfinkel, and Bishop 1978), we use the notion here broadly to refer to the probable effects and costs of an intervention in relation to possible alternatives. If we appraise the results of an experiment from a cost-effectiveness standpoint, we ask "How much of an effect was achieved at what cost (at least in terms of practitioner and client time) and could a comparable effect be achieved by other means at less cost?" Suppose we learn from a single case study that an individualized remedial reading program enabled a child to increase his score on a reading test by ten points and further that it took ten one-hour sessions to achieve this gain. If we have information suggesting that an available group approach (that could reach more children with no greater expenditure of practitioner time) produces results almost as good on the average, we would have questions about the cost-effectiveness of the individualized methods. These questions would prompt further inquiry: Is there reason to believe that this type of child would not have responded to the group approach? If the individualized program seemed to be a little more effective than the group approach, is the slight margin of difference worth the investment if we consider that more children could be helped by group methods?

Use of pragmatic criteria need not necessarily constrain generalization. An intervention may produce only a modest effect. At the same time, it may be simple to learn and may be applied easily and quickly—factors that would enhance its generalizability.

Improving Generalizability

Although the generalizability of single case studies is inherently quite limited, steps can be taken to improve it. Random selection of the experimental case from a well-defined population would avoid a tendency to handpick a case because it seemed well suited to the intervention. Although a report might feature the study of a single case, reference can be made to other single case tests of the intervention if these have been conducted by the investigator. Of particular relevance would be information concerning cases in which the approach had been tried but found unsuitable. Finally, more emphasis could be placed on developing intervention models for particular types of clients or problems and on testing them with representative cases. Single cases studies in which interventions are molded to meet various requirements of the case at hand have considerable value within the context of developmental and operations research, but they provide a poor basis for generalization.

Replication

In our discussion of external validity of single case studies, we have considered one strategy for attempting to develop general knowledge from single case approaches—extrapolation of the results of given studies. A second, and more powerful, strategy to attain this end is replication—or the repeating, with variations, of previous studies to build generalizations through empirical means.

In single case research, replication has been seen as especially important because of limitations on generalizations inherent in a study based on only one case. At the same time, replication is more readily accomplished in single case research than in research involving groups.

Sidman (1960) has distinguished two types of replication in single case experiments: direct and systematic. This distinction has been elaborated upon by Barlow and Hersen (1984) in the context of behavioral treatment of human problems. In direct replication, an investigator (or research team) retests an intervention with the same type of subject and problem and the same setting. Replication of this type is considered to be the first step, since it can establish that the treatment and research procedures used by a particular investigator achieve consistent results with the same kind of client, problem, and so on. In other words, it can show that the success of a single study was not a fluke occasioned, for example, by a client with an exceptional capacity for change. Direct replication provides only a very narrow base for generalization, however. After it has accomplished its objectives—Barlow and Hersen (1984) suggest that a successful experiment and three successful replications of it should be sufficient—systematic replication becomes the next logical step.

In systematic replication, an attempt is made to broaden the scope of generalization by systematically varying practitioners, clients, problems, and settings. If a home notes program has been found to work (through direct replication) with preadolescents, it may be tried with adolescents. If it has proved successful with academic problems, it may be applied to classroom behavior problems, and so on. In this way the range of successful application of a method can be incrementally established. In this process it is vital to have replication by practitioners or researchers other than those involved in the original experiment or in direct replication of it. Ideally, the replicators should have played no part in the development of the intervention and should have no personal investment in its success. Such "independent replication" can help ensure that apparent effects were not due to "experimental demand" (Rosenthal 1966)—that is, to biases resulting from the stake that developers of an intervention might have in the demonstration of its efficacy.

Systematic replication focuses on single methods of intervention varied by practitioners, clients, and so forth. A form of replication both more complex and more easily attuned to the realities of practice is *clinical replication* (Barlow, Hayes, and Nelson 1983; Barlow and Hersen 1984). In clinical replication, combinations of interventions are used with clients with similar clusters of problems—child abusers, for example. This type of replication, Barlow and Hersen (1984) point out, is a form of field-testing of packages of methods that are presumably effective with particular kinds of clients and the usual problems they bring to practitioners. Clinical replication may in fact be carried as a part of ordinary service programs without the design features, such as withdrawal of treatment or multiple baselines, that may be characteristic of more purely research undertakings. However, data describing clients and services need to be obtained as well as measures of change over time.

From such replications one can accumulate evidence on how well combinations of interventions appear to work with particular kinds of clients and on problems and factors differentiating more successful from less successful applications. Details of clinical replication as well as reviews of illustrative series are presented in Barlow, Hayes, and Nelson (1983).

Although the main purpose of replication is to establish generalization, it should also form an empirical basis for building and modifying intervention packages. To the extent that it does, replication becomes a form of developmental research (chapter 2). When to modify the intervention and in what way, become issues in a replication series because making continual modifications of a method may limit its generalizability. Another issue concerns the sequencing of different types of replication. Ideally, the sequence should be direct, systematic and clinical. In social work, however, there is little replication of any kind, either in single case or group research (Coulton 1982). As Barlow, Hayes, and Nelson (1983) suggest, there may be value in clinical replication even if not preceded by the other forms. While direct and systematic replication should be strongly encouraged in social work intervention research, clinical replication merits special emphasis because of its greater feasibility and closer fit to the complexities of social work practice.

CHAPTER 7

GROUP EXPERIMENTS

In this chapter we take up strategies for group experiments, still staying within the context of study of the operation and effects of social work intervention. As in the preceding chapter, we move from the simple to the complex, and so we begin with the most elementary form of group experiment—a design confined to a single group and lacking in control over extraneous factors.

UNCONTROLLED SINGLE GROUP EXPERIMENT

Perhaps the most frequently used evaluative design in social work, the uncontrolled single group experiment (or "quasi-experiment"), may range from a modest test of a specific intervention with a handful of cases to a study of hundreds of cases exposed to a multifaceted program. The logic of the design is, however, no different from that of the uncontrolled single case study. In both single case and group forms of the uncontrolled experiment, intervention programs are administered without manipulation, that is, without delay, interruption, withholding, or other means of determining change in the absence of intervention.

Assessing Intervention Effects

As in the uncontrolled single case experiment, a target is measured before and after the intervention, or an estimate of change is derived from data obtained following the intervention. The guiding hypothesis is that intervention was responsible for observed changes, but it is usually not possible to test this hypothesis adequately, because the design does not control for alternative explanations—history, maturation, and so on, as discussed in relation to its single case counterpart.

Whether measures of change are derived ex post facto or from comparison of before and after assessments, the design is generally (and correctly) considered to be a questionable strategy for assessing intervention effects. Because many types of social work targets tend to improve over time without intervention, studies using the design may in fact give a misleading picture of intervention effects. Persons with a stake in the success of a program expect "positive results" and hope to achieve them. Thus when they learn that two-thirds of the clients receiving a service have improved, they are naturally quite ready to interpret the causes of the improvement to the program and may become impatient with caveats about "alternative explanations."

Such misinterpretations can have unfortunate results. For example, during the late 1950s, a number of demonstrations of casework programs with "multiproblem" families receiving public assistance were conducted (Schlesinger 1963). These studies, which generally used uncontrolled single group designs, were used as the basis for claims about the effectiveness of intensive casework or as a means of enhancing the functioning of multiproblem families and of reducing their "dependency on welfare" (Bell 1961; May 1964). However, when controlled studies of these programs were subsequently conducted (Wallace 1967; Mullen, Chazin, and Feldstein 1972), it was found that families receiving intensive casework did in fact show improvement but not at a significantly greater rate than control families who did not receive this form of service. In retrospect, the service had been oversold with the help of overinterpreted studies.

Although the risk of drawing false conclusions about the effectiveness of intervention is omnipresent in uncontrolled group experiments, such designs can provide rather persuasive evidence on the presence of service effects under certain conditions. These conditions, which involve intervention addressed to stable targets and use of well-explicated practice models, have been previously described for the uncontrolled single case study (chapter 6). The same considerations can be applied to uncontrolled studies consisting of a group of cases.

The Exploratory Experiment

In addition, the uncontrolled group design can serve important exploratory functions, particularly in the development of intervention models (chapter

2). When this function is being served, the design may be appropriately referred to as an exploratory experiment (Reid 1979b). The use of the exploratory experiment in model development is considered in some detail because of its potentially important role in refining intervention approaches for use in practice and for further testing.

The exploratory experiment is most useful when a practice model is at an early stage of development or when it is being adapted to a novel type of problem or population. In such cases, conventional experiments with design controls that might ordinarily be used to test the effectiveness of an intervention make little sense. One cannot hypothesize, as one should in an experiment, that application of X will create Y effect, for it is not clear what X is. Moreover, the risk of obtaining negative findings is high if the intervention itself must be made with considerable trial and error, and if there is uncertainty about what to measure and how. These findings may result in the abandonment of promising intervention strategies or, as is more usually the case, the cessation of further testing of them, before either the intervention or means of evaluating it have been adequately developed.

Of course, not all models need to pass through this stage. A model may not have been field-tested, but its key components may have been, or it may have a very simple structure, so that adequate mapping may be possible from the outset. If so, then a controlled study of its effects may be a logical first step. This course of model development is likely to be rare in social work, where there has been little testing of specific intervention components and where practice approaches tend to be justifiably complicated.

The exploratory experiment consists essentially of a preliminary trial of the model on a small scale—with perhaps from a half dozen to a dozen cases. First, guidelines explicating the model are developed; practitioners, who may be master's students in a field work placement, are trained in its use, and a data collection plan is devised. Particular emphasis is given to securing data on what practitioners do and on what follows their actions. The practitioners themselves supply data through devices such as structured recording forms, ratings, audiotapes, and reports of critical incidents. Clients or other actors in the practice situation may be interviewed. In addition, it is desirable that the model developer herself become a participant-observer (as either a practitioner or supervisor) to acquire firsthand data on the operations of the model.

The main purpose of the experiment is to fill out and correct the rough map laid down in the preliminary formulation of the model. Some questions concern feasibility. Are practitioners able to do the suggested operations? If not, why not? Other questions concern the range and variation of expected events. What kind of case situations will be encountered? What methods, of those suggested, will be used most frequently and what will they look like in actual use? Still other questions are related to possible effects. Because design controls are not used, it is not possible to obtain definitive answers to questions concerning the effectiveness of the practitioners' activities. Nevertheless, one can gather evidence that permits tentative judgments to be made. For example, is the use of an intervention followed by expected changes in the client's behavior? How do practitioners, clients, and collaterals assess the effectiveness of particular interventions? In addition, problems and events not anticipated by the model are bound to occur. Though one cannot plan to collect specific data on what is not anticipated, it is assumed that the more significant of these occurrences will be revealed and will help inform subsequent model development.

A secondary, though still important, purpose of the experiment is to test and refine data collection and measurement procedures. Through this process, one hopes to devise research methods that are maximally sensitive to the practice operations and outcomes of interest in the model.

Data analysis, which makes use of both quantitative and qualitative methods, is directed toward two objectives. The first is a conventional product of exploratory research—the identification of variables and hypotheses for further research. The second purpose is directed at model revisions. The processes by which data influence a reworking of the model are not completely clear, for they are interwoven with such imponderables as the ability to synthesize information and to use it for creative ends. Some aspects can, however, be described.

Much of the analysis is directed toward understanding, distilling, and ordering the mass of events that occurred during the field test. This base can then be used to flesh out the relatively thin sketch that made up the initial formulation of the model. In this way, what practitioners and clients actually did across a range of problems and situations can be used to make judgments about what is to be expected and perhaps what should be done. Innovative work, perhaps stimulated by the model but not specified as a part of it, can be identified, evaluated, and, if it seems promising, incorporated into the next version of the model. Unanticipated problems can be described and new guidelines written to handle them. As noted, the data may well generate hypotheses for further research. Some of these hypotheses may be translated into tentative model guidelines. For example, there may be correlational evidence to suggest that a certain procedure does not work well with a particular type of client. Pending a more definitive test of this hypothesis, the model might be revised to suggest that the procedure in question be used cautiously with this type of client and discontinued if adverse effects appear. Through analysis and application of findings, the developer puts together a revised version of the initial model.

An example of an exploratory experiment at the micro practice level is provided by Rooney (1978, 1981). The model to be developed was a task-centered approach for helping natural parents secure the return of their children from foster care or to prevent such placement. The model design called for a special unit of practitioners to work with child welfare staff, the court, natural and foster parents, and children to identify and alleviate psycosocial problems causing children to be kept in foster care or likely to precipitate placement. Intervention was to be short term; focused on specific, agreed-upon target problems; and organized around problem-solving actions or tasks to be performed by clients and practitioners.

The test of the model consisted of its use with eleven families referred by a cooperating public child welfare agency. Six cases were carried by master's students, whom Rooney supervised, and five by Rooney himself. Primary sources of data were structured narrative tape recordings; practitioner ratings of task progress and outcome; tape recordings of selected sessions; and post-project interviews with clients, student practitioners, child welfare workers, and family court judges.

Of particular interest is how data were used to inform model development, since this key aspect of the exploratory experiment has not been well explicated. The use of data to flesh out vague or empty areas in the map provided by the initial model formulation is well illustrated by observations gathered on family court judges' reactions to specific evidence that parents had accomplished constructive tasks or actions. It was not known at the outset how judges would react or how the evidence could be best presented. Data from the cases indicated that such evidence was viewed favorably and, what is more, the data presented numerous leads about how it might be used more effectively in the future. Although these insights may have been obtained by other means, such as interviews with judges or experienced child care workers, the test-and-observation approach used seemed a very direct way of gaining the needed information.

A rather different use of data is illustrated by an innovation introduced during the project. It consisted of task forms on which practitioners and clients recorded who was to do what, when, and what each in fact did. The use of the innovation was tracked in the data through the forms themselves. Practitioners and clients provided assessments of their value. Findings suggested that the forms were feasible—clients and practitioners did complete them—and that they were useful in helping clients and workers to recall and review one another's tasks. They did not work too well, however, with most adolescent clients, who seemed to react negatively to both the recording and review aspects of the procedure. These findings resulted in incorporation of an improved version of the task forms into the revised model, with the caution not to press their use with adolescent clients. An example of use of an exploratory experiment to test a model of social agency management may be found in Parihar (1984).

The exploratory experiment can provide a fruitful means of using empirical methods to facilitate the early development of crudely formulated practice models. It is an attempt to make more systematic and rigorous the kind of trial-and-error processes that have long been employed by practitioners to improve their efforts. Consequently, there is justification for arguing that its central product—a practice model—can be put to immediate use while further testing and development are being undertaken, if, of course, there is evidence to support the belief that the model is capable of achieving desired results. Granted, at this point, the model will not have been subjected to a rigorous test of effectiveness. But few models have been. Given limited alternatives, a practitioner might sensibly choose to use a well-explicated model that has received some testing rather than poorly formulated methods that may never have been touched by research.

The use in practice of a model at such an early stage of development can, however, be justified only on the basis that better developed tools are lacking and that further work on the model will continue. As a step in a program of developmental research, the exploratory experiment becomes a form of "pilot testing" (Rothman 1980). As Rothman argues, pilot testing is often omitted in the development of programs "in the health, education and welfare fields that are put into widespread and instant operation across the country" (p. 108). As a consequence, such programs may encounter operational difficulties, if not failure to meet their objectives, because of the premature implementation of ideas and approaches.

EQUIVALENT GROUP DESIGNS

In the single case design, control over alternative explanation was achieved by within-case tracking of variation in change targets; variation occurring during periods of intervention was compared with variation when intervention was not used. In group designs, the same control objective is attained by comparisons of variation in change targets between equivalent groups. One group may receive the intervention that may be withheld from a second group; equivalent groups may each receive different interventions. And, of course, many other patterns are possible, as we shall see.

The Classical Design and Variations

The expression "classic experimental design" is commonly used to designate an experiment consisting of two equivalent groups of clients: one group (the experimental group) receives some form of intervention; the other group (the control group) does not. It has been so labeled because it is the most elementary of the controlled group designs and incorporates the basic principles of all such designs.

Random Assignment In this design and in all controlled group designs, equivalence between groups is achieved basically through random assignment of cases (although, as shall be explained, matching may be used as a supplementary device). When we say that cases are randomly assigned to different groups, we mean simply that assignment is determined by chance rather than by other criteria, such as diagnosis or preference of the client.

Assignment is made from a set of cases selected for the experiment according to whatever criteria of problem, age, sex, and so on, are used to define the sample on which the intervention will be tested. Whatever device is used to make the actual assignment—a table of random numbers is probably the best (see chapter 8)—the end result is the same as if a coin were flipped fairly for each case, with "heads" going to the experimental group and "tails" to the control group. If random assignment "works," the original set of cases will be divided into similar—roughly equivalent—sets. If assignment is truly at random, how well it works is largely a function of the size of the pool of cases to which it is applied. If this pool is large—say a hundred or more cases—it is highly likely that the resulting groups will be equivalent. As the pool shrinks, so does this likelihood. With a pool of fifty cases, "straight" random assignment may still work reasonably well, but with twenty cases it may well fail to "deliver" comparable groups.* This is so because, with small numbers, short-term chance effects can produce inequities. (If a coin is flipped a large number of times, a roughly equal distribution of heads and tails will result, but one flipped only ten times might well produce an 8/2 split.)

To avoid such "bad breaks," researchers may resort to precision matching when samples are small. Before random assignment, pairs of cases are matched according to one or more variables thought to affect outcome. The two cases in each pair are then randomly assigned, one to the experimental group and the other to the control group: this ensures that each group will have equal numbers of cases characterized by the variables matched. For example, if sex is thought to be an important variable, pairs would be formed in the following manner: MM; FF; MM. The two males in the first pair would be allocated at random, one to each group; the process is repeated with the second pair, and so on. The experimental and control groups would then be identical in respect to sex distribution.

Subjects may be matched on more than one variable. For instance, if age were added to the cited example, the pairs might look as follows: M 10 yr, M 10 yr; F 8 yr, F 8 yr. It is obvious that the more variables are added the more difficult it is to find cases with the necessary combination of characteristics. Thus, precision matching on more than three variables is rare. Less precise forms of matching (which will not be dealt with here) are also available. Whatever form is used, it must be used in conjunction with random assignment to ensure equivalence of groups.

How does one decide if the experimental and control groups are really equivalent? A common method is to compare the groups on available measures and to apply a test of significance (chapter 11) to any differences to determine if they are within the limits of random variation. Such a test can tell us if the differences between the experimental and control groups are beyond the limits of usual random variation. Knowledge to this effect can lead to a rechecking of assignment procedures on grounds they were not random after all; if, indeed, they prove to have been, then the researcher may decide she is the victim of a bad break. However, initial differences between the two groups that are within the limits of reasonable chance variation—that is, not statistically significant—cannot be ignored. Rather

*The ideas underlying these observations are taken up in chapter 8. In fact, random assignment can be seen as a special case of random sampling.

sizable nonsignificant differences—particularly if samples are small—can occur between experimental and control groups, and these differences can work in the favor of one group or the other. Random assignment then does not guarantee equivalence.

The function of the control group in this design is to provide an estimate of change produced by nonintervention variables. Ideally the controls should not receive any form of intervention (or have any experience) that resembles the interventions received by the experimentals. In social work research, this ideal is seldom, if ever, achieved.

In thinking about control groups, it is helpful to distinguish between two types of clients; those who are actively seeking service and those who are not in the market for service but who would be willing to accept it if offered. With help-seeking clients, a "no-intervention" control group is especially difficult to achieve. Agencies are reluctant to withhold service from people who come to their doors. Moreover, assigning such clients to control groups is no guarantee they will remain isolated from experiences that may compete with the intervention program. Some may seek comparable forms of service elsewhere; others may obtain financial help from friends, clergyman, physicians, and the like.

Nevertheless, some workable solutions are possible. Perhaps the most satisfactory is to use a control condition in which clients are requested to wait for service. This solution works best, of course, if the agency has some form of waiting list anyway and if the waiting period for clients assigned to the control group is kept relatively brief. In one successful use of this strategy, Sloane et al. (1975) held help-seeking clients for a period of six months in a control group. During this period there were regular telephone contacts with the control clients that kept them involved with the agency and may also have performed a quasi-therapeutic function.

The type of contact used in the Sloane study can be expanded into a form of minimal or placebo treatment. Its purpose is not only to keep clients connected with the agency but also to provide control for the "nonspecific" effects of intervention—sympathetic listening and so forth. There are, however, some difficulties with this variation. Because it is difficult to separate these effects from those of the genuine article (chapter 6), the placebo treatment may compete with the experimental intervention; its control function may become somewhat cloudy. In addition, practitioners may have qualms about having clients participate for any length of time in a pseudo-treatment; moreover, there is the delicate problem of informing clients about it—and securing their consent to participate in it—in such a way so as to preserve their expectation that it may have some value for them, as it well might, without leading them to think that it is all the agency has to offer.

Whatever type of control group is used, it is important to remember that any client selected for the study has a chance of being assigned to the control group. Initial interpretations to clients about what might be in store for them must be made accordingly. Also some provision needs to be made for emergencies—situations that cannot wait. In such cases, probably the best solution is to proceed with random assignment but to have an "escape clause" that permits intervention to take place in any control case needing emergency services. Fortunately, in most projects such emergencies do not arise with sufficient frequency to jeopardize the purpose of the control group.

The situation is somewhat different when clients are not seeking anything resembling the kind of service to be tested. The experimenter offers to provide a possibly useful program to a population that would ordinarily not receive it on condition that she be permitted to conduct a controlled study. Under such circumstances, the complaint that service is being unnecessarily withheld if a control group is used is less likely to arise, and control clients are less likely to feel deprived or to seek alternative forms of service. Usually such groups are found in settings—such as schools, hospitals, courts, welfare agencies, or residential institutions-that can facilitate recruitment of potential clients and that can help avoid exposure of controls to competing programs.

There are, of course, certain drawbacks in soliciting the participation of clients in tests of social work interventions. Because they have not sought help, clients may not be motivated to receive it, a factor that may weaken the effectiveness of social work services, which are usually based on the assumption that clients are genuinely interested in receiving them. This explanation has in fact been used to account for failure of casework intervention to show demonstrable effects with such possibly unmotivated groups as predelinquent youngsters and families receiving public assistance (see reviews by Mullen, Dumpson, and Assoc. 1972; Fischer 1976; Wood 1978; and Reid and Hanrahan 1982).

In some situations, the population to be offered the experimental program may be already receiving some form of "lesser" service, such as routine supervision by a probation officer. The control group may then consist of clients so served. In fact, these services are often "mandatory," that is, required by law or regulation, and cannot be withheld. A number of experiments in social work have used some form of lesser treatment "controls" under the assumption that they were receiving little real help—at least not enough to compete with the experimental program. The failure in a number of such studies (for example, Wallace 1967; Mullen, Chazin, and Feldstein 1972) to demonstrate the superiority of experimental programs over such "routine-service" control groups has raised questions about this assumption. Although their negative findings might be explained on the basis that neither experimental nor control clients were helped, the evidence in some of the studies, such as those just cited, is consistent with the possibility that both types of clients received comparable benefit. Although there are studies in which the experimental clients have surpassed routine service controls (Stein, Gambrill, and Wiltse 1978 and Jones 1985), it may usually be more appropriate to view lesser programs as alternate forms of service, as in a comparative design (discussed later) rather than as performing something equivalent to a "no-service" control function. If this were done, then more attention would be paid to the content of the lesser service and to its strengths relative to the experimental program.

It is probably generally true that "captive" control clients—even children in ordinary school settings—are likely to receive help that may be competitive with an experimental program. It is important that close attention be paid to inputs of this kind.

Fundamentally, a "no-treatment" control group, whether it consists of help-seeking or specially recruited clients, gives a picture of what can be expected to happen in the lives of a group of clients who do not receive a systematic intervention with goals and methods similar to that of the experimental program. The functions of this form of control are not necessarily wiped out if clients receive here and there some forms of help of the kind being tested, but it is good to know what this help has amounted to in order to make a valid assessment of the accomplishments of the experimental service.

In the preceding discussion, reference was made to ethical questions concerning use of control groups. These questions merit additional comment in view of the regularity with which they are raised, particularly by persons with program responsibilities. The usual argument is that it is unethical to withhold a service from clients who would benefit from it. The key assumption here is that the service is effective and that if provided would lead to some benefit for the client. Usually the issue is contested over this assumption. A program administrator may claim that a service is (or will be) effective and should not be denied people who need it. From the researcher's stand-

point, however, the effectiveness of the service has not been demonstrated—
otherwise she would not be interested in conducting an experiment to test it.
Until evidence for effectiveness has been obtained, she would argue one
cannot say that clients in a control group are necessarily being deprived of
any benefit. They may do as well as clients who receive the service and, as
some studies have demonstrated, may do better (McCabe et al. 1967; Blenkner, Bloom, and Nielsen 1971; Bloom 1986). This argument may be taken
a step further; the ethics of providing a client with a service that has *not* been
adequately tested may themselves be questioned.

The latter arguments have the greater validity, we think. Upon analysis,
ethical objections to the use of controls usually turn out to be concerns over
placing certain impositions on clients, such as asking them to wait for a
service they want or to give time to assessment procedures from which they
cannot be expected to benefit. Although making demands on clients does
involves real issues, resolutions are possible.

Size and Composition of Samples Since experiments are costly and suitable clients willing to participate in them are often difficult to obtain,
questions concerning sample size assume considerable importance in the
planning stage. Here, as in any group study, a simple answer to the question
of "how many" is "the more, the better." Although true, the answer is not
terribly helpful. Although very large samples are almost always desirable,
practical constraints usually force us to consider the minimum numbers that
may be needed to achieve the central purpose of the experiment—to determine the effectiveness of the intervention tested.

If this purpose is achieved, the numbers of clients in the experimental and
control groups need to be at least great enough so that differences in outcomes can be detected. Customarily, in group experiments these differences
are evaluated through statistical tests of significance (chapter 11), which are
used to discount or rule out variation in outcome that may be due to chance.
Unless differences are great enough to "pass" these tests at acceptable levels,
it is usually concluded that the intervention has failed to demonstrate its
effectiveness.

Although the relation between sample size and significant testing can be
presented only at an intuitive level at this point, some observations can be
made. Significance tests tend to be conservative: a rather large difference in a
small sample may be discounted as an occurrence that may be too likely to
be due to chance to be taken seriously. Suppose, for example, that a re-

searcher tested a social work intervention in a project consisting of twenty clients, divided equally at random into experimental and control groups. Using a dichotomous measure, she finds that nine of the ten clients in the experimental group have improved as opposed to only half the clients in the control group. Although she may find this result exciting, it would fail to "pass" a test of significance at a customary level (the .05 level). If she followed conventional rules of interpretation, she would be forced to conclude that the differences might have been due to chance and would not claim that the experiment had demonstrated the effectiveness of the intervention. Actually, if half the clients in the control group had been classified as improved, all those in the experimental group would have had to be so classified for the differences to be statistically significant at that level.

As can be seen from the example, the size of the sample needed to demonstrate the effects of an intervention (at a given level of significance) depends on the strength of the intervention and the amount of natural variability in the problem—or more simply, on the expected variability of the problem under control and experimental conditions. We are dealing basically with the same factors considered in single subject designs to determine the number of data collection points (the single subject equivalent to sample size).

If the expected variability of the problem in its natural state and response to treatment can be determined, the size of the sample needed to demonstrate effects at a given level of significance can be estimated through a procedure known as *statistical power analysis* (Orme and Combs-Orme 1986; Crane 1976; Cohen 1969), elements of which were in fact applied in analysis of the foregoing example. Whereas expected target variability is usually not known, some educated guesses can often be made on the basis of available research.

If there is no empirical basis for making such estimates, a rule of thumb might be to use a minimum of thirty subjects divided between experimental and control groups. (Recall the difficulty in demonstrating statistical significance with a sample of twenty in the example presented earlier.) The thirty subjects need not necessarily be divided equally between experimental and control groups; there are usually advantages in having the experimental group the larger of the two, for more clients can be given service and more meaningful analyses of change within the experimental group can be conducted.

As noted earlier, however, there are advantages in matching subjects before random assignment if samples are small. Because effective matching reduces extraneous variation between experimental and control groups, somewhat smaller sample sizes, now of course equally divided between experimental and control groups, are possible. For example, in a test of a program to help teenage mothers acquire job-seeking skills, Schinke et al. (1978) found significant differences in a sample of only thirteen experimental and thirteen control clients.

Ideally, experiments should involve tests of interventions with specified types of clients or problems, because our ultimate aim is to develop discriminating knowledge about intervention: what works best with whom. Moreover, if the sample is limited to certain types of targets, extraneous variation is minimized and effects can be demonstrated with smaller samples. (If there is interest in testing an intervention with more than one type of target in a single experiment, clearly defined subgroups of clients or problems should be selected and factorial designs used.)

These ideals may, however, be difficult to realize. It is often difficult to secure a sufficient number of cases if the target group is specifically defined. Moreover, in early stages of the development of an intervention modality (and unfortunately many seem to remain forever in "early stages"), differentiated approaches for different target groups may not yet have emerged.

Evaluating Alternative Explanations The evaluation of the possible effects of extraneous factors on outcome is in principle no different in group experiments than in their single case counterparts. All sources of alternative explanation that need to be taken into account in single case experiments apply as well to group experiments. Some differences and additions in these sources result, however, when equivalent groups are used.

Errors of instrumentation and testing effects are controlled only if they apply equally to both experimental and control groups. For example, there may be reason to doubt that change in the groups has been assessed in an equitable fashion if relevant data have been subjected to the influence of interviewers or judges who had knowledge of which clients were treated and which were not. Expectations that intervention should have positive results may well introduce a proexperimental bias in their collection and evaluation of the data. Measurement error that affects both experimental and control groups equally—for example, a constant bias of judges toward overestimating improvement in all cases—may detract from the sensitivity of outcome measures but would not constitute a source of alternative explanation. In fact, error of this kind might well make genuine results of intervention more difficult to detect.

Additional extraneous factors concern failures to achieve or maintain equivalence among groups. As noted, random assignment does not guarantee equivalence, even if done properly, and random assignment plans are often compromised in the field. Initial differences between experimental and control group clients can then pose a threat to the internal validity of the experiment. This factor, customarily referred to as *selection* (Campbell and Stanley 1963; Cook and Campbell 1979; Krathwohl 1985), produces extraneous variation if one group is favored (or disadvantaged) in respect to the types of clients assigned to it. Selection often operates in conjunction with other factors such as maturation and history. Hence, as a result of a biased assignment or a bad break in random allocation, the experimental group may receive a higher proportion of better motivated clients than the control group. The combination of selection and maturation could account, therefore, for a superior showing of the experimental clients.

Not only must groups be equivalent at the outset in characteristics that may affect outcome, but also this equivalence must be maintained during the experiment. The only differences should be those produced by the intervention program. Equivalence can be jeopardized if clients drop out of either the experimental or control groups. If so, *mortality* (Campbell and Stanley 1963; Cook and Campbell 1979; Krathwohl 1985) becomes a possible source of alternative explanation. Suppose, for example, that clients with little capacity for improvement become discouraged and leave the program while their counterparts remain in the control group in anticipation of being helped subsequently. If these experimental dropouts are not accessible for posttesting, the experimental group may surpass the control group only because the former has lost its "worse" cases.

When dropouts from an experimental group receive a postprogram assessment, it is difficult to know how to evaluate the information. A conservative estimation of program effects would require the retention of their outcome scores in comparisons between experimental and control groups, which would preserve equivalence between the groups. This approach lumps together cases that have completed the program with cases that may have received no service at all; the latter could hardly expect, of course, to show program effects. Neither solution is completely satisfactory; to exclude the dropouts may lead to overrating program effects; to include them, particularly if there are many who have received little service, puts the program to a test that may be unfair and overdemanding. One way out of the dilemma is to present the data both ways (including and excluding dropouts) and let readers draw their own conclusions (Chassan 1967). The ideal solution is, of course, to avoid dropouts in the first place.

A somewhat different form of mortality occurs when clients complete a program but cannot be located or prove uncooperative for purposes of a postprogram assessment. There are grounds for assuming that such "assessment dropouts" tend to have poor outcomes, for they are likely to include "drifters" and dissatisfied customers. Hence, the higher the rate of missing outcome data the more likely it is that program effects will be more apparent than real.

Variations of the Classical Design   Certain variations of the classical design may be particularly useful in social work applications given problems inherent in using no-treatment control groups. The variations considered here should be seen as only illustrative of ways in which the classical design may be shaped to fit the exigencies of practice situations.

As indicated earlier, some of the objections to use of a no-treatment control can be answered by providing clients assigned to a control condition with the treatment at a later point. In a *partial crossover design* the control clients can become a part of the experiment by providing them with the experimental intervention following the control period and then measuring their progress once again after they have received the intervention. In its simplest form, the design can be schematized as in figure 7.1.

This design not only ensures that control clients will receive the benefit of the experimental treatment but also provides an additional test of intervention. Changes in the control clients during the no-treatment condition $(T_1 - T_2)$ can be compared with changes in these clients during the intervention period. In this kind of comparison, which would be similar to the kind made in an AB design, it would be predicted that the control clients' rate of problem change would increase after their "crossover" into the treatment condition. Although this use of clients as their "own controls" does not permit one to rule out maturation and other extraneous factors as possible causes of change, it does provide a useful supplement to the more definitive comparisons between experimentals and controls $(T_1 - T_2)$. It can provide confirmatory evidence that an intervention effect has occurred and can provide additional data on the nature of this effect.

In theory, the design can be extended to a full crossover (Chassan 1967)

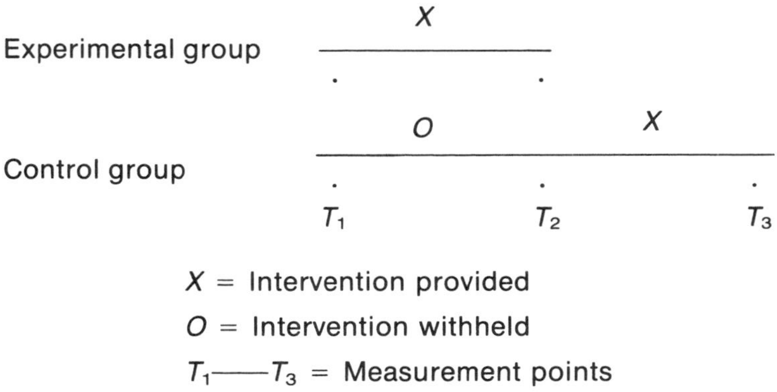

X

Experimental group ───────────

. .

O *X*

Control group ───────────────

. . .

T_1 T_2 T_3

X = Intervention provided
O = Intervention withheld
T_1──T_3 = Measurement points

FIGURE 7.1
Schematic outline of partial crossover

by withdrawing intervention from the experimental group during the second phase $(T_2–T_3)$. Carryover effects from the intervention and a reluctance to withdraw it prematurely are formidable obstacles to this kind of extension. With the partial crossover as presented, the experimental cases, after their assessment at T_2, can be allowed to run their course.

A key consideration in using this design with help-seeking clients is the length of the first phase $(T_1–T_2)$. Ideally, this phase should be kept as short as possible to minimize the time control clients need to be kept waiting. The longer this period, the greater will be the objections to the design and the greater will be the attrition from the control group. If this period is to be kept reasonably brief, say, no more than a few weeks in length, the experimental intervention must be able to show demonstrable results quickly, even though additional effects may be achieved subsequently. Even with a brief initial phase, attrition from the control group may limit the usefulness of the crossover comparison $(T_1–T_2$ versus $T_2–T_3)$. Moreover, any follow-up after T_3 can involve only cases that have received the experimental treatment. This limitation is less serious than it might appear to be with help-seeking controls, who will usually have obtained some form of help in any case by the time of a posttreatment follow-up. Examples of studies using a partial crossover design may be found in Bandura, Blanchard, and Ritter (1969), Reid (1978), and Roskin (1982).

In the previous design, it was seen that a controlled experiment need not involve the entire life of a case, nor need it examine the full effects of an intervention. These principles are more fully exploited in what we refer to as a *micro experiment*.

The purpose of this design is to assess the immediate effects of a specific intervention method. Cases are paired and randomly assigned to experimental and control conditions, with the same practitioner carrying both cases. The cases are handled in a similar fashion until the experimental phase (which may consist of only a single interview). In the experimental cases, a specific method of intervention is used while this method is withheld in the control cases, which may for this brief period receive no treatment at all or a continuation of the form of treatment they had been receiving. Both experimental and control cases are assessed before and after the experimental intervention. The second assessment takes place within a brief period, say up to a week, after the intervention. Assessment is focused on specific changes expected to result from application of the intervention: experimental and control cases are compared on this variable with a check for related changes or side effects. After the experimental or control phases, both cases are treated in ordinary fashion, though they may be followed up at a later point to determine the persistence and longer term influence of the experimental variable.

An example of this design is an early attempt to assess the effectiveness of the TIS (chapter 6), activities intended to help clients plan out, justify, and rehearse problem-solving actions or tasks (Reid 1975a). In brief, thirty-two clients (largely children from a school setting) were randomly assigned to experimental and control conditions. Sixteen student practitioners each carried one experimental and one control case. Experimental and control clients received the same form of task-centered treatment until the fourth interview (approximately) in each case. (The practitioners were not informed of the assignment plan until just before the fourth interview.) At this point the two cases were treated differently: in the experimental case, a task was formulated with the client and TIS activities were applied to it. In the control case, a task was formulated in a similar fashion, but nothing further was done in the interview. No systematic differences could be found in the characteristics of the experimental and control tasks. Progress on each task was reviewed by the practitioner in his next session with the client. On the basis of tape recordings of these reviews, judges independently made ratings of task progress, not knowing which cases were experimental or control. These ratings revealed that almost 70 percent of the experimental tasks in contrast to only 20 percent of the control tasks had been substantially or completely achieved, a statistically significant difference.

As can be seen, the service phase of the experiment took only a week and really affected only a single interview. Although the design yields data on only short-term effects of the method tested, these data can be useful in model development, as they were in the example given.

Comparative Designs

In the comparative or "contrast group" design, two or more experimental interventions are assessed: Its purpose is to test the *relative* effectiveness of the interventions, that is, to determine which is the more (or most) effective of those tested.

As in the classical experiment, clients are randomly assigned to different conditions. Each condition consists, however, of some form of intervention. (To simplify discussion, we assume that two interventions are being compared, which is the usual case; the same design principles apply to comparisons of several interventions.) The interventions compared are considered to be alternative means of achieving common goals in respect to client outcome. Although experimenters may *hypothesize* that one is superior to the other, it is not assumed, or taken for granted, that one will do better, as is the case when an experimental intervention is compared against a "lesser" treatment program. Examples of use of this design in social work include comparisons of structured ·communication training and conjoint marital therapy (Wells, Figurel, and McNamee 1977); of behavioral role play, problem solving, and social group work (Toseland and Rose 1978); of behavioral counseling programs of different lengths (Stuart and Tripodi 1973); and of alternative group work approaches for developing mutual support among community based elderly (Toseland, Sherman, and Bliven 1982). The comparative strategy has several advantages but also some shortcomings. One of its most attractive features is the elimination of the need for a "no-treatment" control and the various problems that accompany it. This advantage is particularly compelling with help-seeking clients, none of whom need to be deprived of service. Concerns about untoward effects on clients are not, however, necessarily eliminated. One program may be regarded by some agency personnel as inferior to the other, and there may thus be reservations about "shortchanging" clients assigned to it. It may also be argued that assignment to a service should be based on diagnostic criteria; assigning clients at random may produce mismatches between client and service. But there are solutions for these difficulties. There are many possible comparisons that involve services neither of which is regarded as clearly superior. Or the design may be structured to permit clients assigned to the presumably "inferior" service to be given, if needed, the "superior" program after the experiment has been completed. Criteria for selection of project cases can be adjusted to exclude cases determined to be inappropriate for either of the services being compared; if so, the argument that professional judgment is needed to assign cases has less force.

A comparative experiment provides data on the *relative* effects of different interventions, a feature with both pluses and minuses. On the positive side, the findings are more likely to be used than those from classical designs. If practitoners are already using some form of the interventions tested, they probably have some conviction that both are effective—otherwise they would not be using them. A classical experiment testing one of these interventions may not alter a practitioner's use of it regardless of outcome: if results are positive, the practitioner may be pleased, but her practice behavior may not be affected, because she had already assumed the intervention was effective; if the results are negative, the practitioner may well discount them, for they would suggest that her practice has been ineffective. An experiment comparing the two interventions, on the other hand, would not challenge the practitioner's convictions that both were effective; ideally, it would present evidence that one was more effective than the other. These findings are more readily accepted and may influence practitioners to make greater use of the methods found more effective.

A comparative test also provides a straightforward means of developing diagnostic criteria and in isolating differential treatment effects. Two methods may be found to differ in their relative effectiveness according to type of client or problem, a finding that may emerge with some definitiveness if clients are randomly assigned to alternative services. Or we may learn that the two interventions affect clients differently: one may be more effective in changing the client's self-concept, the other, in changing the client's behavior.

Finally, as Kazdin observes, a "major contribution of comparative studies often is interim comparisons of the treatments (processes) rather than post-treatment effects (outcome)" (1986:27). For example, in an experiment reported by Jones and her associates (Jones, Neuman, and Shyne 1976; Jones 1985) intensive services designed to prevent placement of children into foster care were compared with routine services. Although the study outcomes, which favored the experimental service, were of primary interest, differences in characteristics between the intensive and routine services were revealing, especially in the subsample followed for a five-year period (Jones 1985). For example, almost as many routine cases as intensive cases received some form of counseling; the main difference occurred in much heavier use of other services, such as financial assistance and help with housing and homemakers in the intensive cases. These findings provide a way of defining apparently successful "intensive services" to the families at risk—a definition at odds with the common notion that "intensive" service in such programs means an emphasis on counseling.

Given the lack of "no-treatment" control, the comparative design does not provide an estimate of the "absolute" effects of either intervention, that is, what either can achieve in relation to whatever clients can accomplish on their own or through unsystematic helping efforts. The seriousness of this limitation depends considerably on the outcome of the comparative study. If one intervention proves relatively more effective than the other, one can argue that it had some degree of absolute effectiveness. In other words, the group receiving the less effective intervention can then be used as one might a control group in a classical design. One alternative explanation is that the "less effective" intervention *worked against* solution of the clients' problems and that the outcomes for the "more effective" intervention were merely the result of spontaneous remission. Suppose the results of an experiment were as follows:

Type of Intervention	Clients Showing Problem Alleviation
Group treatment	55%
Individual treatment	70%

A skeptic might argue that the spontaneous remission could have been close to 70 percent and that those receiving group treatment were "held back" by the intervention. Although this contention cannot be refuted in the absence of a control group, it might be regarded as less than plausible. The results might be reasonably interpreted as providing strong evidence that the individual treatment was genuinely effective.

If there are no significant differences in outcome between the two interventions, spontaneous remission provides a quite plausible interpretation for the findings—usually just as plausible as the one that both were equally effective. All is not lost, however; if one intervention happens to be less costly than the other. It can be said that, whatever they accomplish, one does the job more efficiently and hence might be preferred over the other pending more definitive tests of their relative effectiveness.

The risk of obtaining findings of no difference in comparative tests seems to be high. For example, in reviewing a large number of experiments testing different forms of psychotherapy with one another, Luborsky, Singer, and Luborsky (1975) found few studies that showed significant differences. Several recent comparative tests of social work intervention have also failed to find differences between alternative types of service (Reid and Hanrahan 1982). As Luborsky et al. suggest, this "tie score effect" may reflect the work of generic helping processes. If these processes exert a strong effect relative to the more specific effects of an intervention, it may be difficult to demonstrate clearly that one method is better than the other. While this may be true, one cannot claim that positive but similar outcomes from competing forms of intervention are the result of these helping processes. Maturation and other forms of alternative explanation are hard to rule out. Hence, the risk of "tie scores" becomes a limitation of the comparative design.

In the comparative design, one must face another set of problems that do not arise in the classical design. These problems concern the nature of the interventions to be compared and how they are implemented. They must, of course, be sufficiently distinct that one might reasonably expect differences in outcome, but at the same time they must both be appropriate for the targets selected. Because the comparison is between different types of intervention, these should be administered with the same degree of skill. Given these requirements, the selection and deployment of practitioners raise issues not easily resolved. The ideal solution—to form a sizable pool of practitioners equally adept in both interventions and to allocate them at random to these interventions—is often not feasible. If practitioners are assigned on the basis of their facility with an intervention, differences in practitioner experience, skill, and so on, become potential sources of unwanted variance. In interpreting the findings of a contrast group study, we hope to say that differences in outcomes resulted from differences in the interventions themselves and not from practitioner qualities. When practitioners are assigned to interventions on the basis of their facility with them, usually some attempt is made to match practitioners on characteristics that can be readily measured, such as amount of experience. The matching seldom, however, provides much assurance that key variables, such as level of skill, are adequately equated.

An alternative solution is to use the same practitioners for both methods. This solution works best when practitioners selected are more or less equally skilled in the methods and are not strongly biased in favor of one. Although practitioner characteristics may be controlled by this means, one must contend with another problem: distinctions between the approaches being tested may be blurred by practitioners carrying over methods prescribed for one approach to the other. For example, in a study conducted by one of the authors, the same practitioners were used to implement time-limited and open-ended forms of casework (Reid and Shyne 1969). There was a persistent tendency for practitioners to apply apparently successful elements of the short-term program, such as its stress on relatively specific goals, to the open-ended cases. These problems of "leakage" between interventions may be addressed, and usually controlled in some measure, through initial orientation of practitioners and subsequent monitoring of their work.

Comparative Design with No-Treatment Control   The advantages of both the classical and comparative designs can be realized if a no-treatment control group is added to the latter. The result is a powerful hybrid that permits a comparison of the relative efficacy of two or more interventions and provides an estimate of the absolute effects of each (see, for example, Sloane et al. 1975; Berger and Rose 1977; LeCroy and Rose 1987). Accordingly, if the interventions have similar outcomes, it is possible to say that both were effective (or that neither was).

Most things that are elegant are difficult and costly to create; this design fits that rule. Problems in obtaining an adequate no-treatment control must be resolved; there must be sufficient numbers of clients for at least three groups, the wherewithal to collect data for these numbers, and resources to engineer and oversee the many facets of this more elaborate design. Given the way most experiments evolve, the design is most likely to be considered when there is interest in some form of comparative study. Under these circumstances, it is usually most desirable to add one or more no-treatment control groups if it is possible to do so.

Factorial Experiment   The factorial experiment is a complex form of a comparative design. It can perhaps be best understood by picturing a simple comparative design in which two interventions are compared, say short-term versus long-term treatment for marital problems. Suppose we are also interested in learning about the relative effectiveness of a second contrast in treatment approach for such problems: treatment conducted by means of joint interviews with husband and wife as opposed to treatment done by means of individual interviews with each.

It would, of course, be possible to conduct another experiment in which this second contrast was studied. A factorial design provides a more economical approach: the two contrasts are examined simultaneously. In the example, the clients assigned to the short-term service would be randomly divided into two equal groups: one would be treated by means of joint interviews, the other through individual interviews. The same subdivision would be made for clients assigned to the group scheduled to receive long-term treatment. Table 7.1 shows how the design would look if the project sample consisted of one hundred couples.

An analysis of the example reveals the advantages of this design. As can be seen, the same sample is used for two sets of comparisons (long term versus short term and joint versus individual interviews). In effect two experiments, each with samples sizes of 100, are compressed into one, achieving considerable economy. Moreover, the researcher is able to examine *interactions* between treatment length and type of interview. For example, it may be found that brief intervention is particularly effective when used with joint interviews. In other words, it would be possible to examine the relative effectiveness of four different combinations of interventions. Finally, each contrast provides a control for the other. Thus, in the short-term versus long-term comparison, the deployment of joint and individual interviews is held constant: half the couples receive one type, half the other. In a simple

TABLE 7.1

Layout for a 2 x 2 Factorial Design Testing Length of
Treatment and Type of Interview

Treatment Length	Type of Interview		Total
	Joint	*Individual*	
Long term	25	25	50
Short term	25	25	50
	50	50	100

(nonfactorial) comparison the couples assigned to the briefer treatment might have received a disproportionate amount of joint interviewing as a way of maximizing the clients' involvement in treatment within the available time limits. If the short-term modality then proved more effective than the long-term service, it might have proved impossible to tell if its greater effectiveness was due to its limited structure or to its reliance on joint interviews or some combination of the two. To generalize from the example, the factorial design as opposed to a simple comparative strategy has the advantage of greater economy, greater informational yield (through study of interactions), and greater control over intervention components.

The example involved a comparison of two intervention variables (treatment structure and interview type) with two classifications for each variable (short term/long term; individual/joint). The design can be extended to more than two variables and to more than two classifications of each variable. A form of shorthand has been devised to describe factorial designs in terms of number of variables and number of classifications of each. The design in the example is a 2×2 factorial; if a third variable, say treatment technique, had been added and that variable dichotomized (insight oriented versus supportive), the design would be called a $2 \times 2 \times 2$ factorial. If one of the variables had three classifications, that is, if treatment structure had been divided into short term, moderate length, and long term, a $3 \times 2 \times 2$ factorial would have resulted. And so on.

In the examples given so far, the independent variables—different forms of intervention—have been active. It is also possible to use some combination of active and attribute variables. For instance, a researcher might wish to compare long-term and short-term treatment as used by practitioners with differing amounts of experience (experienced versus inexperienced). Clients could be randomly assigned to practitioners at different experience levels, but experience could not be separated very well from associated factors, such as skill. Or the researcher may wish to examine these methods with different types of clients, those with acute versus those with chronic problems. Although clients could not, of course, be assigned to these conditions, the short-term and long-term interventions could be given similar numbers of clients with each type of problem. Of particular interest would be study of interactions between type of treatment and type of problem.

The factorial experiment shares the basic limitations of its parent—the comparative design. The most important of these limitations—lack of data on absolute effects—can be removed through the addition of a no-treatment control group, which would produce a factorial variation of the design presented in the preceding section.

Additional limitations of the design grow out of its cost and complexity. In its simplest (2×2) version, four groups must be compared, which, if guidelines suggested earlier are followed, would require a sample of sixty clients at a minimum. (This number can be reduced to what might be required for a simple comparative study, say about thirty subjects, if it is decided to concentrate on the effects of the two major variables and to forgo study of interaction. If so, the design is much more economical than two comparative designs.) The simultaneous testing of two independent variables may, however, create certain complications. Each intervention becomes partially defined and hence limited by characteristics of the other. This may be an advantage for control purposes but under certain circumstances may impose undesirable rigidities that may weaken one or both interventions. Thus restricting short-term intervention to individual interviews, as would be done with half the cases, might slow the pace of treatment to the point where necessary goals could not be accomplished within fixed time limits.

Because of its complexity, the design has not been frequently used in field tests of social work intervention though a number of examples can be cited. In one of the earliest applications in social work, Reid and Shyne (1969) used a $2 \times 2 \times 2$ factorial design in a simultaneous test of three pairs of alternative interventions for problems in family relations: short-term service versus continued service; modifying versus supportive casework methods; and treatment conducted by means of joint interviews versus treatment consisting of a combination of individual and joint interviews. (The example provided earlier was a simplified version of that design.) Using a 2×2 factorial design, Schwartz and Sample (1972) compared two different forms of supervision in a public welfare agency; each method was tested under high and low caseload conditions. In perhaps the largest and most complex factorial field experiment in social work to date, Feldman and his associates tested three methods of group work ("social learning," "traditional," and "minimal") with a sample of 701 male youths at a community center (see Feldman, Caplinger, and Wodarski 1983). To determine how antisocial youth might best be treated in a community center setting, group composition was sytematically varied: some groups consisted entirely of "antisocial" boys referred from community agencies; others contained a mixture of such youth and "prosocial" boys who were regularly enrolled in the center's program and were not identified as having specific behavior difficulties; a third group was made up entirely of prosocial boys. A final experimental variable concerned the amount of "experience" of group leaders: graduate social work students versus undergraduate college students who lacked prior social work training or experience. The design (a $2 \times 3 \times 3$ factorial) permitted simultaneous tests of the general and interactive effects of three independent variables (treatment methods, group composition, and practitioner experience). The major outcome variable was an observational measure of the boys' behavior (along an antisocial-social dimension) in the groups. Although the findings revealed that treatment method made no difference in outcome, they did suggest that the groups led by the experienced practitioner did better than those led by the inexperienced. Analysis of interactive effects suggested, however, that inexperienced leaders did relatively better with youngsters in the mixed groups than in groups consisting solely of antisocial or prosocial boys.

NONEQUIVALENT GROUP DESIGNS

When it is not possible to use random assignment to generate equivalent groups, it may still be useful to use experimental designs in which different nonequivalent groups are compared. A nonequivalent group may either be used as a no-treatment control or may be given an alternative form of intervention. (For illustrative studies, see Geismar and Krisberg 1967; Larsen and Mitchell 1980; Florian and Kehat 1987).

The preferred strategy is to use natural groups if they can be located— classes, wards, residential units, caseloads of different practitioners, and so on. Ideally, the researcher hopes to find groups that are "more or less alike" even though their equivalence cannot be ensured. Thus, it may be that two sixth-grade elementary school classes were formed in a manner that might approximate random assignment.

The possible influence of between-group differences in outcome is the primary concern of the researcher. The groups may differ in initial characteristics (selection) or may be exposed to different external events (history) during the experiment, and any of these differences may affect outcome. If the groups are sufficiently large and heterogeneous, and if measures of change in individual members are used as outcome criteria, initial differences affecting outcome can sometimes be dealt with through statistical controls. Suppose a patient self-government program is set up in one ward of a mental hosptial and another ward is used for control purposes and among criterion measures are those relating to patient hospital adjustment and discharge rate. The experimental group is found to contain a higher proportion of patients with acute disorders that may be expected to show a more rapid recovery rate. Hence, the experimental group would be likely to do better for this reason alone. The statistical analysis illustrated in table 7.2 would provide a solution for the problem.

The example provides another illustration of the use of statistical controls (see chapters 4 and 11). The potentially confounding acuteness-chronicity variability is controlled by examining acute and chronic subgroups separately within experimental and control conditions. Although acute patients do better than chronic patients generally, both types fare better under the experimental condition. If such a breakdown had not been made, the experimental group would have shown a much greater degree of superiority on this variable, but it could have been argued that this favorable outcome was due to its having a higher proportion of acute patients. The use of the statistical control weakens that argument, although possible effects of the interaction among patients in the wards introduces an additional complication that we take up in a subsequent use of this example.

No matter how sophisticated the analysis, use of statistical control procedures has a number of limitations in nonequivalent group experiments. The groups must be sufficiently large and varied to permit meaningful statistical anlaysis. If the groups in the example had been very small or if they had been homogeneous—e.g., one consisting of all acute patients, the other of all chronic patients—statistical controls could not have been used. Even when these constraints are not present, statistical controls are fundamentally limited by the scope and quality of the data to which they are applied.

TABLE 7.2

Mean Change in Hospital Adjustment of Patients in Experimental and Control Wards, by Type of Disorder (hypothetical data).

	Experimental Ward Type of Disorder		Control Ward Type of Disorder	
	Acute (N = 30)	Chronic (N = 15)	Acute (N = 12)	Chronic (N = 24)
Mean change in hospital adjustment	+3.2	+.5	+2.1	−1.0

Groups not randomly assigned may differ in ways not measured, and so critical data needed for control purposes may be missing. Or critical variables may be crudely measured. One can go through the motions of statistically controlling for differences, but little control may occur if measurement is fraught with error.

Another means of reducing the influence of extraneous variables in nonequivalent group designs is to use some form of matching. Matching procedures discussed earlier can be used but are not, of course, combined with random assignment. For example, an innovative marital counseling program may be tested in one office of a family agency. Comparison cases may be drawn from another office in which the agency's usual counseling program is offered. Experimental and comparison cases may be matched on two variables thought to have an important influence on outcome: socioeconomic level and degree of marital disturbance (as rated by judges). In this manner each working-class, severely disturbed couple in the experimental group would presumably have its working-class, severely disturbed counterpart in the comparison group.

The major limitation in this procedure is that one cannot ensure equivalence on other variables that may also be important; for example, regardless of their social class or degree of marital disturbance, couples in the "experimental" office may be younger and better motivated than those in the "comparison" office. Without random assignment, these differences cannot be equalized. Whereas matching does not need to be limited to one or two variables, it is often impractical to match for several because of the large number of cases that would be needed to find the correct matches. Moreover, matching is always imprecise; faulty matches may mask differences between the groups. For example, the experimental cases in the preceding example may systematically differ from their control matches in ways that have escaped measurement.

Despite these limitations, matching may still be a useful device when random assignment cannot be used. Sophisticated matching techniques based on factor analysis and other multivariate procedures have been developed and may be considered when potential samples of clients are sufficiently large (Sherwood, Morris, and Sherwood 1975).

Moreover, while cases may be matched in terms of some metric, e.g., ratings of marital adjustment, systematic measurement error may mask actual differences between the samples. For example, it could be that marital cases in the experimental offices given ratings of "severe" are actually in worse shape than "severe" cases in the central office because of ethnic, ecological or other factors not taken into account in the measurement. Finally, the phenomena of "regression to the mean" (chapter 6) may move apparently matched groups in different directions regardless of what kind of services they receive (Kidder and Judd 1986). Suppose cases in the experimental office were characteristically more severe than in the control office. Cases from each office rated "moderately" severe, at the *point of matching*, may undergo different regression effects. As time passes, the ratings of the experimental cases may decline toward a more severe level since a number of the cases in the moderate category would have been on temporary upswings. By the same logic, ratings of control cases in the moderate groups may show improvement! This phenomenon could well nullify or even reverse the effects of a successful service program.

Nonequivalent groups are generally less useful as control devices if the experimental group was formed for the purpose of receiving the intervention. For example, there may be interest in studying the effects of a program designed to improve the communication skills of high school students. The students have "selected themselves" into the experimental group. Any group that might be found or formed for comparison would necessarily differ on motivational and other variables related to the students' self-selection into the training program. These variables could be expected, of course, to have a strong influence on outcome.

Still a nonequivalent control group may have value under such circumstances. Perhaps the most desirable group would be formed from eligible clients who have applied for a program but who could not be absorbed immediately. While such a "waiting-list" control may differ in subtle and important respects from those actually admitted to the program, they would doubtless be more similar to clients in the program than controls chosen from a nonapplicant population. Subjects who may not have applied to a program and who may differ in substantial respects from those in it may still serve certain control purposes. For example, if the criterion measure used to assess gains in an experimental group is one likely to reflect a good deal of change due to normal maturation, a nonequivalent group of subjects may be given the same instrument at two points of time to estimate a base rate of change against which change in the experimental group can be compared. The results obtained from these "limited-purpose controls" must be interpreted with care if they are to be useful. It may be helpful to know that unemployed workers completing a program designed to develop "job-seeking skills" were more successful in obtaining jobs than some other group of unemployed workers, but this finding would provide only one piece of evidence needed to build a convincing case that the program was instrumental in helping the trainees find jobs.

As has been indicated, a nonequivalent group generally provides imperfect or partial control for alternative explanations. In some cases, two or more nonequivalent groups may be used—in the same study or in successive studies—to control for different sources of extraneous variation. This strategy may provide reasonably effective control through what Campbell and Stanley refer to as an "inelegant accumulation of precautionary checks" (1963:227). Not inappropriately, these authors have dubbed this approach a "patched-up design," but the term has an unfortunate negative connotation, conjuring up an image of an old inner tube. In principle, the design is much stronger than one using only a single nonequivalent group and may provide a degree of control comparable to that achieved by an equivalent-groups design. An illustrative study is provided by Brown (1980).

Recall our earlier example of the experiment involving patient self-government. With the use of statistical controls, it was possible to use a second ward to rule out certain extraneous factors that might have caused improvement in the patients' hospital adjustment. But further analysis of the example would suggest an alternative explanation that could not be eliminated by this comparison. It could be argued that the experimental ward with its greater proportion of patients with acute disorders (many of whom were perhaps already recovered) had a much different atmosphere than the control ward in which most of the patients were chronic. The greater improvement of both the acute and chronic patients in the experimental ward might have been in response to this climate rather than to the institution of a self-government program. This alternative explanation might have been tested simultaneously or at a later point by setting up the self-government program in a ward consisting largely of patients with chronic disorders. If the patients in this ward showed a degree of change in hospital adjustment similar to their counterparts in the original experimental ward, then the rival hypothesis that change was due to ward climate could be discounted.

In general, the interpretation of results of nonequivalent-group designs needs to be guided by the kind of logic that can be applied to evaluate the findings of uncontrolled studies. Here, as there, the crucial question is "What plausible alternative explanations need to be ruled out?" If the evidence for an intervention effect in the experimental group is in itself quite persuasive, a nonequivalent group may need only to supply limited data that might help rule out a rival hypothesis of questionable plausibility.

GROUP TIME-SERIES DESIGN

Time-series experiments with single cases were considered at some length in the preceding chapter. The essential characteristics of these designs (repeated measurement, the collection of baseline data before intervention, and experimental manipulations in the form of interrupting and staggering intervention) can be used within the context of group experiments.

In one form of group time-series experiment, unrelated individuals or cases are treated and their progress is measured over time. This form resembles the usual group experiment in that each subject is individually measured and the resulting data are aggregated. For example, Azrin, Naster, and Jones (1973) obtained repeated daily self-reported ratings of marital happiness on twelve couples during a baseline and "placebo treatment" period: they then introduced a form of intervention—reciprocity counseling—while continuing to obtain the daily ratings. An increase in marital happiness following the introduction of the treatment was interpreted as evidence for its effectiveness. This group time-series design is analogous to a variation of the AB single case design. A single-group time-series design provides, of course, a better basis for generalization than its single-case counterpart does. At the same time, the researcher's resources must be spread out over a number of cases. Use of the design may be particularly advantageous if data can be simply and inexpensively collected, as was the case in the study cited.

Time-series group experiments take a somewhat different form when used to study effects of interventions on social systems, such as a classroom or ward. Repeated measurements can be obtained for each individual and aggregated, as in the first form, or measurement may be confined to characteristics of the group as a whole—group cohesion, level of disruptive behavior, and the like. In either circumstance, interest is not centered in individual change but rather in change in the system. Such studies can be seen as a form of single-case time series, with the case being a social system. For example, Hubek and Reid (1980) studied the effects of a self-management program with children excluded from the regular school system because of behavior problems. They selected four classrooms of such children and, using an across-groups multiple baseline design, sequentially introduced a self-management training program in each group. In this program pupils were taught how to control their in-class behavior problems through the recording, evaluation, and reinforcement of their own behaviors. The training program was evaluated by observing the behavior of randomly selected children in each classroom at repeated points. From these observations, measures of inappropriate behavior for each classroom were constructed. It was then possible to document the changes that occurred in the classrooms (not individual pupils) following introduction of the program.

As Tripodi and Harrington (1979) suggest, time-series designs have a potentially broad application in program evaluation. Repeated data on variables such as parole violations, visiting by natural parents, or job placements can be collected before and during the intervention. Programs can be interrupted or introduced sequentially across agencies, offices, and so on. For example, Owan (1978) used a time-series design to evaluate a program in which members of an ethnic group were served by staff drawn from the same group. A branch office of the Social Security Administration (SSA) was opened in Chinatown (New York City) to serve primarily the Chinese-American population that lived in that area. It was staffed entirely by "bilingual-bicultural" (Chinese-American) personnel. Owan compiled time-series data on such outcome variables as processing time and approval rates for claims handled by the new office. Time-series data from other New York offices and from the nationwide SSA program were used for comparison purposes. The pattern of the data suggested that the experimental office very soon began to outperform other New York offices and the national program in respect to the indicators used. The time-series feature of the design provided control for seasonal and other fluctuations that revealed similar trends in all the data sets. As the study illustrates, time-series designs can be used in conjunction with a nonequivalent group comparison and can make use of available data.

THE EXPERIMENTAL INTERVENTION

In any service experiment, great care needs to be given to the planning, implementing, and recording of the interventions to be tested. These considerations are being taken up within the context of the group experiment because of the complexities created by numbers of practitioners and clients. The substance of our observations also applies, however, to single case designs.

In designing an experiment, the researcher usually begins with some conception of the intervention to be tested—the *planned intervention*, one might say. Interest is usually centered in determining the effectiveness of this intervention, however, it may be described. Often this intervention is not well explicated. It may be a complex and vaguely described entity such as "casework" or "counseling" or a procedure that has never been tried. As suggested earlier, exploratory experiments can help "map" interventions prior to a more rigorous testing. But with or without the aid of a pilot study, the researcher attempts to define the experimental interventions at a general level and to operationalize them through specific descriptions of what practitioners are to do in carrying them out. The end product (which may incorporate published or other kinds of available material) is a set of guidelines for practitioners to use in applying the intervention. Even if the practitioner is also the researcher, as in single case or some small group studies, such guidelines are useful in providing a record of what the practitioner/researcher was attempting to test.

The next step is training in use of the intervention, a step that also applies to the practitioner/researcher. At a minimum, the training should involve a recorded trial of the interventions in an actual practice situation. If a group of practitioners is being used, recordings of their tryouts are reviewed and discussed with them. This step also provides a pretest of the guidelines. Feedback from the practitioners can be used to clarify and amplify instructions. Moreover, by providing a sort of pretest of the interventions themselves, the training process provides a final opportunity to modify them before the experiment.

Once the experiment is under way, it is desirable to monitor the implementation of the interventions in at least the practitioners' first cases through tape recordings or other devices and to provide immediate feedback to practitioners concerning deviations or difficulties in implementation. The logistics of this process are often difficult to manage, particularly if there is a sizable number of practitioners to cover and the case flow is heavy. In any event, it is important to have regularly scheduled meetings with practitioners, particularly in the early phases of the experiment, to take up implementation problems.

If the results of the experiment are to be meaningful, it is essential that accurate data be obtained on how the experimental interventions were actually carried out. It does little good to learn that a program was effective (or ineffective) if we do not know what was done. A description of the intervention as planned provides only a statement of intentions and should not be used, as it sometimes is, as a portrayal of the *intervention as implemented*. Hence, a plan for collection of data on service activities should be an integral part of the design of any experiment. Methods of data collection and measurement used to describe interventions are taken up in detail in chapter 13.

Ideally, an experiment should be implemented as planned, but often significant changes will occur during its course. Components of the original intervention may prove unfeasible; practitioners will inevitably improvise, usually in the direction of what appears to be working best from their perspective; often the interventions appear to be unfolding as planned but subsequent analysis reveals major deviations. These modifications alter the working definition of the interventions tested. The experiment informs us about the effectiveness of the intervention as implemented and not as planned. If the program turns out to be a pastiche of improvisations and *ad hoc* compromises, it may offer little basis for generalization. It may have been effective, but it may defy replication. Midstream changes should be kept to a minimum.

GENERALIZATION

The basic considerations presented earlier (chapter 5) concerning generalization from single case experiments apply as well to group experiments. The essential difference is that a group experiment provides a broader, and usually better, foundation for generalization. Although generalization from a group design may be less precise, it is based on a larger and presumably more representative sample of clients, problems, practitioners, and interventions.

Only rarely in service experiments, however, are random sampling methods used to select clients or practitioners, and hence it is usually not possible to generalize within a known margin of error to a larger population (see chapter 8). In other words, generalization usually proceeds without the help of probability theory or statistics.

In generalizing from a group experiment, one begins with the characteristics of the clients and program studied and moves outward. Usually the findings will be most applicable to similar cases dealt with by the same or similar practitioners within the same setting. As these parameters are changed, the risk of error in generalization increases. In forming such judgments one must take into account what is known, or can be reasonably assumed, about the influence of different variables on outcome. For example, there is evidence to suggest that client motivation may be an important variable in the outcome of counseling provided by social workers in family agencies (Ripple 1964; Beck and Jones 1973). Consequently, one would be especially cautious in extrapolating from a family agency program in which the motivation of clients might be questionable.

The size of the sample and knowledge about its representativeness provide additional guidelines. Other things being equal, it is safer to generalize from large samples, say those exceeding a hundred cases, than small ones, say those less than thirty. Although the numbers are less, the same considerations apply to variations in the size of the practitioner sample.

But in any kind of generalization process the representativeness of the sample is always more important than its size. The difficulty with most intervention experiments in social work is that it is hard to know what the sample is representative of—the reason we suggest that one begin with the study at hand and attempt to relate it to similar groups. Still certain assumptions are usually made about representativeness and these need to be examined. It may be assumed, or asserted, that clients served in an experiment are roughly representative of the agency's clientele because no restrictions were placed on intake to the project. It may be found, however, that intake occurred during a time of the year in which referrals from the school system were unusually heavy and that a sizable proportion of clients accepted at intake dropped out of the project and were replaced. In this way, the sample may overrepresent school problems and better motivated clients.

ANALOG STUDIES OF INTERVENTION EFFECTS

Up to this point in the chapter, we have considered the application of experimental design to the study of intervention effects as they occur under field conditions—that is, when services to actual clients with real problems are exposed to experimental testing. As discussed earlier (chapter 4), almost any variable can be simulated and studied under laboratory conditions. This principle has been applied to the study of intervention effects in the helping disciplines (Kazdin 1986).

In essence, an intervention method is tested under conditions that are simulated or are analogous to those characterizing actual helping efforts. Suppose, for example, that an investigator wishes to investigate how different levels of practitioner empathy affect what a person being helped reveals about himself. An experimental study of this problem would be difficult to conduct under field conditions, for practitioners would be reluctant to manipulate the amounts of empathy they displayed with actual clients. Consequently, the researcher might attempt a simulated or analog study. Students taking the role of "clients" might be interviewed about minor "real" problems in their own lives or about fictitious but more serious problems. (In such simulations, it is wise to avoid the more serious problems that students really might have.) The students, who would not be informed about the exact purposes of the experiment, would presumably respond to variations in degree of empathy in a way that would be similar to the responses of actual clients.

There are gradations between simulated and real clients in these experiments. Closer to real clients would be recruited volunteers who might actually have problems (usually in mild form) that could be "treated" in simulations. In their initial experimental tests of their assertiveness training program, McFall and his colleagues (McFall and Twentyman 1973) used student volunteers who had difficulties being assertive. In such cases it may be arguable whether the experiment is better classified as a simulation or the "real thing."

In another variation of simulated study of intervention effects, "real" clients of a service program may serve as volunteers or paid participants. The client subjects may then be exposed to different interventions in a simulated service situation and asked to respond as if they were receiving help. These "clients" might be asked to respond to taped excerpts of actual practitioner-client dialog. The excerpts might be selected to reflect different levels of practitioner empathy; the client volunteers might then be asked to put themselves in the place of the clients on the tapes and rate the amount of practitioner "understanding" reflected in the tapes. The special advantage of such an approach is that one can study the effects of intervention on "clients" who may be close to actual clients in respect to socioeconomic status, educational level, degree of emotional disturbance, and other variables.

Analogs give researchers the opportunity to test intervention-like procedures in controlled experiments that might not be possible to conduct under field conditions. Moreover, in laboratory as opposed to field experiments, experimental variables can usually be more carefully implemented, and their effects can be measured with greater precision, and extraneous factors can be better controlled.

But as a *simulation* an analog study can only approximate the conditions of real interest—those obtaining in the field. Whereas the experiments may have a high degree of internal validity, their external validity, or the extent one can generalize from them, is always problematic. Generalizations to actual client populations may be limited by differences in characteristics between experimental "clients" (who may, for example, be young, middle-class students) and the clients for whom the interventions are intended. Even if subjects are drawn from client populations, they are only pretending to be clients in the experiment and thus may lack the motivation, distress, and problem characteristics of actual clients. Given the artificiality inevitable in an analog study of intervention, one cannot expect experimental variables to "behave" in the same way as they would in reality. Often they operate with *less strength*, since they lack potentiating factors, such as investment or distress, present in field situations. Consequently, a practitioner's expressions of empathy might be expected to be less convincing if evoked by a role played as opposed to a genuine outpouring of feeling. On the other hand, the "problems" to which these weaker interventions are applied may be much more tractable than problems possessed by actual clients. In short, projections from the laboratory to the field can never be readily made.

Still, analog experiments can make an important contribution to the development of intervention approaches. Although a simulation may not provide an adequate basis for asserting how an intervention would work in the field, it might be able to identify promising methods and provide data useful in construction of methods for field trials. Consequently, laboratory experiments can serve a valuable exploratory-formulative function in the development of intervention approaches. Such studies can also be used to test hypotheses from practice theory. For example, in one experiment Loeb, Beck, and Diggory (1971) tested in the laboratory the hypothesis that successful task performance by depressed persons would result in improvements in their self-esteem. Resulting confirmation of this hypothesis in the laboratory test strengthened their theory that use of graded task assignments in treatment would bring about positive changes in depressed patients. Since practice theory is stated in terms sufficiently abstract to cover phenomena in both laboratory and the field—as the hypothesis in the earlier example illustrates—the laboratory experiments can provide a direct means for tests of practice theory.

CHAPTER 8

SAMPLING

In the preceding chapters on research design we have made both explicit and implicit references to sampling. In this chapter we take a closer look at the logic and methods of this process. Our purpose is to provide a general orientation to sampling in its more technical sense. More detailed discussion of sampling theory and procedures may be found in Kish (1965), and Sudman (1976).

While researchers inevitably study specific phenomena—certain individuals, groups, organizations, and so on—they inevitably intend to use their data as a base for making statements about some broader class of phenomena —for example, individuals similar to those studied. Even if these statements take the form of "implications" or "speculations," there is always concern with a bigger picture. If not, there would be little point in doing the study in the first place! In research, the specific phenomena studied are usually referred to as a *"samples"*; a single unit of a sample is called a *sampling element,* and the process of selection is termed *sampling.* The larger classes to which these samples are to be related are known as *populations,* a term that refers generally to any type of unit—people, behaviors, case records, cities, and so on. Regardless of the form sampling takes, the concern is always with the relation between the actual events studied—the sample— and its referent class—the population.

THE NATURE AND PURPOSES OF SAMPLING

Although social workers may not always realize it, they frequently make use of sampling methods in their practice. The social worker may ask parents concerned about their teenage daughter to describe the daughter's behavior at home; from this description, the social worker may tentatively diagnose the daughter as depressed. The *in vivo* interaction between husband and wife during the interview may cause the marriage counselor to perceive their relationship as basically competitive, each trying to control and outdo the other. A supervisor may select several of a worker's case records to read before writing an evaluation of the worker. A school social worker may observe a child's behavior in the classroom and on the playground to understand better what the teacher refers to as the child's aggressive behavior. A planner at United Way may contact a number of people representing different segments of the community to serve as volunteers on a health needs assessment panel.

The case records and the volunteers are obviously samples since in neither case do they constitute the population from which they were drawn; that is, they are not all of the worker's records nor all of the people in the community. In the first example in which the population is easily defined, that is, all of that worker's case records, one may assume that efficiency of time and effort was the supervisor's motivation for selecting a sample. How that sample was selected and which records were read would obviously be of concern to the worker being evaluated. The worker's view of the appropriate sampling method and consequently the "best" sample may not necessarily coincide with the view of a more objective observer. The worker might prefer to handpick the cases while the observer might insist on an unbiased method of selection such as random sampling.

Although the planner is also concerned with efficiency, she is in a very different position from the supervisor who, given the time and desire, could read all of the worker's cases. First, the size of the panel must necessarily be limited. In addition, there are the inherent difficulties of trying to identify all the segments of the community that should be represented and of identifying all the possible representatives of each segment. In this case, sampling not only is desirable but also is the only feasible method. Doubtless, the planner would prefer a purposive sample, that is, people selected by her or the community groups she contacts. The sample could be chosen to meet certain criteria such as knowledgeability about health needs and resources.

The use of sampling methods in the other examples, although more common, may not be so clear. Social workers, as other people do, form impressions and make diagnoses based on observed or described behaviors. These behaviors are not randomly selected; they may be the most salient or problematic in the view of the observer, they may be viewed as symptoms, or they may provide examples or confirmation of an impression, diagnosis, label, or other preconceived way of organizing behavior. This does not make the observed or reported behaviors any less a sample of all of the subject's behaviors in a given situation but refers to the way the sample is selected and how it is used.

The possibility of bias is certainly a possibility in all these examples, but whether or not it is a problem depends on the purpose of the sample. Although the school social worker is looking for aggressive behaviors and therefore pays less attention to the child's other behaviors, she can erroneously use these observations to label the child and react to him as if the aggressiveness were the sum total of the child's personality or can appropriately use one or more of the observed behaviors as the focus of a specific treatment plan with the child. Bias is always a serious problem whenever one is making generalizations or assuming that a set of behaviors, events, attitudes, and so on is representative or typical of a larger population.

Sometimes social workers use sampling in a more structured manner. To illustrate, a counselor may decide to obtain data for a multiple baseline design on four nursery school children referred for withdrawn behavior before initiating a treatment intervention designed to increase their interaction with other children. To obtain baseline measurements on the number of times the four children initiate or respond to attempts at interaction with other children, the counselor decides to observe the children for a half hour of free play during the morning and during the half-hour lunch break (purposive sampling) on a daily basis for a two-week period. She plans to observe each child for five minutes during each designated time period but does not want to observe the children in the same order each time. She puts four different colored marbles, each representing a child, in a large coffee mug, shakes it thoroughly, then blindly draws them out one by one to establish the order of the observations for the fist time period (random sampling). She repeats the process for each time period, writing down the order to be followed for the entire two-week period.

From the foregoing examples, it is clear that the major reason for sampling is feasibility. Often it is impossible to identify all members of a population of interest, for example, homosexuals, drug abusers, or parents of preschool-age children. Even if it were theoretically possible to identify, contact, and study the entire relevant population, time and cost considerations would often make this a prohibitive undertaking. Sampling techniques have been developed that can result in "good samples," that is, samples representative of the population. (Samples need not, however, be representative in every respect, only in those characteristics relevant to the particular study). These techniques involve probability sampling, which is discussed in a later section. The use of such samples may result in more accurate information than might have been obtained if one had studied the entire population. This is so because, with a sample, time, money, and effort can be concentrated to produce better quality research (better instruments, more in-depth information, better trained interviewers or observers, and so on).

Depending on the purpose of the study and the nature of the phenomenon being studied, representatives may not be an important consideration in the selection of a sample. For example, if one is simply interested in identifying variables that may be involved in developing and maintaining egalitarian marriages, an acceptable sample might consist of almost any set of couples known (or believed) to meet certain criteria used by the researchers to define the marital relationship as egalitarian. If, on the other hand, one's interest is in ascertaining the prevalence of egalitarian marriages or factors related to this type of marriage, representative samples of married couples would be necessary. Representativeness is always important when one wants to generalize from the sample to the larger population, that is, when one studies a sample to draw conclusions about the population from which the sample came. Descriptive surveys are the most obvious example of this type of study.

BASIC TYPES OF SAMPLES

Samples are usually divided into two major types: nonprobability and probability. Of the two, nonprobability sampling is used more frequently in social work research. Nonprobability samples, discussed first, are relatively simple and can be described rather briefly. On the other hand, probability sampling involves technical considerations difficult to summarize. Moreover, when it can be used, probability sampling provides a firmer basis for generalization. For these reasons, probability samples are considered in greater depth in a later section.

Nonprobability Samples

For reasons already indicated most samples used by social workers (in their practice and in research) are nonprobability samples. The major advantages of no probability samples generally are convenience and economy. The sampling plans most frequently used are accidental, quota, and purposive.

Accidental samples, sometimes referred to as availability samples or samples of convenience, are, as these names imply, made up of elements selected because they are easy to obtain. This method of sampling is probably the most common. If a student is interested in attitudes toward research of graduate social work students and sends questionnaires to all the Master of Social Work (MSW) degree students in her school, the sample selected is an accidental one. A researcher interested in parent satisfaction in two parent families may select a residential neighborhood and begin knocking on doors to interview people who are at home at the time, who meet the study criteria, and who are willing to participate in the study until the desired sample size is reached. A social worker, wanting to generalize about marital problems, includes in her sample all marital problem cases opened by her agency during a specified period of time. (This is sometimes referred to as a time sample). An investigator wishes to do an exploratory study of needs of migrant workers but has difficulty locating a sample. She asks the subjects she is able to find to give her names of other possible subjects, thereby developing what is appropriately termed a "snowball sample."

Accidental samples have a major shortcoming. Because of biases that may be operating consciously or unconsciously, one does not know how typical the sample is of the population of interest. For example, the students' attitudes about research in the school studied may be different from those of MSW students generally because of factors such as the way research is taught there, the abilities and personalities of the research teachers, and the students' interests and abilities.

Quota sampling differs from accidental sampling only in that it tries to take into account diverse segments of the population that may be important for purposes of the study. To accomplish this, one divides the population into segments or strata based on the selected characteristics, then samples from each stratum. For example, in the parent satisfaction study, it may be as important to obtain research data from fathers as from mothers and from working mothers as from those at home during the day. Since mothers, particularly nonworking mothers, are more likely to be home during the day and mothers may be more likely then fathers to respond to this type of study, interviewers may be instructed to interview only during evenings and weekends and to include fathers and mothers in equal numbers.

The sample might be improved further by stratifying the population on additional variables such as socioeconomic status, racial or ethnic group, age of parents, and number and ages of children. In this way, one could be sure that various segments of the population were included. Practically, stratification is limited to only a few variables because, as variables are added, the sampling plan becomes more complicated and difficult to implement and because the likelihood of few or no elements in certain subgroups increases. Since each subgroup is an accidental sample, the combined sample is accidental and may not be representative of the population.

Purposive or judgmental samples consist of elements (respondents, cases, time segments, and so on) deliberately chosen or handpicked for the study's purposes. In this way, cases may be selected for inclusion because they are thought to be typical of what one is interested in studying. Samples selected in this manner may be especially useful in operations research (chapter 2) and when the function of a study is primarily exploratory (chapter 4). The United Way planner would probably prefer a purposive (handpicked) sample of community people on the health needs assessment panel. The researcher interested in the process of developing and maintaining egalitarian marital relationships would probably select a purposive sample of couples purported to have egalitarian marriages. Like other nonprobability sampling plans, it is risky to use purposive samples for generalizing to larger populations, for we do not know to what extent the samples are representative of populations of interest.

Probability Samples

In probability samples, the likelihood of each element in the population's being included in the sample can be specified. To determine the probability of an element's being selected, one must know at a minimum the size of the population. This is frequently impossible for many phenomena of interest to social workers, such as the number of alcoholics, battered wives, or pregnant teenagers at any one time. Even if one knew the number of alcoholics, the problem would remain of trying to list them or devise some other method of selecting a sample from all alcoholics in the United States, say, in such a way that the probability of each alcoholic's being selected can be specified.

Probability samples are not always necessary and may not even be desirable for certain kinds of research, for example, developing effective treatment methods. Even if probability sampling were the ideal method for a particular study, the difficulty of trying to implement this procedure may not be worth the effort. Since it is impossible to conduct the perfect research study, tradeoffs must be made constantly; probability sampling may be sacrificed for something else (for example, better instruments or more interviews) considered more important. The relative advantages of probability sampling are discussed in a later section; suffice it to say here that this method is more likely to produce representative samples, and this enables the researcher to generalize with more confidence to the population from which the sample came—a crucial consideration in surveys. However, because of attrition the sample obtained may not be the same as the one drawn; whether or not the final sample is still a probability sample depends on whether or not the reason for attrition introduces bias. In addition, it is important to remember that although one may be able to obtain a random sample of students in a particular high school for a study of adolescents' attitudes toward sex, the population of interest is adolescents generally, not just the ones in that high school. Usually the limits of generalizability are only gradually established through replications with different groups under different conditions.

The major types of probability samples are simple random samples, stratified random samples, certain types of cluster samples, and certain types of systematic samples. Some cluster and systematic samples are nonprobability and some are a combination of the two basic types of samples; these differentiations are clarified during the discussion of cluster and systematic sampling plans.

Simple Random Samples   A researcher interested in students' attitudes about an issue on a particular campus who selects "at random" (more precisely, haphazardly) students passing in front of the library to interview does not have a random sample. (The sample obtained in this manner is accidental.) Random sampling involves a very systematic process, which ensures that every element and every combination of elements have a specifiable chance of being chosen. In simple random sampling, each element and combination of elements have the same probability of being selected into the sample. To illustrate, the researcher cited could have obtained a list of all the students on that particular college campus and selected the sample in such a way that every student would have had an equal chance of being interviewed. The researcher might have done this by first numbering consecutively each name on the student list and then using a table of random numbers to decide which students to select. This would result in a random sample of students on that campus.

Tables of random numbers consist of rows and columns of numbers randomly generated. (Pages of random numbers are found in the appendixes of many research methods and statistics books. For example, see Kerlinger 1985.) One uses a table of random numbers by blindly picking a starting point on a page and then going across the rows, down the columns, or diagonally, to obtain numbers to be included in the sample. For example, suppose there were 1,200 students on the campus and the researcher had decided to go down the columns using the first four digits (and ignoring the last digit) in each set of a table of random numbers set up as follows:

    46880
    77775
    00102
    06541
    60697

Two students from these numbers would be selected for the sample: those numbered 10 and 654. The other three numbers in the table (4688, 7777, and 6069) would be disregarded, for they are larger than 1,200. For a sample of N = 100, each student would have 1 in 12 chances of being selected in this manner. Instead of using a table of random numbers, the researcher might have used a list of random numbers generated by a computer; this latter method is less tedious when large populations are involved.

Stratified Random Samples As in quota sampling, the population is first divided into segments or strata based on the characteristics one wants to take into account. Then simple random samples are selected from each stratum in stratified sampling. One purpose of stratification is to ensure that diverse elements of the population considered important for the study purposes are included. In most cases, simple random sampling also accomplishes this goal. There are special cases, however, when stratified random sampling improves on the efficiency or representativeness of the sample. Generally these circumstances occur when heterogeneity exists between the strata and homogeneity within the subgroups on variables of interest in the study. For example, if one is interested in the opinions of social workers in a community concerning a particular issue and has reason to believe that administrators will view the issue very differently from social workers into these two groups, take a random sample from each stratum, and then combine the two sub-samples. First, this guards against the possibility that no or very few administrators will be included, which is possible in simple random sampling. Second, if administrators tend to hold similar opinions and the practitioners hold similar opinions different from the administrators, the representatives of the sample is enhanced.

In stratified random sampling it is necessary to know or have a reasonable estimate of the proportion of people in the population in each of the subgroups. One can sample from each stratum in the same proportions as exist in the population (proportionate sampling) or not (disproportionate sampling). Although it is not necessary to sample in accurate proportions (one may want to oversample administrators, for instance), it is necessary to include enough cases in each stratum to make sure each subgroup is adequately represented and to provide for further categorization, if warranted, in analyzing the data. If the strata are not sampled in the same proportions as exist in the population, then numbers in each subgroup must be weighted in generalizing from the sample to the population.

Sometimes one cannot anticipate the existence of internally homogeneous subgroups in the population with respect to the charcteristics being studied. In this case, one simply stratifies the sample later during the data analysis. For example, during the analysis one could take the simple random sample of social workers and categorize it into administrators and direct practitioners. The effect would be the same as stratification during sampling since the administrators in the simple random sample of social workers constitute a random sample of administrators in the community, and the practitioners in the sample are a random sample of practitioners in the community.

Cluster Samples   For practical reasons, which one of the illustrations that follow will make clear, large-scale surveys generally use cluster or area sampling rather than simple random sampling. With this method of sampling, one can use a single-stage sampling plan by randomly selecting a cluster and obtaining data from all relevant units in the cluster, or one can use a multistage cluster sampling plan. An example of the first would be a sample of all school districts in a randomly selected state. A multistage sampling plan might involve successive random samples to choose a state, a school district, a school, and then inclusion of all the teachers (or a random sample of teachers) in the final sample. Of course, one may select more than one sampling unit (state, school, and so on) at any stage.

Whether or not cluster samples are probability or nonprobability samples depends on whether random selection is used. Multistage sampling may involve both probability and nonprobability sampling since the sampling units at different stages may be selected differently. In the given example, one might choose at the first step a few states purposely selected to represent different regions of the county (nonprobability sampling), from each state randomly select an urban and a rural school district (probability: stratified random), from each district randomly select a school (probability), and from each school select a simple random sample of teachers (probability). Specifying the probability of an element's being selected into a multistage probability cluster sample (where probability sampling is used at every stage) may be very complicated, but it can be done.

It should be obvious to the reader why cluster sampling is usually preferred to random sampling of large populations, particularly if they are widely dispersed. In our example, listing all grade school and high school teachers in the United States is a near impossible task. (Memberships in national professional organizations do not include all eligible professionals.) Even if such a list could be compiled or obtained, selecting a simple or stratified random sample from it would be a huge undertaking and collecting data from such a widely scattered sample would be feasible only by using mail questionnaires. However, a multi-stage cluster sampling plan makes simple random or stratified random sampling quite manageable at every level.

Systematic Sampling   This sampling plan, which involves choosing every *n*th element, is often used by social workers. Every tenth case record in the files or every sixth name on the local NASW membership list may be selected as a sample to study. The sampling interval (for example, ten or six) is obtained by dividing the population by the size of the desired sample. Whether or not systematic samples are probability samples depends on how the first element is selected; probability sampling would require the first element to be randomly selected. (Note that most combinations have no chance of being selected; for this reason, some researchers question whether any systematic sample should be considered a probability sample). In the first example, a number between one and ten would be randomly chosen to determine the first case record for the sample. Thereafter, every tenth case would be selected into the sample. Thus, the probability of a record's being chosen for the sample is one in ten initially but changes after the first record is selected.

Because of this changed probability (either 100 percent or zero), it is important to examine beforehand the files or lists to see how they are constructed. A genuinely random order would result in a random sample. Certain orders may result in a stratified sample. For example, names listed in alphabetical order may stratify the sample on ethnic origin since the "Mac's" and "Mc's" would be together and so forth. Case records filed according to closing date or type of case would be stratified by those principles. In some cases this stratification might be advantageous, but this would need to be evaluated by considering the basis for stratification in relation to the particular study. There are, however, times when the order of the files or lists may result in biased samples. For example, a child welfare agency may keep separate records on foster parents, natural parents, and each child in the family for which the agency has responsibility. If all the records making up a "case" are filed together and in the same order (for example, foster parents first, then natural parents, and then children according to age), the systematic sample would be biased by having large families overrepresented and very possibly by having certain kinds of record (for example, foster parents) overrepresented or underrepresented. The possibility of these biased samples presents serious problems for the researcher.

GENERALIZATION

Making statements about a larger group (population) on the basis of a smaller group (sample) studied is referred to as *generalization*. In this section we focus primarily on generalizing from representative samples in which use is made of probability theory to estimate characteristics of populations from samples. When nonrepresentative samples are used, generalization is guided by the logical considerations set forth in the two previous chapters. These considerations, developed within the context of experimental research, apply as well to naturalistic research. With a nonrepresentative sample, one makes judgments about possible atypicalities and biases of the sample and on the basis of these judgments arrives at informed speculations about larger groups.

With representative samples, however, the process moves more systematically, as the following example shows. Suppose a democratic school of social welfare was considering changing its curriculum slightly to require a statistics course for the MSW degree and decided to base the decision on student opinion. The 400-member student body is polled by asking them to indicate on a ten-point rating scale the extent to which they agree or disagree with making the course a requirement. A rating of 10 would indicate maximum agreement, and a score of 1, maximum disagreement. The school decides to make the statistics course a requirement if the average (mean) student rating is over 5.5 but not to make this change if the mean score is 5.5 or below. Suppose ratings are obtained from all the students and when the scores are added together and divided by 400, the mean score is 4.9. According to the previous decision, the statistics course would not become mandatory.

Since the entire student body was contacted, we know the true population mean (a parameter)—a rarity in social research—and consequently do not have to estimate it from a sample mean (a statistic). Suppose, for illustrative purposes, we randomly selected from this student body a sample of 40 students and calculated the mean of these scores as 5.1. If the school decision had been based on this sample, it would have been the same as the one based on the population value. Suppose three more random samples of 40 students each are drawn from the 400 students (with all students' names replaced before each sample selection), and the calculated sample means are 4.8, 4.7, and 5.7. Two things immediately become apparent: one is that most of the sample means are very close to the population mean, and the other is that if the last sample had been taken as representative of the population on the variable of interest, that is, the student body's wishes concerning the statistics course, the opposite conclusion would have been reached and the course would have been made a requirement. If we randomly selected a large number of samples of size 40 from this population of students, calculated their means, and plotted these means on a graph, we would find that they would distribute themselves around the population mean roughly in the shape of a bell-shaped curve (called a normal curve) as in figure 8.1. This array is called a sampling distribution. In other words, most of the sample

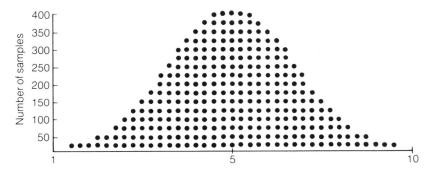

FIGURE 8.1
Sampling distribution of means of sample size 40

means would cluster around the population mean, and the more extreme the sample values, the less likely they would be to occur. If an infinite number of random samples of the same size is taken from the same population, the shape of the sampling distribution of means will be a normal or bell-shaped curve and the most frequently obtained sample mean will be the population mean. This is also true of other sample statistics (standard deviations, medians, proportions, and so on)—all of which could be plotted as sampling distributions. This characteristic of random samples is basic to the notion of generalization and inferential statistics (chapter 11).

In reality we would have only one random sample and no way of knowing for sure whether it is similar to the population on variables of interest or whether it is dissimilar, that is, one of the extreme samples. This is so because we do not know the population values (parameters); if we did, there would be no need to obtain a sample. However, probability theory provides us with some assurance here. First, as we observed in figure 8.1, probability samples are more likely than not to be representative of, although seldom identical to, the population. Second, probability theory enables us to estimate the representativeness or accuracy of the sample. If we take our theoretical sampling distribution of means (an infinite number of samples of the same size), we can calculate a measure of variability (spread or dispersion) around the population mean called the standard error. In effect, the standard error is the standard deviation of the sampling distribution and is a measure of sampling error. We can use the standard error, which takes into account the size of the samples, to determine the probability of obtaining samples with different values (means). According to probability theory, approximately 34 percent of the sample estimates (statistics) will fall within one standard error above the population parameter and 34 percent of the estimates will fall within one standard error below. Thus about two-thirds (68 percent) of the estimates will be within (plus or minus) one standard error. Approximately 95 percent of the sample estimates will fall within two standard errors on either side of the population parameter, and virtually all (more than 99 percent) within three standard errors. This information from probability theory permits us to make inferences about the one sample we have randomly drawn. For example, since we know that 95 percent of the sample means on a given variable will be no larger or smaller than the values representing two standard errors on either side of the population mean, we infer that the chances are 95 percent that our sample mean is between those two values. That is, we are 95 percent confident that our sample mean is within that specified interval. (The use of the standard normal curve with its associated calculated probabilities enables us to make much finer discriminations than those given here.)

Because we do not know the population parameter, we use our sample statistic (for example, the mean) as the best estimate of the parameter. From the preceding discussion, we know that most of the time this will be an accurate estimate and further that we can specify the degree of confidence we can have that the population parameter is within a certain range. Our illustration concerning the statistics course can be used to illuminate these concepts. Suppose the standard error, the sampling error, for the sampling distribution displayed in figure 8.1 was .3. Since we know that the population mean is 4.9, we would expect 68 percent of sample means in a sampling distribution to be between 4.6 and 5.2, 95 percent between 4.3 and 5.5. 99 percent between 4.0 and 5.8, and fewer than 1 percent of the sample means to be smaller than 4.0 or larger than 5.8. Thus, we see that a mean as large as the 5.7 we obtained on one of the four samples we drew initially, which would have resulted in a different conclusion if it had been used to make inferences about the school population, could be expected to occur less than 5 percent of the time. Usually there is no way of knowing if such an unlucky event has occurred, since the population parameter is rarely known. ("Unlucky" refers to the lack of representativeness, although the students at that school may have perceived another referent.)

A less technical and more "consumer-oriented" interpretation of the foregoing may be helpful. When a study makes use of truly random sampling methods, the reader must be alert to two ways in which the sample may give an inaccurate estimation of the means, proportions, and so on, that characterize the population. First, random samples can be expected to vary within a certain range of the population value. For example the report of a poll based on a random sample may say that 55 percent of the voters in a state prefer candidate Brown over her rival but may add the qualification that this estimate may be off by as much as 4 percent. Second, there is always some chance that the sample will fall completely outside the range in which it is expected to vary. Thus not only we expect actual voter preferences for Brown to vary between 51 and 59 percent but even that estimate has a chance of being wrong—say, one in a hundred.

It should also be noted that the population from which a random sample is drawn may not be the population of greatest interest. Thus a study of the attitudes of institutionalized aged may use a random sample of subjects from a particular institution. Although generalizations based on the probability theory can be made about the population of the institution, one may wish to consider what the findings may contribute to understanding of institutionalized aged in general. Generalization beyond that population would need to proceed on logical grounds as would be done for a non-probability sample.

SIZE OF SAMPLE

Decisions about how large a sample to use involve the same considerations as decisions concerning sampling plans. Generally, the larger the sample, the more representative it is likely to be and the greater the chance that the mean is close to the population mean. However, sample size may be completely inrrelevant if conscious or unconscious biases are operating. For example, if a student who detests mathematics had been allowed to choose an accidental sample for the student poll concerning the statistics requirement, it might not have mattered whether 10 or 100 students were polled. However, in the case of probability sampling, the larger the sample, the more likely it is to accurately reflect the population. This is so because, as the size of the sample increases, the sampling error decreases, indicating more cluster around the population parameter. The standard error of the mean is σ/n, where σ is the estimated standard deviation of the population and n is the number of cases in the sample. Thus, as the sample size increases, the denominator becomes larger and the standard error smaller. Again, by making use of probability theory, it is possible to determine how large a sample is needed to achieve a certain degree of precision as measured by the width of the confidence interval. However, the formula requires estimates based on the researcher's judgment and consequently is of limited value for inexperienced researchers. For relatively small populations, some researchers use a sampling fraction of 1/10, which means sampling one-tenth of the population. Intuitively, the reader will perceive that the more homogeneous the population on variables of interest, the smaller the sample needed to reflect the variability in the population. In the final analysis, sample size is usually based on the researcher's judgment, with factors such as time and cost considerations, requirements of planned data analysis, and the like, being taken into account.

Sampling is, after all, only one of many considerations in the planning and implementation of a research study. For example, much of this chapter has dealt with sampling methods designed to prevent bias, but bias can enter into the study at any number of points, for example, in the underlying assumptions of the researcher, in the way data are collected, of in interpretations made of the findings. All the stages of research involve considerations of time, effort, cost, feasibility, appropriateness, desirability, what is possible, and so on. Because resources are inevitably limited, judgments and tradeoffs must be made. Decisions made at one point in the research often have implications for other stages. Consequently, the sampling must be viewed within the context of the entire study, the purpose of the research as the major guiding principle.

CHAPTER 9

MEASUREMENT

Measurement is as much a part of social work practice as relating to clients is. Social workers use measurement procedures in obtaining information about their clients and their problems, in developing treatment strategies, and in evaluating outcomes. Measurement procedures are used in ascertaining the needs of target populations and in evaluating the services or programs that may result. Face sheets, case records, program statistics, annual reports, and the like, contain data resulting from or summarizing these measurements.

Counting the number of clients served or number of dollars spent is readily seen as measurement, as is information about attributes such as the client's age, organizational size, and length of time a program has been in existence. Median family income and mean number of interviews per case are summaries of such measurements. Perhaps less obvious as measurements, but still capable of being quantified, are characteristics such as level of community participation, degree of cooperation, and client satisfaction with service. More difficult to perceive as involving measurement or as capable of being measured are attributes such as the client's sex, religion, occupation, and type of problem. Intuitively, the ease or difficulty in perceiving characteristics as measurable depends on the degree to which they take on properties of the number system. The properties usually considered in this respect are order, distance, and origin. These aspects are discussed further in the section on level of measurement that follows.

DEFINITION

Measurement can be defined in many different ways. The most important differences in meaning for our purposes concern how broadly or narrowly the term is used. References to measuring effectiveness, mental health, or family functioning suggest use of the term in its broadest sense, while counting the number of social workers attending a meeting or the number of agencies in a community providing homemaker service suggests a more restricted usage. In its broadest sense, measurement is used interchangeably with operationalization.

Often, the term measurement is substituted for operational definition, as illustrated by: "In this study, aggression was measured as follows: . . . ," or as Kidder and Judd state, ". . . the procedures for measuring variables are called operational definitions" (1986:40). Viewed broadly then, measurement can be thought of as encompassing the processes necessary to define both the "what" and the "how" to observe and measure; that is, it can include the specification of the indicators selected to represent the major concepts in the study, as well as the categorization or quantification of those indicators. Criteria used to evaluate measurement procedures, such as reliability and validity, are concerned with measurement in this broader sense.

Another common way in which the term *measurement* is used seems to focus on the part of the operational definition that attempts to categorize or quantify the indicators, and consequently, seems more restricted in scope. Suggested originally by Stevens, this definition states that "measurement is the assignment of numerals to objects or events according to rules" (1951:1). In clarifying this definition, Kerlinger (1985) points out that in fact one measures, not objects or events, but rather indicators of the properties or characteristics of objects. For example, it would not be clients or preschool age children that we would measure, or even be interested in measuring, but some attribute that can describe them such as their mental health, intelligence, or aggressiveness. However, since we cannot measure even these characteristics directly, we choose or develop indicators to represent them that we can measure, such as questions answered correctly or hitting others. Generally numbers, which are numerals that have been assigned quantitative meaning, are assigned to or mapped onto the indicators, Kerlinger (1985) warns that the rules used in assigning numbers can be good or bad, and this will determine, other things being equal, whether or not the measurement is sound or poor, even meaningless. To develop good measurements, the rules or assignment or correspondence have to be tied to, or isomorphic with (that is, similar in form to) "reality." Here we are concerned with the fit between the numbers assigned to each of the preschoolers in our sample, for example, and how aggressive each one is. Of course, we cannot determine the goodness of fit precisely or directly, for we cannot know the "true value" of the amount of aggression each child possesses. What we try to do instead is to obtain some indirect evidence of fit by examining various aspects of the measurement (operationalizing) procedure. Essentially we look at two levels of correspondence: one, the fit between the concept (say, aggression) and our indicators of it (say, hitting another child); and the second, the correspondence between the amounts or degrees of the indicator and the meaning of the numbers assigned to represent these amounts. In the first instance, we are referring to operational definitions and are concerned about validity; in the second instance, we are referring to level of measurement and concerned about use of the appropriate measurement scale (that is, nominal, ordinal, and so on).

While definitions of measurement vary, most of the commonly used ones differ along the dimension of inclusiveness. The usage of the term can range from being synonymous with quantification to being interchangeable with operationalization. The broader definitions seem more useful for social work research. Conceiving of measurement as including the operational specification of indicators, as well as their classification or quantification, not only has more utility for the kind of phenomena social workers are usually concerned with in quantitative studies but also permits one to speak of measurement in qualitative studies. Using the term in this broader sense also renders moot the debate over whether nominal measurement, to be discussed in a later section, is in fact measurement.

ROLE OF MEASUREMENT

Measurement is a crucial part of the research process. It plays a vital role in helping us answer research questions and test hypotheses. it is a basic step in the collection and organization of data and a necessary procedure for yielding data that can be analyzed statistically. Inferences about the existence or nonexistence of relationships between variables will be made on the basis of the manipulation of measurements. Consequently, hypotheses will be accepted or rejected on the basis of analyses using measurements that may be viewed as the researcher's approximations to reality.

Measurement provides a bridge between the world of concepts and the empirical world. As Bernard Phillips states, "Measurement . . . [is] the process of creating a correspondence between a concept and data specifying that concept" (1985:108). The relationship of measurement to other aspects of the research process is presented in figure 9.1.

In addition to making hypothesis testing possible, measurement enables us to describe and classify individuals, organizations, cultures, and so on, according to their attributes. It can help us refine our conceptual definitions and gain greater objectivity in our observations. It enables us to discover relationships among variables and makes standardization possible. Measurement also allows us to communicate our research operations more precisely, which is crucial for replication, evaluation of results, and appropriate use of findings.

LEVELS OF MEASUREMENT

There are four commonly accepted levels of measurement, resulting in four types of scales. These are, in ascending order: nominal, ordinal, interval, and ratio. Level of measurement is determined by the extent to which attributes of the variable being measured take on the properties of the number system. At the lowest level, nominal measurement, there is no correspondence between the categories that the variable is partitioned into and the number system. The numerals assigned to various categories of the variable being measured are merely symbols or labels with no number meaning. For this reason some methodologists do not consider the nominal level as measurement but rather as simply nominal classification. At the highest level of measurement (ratio scales), the numbers indicate the actual amount of the

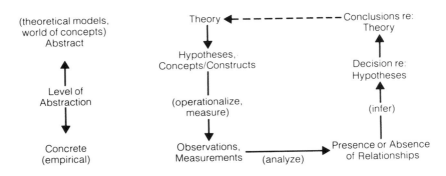

FIGURE 9.1
The relationship of measurement to other parts of the research process

property being measured; consequently, there is perfect correspondence between the attributes being measured and the characteristics or meaning of the numbers assigned to the attributes. Ordinal and interval measurement, as will be shown, fall between these two extremes. Because the level of measurement is related to the degree to which properties being measured take on characteristics of the number system, the arithmetic operations and statistical manipulations that can be performed on data differ according to the level of measurement used. The higher the level of measurement, the more sophisticated the arithmetic operations and statistical tests that can be used. In addition, since the levels of measurement are cumulative (each higher level has the characteristics of all levels below it plus an additional characteristic), operations and tests that are appropriate at lower levels can also be used at higher levels.

Generally researchers aim for the highest level of measurement that is appropriate for variables of interest and that is consistent with their research purposes, because of the increased information to be obtained. At the lowest level where attributes are categorized or classified, we can obtain frequencies or "counts" of the number of cases in each category. At the next level, the data can be ordered and we can determine magnitude, that is, more or less of an attribute. At this point we have moved from qualitative to quantitative data. Even more precise quantitative data are obtained at the two highest levels where the data are referred to as metric. Among the advantages of being able to measure variables on higher level scales are increased precision of description, increased communicability of research operations and results, and increased possibilities for discovering and establishing relationships among phenomena.

Nominal Measurement

Nominal measurement, the lowest level of measurement, is the categorization or classification of objects or properties of objects. It is qualitative, rather than quantitative. Numbers assigned to categories have no numerical meaning but are only names (hence "nominal") or labels for the categories. Suppose we try to classify courses in a school of social welfare according to their major emphasis and our rules call for assigning a 1 to treatment courses, a 2 to social policy courses, a 3 to research methods courses, and so on. No order can be inferred from the numbers; for example, 3 is not more or less, higher or lower, than 2. Nor can any arithmetical operations be used; for example, a 1 and a 2 do not equal a 3. (A treatment course plus a social policy course do not equal a research methods course!) However, cases within a subclass can be counted and cases in one subclass can be compared with cases in other subclasses (on other variables). For example, one could obtain frequencies for the number of treatment courses, social policy courses, and so on. One could compare the mean number of students in treatment courses with the mean number of students in research methods courses, or one could compare the proportion of A's given in social policy courses with the proportion given in research methods courses. As these examples illustrate, nominal measurement is often used in conjunction with other levels of measurement, but that does not affect the level of measurement of the basic variable, the one that is categorized.

Categorization is basic to all measurement. At a minimum we must be able to partition into categories or classes the attributes of a variable. We may classify people into two groups, male or female, on the basis of sex, into several groups according to type of treatment case, into a defined number of categories describing degree of marital satisfaction, or into some large number of categories according to age. On some variables we can categorize cases only into two groups on the basis of presence or absence of some attribute. In developing categories, we need to be concerned about only two criteria; mutual exclusiveness and exhaustiveness. To be mutually exclusive, categories must be unique, distinct, and unambiguous; there must be only one appropriate category for each case. This means that categories must be unidimensional or, if more than one dimension is used, all relevant possible combinations must be included. These categories for religion are mutually exclusive: Catholic, Protestant, and Jew; these are not: Catholic, Protestant, Lutheran and Jew. Attempts to classify cases as child abuse, neglect, or sexual abuse present problems since cases may involve any two or all three. One would need to have categories for all combinations or develop a set of categories for each problem, such as presence or absence of child abuse and so on. Exhaustiveness refers to having a category for each case. To meet this requirement, a category called "other" may need to be added for some variables if the researcher cannot, or chooses not to, specify all possible categories. For example, one might use the following categories for marital status: married, divorced, separated, never married, and other.

Ordinal Measurement

In ordinal measurement not only are objects or characteristics of objects divided into categories, but also the categories can be rank ordered. Relationships of "greater than" or "less than" can be expressed. Ordinal scales are the crudest form of quantitative measurement. Although these scales allow us to express the degree to which objects in a category possess a certain characteristic, they do not allow us to say how much they possess. For example, we might have parents rate their child care arrangement as "very satisfactory," "satisfactory," "unsatisfactory," or "very unsatisfactory." Although this ordinal scale clearly indicates degree of satisfaction, it does not permit us to infer that the distance between "very satisfactory" and "satisfactory" is the same as that between "satisfactory" and "unsatisfactory." Ordinal scales indicate only rank order, not equal intervals or absolute quantities.

Many variables used in social work research and practice are most appropriately measured on ordinal scales. Some examples are socioeconomic status, educational level, severity of problem, and attitude, opinion, and prestige scales. Kerlinger (1985) cautions us that intelligence, aptitude, and personality test scores are also ordinal since they do not indicate the amounts of the traits but rather the rank order positions of the individuals.

Interval Measurement

Not only can categories be rank ordered, but also there are equal intervals between the categories on interval scales. However, there is no natural origin or absolute zero. The commonly cited example of an interval scale is temperature as measured on the Fahrenheit or Celsius scales. (The Kelvin scale, on the other hand, is ratio since it has an absolute zero.) Calendar time, with Christ's birth as the arbitrary origin, is also an interval scale. It is difficult to give other examples, for almost all interval scales are also ratio scales. Attempts have been made to develop interval scales in the social sciences, most notably the Thurstone method of equal-appearing intervals, but there is no consensus that these go beyond ordinal measurement.

Ratio Measurement

Ratio scales have all the properties of the other three scales plus an absolute zero or natural origin. Therefore, ratio measurements indicate absolute amounts. Not only can we say that one person is different from another according to some characteristic (nominal measurement), has more or less of that characteristic (ordinal), and is so many units above or below another person on that characteristic (interval), but also we can now express the difference as a ratio by saying that one person has so many times as much of the characteristic as another person. For example, a person with six dollars has twice as much money as a person with three dollars. Weight, height, and age are usually measured on ratio scales. When we count objects, we are using a ratio scale. Social work practitioners and researchers often use ratio measurement for variables such as number of cases, interviews, problems, agencies; amount of income, welfare grant, and child support (in dollars); and duration or length of interview, case, marriage or employment.

When numerical data are grouped into categories, the result is an ordinal scale. Instead of asking respondents their exact age or income, researchers may develop age or income brackets and ask respondents where they fall, believing that the latter question is less objectionable to most people. Although these groupings cut down on the amount of information obtained, data collected in this manner may be sufficiently precise for the purposes of the research. On the other hand, this method may represent one of the necessary tradeoffs that are inevitable in any study. The same result obtains if numerical data are collected but grouped during the analysis. Whereas the full range of statistical procedures is appropriate for ratio measurements, only those procedures that can be used with ordinal scales are appropriate for the grouped numerical data.

A few comments are in order about the common practice in social work research (indeed, in social research generally) of using arithmetic operations and statistical procedures in analysis of data derived from measurement at the ordinal level. Arithmetic operations, such as addition, subtraction, multiplication, and division, assume at least interval level data. Thus, computation of means, which requires summation and division, strictly speaking, is "inappropriate" for data based on measurement that simply asserts that a is greater than b. Yet measurement of most concepts of interest to social workers does not exceed the ordinal level. Treating ordinal data as if they were at an interval or ratio level is best justified by assuming that most ordinal scales approach interval measurement to some degree. To the extent that they do, treating them as interval scales permits one to make use of a wide range of "more powerful" manipulations and tests that are possible if arithmetic operations are employed. Although this assumption and resulting practice can be defended, one must keep in mind that it invariably introduces an unknown amount of error into what analyses are performed, error that can offset the greater "power" of the arithmetic operations. Hence, ordinal data that have been extensively manipulated by procedures (such as product-moment correlations and factor analysis) that assume interval level measurement must be treated with more than the usual amount of caution.

CRITERIA FOR EVALUATING MEASUREMENT PROCEDURES

Because of the crucial role measurement plays in research—linking theory to reality—the adequacy of measurement procedures is of great concern to researchers, evaluators of research studies, and discriminating users of research findings. The criterion of greatest importance in the evaluation of measurement is *validity*, which refers to the extent to which a measure corresponds to the "true" position of a person or object on the characteristic being measured. A more general way of expressing this idea is to say that validity is a gauge of how well measurement achieves its purposes. If the purpose of the consumer price index is to measure the cost of living, how well does it accomplish this goal? Much more technical definitions of validity, sometimes making use of statistical concepts, have been attempted (see, for example, Kerlinger 1985). But however validity is defined, it is clear that it attempts to capture an elusive property of measurement: "its truth value." For most measures of social phenomena, this value cannot be ascertained in any fundamental sense. There is usually no way of knowing the "true" characteristics of the realities of interest to us. Consequently, validity is inevitably a matter of judgment based on evidence and inference.

Traditionally, one aspect of validity has been treated somewhat separately, perhaps because it does lend itself to more precise assessment. We are referring to the consistency or *reliability* of measurement. While we may not be able to determine if a measure is true, we can determine if it yields consistent or reliable results through means such as repeating the measurement or having it independently applied by two observers. If it does, we have *some* evidence that the instrument is achieving its purposes—at least whatever is being measured is being measured consistently. But we have come only part way: two measurements may be consistent but both may be false. If its application yields inconsistent results, then the instrument has failed an elementary test of validity, and our confidence in its capacity to achieve its purposes is lessened. To put these ideas in concrete form, let us suppose a traveler wants to be sure of the time. He consults his watch but regards it as a fallible measure and so he asks a companion to give him the time. If his companion gives him a time similar to his own, he is reassured that his watch was correct. His "reliability check" has provided some proof of validity. But there is still the chance that both readings may be in error—both the traveler and his companion may have gone through a time zone without resetting their watches (reliability without validity). Obviously, if the initial check had revealed that his companion had a quite different time, the traveler would have received no confirming evidence that his watch was giving him the right (valid) time. Now it is possible that the traveler had the correct time after all. Inconsistent results do not *necessarily* mean that an instrument is in error, but they provide no evidence that it is on the mark.

In addition to needing measurement procedures producing data that are correct, that is, valid and reliable, the researcher also needs to obtain data that are relevant, practical, feasible, and sensitive. Relevance refers to obtaining data that bear upon the research questions, the adequacy of the indicators selected, and the appropriateness of measures for respondents. As an example of the last consideration mentioned, it would be inappropriate and meaningless to ask a respondent if he approved of pending welfare reform legislation if he knew practically nothing about it. Further, the data obtained would be misleading if he responded without the researcher's awareness of his lack of knowledge. Practicality and feasibility refer to matters such as cost in money, time, and effort and to ethical considerations in using the measurement procedures. Cost factors, which pose eternal constraints on research, need no elaboration. Rather stringent procedures for the protection of human subjects have been set up by many research organizations, universities, and governmental funding agencies in efforts to safeguard the rights of, and minimize risks to, individuals. These external controls serve as an impetus to researchers to consider possible ethical issues. Instruments also need to be sensitive, that is, capable of making distinctions fine enough for the purposes they are to serve. In some studies, simply being able to separate individuals correctly into two groups, for example satisfied and not satisfied in terms of marital satisfaction, may be sufficient. Such a crude distinction even if free from error would probably not be adequate in studies where marital satisfaction is a major variable.

Because few if any measuring instruments in the social sciences meet all of these criteria, tradeoffs must be made here as in other aspects of research. Efforts to increase validity and reliability are liable to be costly in terms of money, time and effort. Increased sensitivity often lowers reliability. Because of such problems, researchers are advised to use, when possible, more than one measurement procedure for major variables.

Against the backdrop of these general considerations, we examine in more detail two central aspects of measurement adequacy; reliability and validity. Following convention we treat these aspects separately, although, as we have shown, reliability is a facet of validity. Because reliability is in fact subordinate, it is dealt with first. In discussing both aspects we draw on the typologies and vocabulary developed by Selltiz, Wrightsman and Cook (1976) and widely used by research methodologists (see, for example, Rubin 1983; Phillips 1985).

Reliability

There are different types of reliability, depending on the kind of measurement procedures used and the aspect of reliability one is interested in. The aspects most frequently considered are stability, equivalence, and homogeneity. Stability and equivalence are concerned with external consistency, and homogeneity is concerned with internal consistency. In all these aspects it is assumed that the subjects or respondents remain the same, but the time, instrument, or investigator may vary, depending on the type of reliability being assessed. Generally, the time of administration varies (but not the instrument or the investigator) when stability is the concern, and either the instrument or the investigator varies (but not the time) when equivalence is the issue. When homogeneity is the concern, some items in the instruments are compared to other items and there is no variation of other factors.

Stability Since stability refers to consistency of measures on repeated applications, the appropriate procedure for determining it is comparison of the results of repeated measurements. The variation in results reflect not only errors of measurement but also any fluctuations in the characteristic being measured. Genuine fluctuations or changes complicate attempts to assess stability of the measuring instrument. Attitudes, opinions, perceptions, and emotional states—phenomena that social workers are often interested in— are particularly subject to change.

Test-retest is the most commonly used method of ascertaining reliability when the concern is stability. This method, which involves two applications of the measuring instrument, is applicable to most measurement procedures, including interview schedules and questionnaires. The results of the two measurements are compared and an index of reliability such as a coefficient of correlation can be calculated.

When the measuring instrument consists of a questionnaire, attitude scale, or other device that depends on the responses of the subjects, several phenomena can influence the results on the retest. The measurement procedure itself can affect the characteristic being measured. For example, a respondent may not have thought much about "no-fault" divorce and consequently has formed no opinion about its desirability. Being asked about it, however, might stimulate the respondent's awareness of no-fault divorce, possibly causing him to begin paying attention to publications or discussions about it, so that by the time of the retest he has formed definite opinions about it.

If the interval between the two measurements is short, respondents may remember their earlier answers and simply repeat them upon retest, which can cause an inflated reliability coefficient. On the other hand, the longer the period between the measurements, the more likely there are to be genuine changes in the characteristic one is measuring. The latter results in an underestimate of instrument reliability. This dilemma is difficult to resolve. In an effort to minimize the effects of recall and of genuine change, some researchers suggest an interval of two to four weeks between measurements. Another solution, particularly indicated if recall is likely to be a serious problem, is the use of an alternate form or equivalent instrument the second time. The time interval can then be as short or long as seems appropriate. The major drawback to this solution is the difficulty in finding or developing a truly equivalent measuring instrument. (Note that although an alternate instrument may be used, the concern here is with stability, not equivalence, as discussed later.)

It goes without saying that if one is interested in assessing reliability of an instrument, it is important to administer the instrument each time in as similar a manner as possible, under conditions as similar as possible. For example, very clear instructions, unambiguous wording of questions, and adequate training of interviewers and observers are important to minimize variation in administration. It may not be a fair test of an interview schedule to question a husband about marital satisfaction the first time alone and the second time with his wife present.

Equivalence   When equivalence is the aspect of reliability one is concerned about, the appropriate comparisons are between the results of: 1) different investigators using the same measurement procedures at the same time but independently of one another or 2) different instruments administered at the same time. The first case is more common in social work research. Two or more observers may watch a family planning a trip, and separately record the number of times speeches are directed to various family members; two or more case analysts may be asked to read the same case records and judge the degree of affection exhibited in the parent-child relationship. This type of reliability is generally referred to as interobserver reliability. Depending on the measurement activity engaged in by the investigators, terms such as *interjudge, interrater,* and *intercorder reliability* are sometimes used.

If two or more investigators are to be used to observe, make ratings, code information, and so on, it is crucial to ascertain interobserver reliability after training the investigators in the use of the measuring instruments. Unless there is a high degree of agreement, continued training with special attention to identified problem areas is indicated until satisfactory reliability is achieved. "Satisfactory reliability" is largely a matter of judgment. For example, a correlation coefficient of .80 or a percentage of agreement of 75 may be quite acceptable or again it may not be. The determination depends largely on the purpose of the measurement procedure, the method used to ascertain reliability, and the relevance of that method to the purpose.

A frequently used, and perhaps the simplest, index of interobserver reliability is percentage of agreement. This measure, which is applicable to nominal data, is the number of agreements between observers (usually two) divided by the total number of observations (agreements and disagreements) multiplied by 100. The index is not, however, as straight forward a measure of reliability as it might appear to be. For one thing, a certain amount of agreement between observers may be due to chance. Chance agreement is especially likely to occur when most observations tend to fall in one category. In any case, one may wish to use a refinement of the percentage of agreement that corrects for chance factors, such as Cohen's κ (Cohen 1960). Also the percentage of agreement may take different forms depending on the nature of the data and other circumstances. For example if two observers are coding a behavior that rarely occurs, a simple percentage of agreement may be artificially "high" simply because observers can readily agree on its absence. The fact that they do not agree about the occurrence of the behavior—the crucial part of the reliability test—may escape attention. In such a case the percentage of agreement may be limited to occurrence of behavior as seen by one or both observers. (See Bijou, Peterson, and Ault 1968; and Foster and Cone 1986, for discussion of such variations.)

If the observers were making ratings on ordinal or interval scales instead of using nominal categories, other indexes of agreement are possible, such as Kendall's tau or Spearman's rho (comparing rank orders) or the correlation coefficient r (for interval data.) The coefficients obtained by these methods (and of Cohen's κ) can be tested for significance to see if the level of agreement is likely to have occurred by chance. In reporting interobserver reliability, it is important to indicate not only the percentage of agreement or size of the coefficient but also how it was obtained.

In some cases the appropriate reliability concern is the equivalence of different measuring instruments. Comparisons are made between measures obtained on the same individuals using equivalent instruments or alternate forms of an instrument administered at the same time. As mentioned earlier in our discussion of stability, equivalent instruments are indicated when recall is a serious concern in retesting. The difficulty, however, in constructing equivalent instruments was also mentioned. This involves sampling twice from all potential items that relate to what one is trying to measure in such a manner that individuals tested will be ranked in the same way on both instruments. Thus, the difficulty of developing one instrument that adequately meets all the relevant criteria (validity, reliability, feasibility, and so on) is compounded by having to develop two such instruments. So far, alternate forms have been developed primarily for intelligence and ability tests.

Homogeneity This aspect of reliability is concerned with the internal consistency, or inter-item reliability, of a measuring instrument. The assumption being tested here is that all the items in the instrument are measuring the same characteristic. Several procedures can be used to ascertain the degree of homogeneity. The oldest and perhaps still the most common is the split-half method. The instrument, often a test, is divided into halves, analogous to alternate forms, and the degree of equivalence is ascertained. Traditionally, the test was usually divided by putting the even-numbered items in one half and the odd-numbered items in the other half. More recently, methods have been developed for random assignment of items to halves with corresponding new methods of computing a coefficient of equivalence. (The two best known are coefficient alpha and the Kuder-Richardson formula 20.)

In addition, intercorrelations between responses to all the items in the instrument of correlations between each response and the total test score can be computed. This method not only yields estimates of homogeneity but also helps pinpoint nonequivalent items. Nonequivalent items can then be eliminated to increase the degree of homogeneity. However, there is a point beyond which high intercorrelations among items may be inefficient and dysfunctional; the intercorrelations can be so high that each item adds little or no additional information about the concept being measured. Researchers must also guard against the possibility that high internal consistency is the result of some extraneous factor such as response set or social desirability.

Obviously, homogeneity of the measuring instrument as a whole is not desirable if the instrument is intended to measure several characteristics. Many interview schedules and questionnaires used in social work research attempt to combine the measurement of several concepts in one instrument. For example, in her study of parent satisfaction, Chilman (1979) included measures of other concepts such as parenting, marital satisfaction, attitudes toward children, and job satisfaction. She was interested in ascertaining which factors differentiated highly satisfied parents from those having low satisfaction. One could, of course, ascertain the homogeneity of all items intended to measure the same concept. This might result in a series of estimates of internal consistency, one for each important concept in the study.

Validity

Just as there are different types of reliability, there are also different kinds of validity depending on evidence and procedures used. Similar types may be referred to by different terms adding no little confusion to an already murky subject. We shall focus on three widely recognized types of validity; content, criterion, and construct.

Content Validity This type of validity refers to the representativeness or sampling adequacy of the content of a measuring instrument. Two considerations are relevant in assessing content validity, sometimes called face validity; one is the extent to which the instrument is measuring what it is intended to measure and the other is whether it includes an adequate sample of the behavior. Both aspects are determined on a logical basis; that is, the measurement procedure is inspected and a judgment is made about it in terms of the two considerations listed. To what extent do the questions, observed behavior, and so on, reflect the concept to be measured and not some other concept? To what extent do the items, topics, questions, or behaviors reflect broad and representative coverage of the concept to be measured? Basic to this judgment is the notion of a theoretical universe of items reflecting the concept from which one can choose potential items.

Some universes of content are more obvious than others and consequently judgments about measures of the concepts are easier to make. However, many concepts that social workers are interested in, such as parent-child interaction, marital communication, and life satisfaction, are extremely complex with difficult-to-define universes. As discussed in chapter 3, operational definitions seldom encompass all that is meant by the concept as defined abstractly. Often operational definitions also include parts of other concepts not intended to be measured. How well a concept is operationalized is a gauge of its content validity.

For example, in a check-list instrument designed to determine if parents are providing young children with a minimal acceptable standard of care, there may be agreement that an item such as "keeps harmful substances out of child's reach" would be an appropriate indicator but there may be question about "makes child's bed each day." Further the instrument would need to be examined to ascertain if important indicators of minimal acceptable care had been omitted. The fit between the items and characteristics of subject populations would also be a matter of concern. Keeping harmful objects out of children's reach would not be relevant for children beyond a certain age.

Criterion Validity   This type of validity represents a pragmatic approach to validation. It is particularly appropriate when the purpose of the measurement procedure is to make specific predictions about individuals for selection and placement in jobs, educational and training programs, treatment programs, and so on. In such cases, whatever one is trying to predict (for example, success in a graduate social work program) is the criterion used to estimate validity. In other words, validity is judged according to the accuracy of the predictions to the outside criterion that are made on the basis of the measuring procedure. Hence, the evidence used for criterion validation is empirical.

Criterion-related validation procedures are also used when the major purpose of the instrument is something other than to provide a basis for making predictions about a specific outcome. For example, one may be interested in developing a shorter instrument to measure some characteristic for which a longer, more complicated instrument already exists. Criterion validity would be assessed by the extent to which the results of the shorter instrument corresponded to those obtained on the longer one. Another example is the comparison of results obtained by asking respondents questions designed to elicit information about certain characteristics with observations of behaviors in which those characteristics could be expected to be manifested.

Criterion validity is very important in social work research and in other kinds of applied research, since much of this research is concerned with predicting behavior and outcomes. As previously indicated, it can be a straightforward, practical approach when a good external criterion exists. Usually, however, good criterion measures do not exist for the characteristics our instruments are designed to measure. This poses a serious challenge for the researcher who may need to supplement the most nearly adequate criterion available with other relevant evidence.

There are two types of criterion validity: *concurrent* and *predictive validity*. Both involve prediction, are determined empirically, and use an external criterion. They are distinguished only by whether the criterion data exist concurrently with the results of the measurement procedure or whether these data are obtained at a subsequent time. The importance of this temporal distinction is the practical implication of the necessity of follow-up to ascertain predictive validity.

Construct Validity   In criterion validity, the concern is only with how well one's instrument predicts a criterion, not with why the instrument works. Indeed, one may be measuring some phenomenon other than what was intended but may not discover this with criterion validation procedures if the predictions are reasonably accurate. Such a situation would be revealed through construct validation procedures, however, since construct validity is concerned precisely with what the instrument is measuring.

Construct validity is generally considered to be the most important type of validity. It is concerned with the "meaning" of the instrument, with explaining individual differences in responses, and with identifying the factors or constructs that explain the variance of the measuring instrument. Since constructs cannot be directly observed or measured, their existence must be inferred from other evidence. Generally this involves testing propositions about the relationship of the construct to other variables. Thus, in construct validity, one tries to validate not only the test but also the theory behind the test. This preoccupation with theory, explanatory constructs, and the testing of hypothesized relationships is the distinguishing feature of construct validity. It is primarily the use of empirical data as evidence that distinguishes construct validity from content validity.

According to Cronbach (1970), there are three parts to construct valida-tion: suggesting what constructs possibly account for test performance, deriv-ing hypotheses from the theory involving the construct, and testing the hypotheses empirically. This is nothing less than conducting an empirical study of the constructs involved in one's research. Although Cronbach's formulation indicates a time-consuming, involved process, it also suggests that any testing of hypotheses or empirical study of relationships involves construct validity. In other words, the results of any empirical testing can provide evidence of validity of the constructs involved.

An example of empirical testing of constructs is Miller's (1958) experimen-tal study of the observational process in casework. Miller was interested in learning more about a basic social treatment skill: the ability to understand clients. The central hypothesis of the study was: "The adequacy of the observer's conscious psychological comprehension is said to be positively related to the extent to which he uses free-floating attention and the extent to which his attention is directed internally" (p. 98). Miller had three groups of social work students view the same film of an interview with a client, after which he measured their understanding using the Q technique. (This method is a scaling device in which subjects sort statements into a specified number of piles according to some criterion. See Kerlinger 1985 for a fuller explana-tion.) The Q sorts of a panel of caseworkers with a reputation for expertness served as the criterion of "understanding." Attention, the independent vari-able, was manipulated through information given the groups about the purpose of the study. The "process group" was told the objective was to measure how accurately social workers observed a client's presentation and consequently they should be prepared to write a process record (a step-by-step account). Voluntary and external attention was expected to be high under these conditions. Miller had reasoned that this type of attention would contribute least to psychological comprehension. The "empathic group" was told the research was not a study of individual performance and that they should simply respond to the client naturally. These instructions were ex-pected to promote free-floating and internally directed attention, conditions hypothesized to be most conductive to psychological understanding. The third group was expected to fall between the other two in level of understand-ing. The results indicated that the process group differed significantly from the other two in the expected direction: the process group showed the least adequate understanding of the client. When a check was made on the data to see if the instructions had influenced the form and direction of the subjects' attention, evidence was found that the process group did use more voluntary and external attention than the other two groups did. In addition to its implications for theory and practice, the confirmation of the hypothesis provides evidence supporting the construct validity of the scaling procedures used to measure understanding. Since results turned out as expected, it is assumed that the instrument was successful in assessing understanding. In other words, it is hard to account for the results without concluding that the measurement was achieving its purpose.

There are many approaches to construct validation. One of the most important is the known-groups method. This technique involves administering an instrument to groups of people with "known" characteristics and predicting the direction of differences. For example, a scale designed to measure anxiety might be tested on a group of clients in an outpatient mental health clinic who are being treated for problems of anxiety and on a group of people in the general population.

Convergent validity and discriminant validity are additional forms of construct validation. Convergent validity refers to evidence that different measures of the construct yield similar results; discriminant validity is evidence that one can empirically differentiate the construct from other similar constructs. One should be able to predict which variables are correlated with the construct and how they are correlated. In addition, one should also be able to predict which variables are not correlated with the construct. (See Campbell and Fiske 1959 and Kerlinger 1985 for further discussion of this method.)

Yet another important approach to construct validation is factor analysis, which is discussed in chapter 10. In factor analysis, a large number of measures are reduced into a smaller number of factors that cluster together, that is, measure the same thing. The factors generated by this analytic technique are the constructs underlying the measures. Thus, factor analysis and construct validity are very closely related. In addition, the factors or constructs can be used in further analysis; for example, relationships can be ascertained between the factors and other variables in the study. The interested reader is referred to Harman (1976) for a detailed discussion of the use of factor analysis in determining construct validity. An example may be found in the use of factor analysis by Abell, Jones and Hudson (1984) in their efforts to validate a self report instrument—The Index of Self-Esteem (see also chapter 11).

CHAPTER 10

DATA COLLECTION

Social work practitioners and researchers obtain data by asking people questions, observing them, or using available materials such as case records, organizational budgets, or statistical data. Although their purposes and procedures may differ, both have a need to collect good data, that is, data that are relevant, reliable, valid, and sensitive. In the preceding chapter, we discussed how to evaluate data collected by various means. In this chapter we discuss specific methods of collecting data commonly used in social work.

Throughout this chapter—and throughout the book—references are made to biases that may affect data collection. Before taking up specific data collection methods, it may be well to provide an overview of different forms of bias.

"Bias" in data collection refers to systematic influences that diminish validity of the data: sources of distortion may be found either in the data collection method or in the subjects from whom data are obtained. Bias in the data collection method may be imbedded in the instrument itself. Questions or items may be worded in ways that suggest certain answers or may be skewed by the assumptions on which the instrument is based. When the data collection process can be influenced by a researcher, such as an interviewer or observer, another source of bias is introduced. The collector is then in a position to put her own stamp on the data collected. When data collection is controlled largely by an instrument, as in a standardized interview, this form of bias is of less concern than when use is made of methods, such as unstructured interviewing or observation, that depends to a large extent on the information processing capacities of the collector. Whatever their specific form, instrument and collector biases usually reflect a distortion toward what is *expected*. Thus a researcher or practitioner committed to the theory that delinquents have poor self-concepts may probe interview responses that might lead to evidence of poor self-concept more assiduously than responses pointing in the contrary direction. A more dramatic example is found in the history of science. Hoping to surpass Roentgen's discovery of x-rays, Blondot, a French scientist, developed a theory of N-rays. Blondot and his followers saw N-rays everywhere and published almost a hundred scientific papers on their properties, even though subsequent experiments proved quite conclusively that nothing of the kind existed (de Solla Price 1961).

Bias in the response of subjects (or clients) is a pervasive problem in data collection. Like researchers, subjects are vulnerable to expectancy effects based on prior convictions. An adult child convinced his aging mother cannot care for herself is more likely, when interviewed, to recall examples of confusion than competence in her behavior. In addition, response to questions may be influenced by what the respondent thinks would be appropriate to reveal, would be well received, would create the proper impression, and so on—of what would be the *socially desirable* response under the circumstances. Even if his response is a behavior being observed, the subject (if he is aware of the observation) can produce atypical, often socially desirable reactions.

Regardless of its cause, bias can seldom be completely eliminated. It can however be watched for, controlled, and taken into account in the interpretation of findings.

INTERVIEWS AND QUESTIONNAIRES

Social workers rely more heavily on the interview for collecting data than on any other method. Practitioners and researchers may supplement or verify the information obtained from clients, consumers, and respondents by using other methods, but the interview is the basic data collection method, perhaps because it can be used flexibly to obtain the complex data social workers need. The interview is usually conducted face-to-face with the respondent or, less frequently, over the telephone. A closely related data collection method that also relies on self-report by the respondent is the questionnaire. Unlike the interview, which is oral, the questionnaire calls for written responses and is normally self-administered. Questionnaires may be given to respondents in groups or individually, or they may be sent through the mail. Interviews and questionaires can be developed ad hoc for particular projects or can take the form of "printed" instruments, that is, instruments designed to be standard tools for measuring some phenomenon, such as depression, anomie, marital satisfaction, and so on.

Many different types of information can be elicited through the use of interviews and questionnaires. Simple factual data, such as marital status and occupation of respondents, or number of staff and funding sources of social agencies, are easily obtained. Respondents can also be asked about present or past behavior and experiences of their own or of others. Although some behavior can be observed directly, much cannot be. Some behavior and experiences occur infrequently, are private, or have already happened. Even when observation is possible, asking respondents about behavior may be more feasible and less costly in time, effort, and money. Information about attitudes, feelings, beliefs, perceptions, values, and future plans can be obtained only from the respondent's self-report.

Comparison of Self-Report Methods

The decision to use personal interviews, questionnaires, or telephone interviews depends on a number of diverse factors such as budget and time constraints; purpose of the study and consequently type of information needed; and characteristics, number, and geographical dispersion of desired respondents. Each method has advantages and disadvantages, discussed briefly in what follows.

Questionnaires Compared to the personal interview, the questionnaire is much less expensive and is easier to administer. Because the directions are incorporated in the instrument, the questionnaire requires little skill to administer and in fact is usually self-administered. Consequently, the questionnaire can be mailed to prospective respondents, a procedure that enables the researcher to survey a very large sample that is widely dispersed geographically. A major disadvantage of mailed questionnaires is, however, typically low response rate. Selltiz et al. identify the most important factors affecting the rate of return as:

(1) the sponsorship of the questionnaire; (2) the attractiveness and clarity of the questionnaire format; (3) the length of the questionnaire; (4) the nature of the accompanying cover letter requesting cooperation; (5) the ease of filling out the questionnaire and mailing it back; (6) the inducements offered to reply; (7) the interest

of the questions to the respondent; and (8) the nature of the people to whom the questionnaire is sent. (1976:297)

Some of these factors have implications for the design of the questionnaire, but others are outside of the control of the researcher. Questionnaires are appropriate, for example, only for rather well-educated people. The length —short to encourage returns—curtails the amount of information that can be obtained. The standardized format and prearranged questions also limit the amount and kind of data, which tend to be superficial compared to interview data. Generally respondents may have greater confidence in the anonymity of unsigned questionnaires. However, more sophisticated respondents recognize that numbered questionnaires or use of other codes indicates the existence of a master list by which they can be identified by the researcher. (These codes are often put on questionnaires by researchers to help them identify nonrespondents to send followup requests to in an effort to improve the return rate.)

In-Person Interviews   The in-person interview is capable of eliciting information in larger amounts and in greater depth. It is particularly useful for obtaining data on topics that are complex, highly sensitive, emotionally laden, or relatively unexplored. Questions can be explained and clarified, misunderstandings identified and corrected, and fuller answers and reasons for responses elicited through probing. Almost any group of respondents (poorly educated, illiterates, children, and so on) can be interviewed successfully. Compared to the use of questionnaires, data gathering through the use of in-person interviews is a very time-consuming process. Interviewing can also be a very expensive data collection method. In larger projects, interviewers and coders must be hired, trained, and supervised. Not only must salaries be paid but also travel costs since most research interviewing takes place in respondents' homes. In small-scale projects, however, an investigator (or team) may be able to interview a respectable number of respondents, say from fifteen to fifty, without spending a great deal of money.

Telephone Interviews   Telephone interviews, although not used as often as the other two methods in social work research, combine some of the advantages and disadvantages of both questionnaires and in-person interviews. Like questionnaires, telephone interviews are relatively inexpensive, they permit coverage of a large number of respondents over a wide geographical area, and data can be collected in a fairly short period of time. The response rate is usually good and the opportunity is available to probe, clarify questions, and correct misinterpretations. Telephone interviews are generally shorter than in-person interviews and the amount and type of data that can be collected are more limited. People without telephones or with unlisted numbers present obvious problems for telephone interviews, although a sample can be generated by dialing numbers selected at random from given telephone exchange codes (random digit dialing). Moreover, respondents who live in neighborhoods considered too dangerous for interviewers to enter may be interviewed by telephone. Telephone interviews, like in-person interviews, can be planned in advance with respondents so that a block of time convenient for the respondent can be set aside. Telephone interviews are used frequently for followup by social work researchers and practitioners.

Degree of Structure

Interviews may be as unstructured as nondirective or clinical interviews, or as structured or standardized as self-administered questionnaires, or may fall somewhere in between. Completely standardized interviews and questionnaires consist of predetermined questions and responses. That is, questions are worded in a set manner, the order of questions is always the same, and for each question respondents are given a set of fixed alternative responses from which to choose. Explanations of the study and instructions for filling out the questionnaire or responding to the interview are also standard. To construct a standardized interview schedule or questionnaire, the researcher must already have a fair amount of knowledge about the phenomenon she is studying. She must know not only the relevant questions to ask but also what the possible responses are. If that is the case, a completely structured or standardized instrument should be considered. Such an instrument produces highly comparable data that are relatively quick and easy to analyze because they are already precoded or very nearly so. This type of instrument is particularly suitable for large-scale surveys.

At the other extreme are unstructured interviews in which neither questions nor responses are predetermined. The interviewer obtains information about certain topics but is free to decide the content, wording, and sequence of questions to ask respondents. Because these interviews are very flexible and open, they require knowledgeable interviewers who can control their biases. Not only must the interviewers be skilled, but also they must be clear about the purposes of the study to obtain complete and relevant information. Unstructured interviews are particularly useful when little is known about the phenomenon being studied, as in exploratory research, or for the kind of indepth investigations characteristic of qualitative methodology.

Semistructured interviews fall between the two extremes just discussed and combine elements of the standardized and unstructured interviews. For example, a semistructured interview schedule might consist of open-ended questions with suggested probes to elicit data that respondents might not provide spontaneously. The wording of the questions and probes and the order in which the questions are to be asked are predetermined, but the response categories are not. Other variations are possible. A semistructured instrument might contain both fixed-alternative and open-ended questions; may contain specific or suggested probes; and may or may not allow the interviewer some flexibility in the wording or rephrasing of questions or in asking additional probes. Because of its versatility in being able to combine many of the advantages of both completely structured and unstructured interviews, the semistructured interview is probably used more often by social work researchers than any other type of interview. It is an appropriate and frequently used format for intake interviews as well.

Although it is possible for questionnaires to vary in structure through the use of open-ended questions, less structured questionnaires are generally problematic. Respondents are seldom willing to write much and what is written usually proves difficult to code.

Types of Questions

Questions may be open or closed. Closed or fixed-alternative questions provide categories of responses from which the respondent chooses. Examples of fixed-alternative questions are as follows:

1. Do you currently have a child care arrangement?
   Yes _____
   _____

2. If yes, how satisfactory is this arrangement?
   Very satisfactory___
   Satisfactory   _____
   Unsatisfactory   _____
   Very unsatisfactory   _____

3. What is your yearly family income (before deductions)?

Under 10,000 _____
10–14,999 _____
15–19,999 _____
20–24,999 _____
25–29,999 _____
30,000 or over _____

To develop fixed-alternative items, the researcher needs to know what the relevant responses might be and, in some cases, how they might distribute themselves. For example, the income brackets in the third question just given would be inappropriate for a sample of families on welfare. Not only would it show a lack of sensitivity, it would also yield little variance, for virtually all responses would fall in the first category. Sometimes enough information can be obtained from pretests using open-ended questions to develop appropriate categories for closed questions.

Open-ended questions do not present fixed choices to respondents but allow them to answer in whatever way they choose. For example, dual-career couples in one study (Smith and Reid 1986) were asked:

1. To what extent do each of you feel financially responsible for the other?
2. What are the advantages and disadvantages of the type of financial arrangement that you have?

A technique often used with open questions is going from the general to the specific through the use of probes. The same study provides an illustration of this funnel approach.

3. How do you manage family finances?
   (Probe if not already answered)
   a. Do you pool your incomes, do each of you manage your own money, or some combination?
   b. (If each manages own money): Who pays for what or who contributes what?
   c. Do you have separate or joint checking accounts? Separate or joint savings accounts?

Generally, fixed-alternative questions are most appropriate for factual information and open-ended questions for complex data. Closed items offer the advantage of obtaining uniform data for measurement and thus may be more reliable. Because the wording of the categories defines the dimension the researcher is interested in, the respondents are forced to make comparable responses on the dimensions of interest. For example, responses of dual-career couples to the question, "How much leisure time do you have to spend together?" may include: "Not enough," "About an hour a day," "We usually go out every weekend," "That's the main thing that suffers," and "We make it a point to get away together at least twice a year." If the researcher is interested in a particular dimension such as number of hours per week or the respondents' perception of the adequacy of the amount of leisure time, this interest could be pursued through the use of a fixed-alternative question. Closed questions also help clarify what the question means. For example, the categories "single," "married," "separated," "divorced," and "widowed" help to clarify what is meant by "marital status." Another major advantage of closed questions is the ease of processing the data for analysis; fixed-alternative responses are quickly and easily coded or may even be precoded for direct transferral to data cards.

Disadvantages of closed questions include the difficulty of constructing good categories for some items. If categories are not mutually exclusive and exhaustive, reliability and validity suffer. Inaccuracy results if a major category is omitted and must be included under "other" because some respondents may choose the closest named category instead. Another disadvantage is the superficial nature of responses to fixed-alternative questions. It may be very informative to know why a child care arrangement was satisfactory or unsatisfactory to a parent. To obtain such information, closed questions could be followed by an open question asking the respondent to explain his answer. Respondents can be irritated if they are forced to make a choice when none of the alternatives is acceptable to them. Another serious disadvantage of fixed-alternative questions is that respondents can easily give false information without the researcher's being aware of it. For example, respondents may find it preferable to choose an alternative rather than admit they have no knowledge about the topic or to indicate an opinion when they really have none.

Many of the advantages and disadvantages of open questions are apparent from the preceding discussion. Open-ended questions are flexible, easy to develop and administer, and can be used to develop rapport and encourage the cooperation of the respondent. Ambiguity, misunderstanding, and lack of knowledge are more likely to be detected and the opportunity is available to clear them up. Respondents can provide their own frame of reference and indicate salient dimensions when this is desired by the researcher. In-depth information is more readily obtained through open questions.

Major disadvantages include the lack of comparability in responses, difficulty in developing categories, and time spent in coding. A great deal of effort can be expended in developing a manageable number of nonoverlapping categories for the responses, especially if more than one dimension has been tapped. Sometimes a set of categories for each major dimension tapped needs to be developed for a single open-ended question. In larger projects coders must be trained until a sufficient degree of intercoder reliability is obtained and need to be supervised throughout the coding process. In smaller studies in which a single investigator or a team both collects and codes the data, it is still advisable to have at least more difficult or more important items recorded for reliability purposes.

Scales

In either interviews or questionnaires, scales can be used as a means of eliciting and organizing data. In fact, some printed questionnaires, such as personality and attitude inventories, consist entirely of scales. Some of the more common scaling techniques are briefly considered.

Suppose a researcher is interested in examining clients' perceptions of their social workers in a particular program. From some exploratory research on how clients view social workers in the program, she generates a list of descriptive statements that includes the following:

Was warm and understanding
Helped me get thing I needed
Said things I didn't understand
Gave me useful advice
Helped me learn things about myself
Seemed uninterested in my problems

She assumes that such statements could provide clients with adequate stimuli for revealing their perceptions of their workers but needs to consider the best scaling approach to use.

The simplest method would be to use the statements on a *checklist*—or as a nominal scale. A client would be asked to indicate the statement that best describes his social worker, to check all that apply (and perhaps, in addition, to circle the statement he thought was most descriptive), or to make other choices, such as checking the two most descriptive statements. (In interview formats the statements could be presented on cards.) As the illustration suggests, checklists are simple and quick to complete, but they give minimal information and are subject to social desirability effects. Some clients might tend to check the more positive statements simply to avoid appearing impolite or ungrateful (a social desirability effect).

Usually more information can be extracted if the scale used is at least ordinal level. One approach is to have respondents *rank order* a set of items according to some criterion. To continue with our example, clients could be asked to order the set of statements from "most like" to "least like." The "most like" would receive a 1, the next most like a 2, and so on, until the entire set had been ranked. The chief advantage of rank order scales is that they require the respondent to state his position on each item relative to the others. As a result respondents are prevented from limiting themselves to obvious, perhaps socially desirable, choices and what is more, they must provide discriminations among all options given. For example, one might learn from the rank orders about the relative value accorded advice giving compared to other intervention methods. By the same token, however, measures of "most like," "most important," and so on, yielded by rank order scales are always relative to the other items in the set ranked. Some clients might not have regarded any of the items as descriptive of their workers. Moreover, ranking is a cognitively difficult task for many people, and it is usually assumed that five or six items are about the maximum that most subjects can rank successfully. The difficulties of the task can be lessened by using a *partial rank order scale*. In this manner, subjects could have rank ordered the three statements most descriptive or could have been asked to select the "most like" or "least like" from a set of four statements, among other possibilities.

Another common method—perhaps the most frequently used ordinal scaling approach in data collection—is to have subjects rate each item in a set and then to combine ratings into a total score that would provide a measure of some attribute—*a summated rating scale*. Thus the researcher in our example might have wished to measure the clients' evaluation of their workers on a positive to negative continuum. Statements describing the worker in both positive and negative terms (like those given in the example) would be generated. (A total of fifteen items would usually be regarded as minimal in such scaling.) The client would rate each statement on some type of numerical scale. The client might be asked to indicate where the practitioner might fall on a scale of 1 to 10 with 10 defined as "all the time" and 1 as "none of the time" or words to that effect.

Was warm and understanding

1	2	3	4	5	6	7	8	9	10

none of the time   all of the time

A variation would be to provide descriptive categories for the different scale points.

Was warm and understanding

When categories are used, each category is given a straightforward numerical weight: always = 5; frequently = 4; and so on.

With each item rated, one simply sums the item scores to obtain a total score, giving "reverse" weight to negative items. Summated rating scales are easily administered and scored. Despite the arbitrary assumption that each item is of equal weight and the use of arithmetic procedures with ordinal data, they tend to correlate well with scales in which more elaborate weighting methods are used. They are vulnerable, however, to "halo" effects (the tendency to give items similar ratings) as well as "errors of central tendency" (avoiding extreme values).

It should also be noted that individual items can be treated as separate scales, whether or not ratings are summed. Thus clients' ratings of their workers in respect to their warmth and understanding could be analyzed as a variable in its own right.

A more complicated method of scaling is Guttman or *cumulative scaling*. In the example given, such a scale might be developed if a single dimension could be located and structured in terms of progressive steps or stages. For instance, an aspect of service might involve helping the client secure employment and it might be possible to view the helping process in terms of the following succession of items:

1. Worker discussed possibility of helping me get a job.
2. Worker made active effort to help me get a job.
3. Worker helped me get a job.

In such a succession, it is assumed that each scale point signifies that previous points of the scale have been passed—that is, in order for the worker to help the client get a job, she would ordinarily have made an "active effort," which would have been preceded by "discussion." In this manner, the score informs one exactly how far the worker proceeded in the client's eyes. Although such unidimensional scales have obvious strengths, it is difficult to apply them to complex phenomena and the progression of scale points is always open to question. (Conceivably a worker might help the client get a job without making an "active effort," at least as defined by the client.)

Instrument Construction

The type of instrument to be developed depends on prior decisions such as the specific method of obtaining data and the degree of structure to be used. Although the format and many of the relevant considerations vary, depending on whether one is constructing a self-administered questionnaire, a semistructured interview schedule, or an unstructured interview guide, a great deal of careful planning is necessary in each instance. This planning is focused on procedures—instrument development, training of interviewers, writing instructions for interviewers and respondents, and so on—for obtaining the desired information and reliable, valid data.

Clarity is essential in instrument development. Concerns about clarity that have already been discussed, that is, in formulating hypotheses or research questions and in defining concepts formally and operationally, are paramount at this stage. Clear, precise operational definitions of all the major concepts of the study are crucial, for they provide the basic framework for the construction of the instrument. Now the concern for clarity extends to the wording of questions, to instructions to interviewers and respondents, and to the format of the questionnaire or interview schedule.

Several suggestions can be offered for writing clear, precise, relevant questions. To begin with, the knowledge and understanding level of the respondents must be considered to develop questions relevant to them. Questions should be asked of respondents only if there is reason to believe they have the desired information. For example, one would not ask a parent if his teenage son had ever smoked marijuana. One might, however, ask the parent if he thought his son had smoked marijuana. Another example of an irrelevant question is asking about attitudes or opinions on a topic about which many of the respondents have given little thought. One should avoid professional jargon, slang words, or other words and phrases that the respondents may not understand. Questions about chemical dependencies asked of community residents might need to be worded differently from those asked of pharmacologists. One should be careful, however, not to be patronizing in the wording of questions; this is most apt to occur with certain groups like the poor or minorities.

A number of commonly used terms, which on the surface seem quite clear, must be defined more precisely for research purposes. Examples are income, employment, family, and child care arrangement. Does family mean family of origin, family of procreation, extended family, only members currently residing in the family home, or what? Do child care arrangements include regular school, parents taking care of their own children at home or at work, children taking care of themselves, siblings looking after one another, a neighbor looking in on the children occasionally, some of the above, none of the above? Possible interpretations such as these must be anticipated and specific questions developed to obtain comparable and desired information from respondents. Developing questions that are precise and short, both requirements for clarity, sometimes represents quite a challenge for the researcher.

When possible, time frames and anchor points should be provided for respondents. Instead of asking a student how often he studies in the school library, one might ask how many times he studied in the library for as long as 15 minutes during the past week, specifying when the week began and ended. One might also want estimates of the amount of time spent studying in the library each time or to ascertain if the past week was typical in this regard. Descriptions that serve as anchor points are useful to respondents (or coders) and help to improve consistency of the data.

Clarity and precision also require that questions be simple, not compound. That is, each question should ask about only one idea. Problems arise if it is not clear whether the answer refers to all or part of a question or if it is possible that the responses to the two ideas might be different. "Are you satisfied with your child care arrangement and do you plan to continue it?" is an example of a compound question that should be separated into two questions. Sometimes confusion results from a related practice—the researcher's making an implicit assumption about a phenomenon and then asking the respondent a question based on this assumption. For example, a student researcher known to one of the authors asked recently divorced women a series of questions based on the assumption that their divorces were stressful ("How upsetting was your divorce? Extremely—Moderately—Minimally?") To her surprise (and perhaps dismay) the student discovered that a number of the women interviewed perceived the divorce in positive terms—as a solution rather than as a crisis.

Although the need for unambiguous, specific, relevant questions cannot be stressed too much in the construction of any research instrument, this matter assumes even greater importance in the development of self-administered questionnaires because there is no possibility of additional clarification. Interviewers or the researcher who collects her own data should be very clear about the meaning of each question, the precise information being requested, and the frame of reference intended.

Clarity and specificity are also crucial considerations in writing explanations and instructions on self-administered questionnaires for respondents and on interview schedules for interviewers or for oneself in single-investigator studies. The format of the instrument should be logical and uncluttered, with attention given to clarity in presentation. For example, one should be able to discern immediately which are instructions to the interviewer, which are questions to be asked, which are probes, whether to read response categories to respondents, where and how to record answers to each question, when the topic or frame of reference shifts, and so on. Even if researchers who do their own interviews can keep details in their heads, they may have need in their study reports to convey to others the procedures followed in conducting the interviews.

Among the many other considerations important in instrument construction is the avoidance of bias. Questions should be worded in a neutral manner and in some cases may need to be prefaced with statements designed to cut down on social desirability effects. For example, a question might read, "Some people believe that married couples should have children if they can while other people believe it is all right for married couples to remain childless if they wish. How do you feel about this?" Sometimes it is helpful to preface questions with statements to encourage responses at all. The instrument should also be laid out in such a way as to discourage bias. The order and direction of questions should discourage a string of similar responses, such as all "yeses," or checking straight down the middle or one side of a list of items. Care should also be taken to avoid bias in explaining the purpose of the study, in providing directions for respondents and interviewers, and in selecting questions to be asked.

Finally a trial run, or pretest, of the instrument with a few respondents will provide helpful feedback on such things as appropriateness and scope of the items, completion time, and administration procedures. Also a pretest can provide interviewers with practice in using the instrument.

Selection and Training of Interviewers

A substantial body of literature is available on the advantages and disadvantages of trying to match interviewers to respondents on a number of characteristics such as sex, race, age, and socioeconomic status. (Relevant studies are reviewed by Weiss 1975.) Researchers have found that the amount of data obtained and the way people respond to questions can vary according to the match or lack of match on certain characteristics. Generally the rapport gained from matching must be balanced against possible bias from overidentification. Matching on relevant attributes should be considered, particularly in studies dealing with sensitive issues, but the decision will depend on a number of factors, including the rapport/overidentification equation, feasibility, and costs.

Both social workers and nonsocial workers are used as interviewers in social work research. For most studies, experienced research interviewers, whether social workers or not, are probably preferred. Exploratory studies using unstructured interviews may require interviewers to have some knowledge in the general area being investigated; in social work research, social workers in particular fields such as corrections or child welfare are likely to be preferred as interviewers. Social workers or graduate social work students are often selected as research interviewers because of their interviewing experience. Although social work interviewing and research interviewing are different in a number of ways, some of the skills are the same or are transferable. It is necessary to emphasize the differences in the training of the interviewers for research purposes (Jenkins 1975).

The major differences between interviewing in practice and in research flow from the different purposes of the two activities. The purpose of the social work interview is to provide service to clients; the purpose of the research interview is to obtain data for the study. The practitioner is interested in establishing a professional relationship with the client; the research interviewer tries only to establish rapport to collect the necessary information. The practitioner often plans to see the client over a period of time; the research interviewer usually sees the respondent only once. Consequently, the research interviewer seldom has a second opportunity to ask questions overlooked, clarify ambiguous responses, or pursue fruitful avenues with probes. Unlike the practitioner, the research interviewer has no service to offer the client regardless of what she learns. (The one possible exception is referral if this contingency is planned for in the study.) sometimes, however, respondents are paid for their time.

Regardless of the interviewers' background and experience, training is needed in data collection for the specific study for which they are hired. The content, length, and thoroughness of training will vary depending primarily on the requirements of the study. Generally, the more structured the interview schedule, the less training needed in the use of the instrument itself. Some of the aspects training must deal with are making contact with the prospective respondent (how to present oneself, explain the purpose of the study, handle confidentiality issues, and elicit voluntary cooperation); interviewing techniques including asking questions, probing, responding to comments and questions, remaining objective and neutral; handling various contingencies; and recording information. Role playing is a useful technique in this type of training. If interviews are to be taped, interviewers should be carefully trained in the use of tape recorders for recording interview data. Again practice is important. Because tape recorders are so common (many of the interviewers will probably own one), this training may seem unnecessary. More than one researcher has learned to her chagrin that it is not.

The Interview in Small-Scale Studies

In the foregoing section it was assumed that the study was of sufficient scale to require use of a group of interviewers—hence considerations involving selection and training. Somewhat different considerations apply in small-scale studies in which the researcher is her own interviewer.

In the single case study in which the social worker takes on a practitioner-researcher role, structured interview segments that serve both purposes of research and clinical assessment can be built into the less structured interviewing that serves primarily practice goals (Jayaratne and Levy 1979). For example, a practitioner can conduct assessment interviews at various points in a case to monitor progress on the client's problems. Such interviews can be semistructured and can be guided by specific questions the practitioner prepares in advance. If the client's target problem is fighting with other children, questions can be asked about the frequency and nature of fights the client might have had in a given period. Considerations of clarity and the like suggested earlier apply particularly to this kind of interviewing, which serves research purposes within a practice context. (More generally when the practitioner's primary objective is to elicit data from the client for assessment purposes the interview at that point serves a function similar to the research interview and use certainly can be made of principles and methods of the latter.) The practitioner-researcher can also make use of questionnaires tailor-made for the case at hand or quickly administered standardized instruments such as the Beck Depression Inventory (1967) or scales developed by Hudson

(1982). Assessment devices are reexamined in chapter 12 as tools for use in purely service contexts.

And of course, investigators may do their own interviewing in small-scale studies in which research is the only activity. In any case, researchers who do their own interviewing should apply to themselves the preparatory requirements they would apply to interviewers they might hire. Self-training through pretest interviews is particularly important.

Whether conducting a single case study as a practitioner-researcher or interviewing a small sample of respondents in a research undertaking, the single investigator has to be especially alert to her own biases—in particular, the natural tendency to shape the interview, or what is taken from it, in the direction of the researcher's expectations. A good control for bias, and a means of giving the study greater credibility, is to tape-record the interviews and have samples of the tapes assessed by an independent observer. Fuller discussions of research interviewing may be found in Canter, Brown and Groat (1985) and Mishler (1986).

OBSERVATION

Whether engaged in research or not, all social workers use observation as a way of obtaining information. Observation of behavior is used to obtain descriptive information and frequently to supplement or confirm data obtained by other methods. As a widow talks about the death of her husband, the practitioner may be alert to her affect (vocal quality, facial expression, whether crying or not, and so on), as well as to her words. A marital counselor may notice that a husband constantly interrupts and talks over his wife as the couple describe their symmetrical relationship. An organizer may be aware of the reaction a particular community leader seems to engender in others at meetings. A research interviewer may pick up clues about the quality of the interview data being obtained by observing signs of fatigue or disinterest, distracting influences, and so on.

Social work researchers and practitioners also use systematic observational methods. Empirical practitioners may use systematic observation throughout the intervention process to monitor progress of a case or may have clients observe themselves or family members (see chapter 12). Researchers use observation to study individual and group behavior. Marital communication; parent-child and family interaction; children's behavior in the classroom, at camp, and in other group settings; case studies of mental institutions, hospital emergency rooms, and social service agencies: these are only a few examples of the types of research in which observation may be the primary data collection method.

For reasons that will soon be apparent observation is a demanding, time-consuming, and often expensive method of data collection. Why then use direct observation as the primary data collection technique? Simply put, it is because observation is the best or only method of obtaining certain data. Observation is clearly the best way to study communication patterns, for example, in interaction between dyads such as parent-child or marital partners, or among group members such as families or work groups. Observation may be the best way of obtaining information about other individual or group behavior even when other data sources are possible. For example, a teacher could describe a child's hyperactive behavior in the classroom or group leaders could describe their individual leadership styles. Yet most researchers would agree that, compared to these verbal reports, direct observation would probably yield more objective, systematic data.

Observation provides the researcher with direct access to phenomena under study: she can see or hear what is happening. While the observer's biases and the subject's reactions to being observed are inevitable limitations, distortions inherent in "reported data" can be eliminated. Recent comprehensive reviews of the use of observational methods may be found in Foster and Cone (1986).

If the social work researcher concludes that observation is the appropriate data collection method to use, she must decide specifically what to observe, where and how to observe it, and how to record the data. Involved in each of these decisions is a number of considerations, the most important of which are discussed in this section. Although these points are grouped under one of the major decisions, to some extent the groupings are arbitrary. In fact, most of the topics considered relate to all three decisions. As with other activities of the research process, these decisions are interdependent and overlapping. Consequently, many of the points discussed will need to be considered almost simultaneously regardless of the order in which they are mentioned. It might also be helpful to point out here that observation as a data collection technique can range from being very unstructured, analogous to clinical interviews, to very structured, comparable to standardized interviews.

What to Observe

The purpose of the study provides the general guidelines concerning which behaviors to observe. Operational definitions pinpoint more specifically the behaviors that will serve as indicants of major concepts in the study. The degree of specificity and precision provided by operational definitions may vary, however, by the type of observational study to be undertaken. Essentially, this relates to how structured the observational methods will be, which in turn depends on the state of knowledge about the behaviors to be investigated and the purpose of the study. An exploratory study using unstructured observation will not be able to specify as precisely the relevant behaviors or aspects of behavior to observe as the hypothesis-testing study using structured observation must. In fact, the purpose of the exploratory study may be to ascertain what behaviors are likely given certain conditions or what aspects of behavior are relevant in certain situations. On the other hand, structured observation requires a very detailed level of specificity: that is, one must be able to ascertain exactly which acts or actions constitute each relevant behavior and which do not.

Even in unstructured field observation, the researcher should be as clear as possible about what she is to observe and why. For example, is the purpose of the study to describe a particular group or organization, or is it to be able to generalize about certain kinds of group interaction or organizational behavior? Is the appropriate unit of analysis camp groups, campers, camp counselors or leaders, camper-counselor interaction, or camp behavior in general? Although the focus may shift as the researcher learns more about the group, these shifts should be conscious decisions. With a particular focus of observation in mind the researcher can make decision about the unit of observation she plans to use. Selective options are presented below.

Molar or Molecular Levels   This distinction concerns the level of abstraction in defining what is to be observed. "Molar" (large, generally-defined units) and "molecular" (small, specifically defined units) actually reflect ends of a continuum, with any number of mid-range possibilities. Generally, narrative descriptions or ratings of behavior on scales are used with larger, or molar, units of behavior, while category systems are usually based on smaller, or molecular, units. Describing group leadership styles as democratic, authoritarian, or laissez-faire implies a very molar view of behavior. Still molar, but less so, is the description of a group leader's behavior as "played softball with the boys." A molecular unit would be a single act such as "hit the ball" or "ran to first base." Even smaller units of behavior are "gripped the bat" and "looked at the ball." In observing verbal interaction, one can use larger units of behavior, such as the entire discussion between a husband and wife on a topic or a paragraph of typescript from an audiotape. Alternatively, one could use a molecular unit such as a simple sentence or its equivalent or, smaller still, a word.

Both molar and molecular units have advantages and disadvantages. Generally, molar units are considered to have greater validity, for they tend to capture "natural" behaviors or behavioral sequences. Molecular units may segment behaviors in such a way that the units bear little resemblance to the behaviors. On the other hand, molecular units tend to be more reliable since they can be operationally defined more precisely and are more objective. Molar units involve more complex behavior and thus require more inference on the part of observers.

Units as Events or Time Intervals   An event is a natural unit such as an aggressive act, an instance of prosocial behavior, or the use of the first-person pronoun. Construing units as events is a simple, straightforward way of proceeding with observational research. It is particularly advantageous when phenomena to be observed occur infrequently or if they would be distorted if broken into time intervals. Limitations include difficulties in ascertaining reliability, especially when it is hard to discern when events start and end and when observers overlook events because of their inattentiveness (Cone and Foster 1982). In using time intervals, the researcher observes the occurrence or non-occurrence of some defined behavior within a fixed block of time. Time intervals are generally brief, usually less than 20 seconds. If the behavior—hitting, for example—occurs within the interval, the occurrence is recorded. Different aspects of behavior can be simultaneously observed and recorded, for example, hitting *and* swearing. Interval recording can produce a precise picture of behavior, readily quantified in terms of percents of intervals in which the behavior occurs. Reliability can be readily determined since observers record observations within this same set of intervals. The example below illustrates a recording format and hypothetical observations for two behaviors.

Behavior	Intervals (10 seconds)		
Staring	_ _ _ X X _	_ _ _ _ X X	_ _ _ _ _ _
Head banging	X X _ _ _ _	X _ _ X _ _	_ X _ _ _ _

Time interval units may not be appropriate for infrequently occurring behavior. Also, they may not work well for behavior, the meaning of which may be lost, if fragmented into brief time intervals. Human speech is an example. Finally, time interval observation with its need to maintain constant attention and frequent recording is a demanding task, usually not one for observers like parents and teachers, who must work observation into other activities.

Whatever is selected for observation and whatever form the observational unit takes, some sampling plan must usually be worked out. In some circumstances, to be sure, it may be decided to try to observe the occurrence of a defined event without selectivity. For example, a parent may be instructed to observe and record tantrums whenever they occur, or a client may self-observe all instances of depressive episodes. This type of observation, which Bloom and Fischer (1982) refer to as continuous recording, requires an omnipresent observer for the events in question; it tends to be used in practice applications, as the examples suggest.

Perhaps the most frequently used sampling method in observational research consists of time blocks that may be selected purposively or randomly (chapter 8). A classroom may be observed every other afternoon between two and three p.m. or at three randomly chosen hour periods during the week. Additional sampling frames may involve subjects and settings. In the observation of classrooms, for example, certain children, again purposively or randomly selected, can be observed. Different settings may be sampled, purposively, as a rule, in order to study a behavior in different situations. Assessment of unassertive behavior in a single case might involve sampling of target behaviors at work, at home, and with friends. Observation of subjects in natural versus laboratory settings (discussed below) may also be viewed as a sampling issue.

Where and How to Observe

Several additional considerations are involved in determining how the observations are to be made. These include where and under what conditions the observations will be made, who will make them, the relationship of the observer to the observed, and the degree of structure to be used in making the observations. The extent to which the researcher will have options in these areas depends on the phenomenon she is studying and the research questions or hypotheses.

Some phenomena, such as interaction among children of different races at camp or a child's talking without permission in class, can be observed only in natural or field settings. Other behavior, such as proximal behavior of a young child to his parent or communication patterns among family members, can be studied in laboratory settings. Either type of setting may provide the opportunity for obtaining descriptive data, formulating or testing hypotheses, or conducting experiments. Laboratory settings offer the distinct advantage of a high degree of control over extraneous factors. On the other hand, there may be a question about the artificiality of the behavior and the possibility that the subject's behavior might be influenced by (be reactive to) the observation process. The same question would apply to field observations if the subjects were aware of being observed. One might, however, expect the effect on behavior of being observed to diminish more rapidly in natural settings.

Usually subjects know they are being observed. Many governmental funding sources, universities, and research organizations now have requirements concerning obtaining informed consent as part of their protection of human subjects procedures in research studies. There are still some situations in which it is possible for a researcher to conceal her presence; even when this is not possible, there may still be choices concerning the degree of obtrusiveness of the observer and about what is conveyed to the subject about what is being observed. In field observations of group behavior, a decision must be made about the extent to which the observer will participate in the group's activities. There are obvious implications here about a match between the characteristics of the group and of the observer. The possibilities range from only observing and not participating at all to only ostensibly participating by concealing the observer role from the group. The latter raises questions of ethics and feasibility among others, while the pure observer role tends to keep the researcher on the outside and thus limits the data she can obtain. The role of participant-observer is frequently decided on as the best and most natural strategy. Usually only the fact that the participant-observer is a researcher and a very general explanation of the research purpose are conveyed to the group.

In laboratory settings subjects must be informed about the observation and they must consent to it. Subjects may not be told exactly which behaviors are of interest. For example, a mother may be told that her child's play behavior is being observed when in fact it is her behavior that is of interest. The observer may or may not be engaged in activities (treatment, doing structured tasks, group discussion, or the like) with the subjects. The observer(s) may be in the same room with the subjects in full view or may be in another room behind a screen or one-way mirror. Alternatively, the behavior may be recorded mechanically on film, audiotape, or videotape (see chapter 14). The degree of obtrusiveness of the observation depends on which of these techniques is used and how it is carried out.

The researcher may assume the role of passive observer or may attempt to influence the behavior being observed. The researcher intervenes by manipulating the independent variable in field and laboratory experiments. However, experiments are not the only kind of study in which the researcher may intervene. She may provide structure by way of group tasks or situational tests to observe the behaviors she is interested in. For example, she might ask a family to plan a vacation in order to study their decision making, or she might place a mother and her toddler in a strange room full of toys to observe the toddler's proximal behavior (that is, how long before he will leave his mother's side, how far he will stray from her, and so on). Sometimes the researcher simply tries to control the setting to maximize the chances of being able to observe the behavior she is interested in. For example, interaction between a father and his child is more likely to occur if the two are alone together in a room at the agency than if they are home with the rest of the family involved in normal daily activities.

Recording Observations

Another set of decisions that a researcher collecting data through observation must make revolve around how to record the observations. The method selected for recording observational data depends to some extent on how structured the observations are. In fact, in very structured observation the recording of data is an integral part of data collection. In such cases, observations are made and recorded almost simultaneously.

Among the decisions to be made about the recording of observational data is when it is to be done. Possibilities are on the spot, immediately after the observational period is over, or at a later time from film, videotape, or audiotape. When narrative descriptions or scales are used to summarize behavior, data are recorded after the observational period is over. Most category systems require that data be recorded on the spot or from mechanical recordings. There are obvious advantages to being able to code from recorded observations. Being able to play back allows the coder to catch behavior missed the first time and to check her codes. It also permits the use of several different recording systems for the same observations. In addition, it may be easier to check interobserver, and certainly intraobserver, reliability from recordings than from observations of *in vivo* behavior, that is, behavior as it is occurring. A major disadvantage of recorded observation is the cost involved. If audiotapes must be transcribed before coding, the procedure is even more expensive. Audiotapes are not, of course, appropriate for nonvocal behavior and are of limited value when visual clues would help to interpret the meaning of verbal behavior. A possible disadvantage of films and videotapes is the editing of behavior that may occur if the camera is not able to or does not focus on all relevant behavior at one time (see chapter 14).

The researcher must also decide from whose viewpoint the observations are to be recorded and how much inference she wants the observers to make. Should the behavior be coded from the standpoint of the actor (what was intended), the respondent (how that person interpreted the behavior), or a neutral bystander? Sometimes these viewpoints are the same, but often they are not. One child may lightly tap another child on the arm in an effort to get his attention, the second child may respond to the tap as if it were an aggressive act, while an observer may have seen it as a friendly gesture. Although the observer would not know what was intended unless the first child later made this clear, she might be expected to make inferences about intent from observing the entire behavioral sequence. The same might apply if one of the other viewpoints was selected and inferences needed to be made about the effect or consequences of the behavior. On the other hand, the degree of inference could be minimized by having the observer record only the exact movements or actions that occurred, for example, "One child moved close to the other, raised one arm, brought the arm down and let his hand drop on the other child's shoulder," and so on. This type of recording can be laborious and not very useful for some purposes. Probably most of these studies require the observer to view the behavior from the standpoint of a neutral onlooker and to make a medium degree of inference.

Observational data are recorded in one or more of a variety of forms; the major forms are narrative accounts, ratings on scales, and category systems (Rosen and Polansky 1975). As previously indicated, narratives are particularly suited to unstructured observation such as field research or participant observation. Scales are generally used with more structured observation and category systems with very structured observation. Each form is next discussed briefly.

Narrative accounts are running descriptions of events and large segments of interaction. These descriptions may be only factual accounts, but generally they include the observer's interpretation of the behavior as well. These interpretations should be clearly labeled. Sometimes the observer is able to take brief notes while in the field; in some situations only "mental notes" are advisable. In either case, full field notes should be made daily after the observational period is over. Since it is impossible, and not even desirable, to record everything that occurred during the period of observation, the selection of what to record is guided by the purpose of the study; that is, the most important behaviors, interactions, or events for the study purposes are focused on and recorded as completely as possible. Descriptions of situations observed often include information about the participants, setting, purpose, social behavior, and frequency and duration (Selltiz et al. 1976). Or instead of a full, free-flowing chronological record of behavior, the narrative may be more structured and selective by focusing on critical incidents or collecting anecdotes about the behaviors of interest.

Observations of behavior can also be recorded on scales. Like narratives, the scale ratings are made after the observations are completed, and they constitute a summary evaluation of specific behaviors. For example, observers might be asked to rate the degree of warmth in a parent-child relationship after having observed the parent and child together for a period of time. Generally, observers are asked to make a series of ratings covering different dimensions on the same observational period. In the example cited, other dimensions might include child's initiative in play, child's independence from parent, amount of verbal exchange, parent's attentiveness to child, parental encouragement, and so on. Scales vary in gradations; generally scales with fewer than five points result in distinctions too gross for most studies and those with more than eleven in distinctions too fine for most raters to make without great difficulty. Common biases in rating scale data result from avoidance of extreme ratings (end points of scales), the tendency to give only complimentary ratings, and the halo effect (tendency to give a subject the same rating on all scales). Although these biases cannot be eliminated completely, efforts can be made to minimize them. Clear abstract and operational definitions of the concepts to be rated are necessary prerequisites. Word definitions of the numerical scale gradations are helpful. And, of course, adequate training of the raters in the procedures—both in making the observations and in using the scales—is essential. Sometimes rank-ordering subjects, instead of rating them, can be used to minimize some of the biases. Unlike narratives, both rating and ranking scales produce quantitative data.

Category systems differ from narrative accounts and scales in several ways.

One of the most important is the size of the behavioral unit reflected in the recording: category systems generally use molecular units of behavior. Instead of summarizing overall impressions of behavior during an observational period, category systems usually require the observer to code each separate or isolated behavioral unit as it is being observed. This may take the form of indicating if a particular behavior occurred during a specified time interval, tallying the number of times a behavior occurred during the interval, or coding behavioral units into previously developed categories. The system may require only the behavior of interest to be coded or it may require that additional information about the behavior be coded, such as who initiated the behavior and toward whom it was directed.

An example of a category system is the Bales' (1976) IPA (Interaction Process Analysis) system, which is probably the most widely used verbal interaction system. The IPA, which classifies interaction in groups, uses as the behavioral unit "an act," defined as communication that is equivalent to a single simple sentence. Each act is scored into one of the following twelve categories:

1. Seems friendly
2. Dramatizes
3. Agrees
4. Gives suggestion
5. Gives opinion
6. Gives information
7. Asks for information
8. Asks for opinion
9. Asks for suggestion
10. Disagrees
11. Shows tension
12. Seems unfriendly

As can be seen from these categories, the IPA system captures the type of interaction but not the content. Thus it has utility for a wide range of verbal interactions among two or more people.

AVAILABLE DATA

Another source of data useful for research purposes is information already collected by others for other purposes. These published and unpublished materials come in a variety of forms and from many different sources.

Traditionally, social work researchers have probably made the greatest use of case records and other agency materials, statistical data from agencies and governmental sources, and historical documents. Sources used less often include mass media materials and both public and private documents. Raw data from other studies constitute another little used but potentially important source of data for social work researchers. In this section we describe briefly some of these types and sources of available data. We also indicate how social work researchers use a available data and discuss problems they are likely to encounter in using them.

Sources of Available Data

Data collected by social researchers are increasingly being made available to other researchers for secondary data analysis. This is particularly true of large-scale surveys and evaluation studies. Increasingly, raw data from large investigations are stored in social science data archives or data banks, usually located in universities or research centers, to be readily available to other researchers, including students. Social science data archives are facilities for collecting, processing, preserving, and disseminating computer-readable research data (Geda, 1979). One of the largest such facilities is the Inter-University Consortium for Political and Social Research (ICPSR) at the Institute for Social Research at the University of Michigan. For example, data from the Morgan et al. (1974) panel study of income dynamics (referred to in chapter 4) have been obtained from ICPSR and used by many secondary researchers. Similarly, data from the ongoing National Election Studies, begun in 1952, are obtained from ICPSR by numerous researchers for studies of decision making, group identification, political socialization, and the like. Other archives of particular interest to social work researchers include those based at the National Opinion Research Center at the University of Chicago, the Survey Research Center at the University of California at Berkeley, and the Institute for Poverty Research at the University of Wisconsin. For example, data from the New Jersey Negative Income Tax and from the Rural Income Tax experiments are archived at the University of Wisconsin. Unfortunately, there is no central index of all existing data collections; however, one can request lists of holdings from individual research centers. Depending on how the data archive is funded, a nominal fee may be charged for acquisition of the data. In addition to the large-scale data banks, many university departments and computer centers have local archives for use by that university's faculty and students.

A wide variety of routinely gathered statistical data exists that may be of interest to social work researchers. Such data range from local agency statistics to national statistics compiled by public and private organizations. Several federal government agencies publish massive statistical compilations (and narrative reports) on topics relevant to social work. For example, the Bureau of Labor Statistics in the Department of Labor provides data on topics such as labor force participation, earnings, and unemployment rates; the Bureau of the Census in the Department of Commerce, on population, housing, income, and poverty data, among others; the National Center of Health Statistics in the Department of Health and Human Services, on vital statistics (birth, marriage, divorce, and death rates), health resources and expenditures, and so on; the National Center for Social Statistics, on a variety of topics such as welfare expenditures, child welfare, and juvenile delinquency. An excellent resource is the *American Statistics Index (ASI)*, which is a comprehensive guide to the statistical publications of the United States government. The annual *Statistical Abstract of the United States: National Data Base and Guide to Sources*, summarizes these data. A compilation of data highlighting social and economic trends is contained in volume 3 of the most recent edition of the *Encyclopedia of Social Work* (National Association of Social Workers 1987). In addition to publications available from libraries or obtained by getting on mailing lists, many university libraries have even more of these statistical data available in microform. Additional sources may be found in Mendelsohn (1987).

National voluntary organizations such as Family Service America and the Child Welfare League compile statistical data from their member agencies. The National Association of Social Workers has information on its membership; the Council on Social Work Education, on enrollment in schools of social work; and the United Way, on community fund contributions. An excellent guide to directories of Social Welfare agencies has been provided by Mendelsohn (1987). The National Clearinghouse on Child Neglect and Abuse, an American Humane Association project sponsored by the Office of Child Development, has statistical information on official reports of child abuse and neglect.

Local and state counterparts to many of these national public and private organizations may also be resources for statistical data. Again the data may be in published or unpublished form. For example, states have general information in Blue Books and Statistical Abstracts. Local organizations may need to be contacted for their statistical data.

Social workers are familiar with another kind of available data—social agency records and materials. Case records have frequently been used for research purposes. Research protocols may be filled out by case analysts using these records. Writeups of group treatment or activity group sessions; minutes of agency board meetings, committee meetings, and staff meetings; and agency reports, annual summaries, mission statements, statements of policies and procedures, staff memos, and so on, have also provided research data. Content analysis has been used with these narrative materials (see chapter 14). Although the value of agency records and documents has been recognized by social work research, often collecting and analyzing the data have been laborious procedures. A recent development, computerized information systems, should facilitate these processes, at least for case data. Increasingly, single agency and multiagency systems are being developed. For example, state welfare agencies have slowly been moving toward automation since the early 1970s. Computerized information systems and data archives can be a valuable resource for social work researchers.

Public documents such as congressional hearings, laws enacted by the Congress, Supreme Court cases, and various historical documents are also sources of data readily available to researchers. To illustrate, Janssen (1975) used these materials in his analysis of the politics of children's programs (Head Start, day care, and the child development legislation) from 1962 to 1972. In addition to interviewing key participants, Janssen examined reports of congressional hearings and floor debates and reviewed materials reflecting the politics of the programs—letters, memoranda, policy statements, drafts of legislation, and the like.

The mass media—newspapers, magazines, advertisements, TV, radio, films, public speeches and so on—constitute yet another source. Such materials are usually content analyzed. A related source is professional literature. For example, a number of researchers have analyzed social work journals to study phenomena such as trends in types of research, sex of authors, productivity rankings among schools of social work, and the knowledge base of the profession. To illustrate, content analysis of five major social work journals was undertaken by Kirk and Rosenblatt (1980) in their study of women's contributions to these journals over a forty-four year period.

Personal documents such as autobiographies, diaries, and letters have seldom been used in social work research. However, Chestang (1977) used autobiographies of a number of black persons as the data for his study of the effect of race on the development of coping mechanisms as reflected in the concepts of effectance, competence, adaptation, and the family as a socializing agent.

Using Available Materials as Research Data

There are several good reasons for using existing materials as the data for one's study. Sometimes these are the only available data source. Investigators engaged in historical studies or exploring trends over time must rely on existing materials such as published and unpublished documents and statistical compilations. For example, the Kirk and Rosenblatt (1980) study would have been impossible without such data. Even when it is possible to use other data, there are times when already collected data may be superior to original data that the investigator might collect. Examples are data from well-designed, large-scale evaluations and sample surveys. The research expertise and technical skills, the large field data collection operations, and other resources and facilities employed in these projects are beyond the reach of most researchers. These data provide a rich research resource. Rarely do the collectors of data in these large-scale studies exploit the data fully from all conceivable perspectives. In planning research in a particular area in which a great deal of data are needed, a researcher might be wise to try to track down potentially relevant already collected data. As already indicated, social science data archives constitute an excellent resource.

Other kinds of existing data may also be the best data source available. Although data for some statistical studies could possibly be obtained through a questionnaire survey, existing statistical data may be more accurate, reliable, and comprehensive.

Another reason for using available materials rather than collect original data is that the former is more expedient and economical. Sometimes researchers prefer to collect their own data but do not have the time or resources to do so. As the costs of surveys and large-scale evaluations continue to rise and as funding for research becomes harder to get, the cost of collecting original data will increasingly become insurmountable for many investigators. Secondary data analysis is one solution. Creative use of other investigators' raw data or inventiveness in finding other available materials to test one's hypotheses or answer one's research questions may become increasingly critical for many social work researchers.

Secondary data analysis provides other opportunities for researchers not previously mentioned, many of which are being taken advantage of by social work researchers. For example, independent reanalyses can be conducted to check on the statistical procedures and conclusions of the original research, as was done by Berger and Piliavin (1976). Older data can be reassessed by using other, perhaps newer and more sophisticated, statistical methods, or in light of new findings or theoretical formulations. Secondary researchers can address new issues or use different theoretical approaches with the existing data. Sometimes, longitudinal studies not planned by the original researchers can be executed by secondary investigators if reliable identification of the subjects exists.

On the other hand, a number of disadvantages and problems are often associated with the use of available materials as research data. An initial hurdle may be locating relevant data for one's research purposes. Obtaining the data file can also pose a problem, particularly if the original investigator still has it. She may be reluctant to share it for a number of reasons, including wanting to mine the data to her satisfaction first. Since archiving research data in machine-readable form, particularly in central depositories, is still relatively new, some of these systems are probably not as efficient as they might be. Adequate documentation to facilitate intelligent usage (descriptions of variables and codes, location of variables on tape, description of sample and data collection techniques,and so on) may not be consistently available.

Definitions of terms and adequacy of sampling and data collection methods may constitute problems with already collected data. A basic problem here is lack of information; terms may be inadequately defined or not defined at all; sampling and data collection methods may not be described in enough detail for the researcher to determine their adequacy. Does "married" mean all married persons or only those residing with their spouses? Does "employment" mean full-time employment only or both full and part time? Is the new term *person in column one* now used by the Bureau of the Census the same as *head of household* used by many other governmental agencies? Why are the unemployment rates for black teenagers reported by the National Urban League consistently higher than the Department of Labor's figures? The Bureau of the Census is making concerted efforts now to correct its undercounts of minority persons; if they are successful in the 1980 census, how much of the increase in minorities over previous censuses will represent actual increase and how much better enumerating procedures? Since definitions, sampling plans, and data collection techniques vary across sources and over time, researchers wanting to make comparisons or describe trends may run into difficulty.

Data from other sources may not be consistently available (Shyne 1975). Case records, for example, may have missing face sheet information. The content of the records (forms completed, narrative data, and so on) and the completeness with which information is recorded vary. Such inconsistencies may present serious problems for the researcher, particularly if it results in bias such as having certain kinds of cases overrepresented or underrepresented.

Problems of validity and reliability may also exist. Information on which to make informed judgments about these issues is often lacking. Adequately documented data from other investigations and well-explained statistical data are generally more easily evaluated. This evaluation may be facilitated if other research studies using these data have been reported in the literature, since such reports may comment on evidence of validity and reliability. Otherwise, the investigator will be faced with the difficult question of whether the data are what they seem. How were major terms defined? What constituted a unit? How carefully were the data collected? From whom? When? By whom? What biases are likely to be reflected in the data? Consideration of such questions help the researcher decide how much reliance she can put in the data for her research purposes. As this discussion implies, a careful examination of the data one plans to use is a virtual necessity when using already collected data (Shyne 1975).

Other Uses of Available Data

In addition to being used as the data for one's study, existing materials have other uses in research. We indicate briefly how these data are used in the planning stage and as auxiliary data.

In planning research, the researcher reviews the literature and obtains other relevant information about her topic. She is particularly interested in knowing what other research has been done in the area and what their findings were. These materials may help her formulate her study by indicating fruitful avenues to pursue and how to go about it. For example, the researcher may get ideas helpful to her in the development of specific research questions or in the formulation of hypotheses. Ways of obtaining the necessary data—possible sources, subjects, data collection instruments, and so on—may be suggested.

Already collected data may also be used in an auxiliary manner. They may be used to provide background information for the study and to place the research findings in context. Information from agency reports, for example, may be helpful in describing the setting and the services offered. Statistical data may indicate the extent of the problem being investigated. Research findings from previous studies may provide a basis for comparison for the results of the study. Since random samples are seldom attained, statistical information may provide a check of sorts on one's sample on demographic variables. Available data relevant to the study can also be used to supplement the findings by filling in gaps in knowledge that may help in the interpretation of one's own results and in suggesting directions for further research.

In addition to the sources of available data discussed earlier, we might mention other resources useful in the planning of social work research. Excellent reviews of social service research are found in the three-volume National Association of Social Workers series, edited by Henry Maas (1966, 1971, and 1979), and a comprehensive review of research on psychotherapy is provided by Garfield and Bergin (1986). In addition, reviews of research in specific areas may be found in professional journals. Literature reviews are facilitated considerably by the use of abstracts publications, such as *Social Work Research and Abstracts* (including its 10-year index), *Psychological Abstracts*, and *Sociological Abstracts*. These sources are valuable guides to articles published in a large number of relevant journals. One uses the subject index to locate potentially useful articles abstracted in these reference books. The complete citations for the articles are included in the abstracts.

Many other indexes and abstracts exist for both published and unpublished materials (for example, research in progress). Manual searches, particularly with the help of a good reference librarian, can be competently executed. However, a great deal of time and effort are saved by using computerized data base services for bibliographic searches. Most major university libraries now provide such services, usually at a nominal cost to users. Large numbers of abstracts, indexes, and other information resources can be searched for references on one's topic. Generally, the searches are completed the same day or within a few days at most. Data bases are continually being added to these systems. For example the abstracts published by *Social Work Research and Abstracts* were recently put "online," that is, they are now part of a computerized abstract retrieval system.

CHAPTER 11

DATA ANALYSIS

Probably no other step in the research process is as awe inspiring to the inexperienced researcher, whether social work practitioner or not, as data analysis. Visions of mountains of data, jumbled masses of numbers, and pages of complicated mathematical formulas may be part of the nightmare but are seldom, if ever, part of the reality. One reason is that, in a well-designed research study, the question of what to do with the data has been anticipated and the analysis planned well before the data are collected. The reader will remember that, because the activities in the research process are overlapping and interrelated, with decisions at each stage influenced by earlier decisions and affecting later decisions, ideally the study should be clearly conceptualized from beginning to end during the initial planning stage. This does not mean that all steps are planned in great detail or that modifications or additions will not be made later. But it does mean that all the research procedures need to be planned with enough specificity to allow earlier steps to anticipate the requirements of later ones. For example, concepts that are not measured cannot enter into the data analysis, and the way a variable is measured will determine the kinds of analyses that can be performed with that variable.

Sometimes, however, the research study is not or cannot be so carefully planned. The plan for data analysis and interpretation may have been developed earlier only in a very global and fuzzy manner. By definition, specific and detailed data analysis plans are not possible in most exploratory studies. Or perhaps one is using available data, data collected bysomeone else for another purpose. In such situations, one must plan and do the analysis under the constraints imposed by the data at hand. Regardless of when the plan for analysis and interpretation is made, it is guided by the purpose of the study.

According to Kerlinger (1985), data analysis is "the categorizing, ordering, manipulating, and summarizing of data to obtain answers to research questions" (p. 134). Analysis is accompanied by a closely related procedure, interpretation, which means to explain or find meaning. The findings of a research study are interpreted on two levels. First, the relations within the data of the study are explained. For example, a statistical test may be performed during the analysis for the purpose of ascertaining the strength of relationship between two variables. The results of this test would probably be interpreted immediately and inferences made on the basis of the study data. The second level of interpretation is the one that places the findings in broader perspective. This is done by linking one's results to other knowledge, particularly to other research findings and to theory.

The approach to analysis differs depending on the research questions, the design of the study, and the type of data collected. The major difference is between quantitative and qualitative studies (chapter 4). The major portion of this chapter is devoted to analysis of quantitative data in group designs. Analysis of data from time series designs is then considered. The chapter ends with a brief discussion of qualitative data analysis.

QUANTITATIVE DATA

Our intent is to provide the reader with a conceptual understanding of quantitative data analysis. Statistical methods are discussed only in relation to research: the emphasis is on the logic underlying the use of statistical tools for research purposes rather than on the computations or the statistical procedures per se. Many excellent statistics texts are available for the latter. (For example, Mendenhall, Ott, and Larson 1974; Hoel 1976; Pagano 1986; and Sprinthall 1987 are good elementary books. Hays 1973; Blalock 1979; and Kohler 1985 are excellent for the more advanced student.)

The reader should be warned of the authors' strong bias in favor of the use of multivariate techniques for analysis of quantitative data in social work research. Behavior of interest to social workers is typically complex. Seldom, if ever, does one type of behavior always lead to the same consequence; conversely, a given behavioral or social consequence is seldom, if ever, caused by only one condition. With the possible exception of well-controlled experiments, attempts to explain behavior or social phenomena by looking at only one possible cause are simplistic and misleading. Like Kerlinger (1985), we use the term *multivariate* to refer to more than one independent variable or more than one dependent variable or both. This broad interpretation permits the classification of techniques such as elaboration, factor analysis, and multiple regression analysis as multivariate procedures.

Quantitative data in social work research can be analyzed by hand or by computer. The decision will rest primarily on the amount of data to be analyzed and the number and types of analyses to be performed. The size of the data set depends on the number of cases or units of analysis (subjects, respondents, organizations, and so on) and on the number of variables or individual items of information collected about each case in the sample. If the number of cases is relatively small, some statistical analyses can be performed manually with calculators. Desk computers are also available to perform some statistical computations once the researcher has punched in the raw data. However, even with a small data set, these methods are very time consuming if a number of statistical analyses are to be performed. Hence, except for studies in which the number of cases is very small and the analyses to be performed are few and easily computed by desk equipment at hand, the researcher should plan to use a computer for the data analysis.

Whether the data are to be analyzed by hand or computer, most statistical analyses require that the raw data be in the form of numerical codes. Depending on how the data were collected, much or all may already be in numerical form. The last chapter discussed the use of categories in the collection of data. Here we describe in more detail the steps involved in converting raw data into quantitative form for analysis.

CATEGORIZATION AND CODING

Data must be organized to make them usable for answering the research questions. Categories may need to be developed and the raw data placed into the appropriate categories. Generally, the categories are numbered and the raw data are assigned numbers corresponding to the appropriate category. Although the terms *categorizing* and *coding* are often used interchangeably, we use *categorizing* to refer to the process of developing categories and *coding* to refer to the process of placing data in categories.

As previously indicated some or all of the data may already be classified in this manner. The more structured data collection methods generally require that the data be recorded by using predeveloped categories and scales. Examples are fixed-alternative questions, category systems for observations, checklists, and rating scales. In some cases the subject or respondent has coded the data; that is, he has selected a particular category or scale value for his response. In other cases, the interviewer or observer codes the data as she records it. The data may be completely precoded or may need only to have numbers assigned to categories. Open-ended responses, however, require the development of categories before the raw data can be coded. If narrative records and other unstructured materials such as those resulting from unstructured interviews or observations are to be analyzed quantitatively, these data must also be categorized. Unstructured materials present special problems in quantitative analysis, for they are difficult to categorize. This is discussed further later.

In the study of the Work Incentive Program (WIN) previously referred to (Garvin, Smith, and Reid 1978), responses to an open question asking WIN participants what they liked best about the work-training program included such diverse answers as:

> I learned to type.
> The money is good.
> Nothing.
> Being able to get my G.E.D. (high school equivalent).
> The people (staff) are helpful.
> I like getting out of the house.
> It's all right.
> They got me a job.
> I'm getting what I want.
> Everything.
> Mr. Greene (a counselor).

Since we had about 1,200 such responses and wanted to use them in our analysis, we first had to develop appropriate categories. A perusal of these responses would indicate that they could easily be divided into three categories: responses indicating that the respondent liked something about WIN, those indicating that he did not like anything about the program, and neutral or nonresponsive answers. However, these would not be very useful categories for several reasons: most of the responses would fall into the first category, a great deal of information would be lost, and these categories do not reflect the intent of the question. A more useful category set might include the following:

> Mentioned liking education
> Mentioned liking job training

Mentioned liking job
Mentioned liking staff
Mentioned liking financial aspect
Mentioned liking other benefit

These categories would group the data in a meaningful manner for the purpose of the study, which was to identify incentives and disincentives to participation in WIN. The data themselves would suggest two additional categories: "Did not like anything" and "Inappropriate response." A "No response" category might also be needed to account for all the respondents.

The complete category set just proposed conforms to the basic rules for classification, on the assumption that all the responses indicated only a single "like." We came across two of these rules in our discussion of measurement. At that time we mentioned two criteria for developing categories: mutual exclusiveness and exhaustiveness. This means that it should not be possible to put a response in more than one category within each set and that every response should fit into one of the categories. In grouping data that have already been collected, it is necessary to add two additional rules: 1) categories should be set up according to the research questions and study purpose; and 2) each set of categories must be derived from one classification principle.

If the responses in the WIN illustration were more complex, the data would have to be categorized differently or have special provisions set up for coding in order not to violate the rules. In the study itself some respondents mentioned two or more things they liked, some qualified their positive responses, and some indicated both things they liked and did not like (even though the latter was a separate question). One way to handle these responses would be to develop a set of categories for each aspect we were interested in, such as:

Education: mentioned _____
        not mentioned _____
Job training: mentioned _____
        not mentioned _____

We would probably continue these dichotomous category sets through "Did not like anything." We might also want to add a summary category set indicating the number of different aspects listed that the respondent mentioned liking.

If the responses had been far less complicated than they were with the respondents mentioning only one aspect of occasionally combining certain ones like education and job or job training and job, a single set of categories could be developed that would simply add these combinations to the list of individual aspects mentioned.

Developing categories for materials such as focused interviews, field notes, case records, and minutes of board meetings presents a special challenge when the data have been collected in an unstructured manner. Here we do not have specific questions and responses to suggest classification schemes. We usually have only narrative material and often large quantities of it. Yet if the decision is made to analyze any part of the data by use of quantitative methods, those data must be put in the required form. Since unstructured methods are generally confined to exploratory studies, hypotheses and precise, narrowly focused research questions are not available to guide the categorization of raw data. Consequently, we start from the broader guidelines stemming from the purpose of the study and try to develop more specific questions or working hypotheses based on the data collected. For example, in a study the authors conducted on egalitarian or role-sharing marriages, in-depth interviews with a purposive sample of dual-career couples revealed that some couples who shared the major family roles before having children continued this pattern after starting a family while many others changed to a traditional division-of-labor pattern with the wife responsible for housework and child care and the husband responsible for supporting the family financially (Smith and Reid 1986). Analysis of possible reasons for this pattern suggested the hypothesis that a couple's sharing an egalitarian ideology prior to having children tends to foster continued sharing of roles after the birth of children. The hypothesis required categorizing the data on two variables, extent of shared commitment to egalitarian ideology, and pattern of family responsibilities with infants or small children in the home. Since there was no specific measure of egalitarian ideology, judgments had to be made from responses indicating attitudes toward role sharing, reasons for dividing tasks and responsibilities the way they do, and so on.

To enhance reliability in coding unstructured data, it is particularly important to define categories as clearly as possible with the use of examples to illustrate what is meant by each category. Often specific topics or questions can be identified as containing relevant information for making ratings or other judgments for classification purposes. However, because of the way the data were collected, the same information is not available on all cases.

Missing data and lack of comparability of data are major problems in categorizing unstructured materials for quantitative analysis.

UNIVARIATE ANALYSIS

Univariate analysis is the process of analyzing a single variable for purposes of description (Babbie 1986). This process of examining one variable at a time—displaying the data on a single variable or summarizing it or both—provides useful information to the researcher in and of itself and provides the foundation for more sophisticated analysis. In this section we consider frequency distributions and statistics for summarizing and describing data on single variables.

Frequency Distributions

Usually we want to know how observations are distributed to describe the sample and to plan subsequent analyses. To do this we simply count the number of cases that fall into each category of the variables. These counts are called "frequencies" or sometimes "marginals," since they are found on the margins of the statistical tables. Marginals can be left in numbers representing the actual counts or converted into percentages, which in effect standardizes the data.

If percentages are used, one needs to decide on the base, that is, what constitutes 100 percent of the cases. The most fundamental decision here is whether to use all the cases or to eliminate the ones in the missing data category. Sometimes "undecided," "don't know," and similar categories are eliminated from the base. The decision about the base is determined according the purpose of the analysis and should be made clear in describing the results. For example, if a researcher wants to compare the marital status of her sample with that in another study, she would eliminate any missing data categories, for they would not be meaningful and would be confusing.

Frequency distributions can also be displayed pictorially. Sometimes it is necessary or desirable to categorize some continuous variables into fewer categories for graphic representation. For example, age might be categorized into decades. Descriptions of these graphs and how they are constructed can be found in many elementary statistics books and are not elaborated here. Mendenhall, Ott, and Larson (1974), for example, discuss pie charts, bar graphs, and statistical maps for qualitative data and histograms, frequency polygons, cumulative relative frequency polygons, and time graphs for quantitative data. Although graphs are used most frequently in the presentation of data, they can also be a useful tool in the analysis since they may provide a different perspective on the data.

Descriptive Statistics

We can also summarize data by using numerical descriptive measures. Descriptive statistics for single variables fall into two groups: measures of central tendency and measures of variability (See table 11.1).

Measures of Central Tendency Measures of central tendency locate the center of the distribution; they are single numbers that characterize what is typical or average in the sample. The three measures of central tendency are the arithmetic mean, median, and mode.

The *mean* is the sum of the measurements divided by the number of measurements. Thus it is influenced by both the magnitude of the individual measurements and by the number of measurements in the set. The mean specifies the center of gravity or balance point of the distribution. It is the most stable and versatile of the measures of central tendency and is the most

TABLE 11.1

Outcome Ratings for Five Clients Illustrating Measures of Central Tendency and Variability (hypothetical data)

Client	Rating	Deviation from Mean	Deviation Squared
A	2	−2	4
B	2 (mode)	−2	4
C	6	+2	4
D	7	+3	9
E	3 (median)	−1	1
	5$\overline{)20}$		5$\overline{)22}$ (sum of squares)
	4 (mean)		4.4 (variance)
			$\sqrt{4.4} = 2.1$ (standard deviation)
			$7 - 2 = 5$ (range)

widely used for statistical inference. Although it technically requires interval data, it is often used, albeit inaccurately, with ordinal data.

The *median* is the midpoint of the distribution; that is, half of the measurements are above the median and half below it when the measurements are arranged in order of magnitude. If there is an odd number of measurements, the median is the middle number of the scale; if there is an even number of measurements, it is the average of the two middle observations. Although the median is not as stable as the mean, it is appropriate for ordinal data, as well as interval data. (The reader will remember the cumulative nature of measurement scales.) Medians, unlike means, can also be used for variables that have open-ended categories at the extremes such as "under 21 years old" or "over $50,000." Medians are also more appropriate for certain interval data in which extreme scores would distort the mean; for example, the median is usually used to summarize the income of a sample since one or more very high incomes would inflate the mean and provide a misleading picture of the income level of the sample.

The *mode* is the measurement or value that occurs with the greatest frequency. It is the last stable and least common of the three measures of central tendency. It is, however, the only one that is appropriate for nominal data. Sometimes distributions have more than one mode, which we refer to as bimodal, trimodal, or multimodal, and sometimes there is no mode, as in a flat distribution. Often the mode is used to describe the "typical" value while the mean or median is used to describe the "average" value. Only in perfectly normal distributions do these three measures coincide.

Measures of Variability Numerical summaries of data usually include a second statistic, a measure of variability or dispersion. This measure indicates how widely the measurements scatter around the central value. We mention only three measures of variability here: the range, variance, and standard deviation. Unlike our discussion of the measures of central tendency, we start with the simplest and most easily understood measure of variability. The *range* is the difference between the largest and smallest measurements. This indication of scatter is very unstable and can be misleading, for it depends entirely on the two extreme values. It is, however, a useful statistic in describing small samples.

The most useful and widely employed of the measures of dispersion are the variance and the standard deviation. The *variance* is the sum of the squared deviations of the measurements about their mean, divided by the number of measurements. That is, the mean of the distribution is subtracted from each value in the distribution, each of these deviation scores is squared (resulting in all positive numbers), the squared deviation scores are added, and this sum (called sum of squares) is divided by the number of measurements. (The calculations are illustrated in table 11.1.) The *standard deviation* is the positive square root of the variance. In other words, the standard deviation is a measure of the average distance of values from the mean. Like the mean, it assumes interval data.

Variance and standard deviation are two of the most important concepts in inferential statistics. Variances of different sets of measurements can be meaningfully compared (the greater the dispersion, the larger the variance), but it is difficult to interpret the variance for a single set of measurements. Fortunately, this is not the case with it square root, the standard deviation. In normal or "bell-shaped" distributions, approximately 68 percent of the measurements fall within one standard deviation on either side of the mean. 95 percent within two standard deviations, and more than 99 percent within three standard deviations (see figure 11.5). This fact is useful, not only in interpreting what the standard deviation means, but also in standardizing data measured in different units to permit comparisons to be made in generalizing from samples to populations (inferential statistics). For example, if we learn that an underachieving child has scored "two standard deviations above the mean" on a standardized intelligence test, we know that his score is in the upper 2 to 3 percent of a population of children who have taken the test.

BIVARIATE ANALYSIS

The purpose of the univariate analysis just discussed is to describe respondents or other units of analysis in terms of data collected about them or to make descriptive inferences from the sample to the population (see chapter 8). The primary purpose of bivariate and multivariate analyses is explanation (Babbie 1986), that is, determining what variables are related to what variables and how they are related (Kerlinger 1985). As stated previously, bivariate analysis (analyzing the relationship between two variables) is generally only the first step in the attempt to explain most of the complicated phenomena social workers are interested in. Individual and group behavior or social problems are seldom caused by a single factor; however, this does not mean that social workers are never interested in bivariate relationships. Many of our research questions and hypotheses are posed in this manner; that is, they are concerned with the relationship between two variables. Many of our experiments seek to determine the effect of one independent variable (treatment) on one dependent variable (outcome). But generally the analysis does not end there. If a relationship is found, we want to be able to specify the conditions under which the relationship holds. For example, in which groups (age, sex, race, class, and so on) are the two variables related? With what kinds of behavior or problems is the treatment successful? Multivariate analysis (simultaneously analyzing the relationships among several variables) can help answer these questions. Accordingly, phenomena are explained better. However, bivariate analysis, like univariate analysis, is useful not only for understanding the data but also for serving as a basis for more complicated analysis.

CROSS-TABULATIONS

The notion of tabulating data on a single variable (counting the number of cases in each category) is extended in cross-tabulation by obtaining the joint occurrence of cases in categories on two variables. The result is a contingency table as in table 11.2. The frequencies obtained during the univariate analysis of these hypothetical data would have indicated that the sample contained an equal number of men and women and that half the sample was unemployed. (See row and column totals or marginals.) The two-by-two contingency table reveals that the large proportion of unemployed was due primarily to the women in the sample; three-fourths of the women were unemployed with only one-foruth of the women employed, while the reverse was true for the men.

We might also want to cross-tabulate employment status with age catego-

TABLE 11.2
Employment Status by Sex (hypothetical data)

	Number of Respondents		
	Employed	*Not Employed*	*Total*
Men	75	25	100
Women	25	75	100
Total	100	100	200

ries, race, and other variables that we have reason to believe may be associated with employment status. In like manner, we may want to cross-tabulate sex with other variables to see if the latter are influenced by sex. Some of the variables we cross-tabulate may have more than two categories, resulting in different size contingency tables, such as two-by-three, two-by-five, three-by-four, and so on.

Instead of (or in addition to) frequencies in the tables, we could use percentages. Decisions would have to be made about what base to use and in what direction to percentage. These decisions will depend on the research questions and what makes sense. If one of the variables can logically be considered a dependent variable, the data should be percentaged "in the direction of" the independent variable. Perhaps an illustration using hypothetical data will make these points clearer. Technically, the data in table 11.3 could be converted into percentages as in tables 11.4 or 11.5. However, only table 11.4 is logical in an explanatory sense. Sex may be a determinant (independent variable) of attitude toward WIN (dependent variable), but it does not make sense to think of one's attitude as the cause of one's sex. Table 11.5 may be useful for prediction. For example, if one knew that a person's

TABLE 11.3
Attitude Toward WIN (hypothetical data)

| Attitude | Number of Respondents | | |
	Men	Women	Total
Positive	35	525	560
Neutral	60	100	160
Negative	25	25	50
Total	120	650	770

TABLE 11.4
Attitude Toward WIN (percentages)

Attitude	Men	Women
Positive	29	81
Neutral	50	15
Negative	21	4
Total	100 (N = 120)	100 (N = 650)

attitude toward WIN was positive, she could predict that the person was probably a woman because 94 percent of those with positive attitudes are women (Babbie.)., If one's interest is only in describing subgroups, either table 11.4 or 11.5 is correct. In cases where either variable can be considered the independent variable and either the dependent variable, tables are usually percentaged in both directions during data analysis, particularly if the researcher is interested in explaining both variables.

If we take a closer look at tables 11.4 and 11.5, we see that they give us very different information. For example, table 11.5 tells us that, of the people who had negative attitudes toward WIN, half were women. Looking at 11.4 however, we find that only 4 percent of the women in the sample had negative attitudes. It would be erroneous to conclude from table 11.5 that women were as likely as men to have negative attitudes toward WIN: table 11.4 indicates that in fact men are five times more likely to have negative attitudes. How do we prevent this type of misinterpretation? A basic rule regarding table reading will help: make comparisons in the opposite direction in which tables are percentaged. Accordingly, in table 11.4 we would compare percentages across; for example, we would compare the 21 percent men with negative attitudes to the 4 percent women with negative attitudes. In table 11.5 we would compare the percentages going down and would see from that table that, as attitudes become more positive, the person holding that attitude was more likely to be a woman while the opposite trend held with regard to men.

Our illustrations have dealt with two ways of percentaging tables. There are two other ways. One is to use the total number of cases as the base. In our example, using 770 as the base, we would find that 4.5 percent of the total sample were men with positive attitudes toward WIN, 68 percent women with positive attitudes, and so on. Another way tables may be constructed is by giving only partial information. For example, table 11.4

TABLE 11.5
Attitude Toward WIN (percentages)

Attitude	Men	Women	Total
Positive	6	94	100 (N = 560)
Neutral	37	63	100 (N = 160)
Negative	50	50	100 (N = 50)

might indicate only that 29 percent of the men and 81 percent of the women held positive attitudes toward WIN. These percentages can be directly compared with each other and would not be expected to add up to 100. It would be understood that the other 71 percent of the men and 19 percent of the women held either neutral or negative attitudes about WIN. One further point concerning the construction of tables: one always indicates the numbers that represent 100 percent, as in tables 11.4 and 11.5, the reader can then convert all percentages in the table to actual counts.

Pictorial Descriptions

Like frequency distributions for single variables, the association or relationship between two variables can be depicted in two ways: pictorially and numerically. The contingency table discussed earlier is one way of picturing association. For example, one can look at table 11.4 and "see" the kind of relationship that exists between sex and attitude toward WIN. A more refined way of picturing association is the scattergram, in which the joint occurrences of values on two variables are plotted for each subject. The relationship is demonstrated most clearly when each of the variables can take on several values, that is, has several categories.

For example, suppose we had asked each respondent in the WIN study to rate the program on a five-point scale in which 5 was the most favorable rating and 1 the least positive. Suppose we also knew how long each respondent had been in WIN and wanted to know if people viewed the program more or less positively the longer they participated in it. For each subject we could plot the joint occurrence of these two values (that is, the subjects rating of WIN and the length of time he or she had been in WIN) on a scattergram in which one axis is used for time in WIN and the other for rating of WIN. Figures 11.1 through 11.4 illustrate four possibilities of association between these two variables. Figure 11.1 indicates that, the longer respondents stayed in WIN, the more positive their rating of the program was likely to be. The inverse relationship pictured in figure 11.2 shows exactly the opposite. Unlike figures 11.1 and 11.2, which show a linear (straight-line) relationship, figure 11.3 depicts a more complicated, curvilinear relationship. It indicates that participants tend to have positive attitudes about WIN when they first enter the program, that these attitudes later become less positive, but again become more positive as they stay in the program longer. (One possible explanation for this type of association is that participants enter WIN with high expectations but become disillusioned and less positive about the program if they feel their expectations are not being met. The more positive attitudes for the longer term participants may be largely due to the fact that the disillusioned had dropped out of WIN by that time and those remaining were getting what they wanted from the program.) Figure 11.4 depicts independence; it indicates that knowing how long a participant has been in WIN does not help in the prediction of his rating. Thus, scattergrams indicate several things about the relationship: the shape (linear, curvilinear,

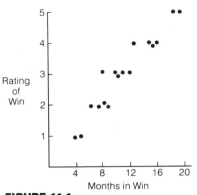

FIGURE 11.1
Positive association

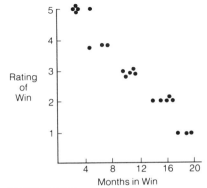

FIGURE 11.2
Negative association

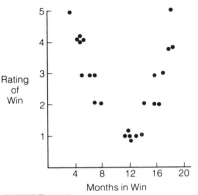

FIGURE 11.3
Curvilinear association

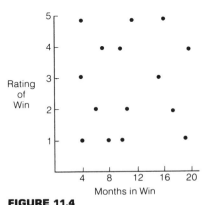

FIGURE 11.4
No asssociation

J-shaped, and so on), the direction (positive or negative as indicated by the slope of the line), and the strength (as indicated by the amount of scatter: the stronger the relationship, the more the points approximate a single smooth line).

Numerical Descriptions

Just as we were able to use means and standard deviations, for example, to describe frequency distributions in terms of average values and amount of scatter, we can use numbers to describe the magnitude or strength of the association between two variables. There are a number of different measures of association. The primary factor determining the appropriate one to use is the way the two variables were measured. Some of the measures that can be used with nominal data are lambda, tau, the phi coefficient, the contingency coefficient, Yule's, Q, and Cramer's V. Examples of measures of association appropriate for ordinal data are gamma, Kendall's coefficient of concordance (W), Somer's D, and Spearman's rank-order correlation coefficient (rho). The degree of linear relationship between two variables measured on interval or ratio scales can be ascertained by using the Pearson product moment correlation coefficient (r) or the coefficient of determination (r^2). The correlation ratio eta can be used when the relationship is nonlinear. Other measures of association are available for various combinations of measurement, such as interval data for one variable and nominal data for the other. Some of the measures of association mentioned earlier are used with data cross-classified in 2×2 tables (for example, the phi coefficient and Yule's Q) while others are used with data in larger tables (for example, the contingency coefficient and gamma, the counterparts to phi and Q).

While all the measures mentioned provide an index of strength of relationship, some indicate additionally the direction of the relationship. Some range from -1 (perfect negative association) through 0 (no association) to $+1$ (perfect positive association). Examples are gamma, Q, rho, and r. Others vary only between 0 and 1 (for example, Kendall's W, r^2, eta, and the measures for nominal data). One of the most important measures of association, the Pearson product-moment correlation (r). which indicates both magnitude and direction of covariation, is a prediction index. A high correlation, say .85 or $-.90$, would enable us to predict the value of one variable from knowing the value on a second variable with a reasonable degree of accuracy. We could predict it with certainty if $r=1$ or -1. Low correlations, say .11 or $-.08$, would make our predictions little more than guesses. The size of r does not, however, tell us the portion of variation on one variable that is explained by the other variable. To determine this, it is necessary to square the correlation coefficient. In other words, a correlation of .80, for example will account for only 64 percent of the variation in the values. It is important to remember that r indicates only linear association. It is also possible for r to be 0 and the two variables to be perfectly correlated in a curvilinear manner. For this reason, one needs to ascertain the shape of the association, which can be done by constructing a scattergram.

INFERENTIAL STATISTICS

Before considering more complex forms of analysis it would be well to examine the role of inferential statistics in evaluating differences or associations obtained from bivariate analysis. As discussed in chapter 5, a common source of uncertainty in research findings is *instability*, that is, the possibility that the findings reflect some chance variation rather than some property of the phenomenon under investigation. Inferential statistics provides logic and testing procedures (tests of significance) that help us to evaluate uncertainties of this kind.

The foundations of inferential statistics and tests of significance were introduced in our discussion of sampling in chapter 8. Whether testing for associations or differences, we expect our measures and statistics to vary somewhat owing simplyto sampling variability. For example, if we compared the means of an experimental group and a control group on an outcome variable after the intervention, we would not expect these two means to be identical whether the intervention had been effective or not. From the discussion in chapter 8 on random samples, we know that samples from the same population will differ by chance but that very large differences seldom occur. Thus, if the means of our experimental and control samples are very similar, we would probably attribute the small difference observed to sampling error. On the other hand, if the differences were very large, we would probably conclude that the intervention made a difference or, in statistical language, that the two groups were not (or no longer, since they should have been alike initially) from the same population. We would have difficulty, however, in trying to make decisions about differences between these two extremes. How large would the difference need to be for us to decide was a real difference and not just sampling error? Our problem is that we have sample statistics but need to know population parameters, which are numerical descriptive measures of the population. Since we do not know these parameters (if we did, we would not have used samples) and cannot engage in repeated sampling to obtain estimates of the parameters, we must make inferences about the population based on our one sample. Inferential statistics provides guidelines to help us with the decisions we must make.

Since inferential statistics is based on probability theory, there is always some risk involved in using statistical procedures to make decisions. On the other hand, no other method of making inferences from samples guarantees certainty either. Inferential statistics has, however, an important virtue that other methods do not: it tells us how much risk we are taking. We know how much reliance we can place on inferences using its procedures since all inferences are accompanied by a measure of their stability.

The notions of probability and sampling distributions of statistics were discussed in chapter 8. Figure 8.1 illustrated that the means from a very large number of random samples of the same size would distribute themselves in a normal or bell-shaped curve. This is a symmetrical curve in which the mean, median, and mode coincide and is the shape that the sampling distributions of many statistics take. In explaining the standard deviation units earlier in this chapter, it was indicated that if the horizontal axis of a normal distribution were divided into standard deviation units and lines were erected at those points, certain probabilities would be associated with these areas. Figure 11.5 illustrates this point. These probabilities hold for all normal frequency distributions of variables and for all sampling distributions of statistics taking this

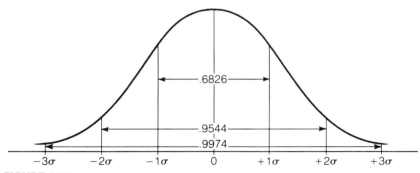

FIGURE 11.5
Normal probability distribution

form. In fact, most statistical texts provide tables that give the probability of the area between the mean and any cutting point, expressed in standard deviation units. From these tables, one can calculate the probability of the area between any two lines erected along the horizontal base. Exactly 95 percent of the statistics in a normal sampling distribution would fall within 1.96 standard deviations on each side of the mean, and 99 percent within 2.56 standard errors.

Statistical Tests

Now, how do we make use of this information in making the decisions we need to about sample data? For example, how do we use it to decide if the differences we have observed are due only to sampling variability? We use it to posit and test the hypothesis that our findings are explained by sampling error or chance. Only if our results would rarely occur by chance, say, less than 1 time in 20, do we rule out sampling error as the explanation and assume that our research hypothesis explains these improbable results. This process of comparing two hypotheses in light of sample evidence is called a test of significance or simply a statistical test.

Although we will use the normal distribution to explain the logic of tests of significance, it is well to keep in mind that not all test statistics assume this form, particularly with small sample. Examples of commonly used test statistics whose distributions take other forms are chi-square, *t* and *F*. For each distribution there are tables for determining the critical areas and probabilities associated with the critical areas for tests of significance. Despite the differences in form, the logic involved in making inferences from sample data is the same.

A statistical test involves four components: a null hypothesis, a research hypothesis, a test statistic (decision maker), and a rejection region (Mendenhall, Ott, and Larson 1974). The null hypothesis is a hypothesis about the population that asserts that sampling error is the explanation for the sample data. This hypothesis may state that a parameter is a specified value, that a parameter falls within a certain interval, that two variables are independent, that there is no difference between two (or more) groups according to some parameter, and so on. We test the null hypothesis and either accept or reject it. If we accept it, we conclude that our sample results could have occurred by chance and are therefore not statistically significant. The research hypothesis or alternate hypothesis is the one we will accept if we reject the null hypothesis, that is, disregard it as an explanation. The research hypothesis may state, for example, that a parameter is not a specified value or is larger than that value, does not fall within a certain interval, that two variables are associated, or that two (or more) groups differ in some specified manner. The last may be expressed by saying the groups are from different populations as evidenced by some parameter. Although the research hypothesis is the one we really want to test, we cannot test it directly. The test statistic, or decision maker, is computed from the sample data. Examples of frequently used test statistics involve means, medians, proportions, variances, frequency distributions, and correlations. The rejection region indicates values for the test statistics that are contradictory to the null hypothesis and consequently imply its rejection. Commonly used rejection regions are illustrated in figures 11.6 and 11.7, which are set up for the test of a null hypothesis of no difference between two groups ($H_o: \mu_1 = \mu_2$ or $\mu_1 - \mu_2 = 0$, where μ is the population mean).

Figure 11.6 indicates that we will accept the null hypothesis of no difference between, say, the experimental and control groups unless the difference between the means of the two samples is large enough to fall in the rejection region, at least 1.96 standard errors from the mean of the sampling distribution of differences between means (μ_1-μ_2). This figure also indicates that 19 times out of 20 we would be correct in our decision but wrong 1 time in 20. We would make an incorrect decision by rejecting the null hypothesis 5 percent of the time when it was, in fact, true. To minimize this risk of accepting chance differences as real, known as Type I error, we could demand even more extreme values, that is, even larger differences before we rejected the null hypothesis. Figure 11.7 illustrates how the risk of being wrong in rejecting the null hypothesis could be cut down to only 1 time in 100. However, we can also err on the other side: accepting the null hypothesis when it is, in fact, false. That is, we may fail to recognize real differences. This is called a Type II error. Unfortunately, these two types of error are inversely related for a given sample size. Researchers sometimes try to determine which type of error would be more serious for their specific study and choose the level of significance accordingly. The level of significance controls the risk of a Type I error.

The probability of Type I error is α (alpha); the probability of Type II error is β (beta); β is more difficult to calculate than α, partly because the calculation of β requires one to make assumptions about the true value, that is, the value under the alternative hypothesis. Generally, researchers are

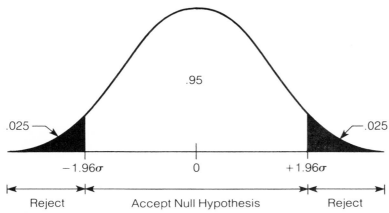

FIGURE 11.6

Rejection region for two-tailed test with $H1:\mu1 \neq \mu2$, when $\alpha = .05$

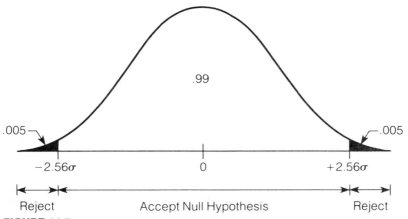

FIGURE 11.7

Rejection region for two-tailed test when $H1:\mu1 \neq \mu2$, when $\alpha = .01$

more concerned about making a Type I error and want a fair amount of evidence before dismissing sampling error as the explanation. They usually set α at a low level and take whatever β accompanies it. Table 11.6 summarizes information concerning Type I and Type II errors.

Most social work researchers appear to use the .05 level of significance. This means that they would describe findings as significant if there was only a 5 percent probability $(p<05)$ that the findings could be explained by chance. They may report findings significant at the .10 level as tendencies.

TABLE 11.6
Decision Table

	Null Hypothesis is:	
Decision	*False*	*True*
Reject the null hypothesis	Correct	Type I error
Accept the null hypothesis	Type II error	Correct

Source: Mendenhall, Ott, and Larson 1974.

However, there may be times when accepting the .10 level of significance is justifiable. Examples are evaluations of treatment with populations where there is little evidence that anything works or in exploratory studies where the goal is hypothesis formulation. Applying very stringent criteria in tests of significance may prevent the researcher from detecting possible clues to be persued further. This is especially true with small samples in which results need to be more extreme (that is, larger differences or stronger associations) to permit rejection of the null hypothesis. The ability of a statistical test to reject the null hypothesis when it is false and the research hypothesis is true is called the power of the test. This term is used to refer to $1-\beta$, a probability statement. As Hays (1973) has observed, "it is literally the probability of finding out that H_o [the null hypothesis] is wrong, given the decision-rule and the true value under H_1 [the alternative hypothesis]" (p. 357). As indicated, one way of increasing the power of a statistical test is to increase the sample size (see also chapter 6).

In figures 11.6 and 11.7, two-tailed tests of significance were assumed: that is, α was divided between the two tails. This is appropriate for nondirectional tests that state only that some difference is to be expected. However, if we are interested in differences in only one direction, then a one-tailed test is more appropriate. For example, we may want to know if the experimental group that received training in a specific knowledge area showed any gains in that area compared to a control group that did not receive the training. In such a case we could use a one-tailed, or directional, test in which α is concentrated in one tail. With an α of .05, the rejection region of a one-tailed test using the normal curve would be enlarged to cover the area in that tail from 1.645 standard deviations from the mean. Given the same α level and the same true alternative, we would increase the power of the test by using a one-tailed test provided the true alternative lies in the direction we think it does. In other words, when a difference is predicted, as noted in chapter 3, a less stringent test is required.

The *t* Test   One of the most common statistical tests is the *t* test, which is most frequently used to compare the means of two samples. Wells, Figurel, and McNamee (1977) made extensive use of this test in their experimental study comparing two methods of marital counseling in a family service setting: group communication training and conjoint therapy. First they compared the groups randomly assigned to the two types of treatment on a number of variables such as age, education, years married, and number of children. In making the comparison, they obtained the means of the two groups on each of the variables and performed *t* tests (independent samples) to see if any of the differences were significant. The researchers also used *t* tests to compare the means of the two groups prior to treatment on the three ordinal scales they selected to measure marital adjustment and relationship. (Note the common violation of the assumption of interval measurement for a test requiring arithmetic operations.) Since none of the differences was significant at the .10 level using two-tailed tests, it was assumed that the two groups were comparable prior to treatment, at least on variables that could be identified as possibly being related to the dependent variable. Another use of the *t* test (dependent samples) was to compare mean change scores on the three measures from pretest to posttest (at termination) and from pretest to follow-up (4 to 5 months after termination) on each group separately. All changes were positive and significant, using one-tailed tests, except one that was positive and showed a trend toward significance $(p < .10)$. A final use of the *t* test (independent samples; two-tailed) was to determine if the mean changes between the two treatment methods were significant. They were not. Therefore, it could not be concluded that one method was more efective than the other since the changes *between* the two groups could have occurred by chance. While the changes that occurred in both groups from the first to the second test were statistically significant, they could have been due to maturation or other extraneous factors. A "no treatment" control group would have been required to rule out such posibilities (see chapter 7).

The *t* test assumes normally distributed populations and interval or ratio data. The *t* distribution is like a flattened normal curve; the smaller the sample, the flatter the *t* distribution. As the sample size increases, the *t* distribution approaches the normal curve. Although we could use the normal curve with its corresponding z statistic with very large samples, we use t to eliminate concern about sample size. Other statistical tests are available for comparing two samples when the assumptions of the t test cannot be met. For example, the Mann-Whitney U can be used with ordinal data with no assumption about the form of the population probability distribution. (Siegel 1956, is an excellent reference for nonparametric procedures.)

The Chi-Square Test The chi-square test is frequently used for qualitative or nominal data. Fischer and Hudson (1976) used the chi-square statistic (X^2) in a secondary analysis of data regarding the effectiveness of casework service to the elderly. (The data were drawn from a well-known study by Blenkner, Bloom and Nielsen 1971). Table 11.7, one of the tables used by Fischer and Hudson, indicates a significant difference between the groups in terms of survival status at follow-up, with the control group being favored. In other words, the probability of obtaining a difference in survival status between the two groups as large as was observed in this sample is less than 1 in 20, and therefore, random error appears to be an unlikely explanation of the differences. Another reanalysis of the same data (Berger and Piliavin, 1976) suggests, however, the groups may have been different initially in spite of random assignment. If so, the differences in table 11.7 may be statistically significant but may be devoid of theoretical or practical significance.

Illustrated here is the general point that statistical tests must be interpreted within the context of the study as a whole. If the groups were comparable at the beginning, we have disconcerting evidence that the service may have contributed to the higher mortality rate of the experimental groups; if the experimentals were worse off initially, then their higher death rate comes as no surprise. One resolution of the issue may be found in Bloom's (1986) insightful review of this controversial study.

Instead of comparing means as the t test does, chi-square in effect compares frequency distributions. The frequencies in each cell of the contingency table are used to calculate the value of chi-square. The greater the deviation of an observed frequency from its "expected" or "chance" value, the greater will be the chi-square for the cell. Thus in table 11.7 one would expect by chance approximately 50 control subjects to be among the survivors —given the total number of control subjects and the total number of survivors $\left(\frac{88 \times 93}{164}\right)$. That 57 were actually still living provides a deviation from chance expectancy. When such deviations are calculated and summed over

TABLE 11.7

Frequency Distribution of Project Participants:
Experimental-Control Group Membership by
Survival Status

	Experimental	Control	Total
Survived	36	57	93
Deceased	40	31	71
Total	76	88	164

Source: Fischer and Hudson 1976.
Note: Chi-square = 4.35, df = 1, $p < .05$.

all cells, the resulting chi-square value (4.35) is sufficiently large to make the null hypothesis untenable at the .05 level. As might be expected, the total chi-square value is evaluated in relationship to the number of cells in the table. This information is conveyed by the number of "degrees of freedom," which begins at 1 in the simplest (2×2) form of the contingency table.

The versatility of chi-square becomes apparent when we recognize that any set of data can be reduced to nominal form. For example, scores on instruments may be divided into the nominal categories of "high" and "low." Although more "powerful" tests, such as the t test, may make fuller use of the information contained in the data, chi-square has the advantage of ease of computation, which the student researcher will appreciate. A few minutes with a pocket calculator, following a simple readily available formula, is all that is needed for most chi-squares. Moreover, the reduction to a nominal level may not waste as much information as may appear since frequently the scores are in the form of ratings or similar measurements which may provide much less than interval measurement in any case.

Evaluation of Significance Testing in Group Designs

By helping to evaluate the possibility that findings may be due to chance variation, tests of significance perform a useful function in social research. But the limitations, and possible abuses, of such tests need to be kept in mind. First of all it must be recognized that in most social work studies, tests of significance are based on a number of challengeable assumptions. For example, relatively few such studies use random samples from large populations. Consequently, in order for tests of significance to be applied, one must assume that whatever group was studied is representative of some population of interest to the researcher. A test of significance tells us then something about the stability of findings, if the study were to be repeated with additional samples from that same population. Keep in mind, however, that the population is actually a construction of the researcher. Actual replications of the study would doubtless make use of different populations. Given this and other assumptions, tests of significance can best be seen as providing a rough criterion that helps us separate findings to be taken seriously from those that may be considered to be unstable, aberrant, unreliable, and so on. They give us a clue to those associations and differences that may be expected to occur again if additional studies were conducted.

While significance tests provide a useful screen for the elimination of inconsequential findings, the screen is used with the smallest amount of error when the associations or differences to be tested are specified in advance. Sometimes researchers proceed with no prior hypothesis but simply look for large associations or differences and apply tests of significance to them. This procedure in effect capitalizes on chance and opens the door to Type I error. It is analogous to placing a bet on a horse after the race is underway. As we know, any set of findings will produce a few that reflect chance occurrences. In fact if we use the .05 level, about one in twenty will be considered large enough to appear stable but will actually reflect the operation of chance. Now if we search simply for large differences or associations, we are bound to find these chance events and claim them as real findings. This practice may still have some justification if the number of tests conducted is small and if due recognition is made for the increased likelihood of Type I error. The practice can be quite misleading if a large number of findings are tested and only those that appear to be "significant" are reported without information about the number of tests run. Thus if we use the .05 level and examine 100 correlations, we are likely to discover five or so that are "significant," even if we are dealing completely with random associations among the variables.

It is important not to confuse statistical significance with theoretical or practical significance. Tests of significance deal only with numbers and are no better than the numbers we have to work with. In experiments, statistically significant differences between treated and untreated groups may reflect the operation of extraneous factors. Tests of significance help us to rule out instability but nothing else. Also whether or not differences turn out to be significant is influenced by the size of the sample. Thus if very large samples are being compared, relatively minor differences or associations may be sufficiently stable to be "significant" but may have little theoretical or practical significance. As suggested, a test of significance gives us really minimal information: Is a difference or association worth taking seriously? Once that fact has been established, we are interested in knowledge that is really more important: the size of the difference or association. For instance, a researcher may report that the outcome shows a significant correlation with practitioner experience, and much may be made of the finding. We may learn, however, that the correlation was based on a study of a large number of cases and is only .15. We know that such a correlation would explain just a little over 2 percent of the variance between the two variables (r^2 equals variance explained), hardly a magnitude to get very excited about! Contrary to the common notion, tests of significance should be given greater weight when samples are small than when they are large (Bakan 1967).

In some circumstances tests of significance are best avoided. For example, the researcher may be dealing for her purposes with an entire population, say the residents of an institution, and may not be interested in extrapolations to other institutions or to points further along in time beyond the one she is studying. Findings should then simply be assessed on the basis of the magnitude of differences or associations. Or the researcher may have conducted an exploratory study without prior hypotheses and may have obtained a large number of findings. As noted earlier, the use of tests of significance may be misleading. The most impressive or most intersting findings can simply be reported without a significance test. Finally we would like to stress that the complexity, or sometimes obfuscation, of the reporting of statistical tests should not prevent consumers from making their own judgments about the meaningfulness of the findings tested. Keeping in mind that tests of significance, regardless of their form, serve only to rule out chance variation as an explanation of the findings, readers can examine the size of differences or associations and, more importantly, what the measures are based on and what they appear to add up to at a substantive level. Additional discussion of issues involved in the use of tests of significance may be found in Cowger (1984) and Glisson (1985).

MULTIVARIATE ANALYSIS

Thus far we have examined different ways of analyzing the relationship between two variables, including methods of determining whether or not a stable relationship exists and of ascertaining the magnitude of the relationship (measures of association). As previously indicated (chapter 3) research in social work is typically concerned with more complex relationships, those occurring among a *set* of variables. To deal with these more complex relationships, we must turn to different forms of multivariate analysis, which we examine in this section.

The Three-Variable Case

The simplest form of multivariate analysis involves three variables. Consideration of analysis at this level reveals basic principles that can be applied to more complex forms.

Chapter 4 introduced the notion of statistical control in examining the relationship between two variables. This technique involves the introduction of a third variable, often referred to as a control variable or test factor, to see what happens to the original two-variable relationship. Sometimes the researcher's interest is simply in eliminating the influence of a third variable from the two-variable relationship. This can be accomplished through contingency analysis with categorical data by examining the two-variable relationship separately for each category of the third variable as was done in table 4.2. With interval or quasi-interval data, a procedure called partial correlation is used. Partial correlation, an important form of statistical control, permits one to control (hold constant) a variable by "partialing out" or eliminating its effect on the correlation between two other variables. In the reduced correlation, the influence of the third variable has been removed from both the variables (that is, the independent and dependent variables). Partial correlation is not limited to three variables; higher order partial correlations can be calculated to control a number of variables.

Often researchers add a third variable to increase their understanding of the original two-variable relationship. This procedure is usually referred to as *elaboration*. By adding a second independent variable, the researcher is able to "see" the relative contribution each independent variable makes in explaining the dependent variable and also the combined effect of the two variables on the dependent variable. In the illustration used in chapter 4, the relationship between father absence and son's self-concept disappeared when social class was introduced into the analysis. In other words, the original relationship turned out to be spurious or "not real" since it was, in fact, due to the third variable, social class.

Sometimes the third variable is an antecedent variable, as was social class, and sometimes it is an intervening variable. If it is antecedent, we say it helps to explain the two-variable relationship. If it is an intervening variable, we say it helps to interpret the relationship. The following hypothetical example illustrates the latter case. Suppose we found that children with lower IQs had higher truancy rates than children with higher IQs. Suppose we also found that children who received lower grades had higher truancy rates than children with higher grades. Further suppose that most but not all of the children with lower IQs received low grades and that most but not all of the children with higher IQs received higher grades. When we controlled grades, suppose we found no correlation between IQs and truancy rates. This would suggest that children who are not successful in school, as indicated by grades, may lose interest in school and therefore are more apt to be truant. Since IQs is related to school achievement, we say we have traced the process by which IQs affects truancy or that we have interpreted the relationship between IQs and truancy by introducing the intervening variable, school achievement. Note that in both this example and the one in chapter 4, the original relationship disappeared when a third variable was added. We called the original relationship spurious when the the third variable was antecedent but said we traced the process when it intervened between the independent and dependent variables. This indicates the importance of the time sequence in trying to establish causality.

Not only may a third variable cause a relationship to be reduced or eliminated, it may also lead to intensification of the relationship within one subgroup and its reduction within another. When this happens, we say we have specified a condition under which the relationship occurs. Conditional relationships refer to the interaction of the two independent variables. When considering contingent relationships, we do not need to be concerned with whether the third variable is antecedent, intervening, or concurrent.

To illustrate, suppose we find a positive relationship between quality of a training program and satisfaction with the program; that is, the higher the quality of the training program according to some specified criteria, the more satisfied trainees are with it. When the relationship is examined separately for trainees with high aspirations and those with low aspirations, it intensifies somewhat for the former group and almost disappears for the latter. In other words, higher quality programs are viewed as more satisfactory by trainees who have higher aspirations, but the quality of the program matters little to trainees with lower aspirations. Level of aspiration helps to clarify the original relationship by specifying a contingent relationship.

The addition of a third variable may also cause a relationship to appear where there was none. This might happen if two variables are associated in opposite directions in subgroups of a third variable. The opposite effects may cancel each other out and conceal a relationship that really exists between the two original variables. For example, there may appear to be no relationship between use of service method and client change, but it may be found that the method helps mild depressives but harms severe depressives. As Lambert, Shapiro, and Bergin (1986) suggest, this canceling out may explain lack of apparent differences between experimental and control groups in studies of the effectiveness of intervention.

We have indicated some of the effects that adding a third variable can cause in a bivariate relationship. The possibilities including having no effect, causing a relationship to disappear, and causing a relationship to emerge. The interested reader will find additional explanations and illustrations of such effects in Rosenberg (1968) and Babbie (1986).

Multiple Variables The reason that adding a third variable can have such strange and diverse consequences for the original two-variable relationship is that the latter is made up of many partial or contingent associations. For example, in the illustration in chapter 4, the total association between father absence and self-concept included partial associations between social class and father absence and social class and self-concept. One could expand that example by substituting other variables as the test variable. One might find that there is a separate relationship between father absence and self-concept for boys and girls; for white and black children; for older and younger children; for first born, middle, and youngest children; for children with authoritarian and permissive parents; and so on. In other words, the total relationship between father absence and self-concept is composed of many partial relationships.

In general, two-variable associations or correlations are composed of many partial associations or partial correlations. Often there is an interaction between these additional variables, that is, associations may exist among them. Hence, their combined effect may not be fully additive. Not only, then, do we need to identify the various contingent associations that comprise the relationship we are interested in, but also we need to understand how these contingent relationships combine. In other words, we need multivariate techniques that permit us to analyze simultaneously the relationships among several variables.

Multiple Regression Analysis

Multiple regression analysis is one of the most powerful tools in this regard; it permits us to study the effects and the magnitude of effects of more than one independent variable on one dependent variable by using principles of correlation and regression. In this very versatile method, the measures of the independent variables can be either continuous or categorical or a mixture of the two.

Fanshel (1977) used multiple regression as one analytic method in his study of parental visiting of foster children that used computerized data on more than 20,000 cases. A series of cross-tabulations had indicated that a number of variables were associated with the dependent variable, parental contact, operationalized as the number of parent visits with their children in foster care. A number of these independent variables were selected for multiple regression analysis to ascertain their combined effect on parental contact. Two of Fanshel's tables are reproduced here to illustrate the separate and combined relationships. Table 11.8 shows the simple correlations be-

TABLE 11.8
Correlations Between Selected Background Variables and Parental Contact for Reported Period (N = 20,214)

	Correlation with Parental Contact (Total Visiting)
Sex (female; MALE)[a]	−.052
Current age of child	.046
Years in care	−.256
Ethnicity (other; BLACK)	−.054
Ethnicity (other; WHITE)	.085
Reason placed (other; DRUG ABUSE)	−.045
Reason placed (other; ABANDONED)	−.110
Reason placed (other; ABUSED)	.016
Reason placed (other; NEGLECT)	.029
Reason placed (other; CHILD BEHAVIOR)	.265
Court status (voluntary; COURT PLACED)	−.030
Discharge objective (other; TO PARENTS)	.387
Discharge objective (other; ADOPTION)	−.275

Source: Fanshel 1977.
[a]The categories indicated by capital letters are those chosen as dichotomous variables, which were coded as 1; those in lower case were coded as 0.

tween each of the independent variables and frequency of parental visiting. Note that many of the variables are coded as dummy variables, a procedure that quantifies categorical variables for use is the analysis. Footnote *a* below table 11.8 indicates how dichotomous variables were coded in dummy variable form. When a variable has more than two categories, this type of coding involves successively dichotomizing the nominal scale so that each category is used to create a variable distinguishing that category from the remaining ones. In creating dummy variables one always has one fewer variables than categories since the categories coded "0" (in this example, female, voluntary, and other) become the reference group for the other categories of that variable and to code them separately would be redundant.

Table 11.8 indicates that three variables are moderately correlated with parental visiting: the social worker's designated discharge objective—that the child is scheduled to be returned to his parents $(r = .387)$; children in care for shorter periods of time $r = .256)$; and children who entered foster care because of their own behavioral difficulty $(r = .265)$. These findings confirmed the results of the cross-tabulations. Statistical tests were not performed on the correlations, since all are statistically significant with an N this large. Instead the magnitudes of the associations were used to guide decisions about the importance of the relationships.

Table 11.9 presents the results of the multiple regression analysis in which the combined influence of the same independent variables listed in table 11.8 is ascertained. The task of multiple regression is to explain the variance in the dependent variable. This involves estimating the contributions to this variance of two or more independent variables. Often the dependent variable is referred to as the criterion variable and the independent variables as predictors. Table 11.9 summarizes the contributions of the selected independent variables in Fanshel's study to the variance in parental contact, the dependent variable. The "Beta" column gives the beta weights, which are called standard partial regression coefficients or sometimes simply standardized regression coefficients. (Beta weights are regression coefficients in standard score form; b weights are regression coefficients in raw score form.) A beta weight expresses the change in the dependent variable that is due to an independent variable when the effect of all other independent variables in that regression analysis are held constant or are controlled. The larger the partial regression coefficient of an independent variable, the stronger that variable is as a predictor of the dependent variable. These coefficients remain the same regardless of the order in which the variables are added to the

TABLE 11.9
Multiple Regression Analysis of Parental Contact (Total Visits)

Independent Variable	Beta	Variance Added	Cumulative Multiple R^2	Unique Variance
Sex (male; FEMALE)[a]	−.066	.003	.003	.000
Current age of child	.129	.002	.005	.006
Years in care	−.150	.100	.105	.001
Age-years in care interaction	−.030	.003	.108	.000
Ethnicity (other; BLACK)	.022	.001	.109	.000
Ethnicity (other; WHITE)	.065	.004	.113	.003
Reason placed (other; DRUG ABUSE)	.003	.000	.113	.000
Reason placed (other; ABANDONED)	−.043	.005	.118	.002
Reason placed (other; ABUSED)	.007	.000	.118	.000
Reason placed (other; NEGLECT)	.038	.001	.119	.001
Reason placed (other; CHILD BEHAVIOR)	.101	.015	.134	.007
Court status (voluntary; COURT PLACED)	−.032	.001	.135	.001
Discharge objective (other; TO PARENTS)	.291	.086	.221	.064
Discharge objective (other; ADOPTION)	−.092	.006	.227	.005

Source: Fanshel 1977.
Number of children = 20,214.
Multiple correlation = .476.
Multiple correlation squared = .227.
[a]The categories indicated by capital letters are those chosen as dichotomous variables, which were coded as 1; those in lower case were coded as 0.

regression mode. (They will change, however, if one or more variables are added to or subtracted from the regression; they may also change from sample to sample.)

The "Variance Added" column indicates the amount of variance each independent variable explains after the independent variables listed above it are controlled. For example, when added first, sex explains .3 percent or three-tenth of a percent of the variance in parental visiting, current age of child explains two-tenths of a percent of the variance after the effect of sex is subtracted; years in care explains 10 percent after the effects of sex and current age are subtracted; and so on. Clearly, the order in which independent variables are added to the analysis is important. The indices in the Variance Added column estimate, then, the variance contributions of each of the independent variables when these variables are in that particular order.

The "Cumulative Multiple R^2" column gives the cumulative total of the values in the Variance Added column. Note that only .227 or 23 percent of the variance in parental visiting is accounted for by the model, that is, by all the independent variables used in the analysis. Thus, more than three-fourths of the variance is left unexplained by the model. This is not unusual in social work research. Generally, models that can explain as much as 15 percent of the variance are considered worthwhile, and one that can explain as much as 30 percent is very good indeed.

The last column "Unique Variance" indicates the amount of variance in parental contact that each of the independent variables explains when all the other variables in the model are held constant. Note, for example, that while sex explains three-tenths of a percent of the variance when it is entered first in the analysis, it makes no unique contribution; that is, it explains nothing over and above what is explained by the other independent variables in the analysis.

The results of the multiple regression analysis again show that the strongest predictor of parental visiting is the discharge objective of the child's return to his parents; its standardized regression coefficient is .291. This variable explains an additional 8.6 percent of the variance and accounts for 6.4 percent of unique variance. No other variable contributes even 1 percent of unique variance. This important study is discussed again in chapter 15. (An excellent reference on multiple regression analysis is Kerlinger and Pedhazur 1973.)

Analysis of Variance and Covariance The *t* test is limited to the comparison of two means; analysis of variance (ANOVA) is used to compare three or more means. For example, a researcher may be interested in comparing the effectiveness of three different methods of treatment (or of leadership styles, work conditions, and so on.) The comparison may involve a decision concerning the differences among the sample means on the dependent variable. The analysis of variance technique can answer the question: Are the differences among sample means large enough to imply a difference among the corresponding population means? Analysis of variance breaks down the total variance in the dependent measures into component variances and pits two sources of variance against each other. In the simplest case, the one-way analysis of variance, the total variance is broken down into between-groups variance (presumably due to the experimental, or independent, variable) and within-groups variance (presumably due to error or randomness). The test-statistic is F; the F ratio consists of between-groups variance in the numerator and within-groups variance in the denominator. Thus, the larger the variance due to the treatment variable compared to error variance, the more likely the result will be statistically significant. As Kerlinger (1985) points out, this is what we seek to accomplish by experimental manipulation: to increase the variance between means. That is, we attempt to make the means different from one another.

More complicated analysis of variance techniques are factorial analysis of variance and analysis of covariance. The results from factorial experimental designs as discussed in chapter 7 can be analyzed by use of factorial analysis of variance. This method analyzes the independent (main effects) and inter-active effects (interaction) of two or more independent variables on a dependent variable. Since F ratios are calculated for each main effect and for each kind of interaction, several hypotheses are tested simultaneously.

Analysis of covariance us used to provide "statistical control" (chapter 4) for initial characteristics that may bias comparisons between groups. The technique is most commonly used in experiments in which methods of assigning subjects to groups fail to produce the desired equivalence. Thus, clients may be assigned nonrandomly to experimental and control groups in a test of a service program. The experimentals may score higher on measures of motivation than the controls and motivation may prove to be correlated with outcome. Analysis of covariance can be used to hold motivation constant in comparisons of the groups on measures of outcome.

An example that illustrates both factorial analysis and analysis of covariance is provided by Feldman, Caplinger, and Wodarski (1983) in their study of the effects of social work experience in clients behavioral change. This complex factorial design was discussed previously in chapter 7. The researchers were particularly interested in identifying clearly the conditions under which experienced and inexperienced therapeutic agents succeed or fail in their treatment efforts. Measures on the dependent variable, client behavioral change, were obtained by having trained observers ascertain the proportion of each youth's total behavioral repertoire that could be regarded as either prosocial, nonsocial, or antisocial. Prior to introducing the treatment, baseline measures of behavior were obtained. These baseline behaviors served as a covariate, that is, they were controlled, in the analysis.

The results of one of the analyses are found in table 11.10. The first

TABLE 11.10

Analyses of Covariance for Mean Observed Proportionate Incidences of Prosocial, Nonsocial, and Antisocial Behavior: End Point Analyses

Source	df	Prosocial MS	Prosocial F	Nonsocial MS	Nonsocial F	Antisocial MS	Antisocial F
Leaders	1	836.17	10.17*	37.69	1.10	669.21	11.48**
Methods	2	28.15	0.34	2.05	0.06	55.37	0.95
Groups	2	223.43	2.72	83.62	2.44	141.89	2.43
Leaders × Methods	2	107.16	1.30	30.03	0.87	130.59	2.24
Leaders × Groups	2	697.83	8.48**	80.31	2.34	573.33	9.83**
Methods × Groups	4	176.93	2.15	97.90	2.58	101.09	2.42
Leaders × Methods × Groups	4	20.70	0.25	24.29	0.71	89.76	1.54
Error	433	82.24		34.32		58.31	
Total	451	95.66		36.05		68.51	

Source: Feldman and Caplinger 1977.
Note: $N = 452$.
$*p < .01.$
$**p < .001.$

column indicates that the total variance was broken down into variance due to three main effects (leaders, methods, and groups), variance due to all possible types of interaction, and variance due to error. (The influence of the covariate, baseline behaviors, has already been removed.) The second column gives the degrees of freedom associated with each source of variance. The remaining six columns list the mean squares and F values for each of the three types of behaviors. The table shows that the only significant differences were found in prosocial and antisocial behavior of the youth between experienced and inexperienced leaders (experienced leaders did better) and in the interaction between leaders and groups (experienced leaders did better than inexperienced leaders with referred and nonreferred groups; inexperienced leaders did better with mixed groups than they did with either referred and non referred groups). None of the other main effects, including treatment method, or interactions made a difference. Schuerman (1983), Kerlinger and Pedhazur 1973; Bock 1975 are good references for a wide variety of multivariate techniques including multiple regression, factor analysis, canonical correlation, discriminant analysis, and multiple analysis of variance and covariance.

Factor Analysis   Factor analysis is another powerful multivariate analytic technique. Like multiple regression analysis and most analyses of variance, it involves complicated computations and requires the use of a computer. Factor analysis is a method of analyzing the intercorrelations within a set of variables. This technique is used to determine the number and nature of the underlying variables called factors among a larger number of measures (Kerlinger 1985). It extracts from a set of measures what the measures have in common (common factor variance) and thus reduces the larger pool of measures to a smaller number of factors. Factors are constructs or abstractions that underlie the set of measures. They are empirical entities without inherent substantive meaning. Although measures such as scales, tests, and questionnaire items are perhaps most frequently used in factor analysis, almost any kind of measure can be factored.

Fortune et al. (1985) factored the responses of 101 social work students to a questionnaire designed to measure their satisfaction with different aspects of field work. Responses entered into the factor analysis consisted of student ratings of satisfaction on seven point scales (7 = very satisfied). Examples of the items rated as well as results of the factor analysis are presented in table 11.11.

The items are organized into factors produced by the analysis. As can be seen, the analysis groups the items into clusters (factors).

The grouping is based on solely statistical considerations—in the pattern of intercorrelation among the items. The factor labels, e.g., Professional Role, are designations devised by the researchers to capture the observed statistical "glue" which joins the items. The labels may or may not correspond to whatever organizing concepts the researchers had in mind in developing the instrument. The "factor loadings" (second column) can be interpreted as correlations between given items and the factors to which they belong. Factor loadings must meet specified criteria of size—in excess of .30 for example—for the item to be considered as belonging to the factor; by the same token, high loadings, for example, in excess of .80, indicate a high degree of correlation with the factor.

By grouping together measures that intercorrelate, factor analysis not only serves to reduce and organize the data, but can generate new measures for use in further data analysis. Thus in the Fortune et al. study the six scales produced by the factor analysis (table 11.11) were in turn correlated with global measures of satisfaction with field agency, field instructor, and field learning. The scales proved to correlate positively with these satisfaction

TABLE 11.11
Average Item Scores and Factor Loadings for Satisfaction and Perceptions
of the Field Placement

Item	Item Mean	
Satisfaction with field agency	5.25	
Satisfaction with field instructor	5.28	
Satisfaction with field learning	5.42	
		Factor Loading
Factor 1: School-Agency Liaison		
My contact with my field liaison has been satisfactory to meet my learning needs	4.10	.918
If there are problems at my field placement, I am comfortable consulting with my field liaison	4.01	.873
When I have problems in my placement I go to my field liaison	3.05	.838
I am aware of the possible roles of my field liaison	4.68	.708
Communication between the school of social work and my agency is adequate	3.99	.663
Factor 2: Professional Role		
I have the same responsibilities as the professional staff at my agency	5.44	8.59
I am included in all agency activities that professional staff are expected to attend	5.54	.825
I have the same privileges as the professional staff at my agency	5.23	.779
I have been able to meet the expectations of my field placement	6.13	.636
I agree with my agency's policies	5.00	.457
Factor 3: Relevant Learning		
I enjoy working with the type of client I serve at my agency	5.94	.840
My field work assignments this year have been relevant to my learning goals	5.64	.751
I was able to actively participate in designing my learning experience	5.54	.616
Factor 4: Supervision		
My field instructor enjoys his/her role as "teacher"	5.79	.770
I have been encouraged to express new or different ideas in my practicum setting	5.30	.654

Item	Item Mean	Factor Loading
Factor 5: Practicality		
My agency provides adequate physical facilities (i.e., desk, office, supplies) for students	5.11	.727
My courses this year have been relevant to my field experience	4.75	.536
Factor 6: Evaluation Anxiety		
There is conflict between the agency and the school's policies concerning expectations for students in the field *	4.39	.716
Having a "pass/fail" system reduces my anxiety concerning my field placement	5.74	.668

Source: Fortune 1985.

* Scoring is reversed (higher = less perceives conflict). On all other items, higher scores indicate more of the quality.

variables. However, a striking exception was the lack of correlation between the School-Agency Liaison Scale and *any* of the satisfaction measures. Thus with the help of factor analytic techniques, the researchers were able to discover an intriguing pattern. While students were less satisfied with School-Agency liaison than with other aspects of field work (as can be seen from Table 11.11) their relative unhappiness with this aspect had little apparent effect on their satisfaction with their agencies, their instructors or their learning. (A good reference on factor analysis is Harman 1976.)

Limitations of Multivariate Analysis

As we indicated at the beginning of this chapter, we believe multivarate techniques hold a great deal of promise for social work research. These techniques handle the complexities of behavioral and social phenomena far better than simpler analyses that deal with two variables at a time. However, even multivariate procedures are limited in the extent to which they reflect the realities of the phenomena of interest to social workers. We mention briefly the major limitations we see in the use of mulivariate analysis, particularly those procedures based on correlation methods.

First, multivariate methods are essentially tools that should be guided, or programmed, intelligently. The researcher must decide what variables go into the analyses and how the analyses are to be performed. These decisions should be informed decisions, based on the researcher's theoretical notions. Accordingly, although multivariate techniques are useful in teasing out possible causal relations, they seldom adequately control the range of extraneous factors that may be influencing dependent variables.

Second, the results of any multivariate analysis are dependent on the particular procedures or routines employed. For example, the solution selected and type of rotation used influence the results of a factor analysis. Similarly, the findings of a multiple regression analysis are affected by the order in which variables are entered into the model and which routine is used to help make this decision.

A third limitation has been referred to but bears repeating. When multivariate techniques are used with ordered data, as is often the case, resulting distortions are compounded in the elaborate manipulations of the data, involving perhaps thousands of calculations that are integral to the use of these techniques.

The quality of the measures themselves usually constitutes another limitation. The imperfections of scales for measuring marital satisfaction, self-concept, group cohesion, and the like, can be clarified sometimes by mutlivariate techniques but cannot be corrected by them.

Finally, reproducibility is always a matter of concern. For example, the "underlying structures" in attitude, client change, or other phenomena that may be revealed by factor analytic techniques may vary considerably from sample to sample. These limitations arise, of course, in the use of simpler methods of analysis. Our essential point here is that the sophistication of analytic techniques and the complex statistical displays that often accompany them should not blind us to what—sometimes what little—is actually being conveyed by the data.

ANALYSIS OF TIME SERIES DATA

Time series data, which consist of repeated measurements over time, can be gathered on samples of all sizes and analyzed in a variety of ways. In this section we shall discuss analysis of time series data obtained in single case designs. This focus reflects growing interest in single case designs in clinical social work and increasing attention by social work researchers to use of statistical techniques in analysis of data emanating from single case studies (Jayaratne 1978; Marsh and Shibano 1984).

Significance Testing

As was observed in chapter 5 the usual method of ruling out instability as a source of alternative explanation in single case time series data is to "eyeball" a graph or other data display and to make a judgment about whether or not observed changes appear greater than those that might have occurred by chance. If changes are of great magnitude and the data base is sufficiently large, the role of chance may be reasonably discounted but often the amount of change is modest or there are few data points. The last consideration is sometimes overlooked. If there are only three or four observations during baseline and a similar number during intervention, a fairly large difference may be a chance artifact. Furthermore experimenters and others who hope that intervention will be successful may understandably overestimate the amount of change that has taken place and erroneously dismiss the possibility of chance influences.

A need for a systematic means of assessing chance factors in time series can therefore be established. Unfortunately, however, time series data do not lend themselves to a straightforward application of standard statistical tests, such as those that have been discussed in preceding sections. The major difficulty is lack of independence between data points in a time series. Standard statistical tests are based on the assumption that data points—or sample elements—are independent of one another. For example, in testing the results of a group experiment it is assumed that the outcome for client A exerts no influence on the outcome for client B. While this assumption may apply reasonably well to the usual group study, it is hard to justify with time series data which by their very nature tend to be serially dependent or autocorrelated. In single case studies different data points concern the same individual, hence any one value is likely to be influenced by its predecessors (serial dependency).

Suppose daily observations are recorded on progress made by a mildly retarded child learning to read out loud. Data points take the form of errors made in reading passages of comparable length and difficulty. It is likely that the data would assume the shape of a learning curve: the number of errors made each day would tend to decrease at a gradual rate over time. The following series of recorded errors might in fact be obtained: 10, 9, 8, 7, 6, 5, 5, 3, 2, 0. It is obvious that how the child performs on a given day is related to his previous performance as his reading improves. Autocorrelation can be seen at a statistical level if one pairs each observation with its successor

(10/9, 9/8, 8/7, 7/6, and so on). As in any correlation with the values in each pair covary. Autocorrelation can also be negative as might occur in rapidly fluctuating behavior and need not be confined to adjacent data points, as might be the case if there is a time lag between a behavior and its consequences. Therefore, a correlation might occur between time points 1, 3, 5, 7, 9 (lag 2); 1, 4, 7, 10 (lag 3); and so on.

In addition, standard statistical tests do not take into account the trends in time series data. In figure 11.8, a marked change in trend occurs coincident with the beginning of treatment. Yet, the means for the baseline and treatment phases are similar; and the *t*-test for differences in means would not reveal a significant difference. Obviously, significance testing would need to determine changes in trends—usually referred to as a change in "slope"—as well as a change in level of magnitude.

More sophisticated approaches to significance testing with time series data have been available for some time (Box and Jenkins 1970; Glass, Willson, and Gottman 1975). These more elaborate methods, referred to generally as time series analysis, ascertain significance of change in slope and level in the light of the nature of autocorrelation found in the series. For a review see Kazdin (1985).

Applications of these techniques to clinical practice have been limited by their computational complexity, which necessitates use of a computer and a usually hard-to-obtain program. Another obstacle has been the requirement for sizeable numbers of observation, often more than would be obtained in a clinical case. Recent work has developed less complex models requiring fewer observations (Gottman 1981; Marsh and Shibano 1984; Rankin and Marsh 1985).

Simple Estimations

Even simpler approaches to the assessment of instability make use of ideas from probability theory but, since they do not take fully into account autocorrelation, can be best seen as statistical short-cuts that can provide estimates of significance. Jayaratne (1978) provides a method of computing autocorrelation between adjacent numbers (lag 1) in a baseline. If this autocorrelation does not prove to be statistically significant, one assumes that the observations are independent and proceeds with standard tests adapted for time series, such as t-tests for level and slope. Since appreciable autocorrelation may be present, but not at a significant level—particularly if the number of observa-

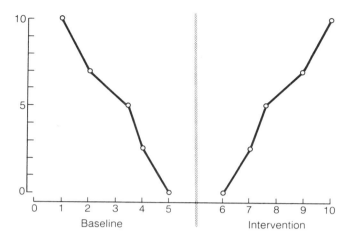

FIGURE 11.8
Contrasting trends but similar means for baseline and intervention periods

tions is small—the problem of serial dependency in data is not completely solved; also, of course, autocorrelation may occur at different lags, a possibility that is not evaluated.

In a method developed by Shewart (1931) and elaborated on Gottman and Leiblum (1974) the standard deviation of baseline data is calculated on the assumption that these data are normally distributed. One determines the number of consecutive observations during the treatment phase that exceed the mean by two standard deviations. Statistical significance can be "claimed," according to Gottman and Leiblum, if two consecutive data points in the treatment phase fall outside the two standard deviation limit. Bloom and Fischer (1982) describe a "frequency procedure" based on similar logic. Through the use of simply computed acceleration lines (White 1974; Gingerich and Feyerherm 1979), a trend in baseline data for a problem can be projected beyond baseline on the assumption that the frequency of the problem would continue to increase in a linear (straight-line) fashion. This projection can be compared with the actual graph obtained during the intervention phase. A discrepancy between the actual and projected graphs can be used as an estimate of the effects of intervention.

Such techniques can provide bench marks for assessing the magnitude of findings. Although probability values that might be ascribed to them may be somewhat metaphorical, the procedures offer a convenient standard for deciding which findings will be taken "seriously." A review that provides useful "how-to" procedures can be found in Bloom and Fischer (1982).

QUALITATIVE ANALYSIS

As qualitative data are collected the researcher begins looking for patterns, themes, or organizing constructs. When these emerge, a tentative analytic framework is developed. The framework may involve the construction of categories or hypotheses or both. Further data collection is guided by this analytic framework, and the usefulness of framework is ascertained. Categories are added or subtracted and hypotheses modified as the new data indicate. This process of sequential analysis and increasingly focused data collection continues until the researcher is satisfied with her understanding of the phenomenon.

As the foregoing suggests, data collection and analysis in qualitative studies are not necessarily separate processes as they are in a quantitative research. To a large extent, data collection and qualitative analysis are interwined with subsequent data collection being influenced by the results of earlier analysis. This may be true whether the qualitative data are collected through field observation, unstructured interviews, or from available materials. However, there is also a stage of intensive qualitative analysis that comes after the completion of data collection. The various materials collected must be pulled together into a coherent whole. Occasionally, even at this final stage of analysis, which occurs just prior to or concurrently with the writing of the research report, more data are collected to check again one's analytic framework.

Two key elements of qualitative analysis have been identified: the integration of analysis and data collection, with each operation guiding the other; and the building of analytic systems from data obtained. In applying the first of these elements the researcher essentially modifies her data collection procedures as she goes along. Suppose for example she wishes to study patterns of division of labor and responsibility among egalitarian "dual-career" marital partners who have young children. A semistructured interview guide informed by available knowledge is developed and used with several couples. In these initial interviews the researcher discovers that although couples agree in principle to share child caring tasks equally, the mothers actually *do* more because their child care standards are more exacting. While the researcher may have anticipated this phenomenon, she may not have given it the attention in her interview guide that it seemed to deserve. After preliminary analysis has led her to conclude that differences in child care standards appear to be important, she expands this area of her inquiry in the next interview, perhaps giving less attention to less fruitful topics. The resulting data may suffer from unevenness but it may illuminate certain aspects of the phenomenon that might otherwise have remained in the shadows.

The process of building concepts and hypotheses from raw data cannot be readily systematized since it involves, among other things, the researcher's prior knowledge of the subject and capacity to think creatively about it. At the simplest level one looks for commonalities or themes in the data. In most couples interviewed does the wife/mother have higher child care standards manifested? Around what types of activities? Although qualitative analysis may not involve counting, the analyst needs to guard continually against natural human tendencies to "see" patterns in the data that in reality have little substance, either because of preconceived notions or a need to present "interesting" findings. Deviant cases are particularly important to note since they may point the way to additional areas for inquiry or theory development. Generalizations or other statements emanating from the analysis should be referenced to actual data, for example, in the form of citations of incidents or quotes from subjects. These references can be used to document the final report.

Constant Comparison   In more extensive applications of qualitative methodology, the researcher may search out differing groups or cases as a means of developing theory. Glaser and Strauss (1967, 1970) describe the logic of this approach, which they refer to as the method of "constant comparison." "Significant categories are first identified . . . during preliminary field work. Comparison groups or cases are then located and chosen in accordance with the purposes of providing new data on categories or combinations of them, suggesting new hypotheses, and verifying initial hypotheses in diverse contexts" (1970:292). For example, in an initial study of client satisfaction with agency services, there may be clues that the most dissatisfied clients were those who sought a concrete service from the agency but were given "counseling" instead. A group of clients who applied for concrete services might then be sought out and studied to check this hypothesis. This group might then be compared with a group that sought counseling services only, and so on. In their single case application of this approach, Butler, Davis, and

Kukkonen (1979) suggest how hypotheses might be developed through a succession of single case studies in a social work context. In a systematic exposition of the constant comparative method, Lincoln and Guba (1985) clarify and extend the original Glaser-Strauss formulation.

Organizing Data Because they consist of words, the data of a qualitative study are difficult to order and summarize. As a first step, the investigator can categorize (code) the data following principles set forth earlier in the chapter. In qualitative coding, however, the purpose is not to reduce data to quantitative form but rather to preserve the detail and richness of the word pictures, which can lead to a "thick description" (Geertz 1973; Lincoln and Guba 1985) of the phenomenon under study. In an example of qualitative analysis in a study of marital case, Reid and Strother (in press) coded all references by either husband or wife or the practitioner to "body language," a focus of treatment in the case. The "body language" code served as a means of identifying instances which were described in detail (rather than as a means of counting references to body language). The investigator can then use these categorizations and descriptions as a basis for identifying themes— or "pattern codes" (Miles and Huberman 1984:67). To continue the body language example, a theme or pattern code emerging from the data was the clients' use of the practitioners focus on body language as a means of exerting self-control over negative expressions of hostile looks or gestures. The practitioner had wanted the clients simply to record instances of "misreading" body language, a task which they ignored.

Coded descriptions can be put on $5'' \times 8''$ cards directly or field notes containing the descriptions can be cut up and stapled to them. A recent development has been the use of microcomputers to store and retrieve such data (Conrad and Reinharz 1984). Whatever form they take, recorded descriptions can be amplified by marginal comments incorporating the investigators' reflections.

An additional (or alternative) mode of data organization is through memos, written to oneself or to colleagues on a research team. Memos consist of ideas, concepts, formulations, and so on, that facilitate the process of data interpretation. They provide stepping stones between the level of data and related codes and the conclusions that will be drawn from the study.

Displays A useful technique for purposes of both data organization and presentation is what Miles and Huberman (1984:79) refer to as a "display."

A qualitative analog to the statistical table, displays take such forms as word tables, charts, diagrams, and the like. Displays organize verbal information in a succinct, structured form so that essential ideas and relationships can be readily discerned. For the researcher "rough and ready" displays can help order and clarify complex data. Final form displays can serve the same function for the user.

The "case process chart" shown in table 11.12 was a display used in a qualitative analysis of a single case (Reid 1988). The display, a form of "effects matrix" (Miles and Huberman 1984:114), traces the process of change in a case involving application of the task-centered family treatment model (Reid 1985). The excerpt given (the first three of six sessions) shows the relation between change in the target problem (quarreling) and its context and use of tasks in the session and at home. The display suggests a close connection between tasks involving mother-daughter activities and the problem of quarreling. The tasks appear to lead to greater activity, which in turn reduces quarreling. The argument that tasks may be a "signed cause" of change (chapter 6) is supported by the sequence of events in the implementation of the first home task. Increased activity following the task is followed by less quarreling. When the task breaks down after Tania's poor score on the quiz and the mother's refusal to continue the task, quarreling increases. This sequence constitutes, in effect, an unplanned withdrawal-reversal design (chapter 6): when the task is followed, the problem changes for the better; when it is not, it changes for the worse. By presenting essential details of the case in a systematic compact form the display provides a picture of the processes of change that would be difficult to duplicate either in narrative form or through quantitative methods (e.g., a graph). (The display also illustrates methods of qualitative single-case study, Reid and Davis 1987; Davis and Reid 1988).

Verification   As noted a potential limitation of qualitative methodology is bias resulting from dependence on the researcher's subjective interpretations of data. Qualitative methodologists have been giving increased attention to ways of controlling for investigator bias (Lincoln and Guba 1985). Essentially, methods of control follow the general principle in reliability and validity testing in which multiple checks are used to evaluate data (chapters 11, 14). The single investigator, herself, can check findings across different types of data sources—e.g., patients, social workers, nurses, and so on, in a study of a hospital ward—or across different methods of data collection—for

TABLE 11.12
Case Process Chart—K Family

Family Situation and Problem—Parents self-referred to family agency for help concerning problems with Tania (T), age 13. Parents black, some college, father (F) on disability; mother (M) works as office manager; T has two siblings, Nora (N) and Jay (J), 8, who is mildly retarded. T and M have been constantly quarreling for several months (at least once a day) over T's behavior—e.g., her clothes, chores at home, her fighting with her siblings and school grades (B's and C's instead of A's). Little interaction between M and T otherwise. F upset over M and T's inability to get along, their doing little together, T's impatience with J. M responsible for discipline though father supports her. She has high expectations for T ("Because she's black and female she needs to be better than average"). M insists on obedience to the rules, wants no back-talk, seldom gives explanations, withdraws privileges, hits when pushed too far. Sees T as the troublemaker in family, seems to favor N who is more conforming, and to be protective of J. Tried individual therapy for T, which T broke off.

Intervention Plan—Family agreed to work on problem of M and T's arguing. Service will consist of six weekly sessions as part of Task-Centered Family Treatment Project. Intervention will focus on tasks in the session involving M, F, and T (session tasks—ST) and tasks to be done at home (home tasks—HT). Session tasks (ST) will be designed to promote family problem solving and development of communication skills. These tasks will be used as the basis for home tasks.

Sessions and Participants	Problem Status	Problem Context	Intervention
1) M, F, T, and N	M: "We argue all the time." At least once a day—over T's clothes, chores, grades. F: "They fight all the time." Several months' duration.	T "mouths off," argues back. M insists T obey, be respectful; seldom gives reasons to T. M and T seldom discuss anything, little interaction when not quarreling.	ST-1: M and T agree to engage in mutually enjoyable activities 3 days a week. T agrees to get 90+ on quizzes. Task (developed from F's suggestion), based on premise that contextual change (M/T relationship) would reduce arguing. Only M, F, and T to attend session to reinforce M/T relationship.

Sessions and Participants	Problem Status	Problem Context	Intervention
			HT-1 Implement activities plan.
2) F, M, T	M and T: Things better then worse. F: "Some improvement."	Did things together (e.g., listen to music), until T got 70 on quiz, then M stopped activities. Hadn't argued much during period when doing things together; more after activities stopped.	ST-2: F and M agree that M resume activities with T regardless of grades, etc. F to increase activities with other children "to be fair." HT-2: M and T to take turns planning joint activities to be done on 3 days and weekend.
3) M, T	M and T: arguing less; 1 argument during week.	M and T did a lot together: shopping, music; M went to T's girl scout meeting; took her to get ears pierced; did their homework together. (M taking class.) Activities occurred on daily basis; more than task called for.	ST-3: M and T asked to discuss one argument and come up with solution. Practitioner stressed "I" statements, asking for and giving reasons for actions. ST-4 and 5: M and T asked to exchange positives about each other. T couldn't think of one—finally said M "could be fun." HT-3: M and T to explain their positions to each other in next argument. F to mediate (F and M's suggestion). HT-2: Repeated.

example, interviews and observations. Interpretations of data can be discussed with a knowledgeable but disinterested peer (Lincoln and Guba 1985:308). A stronger method is to use both multiple data sources and investigators. If there is only a single investigator to collect data, then an independent investigator can be used to reanalyze key pieces of data. Following the logic of the independent analyst, the researcher's entire data set can be thoroughly examined by an independent researcher in a signed audit (Lincoln and Guba 1985).

Use of multiple data sources, data types and investigators, has been elaborated on by qualitative methodologists under the rubric of "triangulation" (Denzin 1978; Lincoln and Guba 1985; Ruckdeschel 1985). Although an important tool in qualitative research, as in quantitative studies (chapters 11 14), triangulation seldom offers clear-cut answers to questions of the credibility of findings. In qualitative studies, it is often difficult to secure comparable readings of the same phenomenon since investigators may follow unique paths in their collection and analysis of data. Moreover, quantitative and qualitative measures are often difficult to use in cross-checking since they may be measuring rather different things. Nevertheless, amassing different types of evidence from different sources, methods, investigators, and so on, can help insure a balanced and comprehensive analysis.

PART THREE

APPLICATIONS IN DATA COLLECTION AND MEASUREMENT

CHAPTER 12

ASSESSMENT

In part 2 we set forth the foundations of research methods as they are, or could be, used in social work. In the remaining chapters, we consider certain applications of these methods of special relevance to the tasks of social workers. A central theme is how data collection and measurement strategies can be employed to generate knowledge and information about the targets, processes, and outcomes of intervention.

Various research strategies can be applied to the task of understanding actual or potential client systems and their problems. Through naturalistic designs, researchers can study client characteristics and problems as they find them and can contribute to explanations of these phenomena. Through experimental designs, theories about human and, hence, client behavior can be tested, at least in the laboratory. Field experiments testing out intervention methods can add to understanding how types of clients and targets respond to methods tested. The data collection and measurement techniques that have been considered are integral to the assessment of any human system.

In this chapter we concentrate on application of research methods to assessment of change targets at two levels: the client system in clinical practice and communities or other population groups at a macro practice level.

RESEARCH PROCEDURES IN CLINICAL ASSESSMENT

In chapter 2, we saw how a scientific viewpoint could influence practice. To review these ideas in relation to assessment, a practitioner who uses an empirical perspective is likely to ground fuzzy diagnostic abstractions like "reality testing" or "enmeshment" with specific indicators, to apply research-based knowledge in an effort to understand client systems, to consider alternative theories and explanations in formulating assessments, and to use research instruments as part of the assessment process. Perhaps the most practical of these ideas is the last. We shall attempt to develop it in more detail below through a survey of kinds of instruments that can be used to measure client systems.

Assessment Interviewing A clinical interview or portions of an interview directed at eliciting data from clients about their functioning, problems, histories and so one, normally uses methods of inquiry similar to those used in research interviewing. Although the purposes of clinical assessment and the research interview differ, both draw on the same repertory of techniques. Thus, criteria for "good questions" (chapter 11) in research interviews and instruments are relevant to assessment interviewing in clinical practice. One type of confluence of research and clinical considerations is represented by the *behavioral interview*, a systematic initial interview conducted within a behavioral treatment framework (Kanfer and Nay 1981; Turkat 1986). By focusing on specific behaviors, their antecedents and consequences, the interviewer attempts to develop an empirically grounded formulation of the client's problems that can serve as a guide to intervention. Principles and techniques of the behavioral interview can be usefully applied to non-behavioral forms of practice.

In another type of assessment interview, topics relating to client functioning or problems are covered through open-ended questions. The resulting data then serve as a basis for rating scales or other measurements. Examples include the Psychiatric Status Schedule (Spitzer et al. 1970), the Social Adjustment Scale (Weissman, Sholomska and John 1981), the Family Functioning Scale (Geismar 1980), and measures of target complaints and problems (Battle et al. 1966; Reid 1978; Mintz and Kiesler 1982).

Goal Attainment Scaling Goal Attainment Scaling (Kiresuk and Sherman 1968; Kiresuk and Lund 1977; Mintz and Kiesler 1982) is a set of procedures for setting up goals during the assessment phase and of evaluating attainment of them at termination or follow-up. The setting of goals is a way of specifying the problems to be worked on and has a definite assessment function. Since goal-setting provides a direction for work, it also provides a way of structuring service. Areas of potential change in a client's life are described, and for each area different possible outcomes in terms of changes that may be achieved are identified and ordered according to levels of treatment success. This information is recorded in a guide, a portion of which is given here together with an illustration of how the scaling process works (figure 12.1)

Naturalistic Observation   The practitioner or an associate (e.g., a teacher or house parent) can observe a client system in some "natural" enviornment, such as a school, a hospital ward, or a home. In this type of observation the observer attempts to be as unobtrusive as possible in order to minimize effects on the client's behavior. Observation may involve either quantitative or qualitative methods or some combination of the two. In using quantitative methods, the practitioner usually records the frequency of a behavior during a specified time period. Various techniques for conducting this form of observation may be found in Bloom and Fischer 1982; Barlow and Hersen 1984 (see also chapter 11). In using qualitative methods, the observer, who would normally be the practitioner, would attempt to identify characteristics of themes of diagnostic interest. For example, in observing a disruptive child in a classroom the practitioner/observer would note the different types of disruptive behavior, the reaction of the teacher and other pupils to disruptive acts, and events preceding them. Counting of specific behaviors would not be considered essential, although it might be done as part of a broader observational process. Notes would be taken and written up in a form of a summary. Careful observations and recording of the sequence of specific events distinguishes a qualitative empirical approach from the kind of global impressions one might obtain through casual observation. Thus, one avoids vague abstractions, such as "showed poor impulse control" but rather states concrete behaviors, such as "repeatedly tapped pencil on desk."

Observation of Task Behavior   Clients may be asked to perform tasks in the practitioner's presence and their behavior may be observed for assessment purposes. For example, a number of approaches using interactional tasks have been devised for marital and family assessment (Filsinger 1983). Such observational devices, which are often time-consuming to administer and score in their entirety, may be adapted for purposes of clinical assessment. In this context the general point can be made that no instrument need to be used either as designed or in its entirety to serve useful functions in clinical assessment.

GOAL ATTAINMENT FOLLOW-UP GUIDE

Check whether or not the Scale has been mutually negotiated between patient and CIC interviewer	SCALE HEADINGS AND SCALE WEIGHTS	
SCALE ATTAINMENT LEVELS	Yes **X** No ___	Yes ___ No **X**
	SCALE 1: Education $(w_1 = 20)$	SCALE 2: Suicide $(w_2 = 30)$
a. most unfavorable treatment outcome thought likely (-2)	Patient has made no attempt to enroll in high school. ∨	Patient has committed suicide
b. less than expected success with treatment (-1)	Patient has enrolled in high school, but at time of follow-up has dropped out.	Patient has acted on at least one suicidal impulse since her first contact with the CIC, but has not succeeded. ∨
c. expected level of treatment success (0)	Patient has enrolled, and is in school at follow-up, but is attending class sporadically (misses an average of more than a third of her classes during a week).	Patient reports she has had at least four suicidal impulses since her first contact with the CIC but has not acted on any of them.
d. more than expected success with treatment $(+1)$	Patient has enrolled, is in school at follow-up, and is attending classes consistently, but has no vocational goals. *	
e. best anticipated success with treatment $(+2)$	Patient has enrolled, is in school at follow-up, is attending classes consistently, and has some vocational goal.	Patient reports she has had no suicidal impulses since her first contact with the CIC. *

Level at Intake: ∨
Level at Follow-up: *

FIGURE 12.1
Sample clinic guide: crisis intervention center (*Source:* Kiresuk 1973; reprinted by permission of the copyright holder, Minneapolis: Medical Research Foundation)

Practitioners can develop their own tasks for assessment or evaluation purposes. A husband and wife may be asked to discuss a problem or parents may be directed to engage in a game or other activity with their child. An adolescent who has difficulty in being assertive may be able to demonstrate the problem in a role play with the practitioner. Because tasks of this kind can be shaped to the particular circumstances of the case at hand, they can often produce observations that approach the validity of those obtained through naturalistic means. Moreover, in many situations, such as family assessment, some practitioner activity, e.g., task setting, is neccesary in order to set the stage for the occurrence of behavior of interest for assessment purposes.

Client Self-Observation   Rather than the practitioner observing clients, clients can be asked to observe themselves and bring in the results. Client self-observation can take a variety of forms, including diaries, logs, simple devices for recording occurrences of one's own behavior or the behavior of a family member; and "self-anchoring" scales (Gingerich 1979). Often self-recording can have beneficial, even if only temporary, effects on behaviors observed. This complicates the use of client self-recording for assessment purposes although usually the clinical benefits provide sufficient compensation. A much greater difficulty is getting clients to do the observation in the first place. A good rule is to keep it simple; another, is not to expect too much. A comprehensive review of self-monitoring procedures may be found in Bornstein, Hamilton and Bornstein (1986).

Standardized Instruments   A standardized, self-report instrument relating to functioning, problems, and the like, is a versatile, easy-to-use tool. Although any standardized instrument, or even a battery, can be used for assessment purposes in clinical work, practitioners prefer what Levitt and Reid (1981) have called "rapid assessment instruments," or RAI's. An RAI is brief (one or two pages), quickly administered (usually in less than 10 minutes), and easily scored. As a result, an RAI can be taken and, if need be, scored within the session. Among the more commonly used RAI's are those that make up the Clinical Measurement Package (Hudson 1982) which includes RAI's to measure self-esteem, marital satisfaction, and family relations; the Beck Depression Inventory (1967); the Locke-Wallace Marital Adjustment Scale (1959); the Dyadic Adjustment Scale (Spanier 1976). Reviews of RAI's for particular areas of practice include group treatment (Edelson 1985) and health care (Ivanoff et al. 1986). A general source for such instruments is Corcoran and Fischer (1987).

RAI's serve three functions in assessment. First, they provide a compact but comprehensive survey of a problem, asking key questions that might not occur to the practitioner, that she may not have time to ask, or that clients may be reluctant to answer frankly, particularly in an interview with other family members present. What is of primary interest in this function is the client's responses to particular items—e.g., "Do you ever think of taking your own life? Second, the client's test scores can be compared with averages from samples of identified populations. For example, a certain score on the Beck Depression Inventory would indicate that a client's responses resemble those of severely depressed patients. Finally, repeat administrations of an RAI can provide measures of change relating to goals of service. Their usefulness with nonverbal, disorganized and resistive clients and helping marital partners better understand each other's perspectives were among more specific advantages cited by family agency practitioners in a trial use of RAI's under ordinary agency conditions (Toseland and Reid 1985). On the other hand, an RAI may not routinely add to what has been obtained from a clinical interview, a limitation cited by practitioners in the same project.

As practice evolution tools, RAI's can provide straightforward and quantified measures of change, independent of the practitioner's judgment. Usually these measures must often be cautiously interpreted, however. They may not necessarily reflect change in the target problem which may not be quite what the RAI measures. Moreoever, the measures may be influenced by the client's defensiveness, wish to impress others, and so on.

Whether used for assessment or evaluation purposes, it is a good idea to examine the client's responses to the instrument items in relation to the totality of one's knowledge of the case. For example, a client who paints a rosy picture of her family at the start of service and a somewhat less rosy one at its conclusion may be providing evidence of a more realistic attitude rather than negative change—or an hypothesis that needs to be evaluated in the light of other case data.

Recording In most cases the bulk of data relating to assessment and intervention will be recorded by the practitioner in narrative form, with such devices as client logs and RAI's providing supplementary information. Whatever style of recording is used, essential data on problems, client characteristics, intervention processes, and change need to be captured. In order to make sure the essentials are systematically preserved, some type of structured recording format is recommended. One may use a general purpose format such as the Structured Clinical Record (Videka-Sherman and Reid 1985) or develop one to fit the situation at hand. Essentially, such a record calls for recording items of information under predetermined headings. For example, a recording format may include such headings as a) Presenting Problem; b) Historical and Contextual Factors; c) Treatment Goals; d) Principal Interventions and Immediate Outcomes; e) Client Situation at Termination. In a structured format, omissions of key data are less likely to occur and can be readily spotted. Moreover, the organization of data facilitates coding, analysis, and communication to others. To this base of organized, essential data, the practitioner can add detailed descriptions for specific purposes, for example, to record in detail an observation of a child.

NEEDS ASSESSMENT

The notion of studying communities or other human aggregations to identify and assess targets for intervention represents one of the oldest uses of operations research in social work. For example, the community survey provided much of the empirical grounding for the social reform movements in the earlier part of this century (Zimbalist 1955). In recent years, the expression "needs assessment" has emerged as an umbrella term to cover various old and new techniques for study of populations as a basis for program planning. Also in recent years, interest and activity in this area have been stimulated by federal requirements for needs assessments as a condition for social and mental health services.

As Stewart (1979) suggests, needs assessment stands for an ill-defined assortment of concepts and methods. The notion of "need" may vary from an abstract indicator of a social problem, such as the youth crime rate in a community, to requests by consumers for particular services. Need may be diversely defined by professionals, government officials, community representatives, and the recipients of service themselves. Assessment techniques may range from judgments about the sentiments of community members expressed at an open hearing to highly sophisticated statistical procedures. Nevertheless, the notion serves the practical function of grouping together a set of approaches all concerned with study of what people may require from the health and welfare system.

Following a classification developed by McKillip (1987), we take up four major categories of needs assessment methods: structured groups; use analysis;

surveys; and social indicators. We discuss each method in turn and then consider likely combinations of methods.

Structured Groups

Perhaps the simplest and least expensive method of assessing need is to assemble relevant groups—of citizens, experts, and so on and to elicit their views of need. Several common techniques will be reviewed.

Community Forum In using the community forum technique (Siegel, Attkisson, and Carson 1978), planners sponsor a meeting of interested members of the community. Sometimes the community members are preselected; at other times the meeting is open to the general public. The meeting is designed to elicit the population's view of the needs of the community in a situation where ideas can flow comfortably. This is certainly the least scientific and systematic of the needs assessment methods. In fact, the forum may degenerate into a session of breastbeating and complaining about the local government or agency and is policies rather than a constructive discussion of the perceived needs of the community. Moreover, if the meetings are open to the general public, the respondents are self-selected. Therefore, the sample is skewed. Ideally, one should hold a series of smaller forums, either centering on specific subject areas or located within different neighborhoods in a community.

The community forum is able to elicit the input of ordinary citizens without structuring their thinking in a preconceived way. If the forum truly has an open agenda, it is conceivable that it could provide an outlet for previously undefined community problems. Questionnaires, surveys, and agenda-controlled discussions all structure the thinking of the respondent. They provide certain definitions that place boundaries on what may appear to be legitimate areas of need or problems. An open meeting provides the opportunity for a spontaneous statement of a previously unperceived need. (This advantage becomes more attractive when one considers the apparent problems with the key informant method discussed later.) Also, as Delbecq (1976) notes the community forum can be good preparation for a survey, for it gives the researcher a preliminary reading of the concerns of community members, how they express these concerns, and the priorities they place on them.

Focused Groups   More structured and systematic than the community forum are "focused groups" (McKillip 1987). A small number of participants, eight to ten, are selected to represent a larger group, for example, tenants in a housing project or parents of mentally retarded children. Views of needs can be elicited through open discussion lead by a moderator who may be the needs assessor. A series of such meetings may be conducted with groups representing different constituencies. Bias in selection of participants is one source of concern. Another is possible disproportionate influence exerted by more vocal or articulate members of the group.

Nominal Groups   A useful method of structuring discussions to maximize the value of the information gained in the community forums or focused groups is the nominal group technique (Delbecq and Van de Ven 1971; Delbecq 1983). The technique evolved from research showing that structured group process enhances creativity (Thompson and Smithburg 1968) and that interaction between group members can prevent some members from openly expressing their ideas and concerns (Taylor, Berry, and Block 1958; Hairston 1979).

First, persons in attendance are divided into smaller groups. The division is made to reflect strata in the larger group, for instance, age, race, or other variables that the organizers consider relevant. Participants are asked to write down the needs they perceive in the community. Delbecq and Van de Ven (1971) recommend asking participants to list not only the needs they have identified but also ways in which existing services have failed to meet those needs. A round-robin is then conducted in each group to list the concerns. Next, each item on the list is discussed and clarified but only briefly, so as to avoid influencing the original thinking behind the expression of the concern. Participants are asked to select individually a given number of concerns or difficulties and then to rank them in importance. These rankings are compiled for each small group and then discussed in the larger group. The information derived from the nominal group method is hard to analyze systematically. Analysis is bound to require considerable interpretation of the data collected. The meeting can also be the occasion of the distribution and return of a questionnaire; however, the sampling difficulties noted earlier would limit the usefulness of the data.

Analyzing Use of Service

In using this method it is assumed that one can extrapolate from persons who have received or are receiving services to the service needs of a larger population (Warheit, Bell, and Schwab 1977). By examining data describing those currently receiving services, one can gain a picture of the characteristics of a potential clientele. On the basis of how often these characteristics appear in the community's population, planners can estimate the need, or demand, for services. For example, if an agency discovers that it serves many recently divorced women, it can estimate potential demand for its services by means such as a study of available data on divorces awarded by courts in the community. If the number of eligibles is known, rates can be computed. Thus, an agency may serve 20 out of every 100 blind persons in a community.

There are several ways in which case data can be collected. One way is through the use of a data sheet completed on each client the agency serves. In addition to fact sheet data, information may be gathered on the presenting problem, treatment or services provided, frequency of treatment, duration of contact with the agency, how the client was referred to the agency, and referrals the agency made for the client (Warheit, Bell, and Schwab 1977).

Another way to develop case data is through secondary analysis of case records. Though there may be some variation between agencies, most collect some general data about each client for their files. Unfortunately, files may be incomplete, and the researcher may end up having to disqualify many cases or to spend precious time gathering the missing data verbally from workers in the agency. Often, even this undesirable method of data collection cannot be used. In addition to the usual distortions present in any form of case recording (chapter 14), records rarely reveal who perceived the problem or need: the practitioner or the client. The data collection process may be facilitated if use data are stored in a computerized information system (Logan 1977), though problems of data quality still remain.

A major drawback of use data is that they can simply affirm existing perceptions of need represented by the services provided and the populations already being served, rather than help the service provider develop a more nearly comprehensive picture of the needs of the community. There is no chance here for an entirely unrecognized need to show itself, for the sample from which data are drawn is biased by definition (Bell et al. 1976).

Moreover, concerns about confidentiality can interfere with the collection of data. Though it is possible for anonymity to be ensured, the sharing of any client information may be against the policy of certain agencies or of private practitioners. However, to get a really balanced picture of clients under treatment, it may be necessary to tap the caseloads of all sorts of service providers. It may be particularly difficult to solicit the participation of private agencies that do not receive substantial public funds. In short, it may be quite difficult either to cover the entire population of service recipients or even to draw a representative random sample.

Because it is necesary to compare use data with data describing the whole population to extrapolate need, one is almost required to use the method in tandem with at least one other data set, such as census data. This is an important drawback. Although agencies usually collect use data routinely, the complexities of comparing use data with other data can considerably increase the cost of using this method.

Another standard against which to compare use data is similar data drawn from previous years. Comparing use data within an agency or community from year to year can allow the agency or community to develop a baseline of need and then to evaluate its performance in meeting that need each year. This is a way in which needs assessment data can be used to evaluate the effectiveness of programs.

In spite of all these difficulties, this method can be useful when its limitations are recognized and accepted. It can give the agency or community a good clear sense of the needs it is already trying to meet. Various methods of analyzing the data collected can reveal the different properties of the data; it is possible that patterns might be detected and used as predictors of problems or clusters of problems that new clients may have. In other words, these patterns could be used to improve agency personnel's understanding of various problems and situations and their subsequent interventions. Problem patterns discovered through this sort of data analysis can also be useful in directing policy decisions.

Surveys

Surveys are used to generate data about needs of communities or target groups through systematic study of samples drawn from these populations. Ideally, these samples are obtained by means of random selection and are representative of the populations from which obtained, although in practice exceptions to this ideal frequently occur (see chapters 4 and 8). Two common types of surveys used in needs assessment are community surveys and surveys of experts, usually referred to as *key informants.*

Community Surveys   In community surveys the focus is usually on assessing perceived needs of respondents who may be clients, members of at-risk populations, or citizens in general. Client surveys generally take form of consumer evaluations (discussed in the following chapter). In surveys of at-risk or potential client populations, emphasis is on determining needs of groups that have not received services. Such surveys generally use "descriptive" designs (chapters 4 and 5) and interviews or questionnaires (chapter 11).

In one example of a survey (Human Services Coordination Alliance, 1976), researchers investigated seven primary needs of the elderly; housing, health/mental health, nutrition, finances, self-sufficiency, social isolation, and transportation. Care was taken to generate a random sample of the target group throughout the designated geographical area. The instrument included some questions that could be coded during the interview, some open-ended questions, and the interviewer's observations. The views of an objective third party were also obtained to verify certain information.

The data analysis focused on identifying sets of circumstances as embodied in combinations of these seven primary needs, and the population's reactions and responses to them. The data were used to rank the counties on each of the seven needs; the results were then mapped providing an overall multidimensional picture of needs throughout the geographic area.

As Cohen, Sills, and Schwebel (1978) point out, the bias and preconceptions of professionals can be inadvertently reflected in the construction of the survey instrument. They discuss a two-stage procedure in which an open-ended survey instrument is administered first to identify the range of problems perceived in the community. A closed-ended survey instrument is then constructed based on the problem categories developed from the previous survey. This second instrument asks respondents if they have difficulties with each problem area, the severity of the difficulty, causes of the problem, solutions attempted, degree of resolution of the problem, and any suggestions respondents may have for services to address these problems. This technique provides an important check on the preconceptions of the professionals executing the community survey.

Advantages of the community survey include opportunity to measure need as perceived by actual or potential consumers. In addition, assessment of need can be based on a *representative* sample of individuals. However, good surveys are expensive and require some expertise to administer. Response rates may also be low, resulting in poor cost-effectiveness (Warheit, Bell, and Schwab 1977). In addition, of course, they suffer from the usual problems, such as social desirability effects and response sets, found in any self-report instrument.

Key Informant The key informant method involves obtaining expert opinions from a selected sample of respondents from the community assumed to have special knowledge of the needs of the overall population. Often agency practitioners themselves are chosen, as well as other community professionals in adjunct occupations. Also included may be various public officials and other community figures who represent sectors or organizations considered to have special knowledge about problems in the community. Advantages of this technique are that it costs very little, and it is easy to obtain a sample.

The choice of key informants should be determined by the questions to be asked or the issues to be addressed. However, the researcher must then decide on a data collection format. Should the data be collected in face-to-face interviews or by means of questionnaires? Should questions be open-ended or closed? If questionnaires are chosen, should they be mailed, administered in person, or used over the telephone? A useful set of guidelines for answering such questions has been provided by the League of California Cities (1975).

The delphi process (Dalkey 1969; Van de Ven and Delbecq 1974) is one way to organize the collection of key informant data. This technique is suited to a situation in which information is gained from key informants individually and through the mail. Participants are asked to respond to a questionnaire examining the problem area under scrutiny in a general way. When the questionnaires are returned, the researcher collates and summarizes the data and sends a report of the results to the respondents. The report is accompanied by a second questionnaire that builds on the first and examines these specific areas in greater depth. One goal of this method is to elicit opinions from each respondent in isolation from one another, so that respondents do not influence each other's thinking. Therefore, this technique would be less appropriate for use in a small, well-knit community.

An example of use of key informants is provided in a study by the Florida Department of Health and Rehabilitation Services (1975). Questionnaires were distributed to professionals invited to attend hearings on the use of federal funds. Most of those in attendance were social service workers; half were direct service providers and most of the remainder were administrators. State social service employees were overrepresented, and since the hearings were held in urban settings throughout the state, rural counties were underrepresented.

The questionnaires were distributed after the representation of materials designed to get the group to think of statewide needs rather than only of their local areas. The questionnaire itself consisted of three parts; first, a listing of needs that respondents were to rate on a five-point scale of importance. Second, the respondents were to list and rank what they considered to be the five most pressing problems. Third, they were to list and rank five target groups in the population that they considered to be most in need of more or better services.

Index scores were then developed from these rankings for the whole state. In addition, the responses were broken down by district and indices developed for each district as well.

Program planners and decision makers use an informal sort of key informant survey with some frequency. Instead of conducting a formal needs assessment, they frequently use informal one-to-one consultations with a representative group of professionals to guide their policy and programming decisions.

However, this informal procedure can be executed in ways that produce more systematic and dependable results. The combination of a carefully chosen sample of key informants, with the use of a qualitative analytic technique in interpreting the data collected, can provide the decision maker with a more dependable and better organized set of impressions on which to base a programming decision.

Research evaluations of key informant approaches have shown mixed results. For example, Booz-Allen Public Administration Service (1973) devised a number of different needs assessment methodologies and tested them in various field sites. The key informant survey, or Informed Community Representatives, as they termed it, proved to be one of the least successful methods in their test. There were problems in choosing respondents and in coding open-ended responses obtained from interviews with them. The respondents had difficulty in handling questions about need that were not related to their own specialized fields or to their own experience. The respondents also had difficulty in estimating quantities of clients with specific problems.

Whereas it seems likely that some of the problems in the Booz-Allen study were a result of their instrument and the interviewers' lack of training in its use, difficulties with the key informant survey were also apparent in a study by Warheit, Buhl, and Bell (1978). They used mailed questionnaires, which yielded a very low return rate—37.5 percent. In this study, the key informant method was compared with mapping of needs based on social indicators drawn from census data. The aim of each analysis was to identify specific areas of need within certain geographic areas.

The use of the social indicators mapping technique enabled the needs assessors to rank different geographic areas within a given community by need level, as identified through the analysis of census data. (See the later discussion for more detailed description of the use of social indicators.) After ranking the geographic areas on the basis of these data, the researchers asked each key informant to assess the extent of need resulting from twenty-two different problems in each geographic area. Using the mapping technique, the researchers were able to clearly differentiate areas of need across the community. However, the key informants were unable to differentiate need from one geographic area to another. "The informants reported high levels of need in all areas on all problems, a finding which may be consonant with the facts" (Warheit, Buhl, and Bell 1978, p. 244). However, the *purpose* of needs assessment is to differentiate all levels of need throughout a community, area, or population. Assessing equal and high levels of need throughout the community, as the key informant method seems frequently to do, makes planning and the allocations of limited resources even more difficult.

More encouraging results were obtained by Deaux and Callahan who compared a random-digit telephone survey and a key informant survey in a state-wide study of health-related behaviors in New Mexico. Respondents in the telephone survey were asked about their own behavior. Key informants were asked to estimate prevalence for the same behaviors. The researchers concluded that "the key informant approach . . . produced prevalence estimates of health-risk behavior that are reliable and apparently more valid than those produced by a telephone survey" (1984:489). Of special interest was evidence that key informants showed consistency in their opinions over a three month period as well as consistency across different disciplines.

In sum, the key informant approach is probably best used to provide an approximate assessment of need. In many situations, however, rough and ready approximations may provide adequate information for planning purposes.

Social Indicators

In its strictest, most traditional sense, "the social indicators method of assessing needs is based on the assumption it is possible to estimate the health and other human service needs of persons on the basis of the geographical, ecological, social, economic and demographic characteristics of the area in which they live" (Warheit, Buhl, and Bell 1978:240). Existing statistical information is used to analyze geographical areas in terms of social indicators thought to be indicative of certain social conditions. These geographic areas, usually census tracts, are ranked for each indicator, and then the rankings are mapped, to provide a multidimensional view of the needs of the overall area (Steward and Poaster 1975). The Mental Health Demographic Profile System (MHDPS) developed by the National Institute of Mental Health (Windle et al. 1975) provides data on indicators that they have shown to be related to levels of mental health functioning. These data are provided by catchment areas and counties, so that needs assessments may be done by local governmental bodies and agencies fairly inexpensively (Goldsmith et al.).

No attempt is made in this kind of analysis to isolate causes or effects. The aim is to demonstrate clusters of indicators that have been shown to signal the coexistence of certain social needs (Bell et al. 1983). This information can then be used to direct social planning. These data help to define the social and demographic boundaries in a community, making the geographical ones less relevant for planning and decision making (Warheit, Buhl, and Bell 1978).

The widespread use of this approach has developed and grown since Bauer's *Social Indicators* was published in 1966. The Warheit-Buhl-Bell (1978) study mentioned earlier is one example of research that verifies the use of a social indicators approach. They found that the mapping of rankings derived by the use of social indicators provided considerable differentiation of needs across geographic areas.

A less traditional definition of social indicators includes any existing statistical data that describe important characteristics of a target population or group. In this way, any regularly kept statistics can be useful. There can be some overlap between the social indicators method and the use method, for many regularly kept statistics that might be applicable are kept by agencies on their clientele. But as a social indicator, statistics on clients served are used to differentiate boundaries of need across geographical areas.

In an example of the use of this sort of statistical data, Rice and Fowler (1973) studied twenty-five geographical areas in Los Angeles County in relation to public mental health facility admission rates. They combined admissions data with census and other data. They were able to successfully predict admission rates from various areas based on statistics describing previous experience with inpatient and outpatient admissions, combined with the use of more traditional social indicators.

Froland (1976) took data that had been collected by another community on its population of substance abusers and compared them with census data describing population characteristics of the state of Oregon. Using these data he delineated areas in the state that could be considered high risk for substance abuse. Projections were then made of need for services in these areas. The projections were found to be consistent with actual service rates.

Less traditional social indicators are subjective measures of life quality. The use of these subjective measures receives support in a study done by Schneider (1975), who found that objective and subjective measures of the quality of life did not match. People did not see quality of their lives as directly related to their socioeconomic status. This finding reinforces the notion that social indicators should not be the sole means of needs assessment used by a community or agency.

COMBINING APPROACHES

Since each method has inherent weaknesses, a needs assessment model, particularly at the level of assessing needs of an entire community, usually contains a combination of approaches. All methods could be used at various intervals to maintain a clear picture of the ever-changing needs of the community. However, this is not financially feasible for most communities.

Since community surveys can reach such a large portion of the population, they can be particularly beneficial when used in concert with other methods. A community survey can generate a large base of information that can then be refined through the use of key informant surveys. Alternately, the community survey can be used to verify data gathered by other methods like use data, community forum, and key informant techniques.

One combination of methods that is particularly appealing, for they appear to complement one another well, is the combined use of social indicators and the community survey. Whereas the survey can be rather costly, the use of social indicators is usually relatively inexpensive. These methods also provide a good check on one another, for the social indicators provide the objective data, while survey provides the subjective side of the picture.

Another likely combination is the use of community surveys with key informant surveys. Although there is no objective measure here as a check, the two subjective measures can provide a two-dimensional view of the articulated needs. One might add the use of data these two subjective measures as a limited objective check. Using these data as the basis for the survey instruments could help to shore up the weaknesses of all three approaches.

A final, but important, issue to consider is the public relations aspect of conducting a needs assessment, and the readiness of the community to make constructive use of the data. If a key informant survey is needed to secure the cooperation of local key professionals and citizens, then its use is advised. The same might be said for the weakest method, the community forum. Luckily, these methods are fairly inexpensive to use. Gauging the readiness of the community or agencies to use the data is crucial from a cost-benefit perspective. It is pointless to invest in sophisticated data collection and analysis if the results will never be taken seriously in the policymaking and planning processes.

USE AS A PLANNING TOOL

The data collection techniques of needs assessment methodology are fairly well developed; however, in viewing the methodology as a planning tool, some important weaknesses become apparent. One weakness is mentioned by Kimmel (1977), who points out that a few tools have been developed for use in transforming the data collected into priorities or planning guidelines. The social indicators method is perhaps the only one with an analytic technique (e.g., mapping) that does part of this job. By graphically displaying the information on census tract or subcommunity maps, areas of intense need can be delineated. Even though areas of a community can be differentially described in this way, some other process is still required to set priorities for which needs are to be addressed when, and which geographic area is the best bet for intervention. Most often, the process used to make the decisions is the political process.

The lack of a stable definition of need is another weakness in the methodology. Clearly, it is often a problem within projects, as values come into conflict, and as assessors try to decide whether need equals demand or is a phenomenon that can be measured against some objective standard. Kimmel

(1977) advocates the development of absolute or comparative standards or criteria for determining need. This may be the way to go when need is being documented to secure federal monies. Each group assessing need must come up with a level or criterion against which to measure need. Again, this criterion is often arrived at through the political process. This is inescapable and may often be the best method.

If needs assessment methods are to be fully used in the planning process, then they must be related to program evaluation. In that way, it would be possible to learn how assessed needs were actually being met by programs developed to meet them. Feedback of this kind would not only facilitate more rational program planning but would also serve as a guide to future needs assessments. In assessing needs, it is important to discriminate between populations that can be effectively served by existing programs and those that cannot be. Needs assessments may be only tenuously related to ensuing programs and tend to be even less well connected to whatever evaluations may follow. These different strands of the planning process could be knit together more closely if greater use were made of principles of developmental research or research and development strategies (chapter 2; Rothman 1980).

CHAPTER 13

MEASURING OUTCOME

To move from assessment of targets to outcome measurement and thence to study of intervention characteristics (the following chapter) seems to be a violation of a natural progression. Doesn't one assess, intervene, and then evaluate? Although this ordering may make sense for many purposes, it introduces, we think, an artificial distinction between "assessment" and "outcome." Actually, the measurement of a target prior to, during, and following intervention can be seen as part of a continuing process of assessment, a point made quite clear in the unbroken lines of a graph in a time series experiment. In any case, it may be better to think of outcome as "outcome of the problem" rather than as "outcome of intervention." Outcome data generally consist in some measure of problem change that may result, and usually does, from the operation of various factors. Intervention can be more appropriately viewed as contributing to outcome rather than being its sole cause, and whether or not it even makes a significant contribution is often a matter of doubt.

OUTCOME CRITERIA

In our conception, then, outcome generally refers to some kind of change in a target system. At the level of the individual (where our attention is centered), outcome may be conceived of in terms such as changes in the person's behavior, attitudes, cognitions, social functioning, problems, emotional distress, environmental circumstances, and status (for example, release from care). We expand this conception, however, to include some related notions. One addition is goal attainment. Although a goal is usually defined as some type of desirable change in behavior, attitudes, and so on, it may be set as maintenance of the status quo, particularly if the state of the target system is expected to worsen in the absence of intervention. Another is the relation of outcome to intervention costs, as in cost-effectiveness or cost-benefit measures. Outcome may also be thought of in terms of consumer satisfaction. For example, did the client regard the service as helpful? A client may positively evaluate service even if no favorable changes have occurred or may feel dissatisfied despite objective evidence of progress. From these conceptions criteria or indicators of outcome are derived.

In operationalizing outcomes for a particular program, one usually develops indicators from the program's objectives (Rossi and Freeman 1985). "What is the program trying to accomplish?" is the customary initial question. To answer this question, it is usually helpful to view program objectives within the framework of the theory in which the program is based. Thus, a program of task-centered intervention is based on the theory that specific problems can be alleviated by tasks carried out by practitioner and clients (Reid and Epstein 1972; Reid 1978, 1985). The theory further predicts that helping clients resolve particular problems through methods prescribed by the approach will have certain additional benefits for them, such as engendering a more positive attitude toward professional helpers and increasing their problem-solving capacity. As the example illustrates, examination of a program's theoretical underpinnings usually reveals that a program has multiple objectives (e.g., immediate problem resolution and enhancement of problem-solving skills) and that its goals can be ordered in a certain sequence (e.g., task accomplishment leads to problem reduction.) With such a map of program goals, one can fashion criteria sensitive to a range of program outcomes. The logic applies to programs of any scope, from those used in single cases to large-scale undertakings.

This process may be difficult, particularly if the program is complex and directed toward vaguely defined objectives and lacking a well-articulated theoretical base. Additional obstacles are posed if those responsible for the program have unrealistic notions of the capabilities of the program or are unable to agree on what its goals should be.

In deriving outcome criteria, one should not be confined to the goals of a program or to its underlying theory. It is important to be aware of unintended consequences of a program (Weiss 1972), particularly of the possibility that a program may have negative effects. Thus, a wider perspective needs to brought to bear, perhaps one informed by other theories. For example, an individualized program may be directed at modifying the behavior of a particular child who has several siblings. The program calls for the mother to reward the child when he behaves in a desired way. Although the goals and theory of the program might limit attention to the mother-child dyad, it would be an oversight, we think, to confine outcome criteria accordingly. A systems perspective on family interaction, if not common sense, would suggest that the mother's rewarding one child might have consequences for her relationships with her other children. Reasonably comprehensive outcome criteria would need to take such "system effects" into account.

The meaning of outcome, and criteria for its assessment, will also vary according to the perspectives of different participants: service practitioners, collaterals, clients, and researchers. Even when outcome considerations are restricted to "objective evidence," what evidence is regarded as a valid measure of outcome and interpretations placed on it can be expected to differ according to different observers. And usually there is little basis for regarding any one vantage point as decisive. Thus the goal of a program may be to alleviate problems in psychosocial functioning. According to the practitioner's criteria, changes in surface problems, which she may regard as "symptoms," may be discounted. Clients may place a high degree of value on changes of this order. A researcher, making judgments on the basis of her interviews with clients, may occupy an intermediate position. Whereas differences in criteria reflecting different actors can be reduced through the development of specific indicators and instructions, they probably cannot be eliminated completely. Outcome assessments obtained from different vantage points tend to show a considerable amount of divergence (Lambert 1983; Kyte 1980). Increasingly, and with good reason, researchers are being advised to incorporate the perspectives of more than one actor in their measures of outcome (Kazdin 1986).

As noted, a program of intervention can be conceptualized in terms of a sequence of goals or outcomes. Task accomplishment leads to problem reduction as in the example given earlier. A program to help patients discharged from mental hospitals become self-sufficient may use on-the-job training in a sheltered workshop as a means of securing job placements in the community. Outcomes for the job-training component could be seen as subsidiary to the outcome of the job placement efforts. Although interest may be centered in the "ultimate" criteria that culminate the sequence, indicators of outcome earlier in the sequence should not be overlooked (Rosen and Proctor 1978). It is important, if possible, to obtain a picture of the chain of events that led to final outcomes. Information of this kind can provide evidence on the effectiveness of the intervention by tracing the process of its impact (chapter 2) and can also help pinpoint weak links in the chain. In some instances, such as programs to prevent teenage pregnancy, the ultimate goals may occur too far in the future to permit feasible follow-up. "Proxy goals" (Rossi and Freeman 1985), such as a change in the teens' sexual behavior, may serve as the best available measure.

Although words such as "final" or "ultimate" may be used to describe the desired end goal of a program, we seldom achieve once-and-for-all solutions. Questions about the durability of effects inevitably contribute additional complexities to decisions about outcome criteria. Usually priority is given, and with good reason, to indicators of the immediate effects of a program. There is little point in worrying about durability of gains if no gains had occurred. In most social work programs, such effects, if they are found at all, occur by the time of the termination of service or shortly thereafter.

But the durability of effects is usually accorded an almost equivalent importance. In fact, in some types of program, interest in durability may be paramount. The immediate effects of a program may have already been established; one wishes to learn if these effects persist over time. (A good deal of behavior modification fits this case.) In other situations, target problems presumably affected by the program may occur at a relatively low frequency. A fair amount of time may need to pass before one can establish that the intervention has done its work. Programs designed to reduce delinquent behavior provide examples. Finally, a premium may be placed on durability in the outcomes of long-term counseling or of other programs that attempt to bring about fundamental changes in the client's functioning.

Thus far we have considered the breadth or range of outcome criteria across various areas. We now turn to questions of depth, or to the movement from the abstract to the concrete in the development of criteria. One may begin with a global conception of outcome, such as "increased independent functioning," and attempt to fashion definitional chains encompassing an array of more specific indicators. In one chain this conception may be specified as "improvement in self-care routines" which in turn may be further specified (in part) as "increased ability to dress self." Even indicators that are fairly specific to begin with further specification. Thus outcome in a single case study may concern reduction in a child's getting out of his seat without permission—a complex behavior that would need to be specified in terms of the rules governing the movement of children in the classroom.

In general, the considerations presented in chapters 3 and 9 relating to developing indicators for concepts apply here. In applying these considerations to the generation of outcome indicators, it is important, we think, to keep certain principles in mind. First, global concepts of outcome should always be defined in terms that are as specific as possible. Global concepts such as "improvement" and "positive change" should always be so articulated, even though inherent difficulties in spelling them out may make it tempting to leave their interpretation to practitioners, judges, or clients. Second, in explicating criteria an attempt should be made to include indicators sensitive to what might be called the "smallest measurable increments of effect." Given the difficulties in demonstrating the effectiveness of many forms of social work intervention, the researcher should try to include indicators that relate to minor or subtle changes, goal achievements, and the like. The evaluation instrument developed by Beck and Jones (1973) provides an excellent illustration of this principle.

Finally, attention needs to be given to the practical significance of changes resulting from the program. Although it is well to measure subtle effects, it is also important to be able to identify proportions of clients who have achieved a level of change commensurate with the goals of a program. Thus, clients in a program may change to a statistically significant degree (when compared with a control group) but few clients may have attained adequate resolutions of the problems that occasioned service. Such paradoxical results have generated considerable interest in establishing criteria for "clinical significance" (Jacobson, Follette, and Revensdorf 1984). Clients treated for depression might be judged to have improved to a clinically significant degree if they are free of depressive symptoms at the close of service. Various criteria may have been suggested to determine what might be regarded as clinically significant, most of which involve measurement of degree of change in standardized scores from pre-service to post-service—for example, change in scores from a pathological to normal range (Jacobson, Follette and Revensdorf 1984; Christensen and Mendoza 1986). Criteria of this kind are limited to problems for which good standardized instruments exist, a shortcoming in various types of social work practice, e.g., in child welfare, youth services, and hospitals settings, in which such instruments may not be available. Still the general thrust of the clinical significance movement, which calls for setting standards of decisive progress and for reporting proportions of clients who meet those standards, applies to all forms of social work practice.

FROM CRITERIA TO DATA

A final step in the specification of outcome measures is consideration of how data are actually derived. Although outcome measures can take the form of direct evaluations of service, as when clients are asked what they thought of a program, almost all measures involve some calibration of change in some target that the intervention has presumably affected. The more common means of calibration are briefly reviewed.

The simplest means is to obtain retrospective estimates from clients, practitioners, or others who in effect are asked for their opinions about change in target problems, systems, and the like, since the beginning of intervention. Like most ex post facto data, retrospective assessments of change may suffer from respondent memory loss and the influence of recent events. The desire of respondents to see benefits from intervention may result in exaggerations of amounts of change that have occurred. To provide more information than error, these retrospective approaches should not be limited to global impressions but should rather cover aspects of change in a detailed and comprehensive manner.

A more rigorous method of deriving measures of change is to obtain one measure of the status of the target prior to intervention (premeasure) and a second measure (postmeasure) following the intervention. The change score is obtained by subtracting the premeasure from the postmeasure. Thus, if a family is rated five on the Geismar Family-Functioning Scale (Geismar 1980) at case opening and seven at case closing, a change score of +2 is recorded. In principle, the procedure is the same as weighing oneself before and after a period of dieting and measuring change in terms of pounds gained or lost. In measurement of intervention outcomes, however, subtractive measures of "gain scores" tend to be vulnerable to certain kinds of imprecision that need to be taken into account in their use. First, if the measure has some degree of unreliability, as is usually the case, it must be kept in mind that the unreliability of the change score reflects an *accumulation* of the unreliability of both the before and after measures (see, for example, Gulliksen 1950). An intuitive sense of this problem can be grasped if one imagines a bathroom scale as fluctuating within two pounds, which is a way of stating its unreliability. The scale will be "off" by a maximum of only two pounds if it is used as a measure of weight at a given point of time. If used to measure weight change, however, the scale could give a reading of gain or loss that could be off by as much as four pounds. Moreover, if the measurement level of a scale is no more than ordinal (chapter 8), as is often the case, subtracting prescores from postscores conveys a somewhat spurious precision. Finally, subtractive measurements of change may be insensitive to subtle changes. Thus, a client may fall exactly at midscale in a rating of social adjustment at two points of time, but still his adjustment may have improved in ways not great enough to be detected by the second measurement.

Alternatives to retrospective and subtractive approaches are measures of change based on judges' comparisons of before-and-after data. In this method, a trained judge compares data on targets obtained before and after intervention and makes a rating of change on scales developed for the purpose. Ideally, the judges are unaware that intervention has occurred in the interim and can even be kept in the dark about which set of data was obtained before intervention and which after. In other words, judges can simply be asked to assess change between two "pictures" of a case, without knowing anything additional. A principal advantage of this method over the preceding measures is its greater sensitivity, a particular strength in evaluation of social work intervention where changes are frequently in the "modest" range. Thus a small, but important, decrease in the intensity of a couple's quarreling may be apparent from comparing interview data obtained from the couple at different points of time, a decrease that might not be detected in retrospective or subtractive measures. The assessments of judges must, however, be based on data, such as interview protocols, that may have significant limitations. Also one does sacrifice information about level: the position of a target before intervention as might be compared to general norms. These drawbacks may be more than offset by gains in sensitivity if change is difficult to detect through the use of before-and-after measures.

Another approach consists of repeated measures over time. Assessments of change are then based on evaluations of variability, level, and trend of the series of measures as discussed in chapter 6. As can be seen, such a time series is an extension of pre-post measurement. Measures are now obtained not only before and after intervention but also during its course. Since it incorporates pre-post measurement and provides in addition continual readings of the course of change during intervention. time series measurement might be seen as clearly superior albeit more costly. But repeated measures can create their own special kinds of distortions: for example, clients may remember previous responses on a test, or their behavior may be influenced by repeated testing or observation. Moreover, it may be difficult to withhold from the data collector knowledge that clients are receiving intervention, knowledge that could be a source of bias.

Any of the foregoing measures can be used to compare treated and untreated groups or groups receiving different forms of treatment. When between-group comparisons are to be made, still other procedures can be applied. If the groups were formed through random assignment and were assumed to be equivalent prior to the experiment, a meaningful comparison can be based on posttest scores only. Since the groups supposedly had equivalent initial scores, the differences at posttest provide a relative measure of differences in amount of change between the groups. The main advantage of this procedure is to eliminate the need of a premeasure, particularly in situations when such a measure might influence the outcome of the experiment (testing effects). When groups are not equivalent, comparisons can be made using posttest scores with statistical adjustment or control (analysis of covariance) used to eliminate effects of differences in pretest scores. Covariance analysis (as illustrated in chapter 11) can also be used with randomly assigned groups to adjust for the effects of random difference in initial scores (Cook and Campbell 1979).

APPROACHES TO MEASUREMENT

In a broad sense, the measurement of outcome comprises the various steps that take place in the translation of outcome criteria to refined data. As we have seen, they include the development of instruments, obtaining raw data from particular sources, and transforming these data into final measures of change. We now take a clear look at these complex processes, beginning with a dimension of major importance—the source from which data are obtained.

Source of Data

Almost any approach to the measurement of outcome can be traced to one ultimate source: the client himself. Data supplied by practitioners are obtained from records concerning the client's status or functioning. The client is a more direct source of measurement when his behavior is observed, when he is interviewed about changes in his problem or his situation, or when his evaluations of service are elicited.

Clients Approaches in which the client provides data directly through behavior, self-report, or other means make up the back-bone of most attempts to measure outcome. For this reason, they are considered first and in greater detail.

A central consideration when the client is the source of data is the extent to which the amount and kind of information provided the researcher are under the client's cognitive control. At one extreme would fall measures of client opinion about a program and measures based on the client's own report of change. At the other extreme are observations of the client's behavior in a natural setting or his performance of a task in the laboratory.

If information is dependent on the client's memory or judgment, there is considerable opportunity for distortions or biases to affect the data. The client, like any person, is limited by his ability to recall events in the past, and moreover his recall may be influenced by his own involvement in the program. Anticipation of help and need to justify investments may cause him to give an erroneously favorable picture of the program's impact. Social desirability effects may be additional sources of bias. If the client perceives a data collector as a representative of the program, the client may give a response that would make the program look good to please his interrogator. "Polite lying" to people responsible for providing service is a natural reaction: indifferent meals suddenly become "fine" when we are asked our opinions of them by waiters and maitre d's. When the client is dependent on the program for important resources, such as income, housing, or health care, he may be reluctant to be critical because of his wish to "stay out of trouble." Sample attrition or mortality may add further distortion. As noted in chapter 7, clients willing to cooperate in an outcome study are more likely to give positive evaluations than dropouts are.

Despite these limitations, client self-report data provide a unique perspective on outcome in evaluating programs designed to change phenomena that researchers cannot readily observe—for example, family interaction in the home. To control for biases associated with memory, social desirability and the like, an attempt should be made to pin measures to specific events and, if possible, to obtain self-report data (on initial status) prior to service as well as data relating to change during the course of service. For example, self-report data can be obtained by practitioners during the course of service interviews (Reid 1988). Additionally, or alternatively, standardized self-report measures (chapter 11) can be used before, during, and at the end of treatment. If only post-service ratings are possible, clients can be asked to do retrospective ratings of how problems were before service began and then to rerate how these problems are "now," so that measures of change can be calculated. As Beutler and Crago (1983) suggest, such anchored change measures are preferable to the more common client post-service ratings of improvement which appear to be heavily influenced by the clients' current sense of well being. (Specific procedures for before-and-now ratings can be found in Beutler and Crago 1983).

Client ratings of *satisfaction* with service are another kind of commonly obtained measure, one that is conceptually distinct from data relating to change, improvement, and the like. (Clients can be satisfied with a service that has produced little change in their lives, or vice-versa). Global ratings of satisfaction with service tend to be quite positive. For example, compilations of studies of client satisfaction with mental health services have reported satisfaction rates that generally range from 70 to 85 percent (Berger 1983; Lehman and Zastowny 1983; Lebow 1983). It is impossible to determine to what extent these added rates reflect genuine satisfaction as opposed to sampling bias, self-justification, social desirability, and other types of distortion, but it is reasonable to suppose that they contribute to some amount of "exaggeration of benefit" or inflation in a positive direction.

Conservative interpretations of data are justified as a rule. Thus, if 20 percent of the clients receiving services say they are "very satisfied," 50 percent "satisfied," and the remaining 30 percent "dissatisfied," it would be more reasonable to conclude that an alarming number of clients had reservations about the program (almost a third expressed dissatisfaction) than to suggest that 70 percent were "satisfied customers." (A client rating of "satisfied" can almost be interpreted as a neutral response if a "very satisfied" option is available.) This is not to say that one can dismiss the possibility of negative bias in client self-reports, particularly if there is reason to suppose that clients resented an "imposed service."

A movement toward more meaningful interpretation of client satisfaction ratings is reflected in the work of Lehmann and Zastowny (1983) to establish, through analysis of available studies, norms for different types of client populations and programs in mental health. Until such norms are developed the kind of averages and corrections just described can be used as rough guides in interpreting consumer satisfaction in a given study. Usually more useful than ratings of satisfaction for programs as a whole are client evaluations of specific components. An example is provided by client dissatisfaction with time-limits in short-term treatment (for a review see O'Conner and Reid 1986).

When outcome measures are based on observations of the client's behavior in natural situations or performance of structured tasks, then distortions of the kind considered above are less likely to occur. One must still be concerned with the client's reactions to being observed or tested, reactions that may produce atypical—often atypically positive—responses. Although the client's selective recall may not be an issue, the researcher must now pay attention to the representativeness of what has been observed or tested. Do the observation periods reflect a fair sample of the client's behavior? Does a role-play test of assertiveness cover typical situations in which assertive responses may be called for?

Practitioners The practitioner is frequently used as a source of data on client change. Data can usually be readily obtained from practitioners at minimal cost. Also, the practitioner has firsthand knowledge of changes in the client's life and circumstances that may be associated with intervention and, as we have noted, brings to bear a perspective informed by professional knowledge.

Outcome data may be obtained directly from practitioners by means such as questionnaires, precoded recording forms, scales, or interviews. Less direct means usually involve coding of the practitioners' written narrative recordings. The more direct means are almost invariably superior, given the additional sources of error inherent in narrative although it may be necessary to use the latter in ex post facto studies.

The most important limitation of the practitioner as a source of outcome data is probably bias resulting from her involvement in the intervention. Artisans are seldom considered to be the best judges of their own work. Even if they attempt to be strictly honest in their appraisals, they may be inclined to give more weight to positive changes than an objective observer might; on the other hand, their perceptions may be influenced by self-critical tendencies, with the result that gains others may see are downplayed. Since it is impossible to predict the amount or direction of these biases, one can only place a large question mark alongside the outcome data obtained from the practitioner.

Another limitation grows out of difficulties in training practitioners to apply criteria developed to assess change. Practitioners may have their own notions about what constitutes improvement, goal attainment, and the like, which they may find difficult to give up and which may vary considerably from one practitioner to the next. Moreover, the time needed to train practitioners to view change in some standard manner may be lacking. Practitioners may then be given crudely defined scales or other instruments in the naive hope that their judgments will be based on common standards. Like judges and coders, practitioners need to be given well-developed instruments and to be trained in their use.

Finally, data supplied by the practitioner are limited by her own knowledge of the client and his situation. This knowledge may be highly selective, particularly if it is limited to what clients have discussed in clinical interviews. Although clients may be more open with their practitioners than with research interviewers, what the clients reveal to their helpers can still be partial and distorted. Practitioners are in a better position if they have had the opportunity to obtain information about the client from a variety of sources, including observation of the client in interaction with others.

Collaterals Outcome data may be obtained from persons involved in a case—relatives, teachers, houseparents, and so forth—who have firsthand knowledge of the client. The idea can be extended to include persons (sometimes called "informants"or significant others) who know the client but who may not have any connection with the case; for example, the client may be asked to nominate a friend to serve this role (Sloane et al. 1975).

Since they usually have less of a personal stake in the intervention process, collaterals may be more objective in their appraisal of change than either practitioner or client. They may also have access to data, such as the client's behavior in a classroom or on a ward, that is beyond the scope of the practitioner's knowledge and that the client himself for any number of reasons may not be able to recall accurately.

Standardized instruments have been developed expressly for gathering information from collaterals. One of the best known is the Katz Adjustment Scale—Relatives Form (KAS-R) (Katz and Lyerly 1963). Some instruments are designed to elicit both self-report data from the clients and data from those who know the client. The Psychological Adjustment to Illness Scale (Derogatis 1976) is an example. A review of such instruments may be found in Davidson and Davidson (1983).

While collateral data can provide an important perspective on outcome, their value in a given study needs to be carefully weighed. It cannot be assumed that collaterals have no personal investment in the outcome of intervention—in some cases they may have been involved in implementing the program; in others they may have the hope or expectation that the client will improve. On close inspection, one may find that the collateral's actual knowledge of the client may be more limited than initially assumed. For example, teachers' observations of their pupils' in-class behavior have been found to suffer from a considerable margin of error (Green and Wright 1979). And, of course, the collateral's knowledge of the client is invariably confined to only certain aspects of the client's functioning. It may be even more difficult to orient collaterals than practitioners to criteria for assessing outcome since, among other reasons, there are usually more of the former. Consequently, collaterals can probably be best used if emphasis is placed on specific data pertaining to the client rather than on their global judgments about change, although these judgments may be of interest as indicators of how the results of the program are perceived by others.

Recorded Information Various kinds of recorded information (available data) about the client—grades, contacts with police, admissions and discharges from institutions, and so forth—may be used as the basis of outcome measures. These data, which are usually collected by persons who are not a part of the intervention program, have the advantage of being free from bias resulting from case involvement. (Routine case information recorded by practitioners and collaterals would be exceptions if included here.) Moreover, they are the best, and often the only, source of data pertaining to contacts and status changes with human service organizations—hospitals, welfare departments, correctional facilities, and the like.

As Shyne (1975) points out, a first consideration in use of recorded information is its "consistent availability." Data records may contain omissions, and official criteria used for defining categories of interest—such as what constitutes a police contact or job placement—may vary over time. She wisely suggests that the investigator spotcheck recorded information before deciding to use it.

It is also important to determine how such data were obtained, by whom, and under what instructions and what conditions. One can then indicate possible sourses of bias or inaccuracy in the data. In other words, the data collection processes used to produce the information need to be looked upon in the same critical light as one would regard any method of data collection used in a study. In this respect, assessments of data quality by staff who collect and use the information may be quite instructive. The error of assuming that records labeled "official" are thereby accurate should be avoided at all costs.

Since available data generally take some standard form—occurrence of police contacts, rehospitalizations, and the like—the researcher needs to determine if the data provide reasonable indicators of outcome for the usual case in the program to be evaluated. An aftercare program may provide useful services to patients while they are in the community but may not be really designed to avoid rehospitalization. In some cases, the program may, with good reason, be instrumental in bringing about a patient's readmission.

For this reason and others, available data can often be misleading if used in an undiscriminating way. Thus the frequency of police contacts, school disciplinary reports, infractions of housing project rules, and the like, may give a false picture unless some measure of "severity" is obtained. As Berleman has commented in respect to one such indicator, "to accept only the frequency of [school] disciplinary contacts without reference to the severity of those contacts means that 'chewing gum and eating candy' is indistinguishable from 'breaking or damaging school property' " (1976:173).

Research Judges and Expert Observers Researchers play an intermediary role in the use of any source of data. Usually this role is limited to collecting data by means of observation codes, interview schedules, or other devices in which the researchers' own interpretations of the data are minimized. In this capacity, the researcher serves as a channel, albeit an imperfect one, for conveying information from the source. A researcher can be considered a data source in her own right, however, if she is expected to make use of a high degree of judgment in her assessments of the data. The product is a measure of change based on the researcher's judgment. In general, research judges make judgments about raw data supplied by a variety of sources—clients, practitioners, recorded information, and the like. The same function is sometimes performed by persons designated as coders and analysts. We use the term *judge* as a generic designation for any person responsible for making relatively complex judgments about previously collected data. One use of judges in measuring change was considered in the previous section.

When judges are used as sources of data, one places confidence in the judge's capacities to process and organize complex data and to produce measurements of acceptable reliability and validity (Shyne 1959). To help ensure that this confidence is warranted, judges may have to meet various requirements. For example, to qualify as judges, persons may need to have professional credentials or credentials plus practice experience. Special training (sometimes quite extensive) in the judgment tasks is usually needed.

Qualifications and training requirements vary considerably, however. Highly structured judgment tasks in which rules for making judgments are explicit may not require professional credentials; for example, graduate social work students may be used. Training time may be confined to a few hours if the judgment tasks are highly structured and limited. In some cases judge training and instrument development may take place simultaneously; judgment criteria are developed by having judges review raw data, make judgments about them, and write out the criteria they use. Differences in judgments and criteria are discussed in group meetings and the discussions are used as a basis for redrafts of the instrument. This process may be quite time conuming.

Regardless of the initial shape of the instrument, training is usually continued until judges have reached an acceptable level of reliability in trial applications of the judging instrument (see chapter 8). If an adequate reliability level cannot be reached, the instrument may need to be revised or an alternative means of measurement developed.

In addition to making judgments based on already collected data, researchers may make judgments about data they themselves collect through observation, interviews, and so forth. Although the term judge is sometimes extended to describe this role, we prefer "expert observer" (Auerbach 1983), a designation which suggests that the researcher is functioning both as a data collector (observer) and judge (expert). The usual instrument used by expert observers is some form of assessment interview, as discussed in the preceding chapter. The interview generates data which the observer uses as a basis for ratings or other judgments concerning functioning, change, and so on. Several standardized interview schedules have been developed, as previously noted (page 296). Risks inherent in placing faith in the skills and knowledge of the expert observer can be offset by having the expert tape record interviews and having judges make independent ratings from the tapes.

Problems of Choice As a general principle of outcome measurement, one wishes to obtain, whenever possible, multiple readings of change. This principle applies to selecting sources of data.

As a rule, the client should be, we think, the primary data source. Ideally, there should be data, such as observational measures, that are not dependent on the client's recall or evaluation, but they should be combined with data from the client's own perspective. When service involves multiple clients, such as family treatment, data should be supplied by different members of the system, independently if possible.

Use of data from collaterals or available data should be governed by the availability of collaterals or records capable of generating accurate and pertinent assessments of change. The need for such data becomes accentuated when one must rely on the client's self-report, and particularly when there is reason to doubt the credibility of the client's own account. Data from practitioners are readily obtainable and should be secured as a matter of course though they may be given less weight than data from other sources. While costly, judges and research observers can be used to advantage when outcome criteria and presumed changes relate to complex, diverse, and subtle phenomena.

Standardization-Individuation

Instruments vary in the extent to which they can be adapted to fit the particular characteristics of the individual case. At one extreme, an instrument may be designed to be constant in form, content, and application procedures across all cases; at the other, an instrument can be constructed to fit the requirements of a particular case and may have no life beyond that case. These extremes represent ends of a standardization-individuation continuum that, as we shall show, is of considerable importance in measurement of outcome.

Standardized Instruments A standardized instrument is one that exposes different subjects to the same test stimuli, attempts to elicit the same kind of information from each subject through fixed-alternative items, and uses the same set of procedures for processing and interpreting the information. A researcher may develop her own standardized instrument for a given project or make use of existing instruments constructed to measure a particular kind of phenomenon—depression, self-concept, family interaction, and so on. Reviews of standardized instruments that can be used to measure change associated with psychotherapy and other forms of interpersonal treatment may be found in Lambert, Christensen, and DeJulio (1983); Ciminero, Calhoun and Adams (1986); see also chapter 12.

The primary rationale for using a standardized instrument in the study of outcome is to enhance comparability of measurement across client systems. Measurement bias or other forms of error resulting from variation in instrument items, testing procedures, and so on, are, at least in theory, reduced. Standardized instruments have additional advantages of efficiency and economy since they require no variation from case to case. If the outcomes of an intervention program can be appropriately assessed by an available instrument, additional advantages accrue. Usually such instruments have been developed systematically by knowledgeable researchers. An available instrument may already have been used in a number of studies so that a good deal of evidence on its validity, reliability, and other measurement properties may have gathered. Normative data in the form of scores of various groups of subjects may exist. These norms can be used for comparative purposes. Thus, if the Beck Depression Inventory (Beck 1967) were used to evaluate the outcome of a program for depressed clients, a researcher could assess the severity of the degree of depression in her sample of clients before intervention by comparing initial scores of her clients to the inventory scores of a large number of depressed persons. These normative data provide "benchmark" scores indicating different degrees of depression, scores that have been validated against the diagnostic judgments of psychiatrists. Moreover, the gains made by depressed clients in her study could be compared with gains, again as measured by the Inventory, of depressives treated in other programs.

The advantages of standardized instruments in the measurement of outcome are counterbalanced by a number of limitations. Although a standardized instrument exposes different subjects to the same stimuli, this constancy of exposure does not guarantee that the stimuli will be interpreted in the same fashion or responded to with the same degree of accuracy. Thus subjects may vary considerably in the meanings they ascribe to "feeling blue," in how well they recall such episodes, their frankness in admitting to such feelings, and so on. Given such variation, one cannot assert that two clients with the same "depression score" are equally depressed. A high degree of equivalence betwween scores and phenomena measured occurs only when an instrument is responded to in a constant fashion, as would be the case in determining the weight of subjects with a set of accurate scales. When instrument stimuli evoke variable responses, as is the case with most standardized instruments used to measure the outcome of social work intervention, the relations of scores to phenomena measured must be assessed, and then only in approximate fashion, through complex validation procedures (see chapter 8 and later here).

Since items on a standardized instrument must be cast in general terms to be applicable to a wide range of subjects and their circumstances, they are often global and vague (I feel at ease with other people: never ___; sometimes ___; usually ___; always ___). Not only do these items fail to provide much precise reliable information, but also their lack of specificity makes it easy for clients to exercise their biases.

Unwanted variability or error of the kind considered thus far applies, for the most part, to client self-report instruments, which, of course, make up the bulk of standardized instruments. Standardized measures based on direct observations of behavior such as the Bales Inventory (1950) would not have this particular problem but would be subject to error resulting from observer variation.

Even if they measure what they purport to measure reasonably well, standardized instruments are usually limited in their sensitivity to the range and detail of particular changes that may occur in the client systems under study. These limitations are most obvious when an instrument measures change in only one kind of target in a project that may be addressed to a variety of targets. Thus an instrument designed to measure change in adolescents' self-concept may frequently miss the mark if self-concept is not an issue in a large proportion of cases in a program being evaluated. This lack of case relevance can result in an underestimation of intervention effects. To continue with the example, changes in self-concept may occur as a result of intervention but in not enough cases to show a statistically significant result since cases in which it was not a target may show no change.

Standardized instruments may be relevant in a general way to the change target but still not sensitive enough to capture the relatively subtle (but meaningful) changes that may result from intervention. A client may label himself (correctly) as "shy" on a standardized instrument before and after intervention but still may have made significant improvement in his ability to initiate social relationships. More generally, the change experienced by a client system may be characterized by a particular configuration that a standardized instrument or even several may not detect. Certain problems are handled a little better—there is some increase in self-confidence, conflicts in family relationships have lessened somewhat. It all may add up to substantial improvement, but no one piece of the pattern is striking enough to be detected by the instrument.

The advantages of existing (as opposed to *ad hoc*) standardized instruments have been noted, but we would like to convey some specific words of caution about them. An author of a published instrument may report an impressive amount of data on the instrument's reliability, validity, factor structure, and so on, and such data may be, of course, quite useful in evaluating the instrument. Because the instrument is the author's own, the data may be presented in a favorable light and may need to be examined critically. It may pay to search the literature for a more objective appraisal of the instrument or to consult the most recent edition of the *Mental Measurements Yearbook* (Buros 1978), a reference work that publishes reviews of a large number of printed instruments.

Particular attention needs to be given to validity data. It is a common error to regard an instrument as "having been validated" simply because there is evidence that it can discriminate between groups of subjects, for example, between psychiatric patients and normals, or that it correlates with other measures, such as other standardized tests or ratings of clinicians. To reiterate a point made earlier (chapter 9), instrument validity is always a matter of degree and seldom "established" in any final sense. Validity data must be related to the purposes the potential user has in mind. For example, an instrument to measure perceived "powerlessness" may have shown predicted differences between middle- and lower-class subjects, but this does not mean that it can discriminate between groups of lower-class subjects. If an investigator uses the instrument to test the effects of a program with an exclusively lower-class clientele, she does so on faith that it can detect meaningful differences within such a clientele. Moreover, validity evidence may be based on correlations with similar instruments, which may share similar biases, or the evidence may rest on statistically significant but essentially weak associations with criterion variables.

The researcher needs further to examine the fit between items used in the instrument and the subjects in her own study. A test of assertiveness that contains youth-oriented items, with references to dating and the like, may not provide a meaningful measure of this variable in a group of senior citizens. Similarly, normative data compiled by the instrument developers must be examined for relevance to the sample at hand.

Particularized Instruments   An instrument can be said to be particularized if it enables a researcher to accomplish two goals: 1) to adapt the change measure to the individual characteristics of the case and 2) to rate or score particularized measures of changes on some common scale of measurement. As this definition suggests, particularized instruments attempt to achieve greater sensitivity to idiosyncratic patterns of change but at the same time to permit the amount of change to be compared across cases.

A particularized instrument usually asks in effect "How much change or progress has occurred in respect to the particular problems, symptoms, goals, and the like, that are at issue in the case at hand?" For example, in an approach used by one of the authors (Reid 1978), target problems in a case were identified and data on the status of the problems were obtained prior to and following either task-centered intervention or a minimal intervention control. Judges reviewed the two sets of data on problem status (without knowing what kind of intervention had taken place in the interim) and made judgments about the amount of change that had occurred in each problem. The judges used scales to rate problem change. If a couple had, say, five quarrels during the preintervention period but only three quarrels during a postintervention period of comparable time, the judge (following guidelines for assessing change in problem frequency) would rate the problem of quarreling as showing a "moderate" degree of alleviation on a scale to measure problem change. Such an approach is more sensitive than a standardized instrument to the specific and often modest changes that might be associated with intervention but still provides a basis for across-case comparison.

Similar to the problem change measure just described is the use of "target complaints" to evaluate changes in adult outpatients in mental health settings. (Battle et al. 1966; Mintz and Kiesler 1982). Perhaps the best known and most widely used of the particularized approaches is Goal Attainment Scaling (Kiresuk and Sherman 1968; Kiresuk 1973; Kiresuk and Lund 1977). (See also chapter 11.) In Goal Attainment Scaling, outcome is evaluated in terms of progress clients have made toward goals established at the beginning of service. Progress (or regression) is assessed on five point scales by practitioners, judges, collaterals, or the clients themselves. The scales may be further refined by weighting the goals according to their importance. An excellent review of both target complaint measures and Goal Attainment Scaling may be found in Mintz and Kiesler (1982).

The major limitation of particularized instruments is the reciprocal of its strength. If each case is measured on its own terms, there are obvious problems in making comparisons among cases or in giving any precise interpretation to ratings on the common scales used to record amounts of change. Thus the problems in one case may be trivial in comparison to those in another case. A rating of "slight improvement" made for both cases would obviously have much different meanings. And, of course, statements about slight or considerable amounts of problem alleviation, goal attainment, symptom relief, and so on, say little about what in fact was changed. As we have seen, standardized instruments are also affected by this kind of limitation; it becomes more of a factor, however, in particularized approaches to outcome measurement.

Ideographic Instruments An extreme of individuation is reached in the ideographic instrument, which is directed exclusively toward measurement of the phenomena in a particular case. For instance, if an intervention target in a single case study was the aggressive behavior of a particular child, an ideographic instrument might be constructed to measure that child's aggression. Aggression would be operationally defined in relation to the child's behavior, and observation codes or other means of measuring only his behavior would be developed. By definition, ideographic instruments are limited to single case studies and are widely used in that form of research. It is possible, of course, to use standardized or particularized instruments in single case studies.

In a study of intervention in the single case, the ideographic instrument can yield specific evidence of change directly related to the targets and purpose of the intervention. As a result, it may be possible to obtain a detailed and sensitive account of change that might never emerge if a standardized measure were used. For example, in one case a mother's communication with her ten-year-old son was characterized by an unusually heavy use of "rhetorical" questions containing abstract terms ("Don't you realize what will happen to you if you go on behaving this way?"). Such questions, which had obviously hostile overtones, seemed confusing to the child, who seldom answered them. Now if an attempt were made to improve the mother's communication with her son, an obvious target would be her use of "rhetorical" questions. A standardized instrument to measure "clarity" in communication (Riskin 1971) might have been used and might have detected change in the mother's communication with her child. An ideographic instrument designed to measure change in use of rhetorical questions would be more closely fitted to that target and would be more likely to detect changes relating to it. In any case, there would be interest in knowing how that particular target might be affected by intervention—knowledge that could only be gained through an ideographic instrument.

While an ideographic instrument may yield highly informative data about a particular case, its usefulness is limited to that case, an obvious drawback. Moreover, an ideographic instrument provides no information about where a case might stand in relation to norms. Normative data are not essential if one wishes only to determine whether or not change has occurred in the case but are useful in assessing the significance of the change. For example, it may be helpful to learn that a child completing an individualized remedial reading program has improved one grade level, as measured by a standardized reading test.

Decisions about Type of Instrument The ideal outcome instrument would be standard in form to ensure uniform interpretation of scores and comparisons with other data but at the same time sensitive to change resulting from intervention. In the area of psychotherapy outcome research, an attempt has been made to identify a "core battery" of such instruments that might attain this ideal (Waskow and Parloff 1975; Kolotkin and Johnson 1983). But, as Bergin and Lambert have observed, "diverse treatment samples, differences concerning valued directions of change, as well as theoretical and conceptual preferences, all make the possibility of an effectively applied, single case battery doubtful" (1978:176). The possibility is much more doubtful in the more diverse arena of social work intervention.

Whether standardized instruments are used in combination or singly, their overall utility in outcome measurement is rather limited in our judgment. Bergin, Shapiro, and Lambert's conclusion that particularized instruments may be more useful than standardized approaches in study of the outcomes of psychotherapy applies with even greater force to outcome research in social work. As they comment, "trends to specify and to individually tailor criteria offer a strong antidote to the vague and unimpressive conclusions so often reported in the outcome literature" (1986:191).

Standardized instruments may be useful, particularly when the targets of intervention are relatively homogeneous. For example, if a program were directed exclusively at helping mentally retarded persons find employment, uniform questions about type of work found, wages, job satisfaction, and so forth, would make sense. If targets are relatively homogeneous and if there is an existing standardized instrument designed to measure change in that type of target, then the advantages in using a well-developed instrument may be compelling.

When change targets are heterogeneous, as is often the case, a standardized instrument may be too "blunt" to detect the variety of changes at issue. A particularized instrument may be needed. There may be little doubt on this score when targets are obviously heterogeneous, as would be the case in a counseling program addressed to a variety of psychosocial problems. The matter is not as clear when targets fall within the same class but still reflect considerable diversity. Marital problems are a case in point. In one situation, a problem may center on sexual difficulties; in another, on quarrels about money. A particularized instrument may be preferable to a standardized measure.

A common and reasonable strategy is to use a combination of standardized and particularized instruments, particularly when targets, as in the example given, have some degree of similarity and standardized instruments to measure them are available.

There may also be advantages in using standardized instruments in single case studies in which ideographic instruments generate the major measure of change. If a standardized instrument appropriate to the target and change goals can be found, its use may help locate the case in relation to other cases of that type.

VARIATION IN OUTCOME MEASURES

We have shown how measurement can vary in terms of data source and degree of individuation. We now turn to problems that arise from the inevitable variation when multiple measures are obtained from multiple sources.

The researcher hopes, of course, that use of different measures of outcome will yield similar results, but unfortunately her hopes are frequently, if not usually, unrealized. In a review of forty-four studies in which outcome data were derived from different sources (client, intervener, judge), Kyte (1980) found only three that reported uniformly high correlations (correlations exceeding .65); nine reported moderate levels of agreement ($r = .35-.65$); in twelve studies agreement was generally low (correlations below .35). The remaining (twenty) studies revealed a broader span of correlations, usually in the low to moderate range. Such patterns are often found in outcome studies, a phenomenon referred to as lack of "intersource consensus" (Lambert 1983, Bostwick and Bostwick 1987).

The magnitude of correlation between scores of different instruments tells only part of the story, however. A correlation may be relatively high, but still one source may be consistently higher or lower than another. The following hypothetical data illustrate the point:

Outcome Ratings by Source

Case	Practitioner	Judge
A	5	4
B	6	5
C	7	6

The correlation in this series is at a maximum ($r = 1.00$), indicating that the scores covary perfectly but at the same time one source, the practitioner, is consistently higher than the judge. A pattern similar to the one illustrated was in fact found for one of the studies in the Kyte review that reported a high level of intersource agreement (Reid 1975). Analysis of outcome studies from this perspective has revealed abundant evidence of systematic differences among sources in *level* of outcome assessment (Kyte 1980). Perhaps the most consistent pattern is the apparent tendency of practitioners to rate outcome more *conservatively* than their clients.

When different outcome measures are well correlated and do not show systematic discrepancies in level, one has reasonable grounds for assuming that the scores are measuring the same phenomenon in a similar manner and hence one can combine the scores through averaging or other means. When variation among measures is a significant factor, as is more often the case, a simple aggregation of data may present a misleading picture. Results from different instruments or sources are best presented separately. Disparate measures should be combined only if the results of separate analyses have been made clear.

Variation among data sources in assessments of the outcome of services is of course much more than a technical problem of measurement. To put it simply, different sources of effectiveness data—practitioners, clients, collaterals, research observers, and so on—may have differing conceptions of what is effective. The same applies to different actors who make judgments about these data—managers, staffs of funding agencies, and the like.

Much of this divergence appears due to value differences (Strupp and Hadley 1977; Bergin 1980). The notion of effectiveness inevitably incorporates a value component. In the language of the human services, to be effective means to achieve a desired effect—"intended goals" to use Bielawski and Epstein's terms (1984). A program that is designed to reduce delinquency but manages to increase it would not be seen as effective, though we may speak of its negative *effects*.

It does not stretch one's imagination to see how value differences can complicate assessment of effectiveness. For example, a divorce as an outcome of marital counseling may be viewed as the optimal solution by the husband, a disaster by his wife, as deplorable by the religious organization that funds the agency, and as regrettable but necessary by the practitioner. In addition different sources have access to different information. Clients know details of life at home that practitioners do not have; practitioners may have information about norms of family life that clients lack, and so on. While such disparity is often viewed as a measurement issue, its roots lie in conceptual and value orientations. These differences are not always reconcilable or averageable.

Researchers can handle such discrepancies by reporting them and discussing reasons for the variation. For program people the task is not confined to paper. Programs may need to be restructured to accommodate different value positions; often choices must be made between which goals to emphasize or pursue. For example, an adoption program for older emotionally disturbed children was effective from an agency perspective since "good homes" were found for large numbers of children who might otherwise have had to remain in an institutional setting (Reid, Kagan, Kaminsky, and Helmer 1987). However, its effectiveness was questioned by many of the adopting parents who found raising the children more then they had bargained for. "How can the needs of such children be squared with those of the adopting parents?," was one of a number of issues raised by divergences in point of view about the effectiveness of the program.

CHAPTER 14

STUDY OF INTERVENTION CHARACTERISTICS

As observed in chapter 7, a study of the effects of intervention, whether the study is experimental or naturalistic, is based on the assumption that one can determine the nature of the intervention tested. Because social work interventions tend to be relatively complex, a systematic study of the nature of the intervention itself is usually needed. At a minimum, such an investigation should yield a reasonably accurate picture of the intervention or interventions tested. It is also desirable to determine how different types of intervention used may correlate with outcome.

Study of the characteristics and correlates of intervention need not, of course, occur as a part of an outcome study. For example, exploratory or descriptive studies may be conducted to formulate or depict interventions in models of practice, programs, settings, and so forth.

The need for basic descriptive data on the nature of social work intervention has long been recognized, and there have been repeated calls for research addressed to this need (Briar 1974). Whether one is attempting to teach intervention to students or to interpret social work to funding sources, empirically based knowledge of what social workers do is of vital importance.

To questions of "What does intervention look like?" can be added questions of "What makes it look that way?" How do experience and training influence practice? How are social workers' activities shaped by their diagnostic assessments? And so on.

The considerable variety of forms that intervention may assume makes it difficult to generalize about research approaches. Ideally, generalizations would need to span a range in which one finds disparate activities such as interview techniques, social action, and foster care. In the review that follows, we continue our focus on activities involving direct work with clients but at points extend our discussion to measurement of other facets of social work practice.

Practitioner Report Data

Traditionally, investigations of social work intervention have relied on practitioner reports of their activities. Whatever variety they assume—several of the more important are considered here—practitioner reports may be considered to be a form of participant observation data with its particular combination of strengths (observations based on firsthand knowledge) and weaknesses (biases resulting from personal involvement) (See chapters 4 and 10; also see the final section of the present chapter.)

Discursive Narratives In considering practitioner reports, an obvious starting point is the large volume of data that practitioners themselves accumulate as part of their routine recording procedures. The data are readily available and have cost the researcher nothing to collect. Most service programs use the discursive narrative case record, which is likely to be a highly selective chronology of what has taken place in the case. Samples of case records (or samples from records) may be used as a basis for studying practitioner activity or other forms of intervention. Interventions may be coded with some form of a content analysis instrument (see later discussion) or reviewed in a more impressionistic fashion.

The limitations of narrative case records as a basis for measurement of intervention are well known. Incompleteness, inaccuracy, selectivity, and bias in recording are typical problems. Their summarized and uneven character usually precludes any sort of fine-grained analysis of what practitioners do.

Still, narrative records have their uses in research. They provide an excellent means of gaining an overview of the activities of a complex program. Spotiness in recording is not a problem if one wishes only to acquire a sense of the type and range of interventions taking place. In this respect, the narrative record gives one a sense of the configuration of program activities that one might not obtain from data in more atomistic form, such as the number of different types of specific interventions used. And often, of course, narrative records are the only data on intervention that can be secured, as is the case when the decision to evaluatae a program is not made until the program is well along or completed. Moreover, they may be the only source of data in historical studies of intervention.

Systematic Recording The utility of the case record can be increased manyfold if provisions are made to build in systematic recording procedures. The resulting record can serve multiple purposes: clinical, supervisory, administrative, and research. A number of formats for systematic case recordings have been developed (Weed 1969; Kane 1974; Videka-Sherman and Reid 1982; Kagle 1984). These formats require the collection of specific kinds of case data organized under predetermined headings. Omissions of key data are less likely to occur and can be readily spotted (and possibly corrected) when they do. Moreover, the organization of the data facilitates coding and analysis.

For example the Structured Clinical Record (Videka-Sherman and Reid 1982) provides a means of tracking problems, goals, interventions, and outcomes in a case regardless of the service model employed. Kagle (1984) describes two useful systematic recording devices: the Chronolog, which lists activities with clients in a chronological order and the Progress Log, which records specific attitudes, feelings, or actions that represent the client's response to service." (1984:48) More highly structured forms may consist of precoded items, such as checklists (Seaberg 1965, 1970).

Structured recording can be done on a routine basis. If so, the resulting data can be incorporated as part of an agency information system. Recording of this kind can, of course, be limited to special projects. For example, Biddle and Biddle (1965) used a method of systematic recording for translating the field notes of community workers into coherent records of the community development process. Their goal was to use these data as the basis for theory development. Participants in a community development effort would periodically transcribe their notes onto structured recording forms. These individual forms were then analyzed to identify the processes used to achieve certain goals.

Critical Incidents and Events The researcher may wish to concentrate on specific types of intervention that may occur now and then in the course of complex practice situations and to have reasonably full descriptions of those interventions. If so, she may ask practitioners to record incidents of the occurrence of the intervention of interest. The incidents (which may be recorded on cards) may describe what the practitioner did and possibly her perception of the immediate consequences of her actions. In this way, practitioners might record, for example, the substance of contacts with physicians or attempts to use verbal limit setting with acting-out youngsters. When actions reported can be categorized as effective or ineffective, the method may be considered to be an application of the critical incident technique as developed by Flanagan (1954). (To be "critical" in Flanagan's terms an incident should have clear-cut consequences.) In a study by Thomas et al. (1987), practitioners applying a new model of case management were asked to record incidents involving "instances of failure to carry out a procedure because it is incomplete, not specific, or both" (p. 47). Analysis of the incidents enabled the researchers to make judgments about how well the procedures were described and to identify areas that needed attention.

In a study of intervention processes, a critical incident can be seen as a type of "event." Events can comprise a range of episodes, occurrences, etc., of interest to the researchers. For example, Mahrer and Nadler (1986) review use of "good moments," which they define as "epochs of a few seconds or more wherein the client is manifesting therapeutic process, movement, improvement, progress, or change" (p. 14). Although their compilation of types of good moments emphasizes client rather than practitioner behavior, the focus is on specific occurrences within an intervention context, such as "provision of personal material about self and/or interpersonal relationships or expression of insight-understanding." Analysis of such episodes is designed to illuminate the practitioner-client interactions that give rise to them and hence can be seen as integral to the study of intervention characteristics. In fact, study of specific client behaviors in relation to specific practitioner activities enables researchers to break down the artificial distinctions between the "processes" and "outcomes" of intervention. Reid (1985) and Davis and Reid (1988) use a broader definition of event ("an informative event") to include both practitioner and client actions. Recent examples of use of events in intervention research can be found in Rice and Greenberg (1984) and Yalom (1985).

Interviews and Questionnaires Interviews and questionnaires provide additional means of securing practitioner self-report data on intervention. Semistructured interviews are particularly useful when one wishes to obtain exploratory data on the range and variety of interventions the practitioner might use, or if other forms of data collection, such as written or tape recordings, are not feasible or would not give an adequate accounting of the practitioner's work. For example, Rooney (1985) interviewed 28 practitioners six months after they had received training in task-centered practice to determine the extent and variety of use of task-centered methods in the post-training period. Also, an interview may be the method of choice if one wishes to investigate the practitioner's rationale for her behavior or to elicit the practitioner's "expert" knowledge. Thus, Fortune (1985) interviewed practitioners about criteria they used in termination. Practitioners can be interviewed about their practice in general as in the Fortune study, or about specific cases they have dealt with, as did Abramson (1985) in her study of hospital discharge planning.

If a researcher wishes to obtain a picture of the activities of a large number of practitioners, a self-administered questionnaire may be the instrument of choice. In one study illustrating this methodology, Cocozzelli (1987) compared the theoretical orientation and the self-reported practice behavior of 199 clinical social workers through questionnaires distributed through agency administration. In another investigation, Teare (1979) studied tasks of workers in a large state public welfare agency by means of an original self-administered instrument (the Job Analysis Survey).

The Client's Impressions

The client himself may provide data on intervention processes, usually by means of a questionnaire or an interview. A frequent purpose in collecting such data is to determine the client's subjective perception of his service experience. It may be assumed that clients are unable to give an adequate accounting of complex and technical interventions, but there may be interest in ascertaining the client's view of them for its own sake. In order for certain interventions to work, the client may need to have a cognitive grasp of what is going on or at least the interventions may need to make sense to him. For example, it has been found (Mayer and Timms 1970) that working-class clients may be mystified by insight-oriented counseling, particularly when they have sought help for concrete problems. In another instance, clients in a work-training program were found to have misinterpreted a monetary incentive for participation as a training allowance (Smith and O'Brien 1978). The identification of these misperceptions can serve as a basis for orienting clients or for providing them with a different type of service altogether. Clients may be also used as sources of descriptive data on program operations, particularly if other sources are unavailable or inadequate. For some services—homemakers, for example—clients may be in a better position to describe concrete aspects of the service than anyone else.

Direct and Electronic Observation

Whether obtained from practitioner or client, recollections of intervention characteristics are inherently limited: participants cannot be expected to recall the nature or sequence of complex interventions with a high degree of accuracy and, because they are emotionally involved in the process, their objectivity is always problematic. To obtain data free of these limitations, the researcher must find ways of studying practitioners in action. A principal means is through observation of actual intervention processes.

Audiotape Audiotape recording is relatively inexpensive and in most situations does not seem to engender reactive effects of any duration. Clients normally accept recording procedures. Resistance is more likely to come from practitioners, although practitioner reluctance to be taped is becoming less of a problem as tape recording is becoming more common in routine practice. Safeguards to client confidentiality can be spelled out in forms that clients approve and sign.

Audio recording works best, of course, when intervention consists of face-to-face interaction between practitioners and clients. This kind of recording encounters greater obstacles as one moves out into the community, for practitioners, collaterals, or other professionals may be reluctant to get involved in the recording process. Still, with some effort and ingenuity, a good deal of this communication, even including telephone calls, can be tape recorded. Audiotapes record, of course, only vocal communication, but some reflection will reveal that most of the significant communication events in most social work intervention are reflected in language and paralanguage, including voice expressions. To the extent that important communication processes are kinesthetic (for example, body movements and facial expressions), then audio is less useful, as might be the case in family treatment sessions involving children.

The sound quality of audiotapes is an important aspect that is frequently not thought of until the researcher, to her dismay, discovers that her precious tapes, obtained by considerable effort, are inaudible and virtually useless. It pays, literally, to have decent though not necessarily expensive equipment and to train practitioners in its use. Specifics such as testing equipment before and during the session and watching the sound level indicator should be stressed. Lapel microphones are particularly useful. If only one microphone is used, it should be carefully placed so that it picks up the voices of all participants.

Videotape Videotaping is both more expensive and intrusive. As suggested earlier, researchers should take a hard look at what its use might contribute over audio recording. When video is used, camera work becomes an important factor. One may be able to include all participants by using a fixed-camera position, but the advantages of close-ups are lost. If the camera is moved, then some selection occurs. The person operating the camera, who may be a technician, then, in effect, has a good deal of influence over which visual data are obtained.

Whatever type of tape is used, electronic recording simply reproduces the volume and complexity of the intervention processes observed. Tape simply preserves sense impressions and permits them to be repeated, which is a considerable advantage, but it does nothing to further the analytic process.

Direct Observation Research observers can observe intervention processes directly as they occur. The observers may be physically present or may watch the action through one-way mirrors. The direct observer has the simple but powerful advantage of "being there." She can take into account the full range of events that may be occurring without restrictions imposed by the reports of others or the limited scope of electronic recording (discussed above). However, direct observation of social work processes must contend with several obstacles. First, the presence of an observer may be distracting, especially in such forms of practice as individual and family treatment. (While one-way mirrors provide an answer, many facilities do not have this kind of equipment). Second, it is difficult for the observer to process the complexities of live social work intervention. Observation codes, ratings, and the like must usually be kept at a simple level. Finally, since two observers are generally involved (for reliability purposes) and often must observe on repeated occasions, logistics often become troublesome. For these reasons direct observation tends to be used to observe interventions when the observers' presence is less disruptive and when electronic recording may present problems—for example, work with client or community groups.

For example, in the St. Louis experiment discussed in chapter 11 (Feldman,

Caplinger, and Wodarski 1983), observers rated group leaders' style of method as "minimal," behavioral, or traditional. The observers (who were simultaneously observing and coding the boys' behavior) rated the leadership styles at four points during the project. Although these global ratings were simple, bias was controlled by keeping the observer "blind" as to which leadership style was supposed to be used. The resulting data were useful in interpreting the results of the experiment. Thus only a quarter of the "traditional-method" leaders were found to implement this method adequately; by contrast almost two thirds of the "behavioral-method" leaders were rated as having made adequate implementation of their method (p. 220). (The findings underscore the point made in chapter 7 about the importance of measuring service inputs in an experiment).

In this example use of direct observers and simple ratings were appropriate to the nature of the treatment, which involved the work of numerous leaders with a groups of active boys in a context in which the observers' presence was probably not a significant distraction. When a more fine-grained analysis is desirable or when an observer's presence would be intrusive, researchers are likely to turn to indirect (electronic) means of recording.

Analysis and Instrumentation   Audio or video tapes of intervention with typescripts made from them, provide an abundance of data that can be examined through a variety of methods—ratings, event and time interval coding (chapter 11), qualitative analysis, and so on. A common methodology involves the construction and application of coding schemes. In the context of communications data of this kind this methodology is frequently referred to as *content analysis* (Krippendorf 1980; Fortune 1981; Allen-Meares 1984).

A principal type of instrument used in content analysis is referred to as an intervention typology. Such a system is designed to classify (code) discrete intervention methods, such as facilitating negotiation, providing reinforcement, or advocacy. Most research on intervention characteristics in social work has concentrated on clinical interviews, and hence most available instruments reflect that emphasis. Examples of intervention typologies related to social work intervention may be found in Hollis (1972), Reid (1978), and Basso (1985). A typology for counseling and psychotherapy has been developed by Hill (1986) and one for family therapy, by Pinsof (1986). Additional material on typologies, including an example of an instrument and discussion of reliability considerations may be found in Reid and Smith (1981).

Intervention typologies represent only one form of content analysis. Almost any recordable aspect of practitioner intervention can be investigated through one kind of content analysis scheme or another. For example, extensive use has been made of content analysis to study practitioner skills and attributes such as empathic responding, expressiveness, and warmth (Rice and Greenberg 1984; Orlinsky and Howard 1986).

In recent years considerable attention has been given to the processes of change occurring within courses of intervention, including both practitioner and client activities as well as evidence of immediate change that may result. This new approach has been referred to as "change process research" (Greenberg 1986:4). In the words of Elliot, this research strategy is a "discovery-oriented approach to significant change events" (1984:249). The emphasis is on study of the link between specific treatment activities and specific *immediate* outcomes—for example, "change that is evident in the session" (Greenberg 1986:4). This is in contrast to the conventional practice of linking gross measures of intervention to gross measures of outcome at termination. Further an attempt is made to isolate key events *in context* on the assumption that certain episodes of process may be critical to change while others may not be. In this strategy one rejects the "myth of homogeneous process" (Rice and Greenberg 1984) in which a given unit in a process category is seen as more or less equal to any other unit in that category regardless of the context in which it occurs. Thus as Elliot observes, research on "empathy in which empathy ratings are averaged across interviews or cases are insensitive to the possibility that empathy may play a crucial role only at certain moments in a helping relationship—for example, following a new and highly intimate disclosure" (1983:114). This is not to dismiss the sizeable body of research based on the assumption of homogeneous process but rather to say it has left untouched important areas of inquiry that may be fruitfully pursued by intensive study of change events in context.

In this evolving approach, change events are investigated in depth in relatively small units of process—single sessions in small groups of cases (Henry, Schacht, and Strupp 1986), single cases (Hill, Carter, and O'Farrell 1983); Reid and Davis (1987); Davis and Reid (1988) and single episodes within sessions (Elliot 1983a). Both quantitative and qualitative methods may be employed, often in combination. For example, Elliot (1983a) used a mix of seventeen quantitative and qualitative techniques in his analysis of a single psychotherapeutic episode. Such mixes can combine the capacity of quantitative measures to reveal statistical patterns in objective communication data with the ability of qualitative analysis to depict contextual features and capture the more elusive complexities of process.

In change process research both practitioner and client behavior may fall within the focus of study on grounds that the intervention process is not simply a function of the practitioner's methods but is rather part of a system that comprises the practitioner, clients, and often others (Gurman, Kniskern, and Pinsof 1986). Some studies may focus on the interrelationship of client and practitioner activities (Reid and Strother in press); others may concentrate on the client's behavior (Sherman and Skinner in press).

Intervention Analogs

The study of social work intervention as it actually occurs must contend with a number of obstacles. Investigation of practitioner behavior in detail can be a time-consuming and costly business. The complexities of intervention are difficult to sort out, as well as the multitude of variables that affect what the practitioner does. Moreover, it may not be feasible to control for certain variables that may affect the practitioner's actions. Accordingly, if an investigator were interested in determining the effffects of the client's race (black versus white) on how clients were treated, a design executed in the field would ideally require that a sizable group of practitioners treat black and white clients matched on all other influential variables.

One answer to such problems is to study intervention through use of practice analogs that the investigator can shape according to the specific purposes of the study. Thus, two case summaries can be developed, identical in all respects except that in one the client is presented as white and in the other as black. These different "cases" can be randomly assigned to practitioner-subjects who are then asked to assess and treat them as they would in their practice. The influence of the independent variable, the race of the client, can be discerned from differences in practitioner responses to different forms of the case.

Types of Analog Two major types of analog are used to study practitioner behavior. The most common variety consists of some form of stimulus material, such as a case summary, a film, or videotape of an interview, to which practitioner-subjects are asked to respond as they would if confronted with such a situation in their practice. Since subjects are presented with a stimulus situation to which they then respond, the term *stimulus-response analog* seems appropriate to describe this type. In an early example (Strupp

1958), clinicians, including social workers, viewed a film of an actual interview that was stopped periodically; the clinicians were then asked to write out how they would respond to the "client" if they were conducting the interview. In a study of decision making in an adoption agency (Brieland 1959), child welfare workers listened to audiotape recordings of interviews with prospective adoptive parents and then indicated, among other things, whether or not they would recommend that the parents be given a child for adoption. In a study of practitioner empathy (Jackson 1987) practitioners responded to filmed vignettes depicting natural interactions between people. A number of studies in social work have used "paper" analogs in which stimulus material takes the form of written case summaries (Reid 1967; Miller 1974; Dailey 1980; Davis and Carlson 1981; Gingerich, Kleczewski, and Kirk 1982; and Franklin 1985).

An example of a paper stimulus-response analog is provided by Miller (1974), who studied the influence of patient sex on diagnosis and treatment. A sample of sixty-seven social workers, psychologists, and psychiatrists from a teaching hospital was selected. Two forms of analog were distributed to the sample at random; in one form the subject was presented as female and in the other as male. The subject, a young adult who had sought help for psychosomatic complaints and mild depression, was characterized in the case summary as passive, as an excerpt from the male form of the analog illustrates.

Presenting Problem

Mr. S. explained that the onset of his headaches began a few months ago. (There was nothing revealed in his history to explain this.) He would get the headaches following "a hard day at work." He finds it increasingly hard to get up in the morning to go to work and has been feeling "down in the dumps" for a few months. He works at an employment agency as an employment counselor. Mr. S. states that on the whole he likes his job, but it involves a lot of "hassles and petty haggling," which he doesn't like. He thought that this was due to the fact that all the counselors worked on a commission basis. He complained about the overly "pushy" counselors at his job. He was recently offered a promotion to an administrative level but turned this down feeling that he could do a better job where he was now. He rationalized further—saying the pay was practically the same. He grinned self-consciously as he said that he thought that the "Peter Principle" would be in operation if he took the job offered. He has always done better in a job dealing directly with people and didn't really aspire to a higher position at the administrative level.

The subjects completed a series of items indicating how they would diagnose and treat the client. As predicted, subjects receiving the male form were significantly more likely to view the client's "passivity" as a central focus of treatment than subjects receiving the female form. Moreover, social workers in the sample who were given the male client were unexpectedly found to favor interpretive, insight-oriented treatment over supportive, relationship treatment; for social workers given the female client, these choices were reversed! Hence, the sex of the client was found to make a difference in treatment planning, both in expected and unexpected directions. The findings illustrate how analogs can be used to both test and develop theory about intervention—a point we return to subsequently.

The second major type of analog uses a person or interactive computer program to portray a client. Since the practitioner-subject's behavior is then studied as it occurs in interaction with "the client," this type of analog can be described as *interactive*. For example, Thomas and McLeod (1960) used an actress to portray a client in a study of caseworker performance in a public welfare setting. Although practitioners knew they were interacting with a client substitute, they did not know that the actress-client was following a memorized script in her responses. In studies of skill training, students have interviewed one another concerning minor real-life problems (Katz 1979) or have role played "clients" with more serious (but fictitious) problems (Zastrow and Navarre 1979).

Validity of Analogs   As the foregoing examples suggest, analogs provide a wide variety of ways of studying practitioner behavior under controlled conditions. Measurement of practitioner behavior can be quite rigorous. For example, response alternatives can be carefully defined and then refined through pretesting. Moreover, analogs have the advantages of economy and feasibility. One does not have to collect and analyze hours of tape recording or to make any intrusions in practice situations. All these pluses must be weighed, however, against a profound limitation, and that concerns the validity of this type of instrument.

Like any instrument, the validity of an analog can be thought of in terms of its capacity to measure what it purports to measure. Since, in the present context, an analog is viewed as a way of measuring practitioner behavior in actual practice situations, the validity of an analog must be evaluated in terms of its relation to what practitioners actually do.

In considering validity issues, we focus first on the stimulus-response analog, the type most commonly used. Like any test, an analog can be validated against some criterion measure. For an analog the criterion would be some measure of actual practitioner behavior. This kind of empirical validation has been rarely attempted with analogs, however. One reason has been that most analogs have been devised for purposes of particular studies and do not seem to be sufficiently reusable to warrant elaborate empirical validation procedures. Also it would prove quite difficult to secure the necessary measures of practitioner behavior in actual practice situations since the analogs tend to be rather specific to the kinds of case situations studied.

Usually stress is placed on content validity, which involves evaluating the analog in terms of how well its content seems to tap desired practice variables. Most of the content validity issues grow out of the artificiality of the analog situation. Whether the case takes the form of an individual client, a group, or a community, it is likely to strike the practitioner-subject as something quite different from the real thing. The information provided is limited, much more so than might be true in an actual situation, and the subject is not able to get additional information through normal processes of interaction. Variables of interest may not have the same strength on tape or on paper as they would in reality. It is one thing to react to a psychotic client in the flesh; it is quite another to react to a written description of such a client. As Fanshel (1963) has observed, subjects responding to analogs are not held accountable for their behavior in the way they would be in actual practice. In responding to analogs, practitioners have more time to think than they would in practice and as a result may be more inclined to give "textbook" answers. An analog may limit the practitioner's choice of response in various ways, such as requiring her to select a preferred intervention among several possibilities. Such problems of "response reality," to use Thomas' (1962) phrase, become particularly acute when none of the options offered reflect what the practitioner would actually do under the circumstances.

In addition, sampling constraints in use of analogs must be recognized. Most analogs present subjects with one or a very small number of case situations, and a sampling of practitioner responses is normally quite circumscribed.

With the exception of the last consideration, which applies to any form of analog, content validity problems may be less serious when highly naturalistic analogs, such as actors or actressses taking the roles of clients, are used. While their content validity may be greater, these naturalistic analogs are expensive and difficult to engineer, especially since they must be "administered" to practitioners one at a time.

Construct validation offers another and in some ways more decisive approach to the problem. This approach to validation is best used when the analog tests a theory-based hypothesis, preferably one for which some evidence has already been accumulated from nonanalog research. Confirmation of the hypothesis provides some evidence that the analog has, in fact, measured what it was designed to measure; otherwise, the hypothesis would not have been confirmed. Miller's study, just referred to, provides an example. If the hypothesis fails to be confirmed in the analog test, one must then face the possibility that the hypothesis itself was correct but that the instrument proved to be an invalid means of testing it. In other words, a failed hypothesis provides no evidence for construct validity.

More generally, the usefulness for analogs is clearest when they are used in theory-related research. By confirming hypotheses, they can strengthen theories of practitioner behavior. They can also serve an exploratory function by suggesting ways of responding not accounted for by theory (again the Miller study is illustrative.) In the latter case, they produce hypotheses, which need to be tested through additional research, preferably based in some part on the study of actual practice behavior.

Construction of Analogs In research built around original analogs, the construction of the analog itself is usually the most demanding and time-consuming task of the entire study. Although the many intricacies of the process cannot be fully dealt with here, we can offer some general guidelines and a few specific suggestions that may prove helpful. Again we assume that the analog consists of a practice situation presented in writing or on tape.

It goes without saying that we should have a reasonably well-developed research question or hypothesis before beginning work on the analog, but it usually pays to think of instrumentation possibilities before coming to closure on the research problem. This step may well lead to modification of the problem or will at least test its clarity. The practice situation devised for the analog should then be constructed to achieve the researcher's purposes as they evolve from a process that involves some going back and forth between the problem and the instrument.

In developing the practice situation, one needs to build in the stimuli needed to bring forth the desired variation in responses. In this manner, if a researcher is interested in determining how social workers with a psychodynamic orientation to practice might differ in their interventions from behaviorally oriented social workers, she would want to incorporate case material that would be likely to elicit hypothesized differences. If the analog is good, it should be one that would provoke controversy among the study's subjects if they were to react to it as a group. To be avoided are situations that all subjects would handle in pretty much the same way. For this reason, analogs should usually be invented rather than rooted in actual situations. It is usually not difficult to develop fictitious analogs in the form of case summaries that will be accepted by practitioner-subjects as realistic. Presenting case material in the form of audiotape or videotape recording does not guarantee realism. Amateurish acting is often readily detected. Still the subject's awareness that the practice situation is contrived is not necessarily a fatal limitation. It need only be sufficiently "realistic" to evoke the kinds of responses a practitioner would make if it were in fact real.

Usually the problem is not so much the subject's sense that the case lacks realism as it is that the analog case material is not likely to have as strong an impact as a real-life case would. Consequently, features of the analog case that the researcher wants the subjects to react to need to be made strong and vivid. For example, if the researcher is interested in how subjects would deal with a child who is physically acting out, the child's acting-out behavior should be of a serious nature and should be described in graphic detail. If the researcher plans to compare practitioner responses to such a child with a child whose acting out is confined to a verbal level, the differences between alternative forms of the analog should be sharply delineated in this respect. The need to hit subjects "between the eyes" with strong representations of stimulus material must be balanced, however, against a need to have the case representative of practice situations to which the researcher may wish to generalize.

With the stimulus-response analog, subjects may use any of the forms of response applicable to questionnaires. If practitioners are given a range of interventions to choose from, it is important that these possible responses be described in concrete terms. One should avoid vague generalizations such as "providing counseling." Having subjects rank-order responses (putting them in order of preference) may be better than having them simply select the response most preferred from a set. In such instruments, subjects have a tendency to select relatively neutral or "safe" responses if such are offered. Rank-ordering forces subjects to indicate how they stand in relation to all response possibilities.

At various points in analog construction, the researcher may wish to obtain the assistance of others. An expert (or a small panel of experts) may be asked to evaluate the stimulus material for realism, to suggest varieties of possible responses, or to classify responses already selected. A pretest given to a small group (six to ten) subjects will help identify problems in interpretation of instructions and responses that reveal little discrimination.

Participant Observation

Finally we would like to consider briefly an approach that usually includes some of the methods of studying intervention that have been taken up in earlier sections. We have in mind a more extensive and systematic use of participant observation than one finds in data recorded by practitioners on their own intervention activities. The participant-observer may occupy a range of roles reflecting different degrees of involvement in the intervention process under study. She may be a practitioner who conducts a special study of her own intervention technique or a practitioner who investigates a larger service system of which she is a part (she may assume a part-time or temporary role in such a system to study it), or she may be primarily an observer whose participation is limited largely to applying her own firsthand knowledge of the situation to the analysis of her observations.

Participant observation is particularly well suited to the study of complex service systems that may involve a variety of activities by different personnel. For example, there may be interest in investigating the treatment of older residents in an institutional setting, the "processing" of children admitted to a hospital, or a community's approach to dealing with delinquent youth. While useful, data obtained from sources such as records, surveys, and structured observation might not yield a coherent, comprehensive picture of the service system. A single participant-observer, or team of observers, can observe the various facets of the system in operation and seek out data needed to put together a view of the whole. As noted, participant observation is usually not confined to observation in the strict sense of the term. Accordingly, in a study of service systems the participant-observer may interview service providers (often in the form of brief, informal conversations) or review records and other documents. In addition to providing a unified description of a service system, investigators can also identify flaws and trouble spots that may not surface in data obtained from official records, questionnaires, formal interviews, or other conventional means. Like the investigative reporter, the participant-observer can dig beneath surface images of what is going on. In his participant-observation study of services to senile elderly in a particular community, Frankfather first describes a hospital ward in terms that one might obtain from an official description.

Service A is administered by the supervising psychiatrist and chief resident, a third year psychiatric resident. Ward staff, nurses, social workers and attendants are organized in six teams led by first-year psychiatric residents. Patient population [including the elderly] ranges from 25 to 30 and each patient is assigned to a specific psychiatric resident and team. (1977:111)

A rather different (though not necessarily contradictory) impression of service A is obtained when we see it through the investigator's eyes:

The paint is filthy and peeling. . . . The room is lined with ragged, sometimes cushionless couches. . . . The remains of lunch are left lying around until dinner time. This provides some patients, usually the elderly, with an opportunity to go picking among the left-overs during the day. (p. 111)

Investigator subjectivity and bias are, of course, inherent limitations in studies based largely on participant observation. But these limitations may be well worth accepting to obtain accounts that report on facets of programs that may otherwise not be brought to light.

Frankfather's research provides an example of use of participant observation to study a community service system. Another illustration of the application of this kind of methodology is found in the work of Bailey (1974), who studied in depth the operations of a social action organization. Using participant observation and interviews, Bailey obtained data not only from the staff members but also from professionals in the community and clients served by the organization.

In summary, participant observation offers a flexible and searching method for the study of service inputs, particularly complex service systems. Although results may be colored by the idiosyncratic perceptions of the observer, they may yield a view of the whole, as well as critical insights, that may not be attainable by other means.

REFERENCES

Note: SHR numbers can be used to obtain documents cited from Project Share, National Clearinghouse for Improving the Management of Human Services, P.O. Box 2309, Rockville, Md. 20852.

Abell, Neil, Barry L. Jones, and Walter W. Hudson. 1984. "Revalidation of the Index of Self-Esteem." *Social Work Research and Abstracts* 20:11–16.

Abramson, Julie. 1985. "Disagreement Among Principals in the Discharge Planning Process." *Discharge Planning Update* 6:4–10.

Achenbach, Thomas. 1982. "Research Mehods in Developmental Psychopathology: In Kendall and Butcher, eds., *Handbook of Research Methods in Clinical Psychology*, q.v.

Adams, Gerald R. and Jay D. Schvaneveldt. 1985. *Understanding Research Methods*. New York: Longman.

Allen-Meares, Paula. 1984. "Content Analysis: It Does Have a Place in Social Work Research." *Journal of Social Service Research* 7:51–68.

Andreoni, V. James. 1980. "A Case Study in Promoting Personal Hygiene in an Adolescent Male." Manuscript. University of Wisconsin, Milwaukee.

Argyris, Chris and Donald A. Schön. 1974. *Theory in Practice: Increasing Professional Effectiveness*. San Francisco: Jossey-Bass.

Atherton, Charles R. and David L. Klemmack. 1982. *Research Methods in Social Work: An Introduction*. Lexington, Mass.: D.C. Heath.

Attkisson, Clifford C., William A. Hargreaves, Mardi J. Horowitz, and James E. Sorenson. 1978. *Evaluation of Human Service Programs*. New York: Academic Press.

Auerbach, Arthur H. 1983. "Assessment of Psychotherapy Outcome from the Viewpoint of Expert Observer." In Lambert, Christensen, and DeJulio, eds., *The Assessment of Psychotherapy Outcome*, q.v.

Austin, Lucille N. 1948. "Trends in Differential Treatment in Social Casework." *Journal of Social Casework* 29:203–211.

Azrin, Nathan H., Barry J. Naster, and Robert Jones. 1973. "Reciprocity Counseling: A Rapid Learning-Based Procedure for Marital Counseling." *Behavior Research and Therapy* 11:365–382.

Babbie, Earl. 1986. *The Practice of Social Work Research*. Fourth Edition. Belmont, Calif.: Wadsworth.

Bailey, Robert, Jr. 1974. *Radicals in Urban Politics: The Alinsky Approach*. Chicago: University of Chicago Press.

Bakan, David. 1967. *On Method: Toward a Reconstruction of Psychological Investigation*. San Francisco: Jossey-Bass.

Bales, Robert F. 1969. *Personality and Interpersonal Behavior*. New York: Holt, Rinehart and Winston.

—— 1976. *Interaction Process Analysis: A Method for the Study of Small Groups*. Chicago: University of Chicago Press.

Barlow, David and Michael Hersen. 1984. *Single-Case Designs: Strategies for Study of Behavioral Change*. 2d ed. New York: Pergamon Press.

Barlow, David H., Steven C. Hayes, and Rosemary O. Nelson. 1983. *The Scientist Practicioner: Research and Accountability in Clinical and Educational Settings*. New York: Pergamon Press.

Barth, Richard et al. 1987. "Contributors to Reunification of Permanent Out-of-Home Care for Physically Abused Children." *Journal of Social Service Research* 9:31–45.

Basso, Robert. 1985. "Teacher and Student Problem Solving Activities in Educational Supervisory Sessions." *Journal of Social Work Education*. 23: 67–73.

Battle, C. C., Stanley D. Imber, Rudolph Hoehn-Saric, Anthony R. Stone, Earle H. Nash, and Jerome D. Frank. 1966. "Target Complaints as Criteria of Improvement." *American Journal of Psychotherapy* 20:184–192.

Bauer, Raymond A., ed. 1966. *Social Indicators*. Cambridge, Mass.: MIT Press.

Beck, Aaron T. 1967. *Depression: Clinical, Experimental and Theoretical Aspects*. New York: Harper and Row. Republished as *Depression: Causes and Treatment*. Philadelphia: University of Pennsylvania Press, 1972.

Beck, Dorothy Fahs and Mary Ann Jones. 1973. *Progress on Family Problems*. New York: Family Service Association of America.

—— 1980. *How to Conduct a Client Follow-Up Study*. New York: Family Service Association of America.

Bell, Roger A. 1976. "The Use of a Convergent Assessment Model in the Determination of Health Status and Assessment of Need." In Roger A. Bell et al., eds. *Need Assessment in Health and Human Services*, q.v.

Bell, Roger A. et al., eds. 1976. *Need Assessment in Health and Human Services: Proceedings of the Louisville National Conference, Louisville University, Kentucky*. Rockville, Md.: Health Resources Administration. SHR-0001452.

Bell, Roger A., Martin Sundel, Joseph F. Aponte, Stanley A. Murrel, and Elizabeth Lin, eds. 1983. *Assessing Health and Human Service Needs*. New York: Human Sciences Press.

Bell, Winifred. 1961. "The Practical Value of Social Work Service: Preliminary Report on Ten Demonstration Projects in Public Assistance." New York School of Social Work, Columbia University.

Berger, Michael. 1983. "Toward Maximizing the Utility of Consumer Satisfaction as an Outcome." In Lambert, Christensen, and DeJulio, eds., *The Assessment of Psychotherapy Outcome*, q.v.

Berger, Raymond and Irving Piliavin, 1976. "The Effect of Casework: A Research Note." *Social Work* 21:205–208.

Berger, Raymond M. and Sheldon D. Rose. 1977. "Interpersonal Skill Training with Institutionalized Elderly Patients." *Journal of Gerontology* 32:346–353.

Bergin, Allen E. 1980. "Negative Effects Revisited: A Reply." *Professional Psychology* 11:93–100.

Berleman, William C. 1976. "A Cautionary Cheer: Some Reservations Regarding the Interpretation of Findings." In Joel Fischer, *The Effectiveness of Social Casework*, q.v.

Berleman, William C., James R. Seaberg, and Thomas Steinburn. 1972. "The Delinquency Prevention Experiment of the Seattle Atlantic Street Center: A Final Evaluation." *Social Service Review* 46:323–346.

Beutler, Larry E. and Marjorie Crago. 1983. "Self-Report Measures of Psychotherapy Outcome." In Lambert, Christensen, and DeJulio, eds., *The Assessment of Psychotherapy Outcome*. New York: Wiley.

Bickman, Leonard. 1976. "Data Collection 1: Observational Methods." In Claire Selltiz, Lawrence Wrightsman, and Stuart W. Cook, eds., *Research Methods in Social Relations*, q.v.

Biddle, Willilam W. and Loureide J. Biddle. 1965. *The Community Development Process: The Rediscovery of Local Initiative*. New York: Holt, Rinehart, and Winston.

Bielawaski, Barbara and Irwin Epstein. 1984. "Assessing Program Stabilization: An Extension of the Differential Evaluation Model." *Administration in Social Work*. 8:13–23.

Bijou, Sidney W., Robert F. Peterson, and Marion H. Ault. 1968. "A Method to Integrate Descriptive and Experimental Field Studies at the Level of Data and Empirical Concepts." *Journal of Applied Behavior Analysis* 1:175–191.

Black, James A. and Dean J. Champion. 1976. *Methods and Issues in Social Research*. New York: Wiley.

Blackman, Donald K., Carolyn Gehle, and Elsie M. Pinkston, 1979. "Modifying Eating Habits of the Institutionalized Elderly." *Social Work Research and Abstracts* 15(3):18–249.

Blalock, Hubert M. Jr. 1979. *Social Statistics*. 2d ed. New York: McGraw-Hill.

Blenkner, Margaret, Martin Bloom, and Margaret Nielson. 1971. "A Research and Demonstration Project of Protective Services." *Social Casework* 52:483–499.

Bloom, Martin. 1986. *The Experience of Research*. New York: MacMillan.

Bloom, Martin and Joel Fischer. 1982. *Evaluating Practice: Guidelines for the Accountable Professional*. Englewood Cliffs, N.J.: Prentice-Hall.

Blythe, Betty and Scott Briar. 1985. "Developing Empirically Based Models of Practice." *Social Work* 30:483–488.

Bock, R. Darrell. 1975. *Multivariate Statistical Methods in Behavioral Research.* New York: McGraw-Hill.

Booz-Allen Public Administration Services, Inc. 1973. *Assessing Social Service Needs and Resources.* Washington, D.C. SHR-0000515.

Bornstein, Phillip H., Scott B. Hamilton, and Marcy Tepper Bornstein. 1986. "Self Monitoring Procedures." In Ciminero, Calhoun, and Adams, eds., *Handbook of Behavioral Assessment*, q.v.

Bostwick, Nancy K. and Gerald J. Bostwick. 1987. "Intersource Consensus and Outcome Evaluation." In Naomi Gottlieb, ed., *Prospectives on Direct Practice Evaluation.* University of Washington, Center for Social Welfare Research, Seattle.

Box, George, E. P. and Gwilym M. Jenkins. 1970. *Time-Series Analysis: Forecasting and Control.* San Francisco: Holden-Day.

Briar, Scott. 1973. "The Age of Accountability." *Social Work* 18:2.

——— 1974. "What Do Social Workers Do?" *Social Work* 19:386.

——— 1980. "Toward the Integration of Practice and Research." In Fanshel, ed., *Future of Social Work Research*, q.v.

Briar, Scott and Betty J. Blythe. 1985. "Agency Support for Evaluating the Outcomes of Social Work Services." *Administration in Social Work* 9:25–36.

Briar, Scott and Henry Miller. 1971. *Problems and Issues in Social Casework.* New York: Columbia University Press.

Brieland, Donald. 1959. "An Experimental Study of the Selection of Adoptive Parents at Intake." New York: Child Welfare League of America.

Brown, Lester. 1980. "Client Problem-Solving Learning in Task-Centered Social Treatment." Ph.D. dissertation. University of Chicago.

Broxmeyer, Neal. 1978. "Practitioner-Research in Treating a Borderline Child." *Social Work Research and Abstracts* 14(4):5–11.

Buckley, Walter. 1967. *Sociology and Modern Systems Theory.* Englewood Cliffs, N.J.: Prentice-Hall.

Buros, Oscar, ed. 1978. *The Mental Measurements Yearbook.* 8th ed. Highland Park, N.J.: Gryphon Press.

Butler, Harry, Inger Davis, and Ruth Kukkonen. 1979. "The Logic of Case Comparison." *Social Work Research and Abstracts* 15(3):3–11.

Cagle, Lawrence T. 1984. "Using Social Indicators to Assess Mental Health Needs: Lessons from a Statewide Study." *Evaluation Review* 8:389–412.

Campbell, Donald T. 1969. "Reforms as Experiments." *American Psychologist* 24:409–429.

Campbell, Donald T. and Donald W. Fiske. 1959. "Convergent and Discriminant Validation by the Multirait-Multimethod Matrix." *Psychological Bulletin* 56:81–105.

Campbell, Donald T. and Julian C. Stanley. 1963. "Experimental and Quasi-Experimental Designs for Research on Teaching." In N. L. Gage, ed., *Handbook of Research on Teaching.* Chicago: Rand McNally.

Canter, D., J. Brown, and L. Groat. 1985. "A Multiple Sorting Procedure for Studying Conceptual Systems." In M. Brenner, J. Brown, and D. Canter, eds., *The Research Interview: Uses and Approaches*. London: Academic Press.

Chapin, F. Stuart. 1955. *Experimental Designs in Sociological Research*, rev. ed. Cambridge, Mass.: Harvard University Press.

Chassan, J. B. 1967. *Research Design in Clinical Psychology and Psychiatry*. New York: Appleton-Century-Crofts.

Chestang, Leon W. 1977. "Achievement and Self-Esteem among Black Americans: A Study of Twenty Lives." Ph.D. dissertation, University of Chicago.

Chilman, Catherine S. 1979. "Parent Satisfactions-Dissatisfactions and Their Correlates." *Social Service Review* 53:195–213.

Christensen, Larry and Jorge L. Mendoza. 1986. "A Method of Assessing Change in Single Subject: An Alteration of the RC Index". *Behavior Therapy* 17:305–308.

Ciminero, Anthony, R., Karen S. Calhoun, and Henry E. Adams, eds. 1986. *Handbook of Behavioral Assessment*. 2d ed. New York: Wiley.

Clark, Frank W., Morton L., Arkava, and Associates, eds. 1979. *The Pursuit of Competence in Social Work*. San Francisco: Jossey-Bass.

Cocozzelli, Carmelo. 1987. "A Psychometric Study of the Theoretical Orientations of Clinical Social Workers." *Journal of Social Service Research* 9:47–70.

Cohen, Jacob. 1960. "A Coefficient of Agreement for Nominal Scales." *Educational and Psychological Measurement* 20:37–46.

—— 1969. *Statistical Power Analysis for the Behavioral Sciences*. New York: Academic Press.

Cohen, Mark W., Grayce M. Sills, and Andrew I. Schwebel. 1977. "A Two Stage Process for Surveying Community Needs." *Journal of Community Development Society* 8:54–61.

Cone, John D. and Sharon L. Foster. 1982. "Direct Observation in Clinical Psychology." In Kendall and Butcher, eds., *Handbook of Research Methods in Clinical Psychology*, q.v.

Conrad, P. and S. Reinharz. 1984. "Computers and Qualitative Data." *Qualitative Sociology* 7:1–2.

Cook, Thomas D. and Donald T. Campbell. 1979. *Quasi-Experimentation: Design and Analysis Issues for Field Settings*. Chicago: Rand-McNally.

Corcoran, Kevin J. and Anita K. Bryce. 1983. "Intervention in the Experience of Burnout: Effects of Skill Development." *Journal of Social Service Research* 7:71–79.

Corcoran, Kevin and Joel Fischer. 1987. *Measures for Clinical Practice: A Source Book*. New York: Free Press.

Coulton, Claudia J. 1982. "The Need for Replication in Social Work Research." *Social Work Research & Abstracts* 18:2.

Cousins, Peter C. and Thomas A. Power. 1986. "Quantifying Family Process: Issues in the Analysis of Interaction Sequences." *Family Process* 25:89–105.

Cowger, Charles. 1984. "Statistical Significance Tests: Scientific Ritualism or Scientific Method?" *Social Service Review* 58:358–372.

Craig, Maude M. and Phillip W. Furst. 1965. "What Happens after Treatment? A Study of Potentially Delinquent Boys." *Social Service Review* 39:165–171.

Crane, John A. 1976. "The Power of Social Intervention Experiments to Discriminate Differences between Experimental and Control Groups." *Social Service Review* 59:224–242.

Cronbach, Lee J. 1970. *Essentials of Psychological Testing.* 3d ed. New York: Harper and Row.

Cunningham, Gloria. 1978. "Workers' Support of Clients' Problem-Solving." *Social Work Research and Abstracts* 14(1):3–10.

Dailey, Dennis M. 1980. "Are Social Workers Sexists? A Replication." *Social Work* 25:46–50.

Dalkey, N. C. 1969. *The Delphi Method: An Experimental Study of Group Opinion.* Santa Monica, Calif.: Rand Corp.

Davidson, Christine V. and Ronald H. Davidson. 1983. "The Significant Other as Data Source and Data Problem in Psychotherapy Outcome Research." In Lambert, Christensen, and DeJulio, eds., *The Assessment of Psychotherapy Outcome,* q.v.

Davis, Inger P. 1975. "Advice-giving in Parent Counseling." *Social Casework* 56:343–347.

Davis, Inger P. and William J. Reid. 1988. "Event Analysis in Clinical Practice and Process Research." *Social Casework.* 69(5):298–306.

Davis, Liane V. and Bonnie E. Carlson. 1981. "Attitudes of Service Providers Toward Domestic Violence." *Social Work Research and Abstracts* 17:34–39.

Dean, Ruth and Helen Reinherz. 1987. "Psychodynamic Practice and Single System Design: The Odd Couple." In Naomi Gottlieb, ed., *Prospectives on Direct Practice Evaluation.* University of Washington, Center for Social Welfare Research, Seattle.

Deaux, Edward and John W. Callahan. 1984. "Estimating Statewide Health-Risk Behavior: A Comparison of Telephone and Key Informant Survey Approaches." *Evaluation Review* 8:467–492.

Delbecq, Andre L. 1976. "The Use of the Nominal Group Method in the Assessment of Community Needs." Bell et al., eds. *Need Assessment in Health and Human Services,* q.v.

—— 1983. "The Nominal Group as a Technique for Understanding the Qualitative Dimensions of Client Needs." Bell et al., eds., *Assessing Health and Human Service Needs,* q.v.

Delbecq, Andre L. and Andrew H. Van De Ven. 1971. "A Group Process Model for Problem Identification and Program Planning." *Journal of Applied Behavioral Science* 7:446–492.

Denzin, Norman K. 1978. *Sociological Methods: A Source Book.* 2d ed., New York: McGraw-Hill.

Derogatis, Leonard 1976. *Scoring and Procedures Manual for PAIS.* Baltimore: Clinical Psychometric Research.

de Solla Price, Derek J. 1961. *Science Since Babylon.* New Haven: Yale University Press.

Dollard, John and O. Herbert Mowrer. 1947. "A Method of Measuring Tension in Written Documents." *Journal of Abnormal and Social Psychology* 42:3–32.

Dubos, René. 1965. "Science and Man's Nature." *Daedalus* 94:223–44.

Dunham, H. Warren. 1976. "The Epidemiological Study of Mental Illness: Its Value for Needs Assessment." Bell et al., eds., *Need Assessment in Health and Human Services*, q.v.

Edelson, Jeffrey L. 1985. "Rapid-Assessment Instruments for Evaluating Practice with Children and Youth." *Journal of Social Service Research* 8:17–32.

Ell, Kathleen and L. Julian Haywood. 1984. "Social Support and Recovery from Myocardial Infarction: A Panel Study." *Journal of Social Service Research* 7:1–19.

Elliot, Robert. 1983. "That in Your Hands: A Comprehensive Process Analysis of a Significant Event in Psychotherapy." *Psychiatry* 46:113–129.

—— 1984. "A Discovery-Oriented Approach to Significant Change in Psychotherapy: Interpersonal Process Recall and Comprehensive Process Analysis." In Laura N. Rice and Leslie S. Greenberg, eds., *Patterns of Change: Intensive Analysis of Psychotherapy Process*. New York: Guilford Press.

Ewalt, Patricia L. and Janice Kutz, 1976. "An Examination of Advice Giving as a Therapeutic Intervention." *Smith College Studies in Social Work*. 47:3–19.

Fanshel, David. 1963. "Commentary on 'Clinical Judgment in Foster Care Placement." *Child Welfare* 42:169–172.

—— 1976. "Computerized Information Systems and Foster Care: The New York City Experience with CWIS." *Children Today* 44:14–18.

—— 1977. "Parental Visiting of Foster Children: A Computerized Study." *Social Work Research and Abstracts* 13(3):2–10.

—— 1980. "The Future of Social Work Research: Strategies for the Coming Years." In Fanshel, ed., *Future of Social Work Research*, q.v.

Fanshel, David, ed. 1980. *Future of Social Work Research*. Washington, D.C.: National Association of Social Workers.

Fanshel, David and Eugene B. Shinn. 1978. *Children in Foster Care: A Longitudinal Investigation*. New York: Columbia University Press.

Feldman, Ronald A. and Timothy E. Caplinger. 1977. "Social Work Experience and Client Behavioral Change: A Multivariate Analysis of Process and Outcome." *Journal of Social Service Research* 1:5–33.

Feldman, Ronald A., Timothy E. Caplinger, and John S. Wodarski. 1983. *The St. Louis Conundrum: The Effective Treatment of Antisocial Youths*. Englewood Cliffs, N.J.: Prentice-Hall.

Filsinger, Erik E. 1983. "Choices Among Marital Observation Coding Systems." *Family Process* 22:317–335.

Finch, Stephen and David Fanshel. 1985. "Testing the Quality of Discharge Patterns in Foster Care." *Social Work Research and Abstracts* 21:3–10.

Finlay, Donald G. 1977. "Changing Problem Drinkers." *Social Work Research and Abstracts* 13(4):30–37.

Fischer, Joel. 1973. "Is Casework Effective? A Review." *Social Work* 18:5–20.

—— 1976. *The Effectiveness of Social Casework*. Springfield, Ill. Charles C. Thomas.

—— 1978. *Effective Casework Practice: An Eclectic Approach.* New York: McGraw-Hill.
Fischer, Joel, Diane D. Dulaney, Rosemary T. Fazio, Mary T. Hudak, and Ethel Zivotofsky. 1976. "Are Social Workers Sexists?" *Social Work* 21:428–433.
Fischer, Joel and Walter Hudson. 1976. "An Effect of Casework? Back to the Drawing Board." *Social Work* 21:347–349.
Fischer, Seymour and Roger P. Greenberg. 1977. *The Scientific Credibility of Freud's Theories and Therapy.* New York: Basic Books.
Flanagan, J. C. 1954. "The Critical Incident Technique." *Psychological Bulletin* 51:327–58.
Florian, Victor and Dov Kehat. 1987. "Changing High School Student's Attitudes Toward Disabled People." *Health and Social Work* 12:57–63.
Florida State Department of Health and Rehabilitation Services. 1975. *Key Informant Assessment of the Needs of Florida Residents: Title XX of the Social Security Act.* SHR-0000501.
Fortune, Anne E. 1979A. "Communication in Task-Centered Treatment." *Social Work* 24:390–396.
—— 1979b. "Problem-Solving Processes in Task-Centered Treatment with Adults and Children." *Journal of Social Service Research* 2:357–371.
—— 1981. "Communication Processes in Social Work Practice." *Social Service Review* 55:93–128.
—— 1985. "Planning Duration and Termination of Treatment." *Social Service Review* 59:647–661.
Fortune, Anne E. et al. 1985. "Student Satisfaction with Field Placement." *Journal of Social Work Education* 21:92–104.
Foster, Sharon L. and John D. Cone. 1986. "Design and Use of Direct Observation." In Ciminero, Calhoun, and Adams, eds., *Handbook of Behavioral Assessment*, q.v.
Frankfather, Dwight. 1977. *The Aged in the Community.* New York: Praeger.
Franklin, Donna L. 1985. "Differential Clinical Assessments: The Influence of Class and Race." *Social Service Review* 59:44–61.
Froland, Charles. 1976. *Substance Abuse in Oregon: Identifying Potential Clientele, Problem Trends, and Service Related Needs. Technical Report.* Salem, Oregon: State Mental Health Division, Management Support Services. SHR-0001804.
Gallo, Frank. 1984. "Social Support Networks and the Health of Elderly Persons." *Social Work Research and Abstracts* 20:13–19.
Gambrill, Eileen D. 1977. *Behavior Modification: Handbook of Assessment, Intervention, and Evaluation.* San Francisco: Jossey-Bass.
Garfield, Sol L. and Allen E. Bergin, eds. 1978. *Handbook of Psychotherapy and Behavior Change: An Empirical Analysis.* 2d ed. New York: Wiley.
—— 1986. *Handbook of Psychotherapy and Change.* New York: Wiley.
Garvin, Charles D. and Brett A. Seabury. 1984. *Interpersonal Practice in Social Work Processes and Procedures.* Englewood Cliffs, N.J.: Prentice-Hall.

Garvin, Charles D., Audrey D. Smith, and William J. Reid, eds. 1978. *The Work Incentive Experience*. Montclair, N.J.: Allanheld, Osmun.

Gary, Lawrence E. 1985. "Depressive Symptoms and Black Men." *Social Work Research and Abstracts* 21:21–29.

Geda, Carolyn L. 1979. "Social Science Data Archives." *The American Archivist* 42:158–166.

Geertz, Clifford. 1973. "Thick Description: Toward an Interpretive Theory of Culture." In Clifford Geertz, ed., *The Interpretation of Cultures*. New York: Basic Books.

Geismar, Ludwig L. 1980. *Family and Community Functioning*. 2d ed. Metuchen, N.J.: Scarecrow Press.

——1982. "Comments on the 'Obsolete Scientific Imperative in Social Work Research.'" *Social Service Review* 56:311–312.

Geismar, Ludwig L. and Jane Krisberg. 1966. "The Family Life Improvement Project: An Experiment in Preventive Intervention: Part II." *Social Casework* 47:563–570.

Germain, Carel. 1970. "Casework and Science: A Historical Encounter." In Robert W. Roberts and Robert H. Nee, eds., *Theories of Social Casework*. Chicago: University of Chicago Press.

Gilbert, J. P., R. J. Light, and F. Mosteller. 1975. "Assessing Social Innovations: An Empirical Base for Policy." In C. A. Benjnett and A. A. Lumdsaine, eds., *Evaluation and Experiment*. New York: Academic Press.

Gingerich, Wallace A. 1979. "Procudure for Evaluating Clinical Practice." *Health and Social Work* 2:105–130.

Gingerich, Wallace and W. Feyerherm. 1979. "The Celebration Line for Assessing Client Change." *Journal of Social Service Research* 3:99–113.

Gingerich, Wallace A., Mark Kleczewski, and Stuart A. Kirk. 1982. "Name Calling in Social Work." *Social Service Review* 56:366–374.

Glaser, Barney G. and Anselm L. Strauss. 1967. *The Discovery of Grounded Theory: Strategies for Qualitative Research*. Chicago: Aldine.

—— 1970. "Discovery of Substantive Theory: A Basic Strategy Underlying Qualitative Research." In William Filstead, ed., *Qualitative Methodology*. Chicago: Markham.

Glass, Gene V., Vernon L. Willson, and John M. Gottman, 1975. *Design and Analysis of Time Series Experiments*. Boulder: Colorado Associated University Press.

Glisson, Charles. 1985. "In Defense of Statistical Tests of Significance." *Social Service Review*: 59:377–386.

Goldberg, Gertrude S., Ruth Kantrow, Eleanor Kremen, and Leah Lauter. 1986. "Spouseless, Childless, Elderly Women and Their Social Supports." *Social Work* 31:104–112.

Goldsmith, Harold, F, D. J. Jackson, S. Doenhoefer, W. Johnson, D. L. Tweed, D. Stiles, J. D. Barbano, and G. Warheit. 1984. "The Health Demographic Profile System's Inventory of Small Area Social Indicators" (1984-455-749/20133). Washington, D.C.: Superintendent of Public Documents.

Goldstein, Arnold P. 1973. *Structured Learning Therapy*. New York: Academic Press.

Goldstein, Arnold P., Kenneth Heller, and Lee B. Sechrest. 1966. *Psychotherapy and the Psychology of Behavior Change*. New York: Wiley.

Goode, William J. and Paul K. Hatt. *Methods in Social Research*. New York: McGraw-Hill.

Gottman, John. 1981. *Time Series Analysis*. Cambridge: Cambridge University Press.

Gottman, John M. and Sandra R. Leiblum. 1974. *How To Do Psychotherapy and How To Evaluate It*. New York: Hold, Rinehart, and Winston.

Green, Glenn R. and J. E. Wright. 1979. "The Retrospective Approach to Collecting Baseline Data." *Social Work Research and Abstracts* 15(3):25–31.

Greenberg, Leslie S. 1986. "Change Process Research." *Journal of Consulting and Clinical Psychology* 54:4–9.

Greenberg, Leslie S. and William M. Pinsof, eds. 1986. *The Psychotherapeutic Process: A Research Handbook*. New York: Guilford Press.

Gulliksen, Harold. 1950. *Theory of Mental Tests*. New York: Wiley.

Gurman, Alan S., David P. Kniskern, and William M. Pinsoff. 1986. "Research on Marital and Family Therapies." In Garfield and Bergin, eds., *Handbook of Psychotherapy and Behavior Change*, q.v.

Gurman, Alan S. and Andrew M. Razin, eds. 1977. *Effective Psychotherapy: A Handbook of Research*. New York: Pergamon Press.

Gynther, Malcolm and Samuel Green. 1982. "Methodological Problems in Research with Self Report Inventories." in Kendall and Butcher, eds., *Handbook of Research Methods in Clinical Psychology*, q.v.

Hagedorn, Homer J., Kenneth J. Beck, Stephen F. Neubert, and Stanley H. Werlin. 1976. *A Working Manual of Simple Program Evaluation Techniques for Community Mental Health Centers*. U.S. Department of Health, Education, and Welfare Pub. No. [ADM] 76-404. Washington, D.C.: GPO.

Hairston, Creasie Finney. 1979. "The Nominal Group Technique in Organizational Research." *Social Work Research and Abstracts* 15(3):12–17.

Hall, James A. and Sheldon D. Rose. 1987. "Evaluation of Parent Training in Groups for Parent-Adolescent Conflict." *Social Work Research and Abstracts* 23:3–8.

Hall, R. U., ed. 1971. *Behavior Management Series: Part II, Basic Principles*. Lawrence, Kansas: H & H Enterprises.

Hanrahan, Pat and William J. Reid. 1984. "Choosing Effective Interventions." *Social Service Review* 58:244–258.

Hargreaves, William A., James E. Sorenson, and C. Clifford Attkisson, eds. 1977. *Resource Materials for Community Mental Health Program Evaluation*. 2d ed. U. S. Department of Health, Education, and Welfare Pub. No. [ADM] 77-328. Washington, D.C.: GPO.

Harman, Harry. 1976. *Modern Factor Analysis*. 3d ed. Chicago: University of Chicago Press.

Hartman, Ann. 1974. "The Generic Stance and the Family Agency." *Social Casework* 55:199–208.

Haworth, G. O. 1984. "Social Work Research, Practice and Paradigms." *Social Service Review* 58:343–357.

Haynes, Jeanne. 1977. "Application of Single Subject Design to Psychosocial Casework." Paper presented at Annual Program Meeting, Council on Social Work Education.

Hays, William L. 1973. *Statistics for the Social Sciences*. 2d ed. New York: Holt, Rinehart and Winston.

Hedlund, James, Bruce Vieweg, and Dong Cho. 1985. "Mental Health Computing in the 1980's: General Information Systems and Clinical Documentation." *Computers in Human Service* 1:3–33.

Heineman, Martha B. 1981. "The Obsolete Scientific Imperative in Social Work Research." *Social Service Review* 55:373–397.

Heineman-Pieper, Martha B. 1985. "The Future of Social Work Research." *Social Work Research and Abstracts* 21:3–11.

Henry, William P., Thomas E. Schacht, and Hans H. Strupp. 1986. "Structural Analysis of Social Behavior: Application to a Study of Interpersonal Process in Differential Psychotherapeutic Outcome." *Journal of Consulting and Clinical Psychology* 54:27–31.

Hill, Clara E. 1986. "Verbal Response Modes Category Systems." In Greenberg and Pinsof, eds., *The Psychotherapeutic Process: A Research Handbook*, q.v.

Hill, Clara E., J. A. Carter, and M. K. O'Farrell. 1983. "A Case Study of the Process and Outcome of Time-Limited Counseling." *Journal Counseling Psychology* 30:3–18.

Hoel, Paul G. 1976. *Elementary Statistics*. 4th ed. New York: Wiley.

Hollis, Florence. 1949. "The Techniques of Casework." *Journal of Social Casework* 30:235–244.

—— 1963. "Contemporary Issues for Caseworkers." In Howard J. Parad and Roger R. Miller, eds., *Ego-Oriented Casework*. New York: Family Service Association of America.

—— 1972. *Casework: A Psychosocial Therapy*. 2d ed. New York: Random House.

Hollis, Florence and Mary E. Woods. 1981. *Casework: A Psychosocial Therapy*. New York: Random House.

Hopps, June and Elaine Pinderhughes. 1987. "Profession of Social Work Contemporary Characteristics." In Anne Minahan, ed., *Encyclopedia of Social Work*, q.v.

Hubek, Marilyn M. and William J. Reid, 1982. "Components of Self-Management in Special Education Classes." In Robert T. Constable and John P. Flynn, eds., *School Social Work: Practice and Research Perspectives*. Homewood, Ill.: Dorsey Press.

Hudson, Walter W. 1982. "The Clinical Measurement Package: A Field Manual." Homewood, Ill.: Dorsey Press.

Human Services Coordination Alliance, Inc., 1976. *Let Older People Speak for Themselves: An Assessment of Need in the KIPDA Area Development District*. Louisville, Ky.: Prepared for the Administration on the Aging. SHR 0001058.

Hunt, J. McVicker. 1948. "Measuring Movement in Casework." *Journal of Social Casework* 29:343–351.

Ivanoff, Andre et al. 1986. "Standardized Measurement in Clinical Social Work: Annotated Bibliography." Presented at the meeting of the Council on Social Work Education, Miami, Florida, March 1986.

Ivanoff, Andre, Betty J. Blythe and Scott Briar. 1987. "The Empirical Clinical Practice Debate." *Social Casework* 68:290–298.

Jackson, Eugene, 1987. "Specificity and Generality of Internal Empathy in Facilitative Behavior and Communicative Empathy: A Path-Analytic Study." *Social Work Research and Aspects* 23:4–9.

Jacobson, Neil S., William C. Follette, and Dirk Revensdorf. 1984. "Psychotherapy Outcome Research: Methods for Reporting Variability and Evaluating Clinical Significance." *Behavior Therapy* 15:336–352.

Janssen, Bruce. 1975. "History and Politics of Selected Children's Programs and Related Legislation in the Context of Four Models of Political Behavior." Ph.D. dissertation. University of Chicago.

Jayaratne, Srinika. 1978. "Analytic Procedures for Single-Subject Designs." *Social Work Research and Abstracts* 14(3):30–40.

Jayaratne, Srinika and R. Levy. 1979. *Empirical Clinical Practice*. New York: Columbia University Press.

Jenkins, Shirley. 1975. "Collecting Data by Questionnaire and Interview." In Normal Polansky, ed. *Social Service Research*, q.v.

Johnson, S. M. and G. White. 1971. "Self Observation as an Agent of Behavioral Change." *Behavior Therapy* 2:488–497.

Jones, Mary Ann. 1985. *A Second Chance for Families: Five Years Later*. New York: Child Welfare League of America.

Jones, Mary Ann, Renee Neuman, and Ann W. Shyne. 1976. *A Second Chance for Families: Evaluation of a Program to Reduce Foster Care*. New York: Child Welfare League of America.

Kagan, Leonard S. and Ann W. Shyne. 1965. "Tender-Minded and Tough-Minded Approaches in Evaluative Research." Symposium on Individual and Family Measurement, National Conference on Social Welfare. Atlantic City, N.J.

Kagle, Jill D. 1984. "Restoring the Clinical Record." *Social Work* 29:46–50.

Kane, Rosalie A. 1974. "Look to the Record." *Social Work* 19:412–419.

Kanfer, F. H. and W. Robert May. 1981. "Behavioral Assessment: Toward and Integration of Epistemological and Methodological Issues." In G. T. Wilson and C. M. Franks, eds., *Behavior Therapy and Its Foundations*. New York: Guilford Press.

Kaplan, Abraham. 1964. *The Conduct of Inquiry: Methodology for Behavioral Science*. San Francisco: Chandler.

Karger, H.J. 1983. "Science, Research, and Social Work: Who Controls the Profession?" *Social Work* 28:200–205.

Karpf, Maurice J. 1931. *The Scientific Basis of Social Work*. New York: Columbia University Press.

Katz, David. 1979. "Laboratory Training to Enhance Interviewing Skills." In Frank W. Clark, Morton L. Arkava, and Associates, eds., *The Pursuit of Competence in Social Work*, q.v.

Katz, M. and S. Lyerly. 1963. "Methods for Measuring Adjustment and Social Behavior in the Community: Rationale Description, Discriminative Validity and Scale Development." *Psychological Reports* 13:503–535.

Kazdin, Alan E. 1976. "Statistical Analyses for Single-Case Experimental Designs." In Michel Hersen and David H. Barlow, eds., *Single Case Experimental Designs*, q.v.

—— 1981. "Drawing Valid Inferences from Case Studies." *Journal of Consulting and Clinical Psychology* 49:183–192.

—— 1982. "Single Case Experimental Designs." In Kendall and Butcher, eds., *Handbook of Research Methods in Clinical Psychology*, q.v.

—— 1986. "Research Designs and Methodology." In Garfield and Bergin, eds., *Handbok of Psychotherapy and Behavior Change*, q.v.

Kendall, Philip C. and James N. Butcher, eds., *Handbook of Research Methods in Clinical Psychology*. New York: Wiley.

Kennedy, Wallace A. 1965. "School Phobia: Rapid Treatment of Fifty Cases." *Journal of Abnormal Psychology* 70:286.

Kerlinger, Fred N. 1973. *Foundations of Behavioral Research*. 2d ed. New York: Holt, Rinehart and Winston.

—— 1985. *Foundations of Behavioral Research*. 3d ed. New York: Holt, Rinehart, and Winston.

Kerlinger, Fred N. and Elazar J. Pedhazur. 1973. *Multiple Regression in Behavioral Research*. New York: Holt, Rinehart and Winston.

Kidder, Louise H. and Charles M. Judd. 1986. *Research Methods in Social Relations*. New York: Holt, Reinhart and Winston.

Kiesler, Donald J. 1973. *The Process of Psychotherapy: Empirical Foundations and Systems of Analysis*. Chicago: Aldine Press.

Kimmel, Wayne A. 1977. *Needs Assessment: A Critical Perspective*. Prepared for the Office of Program Systems, Office of the Assistant Secretary for Planning and Evaluation, Department of Health, Education, and Welfare.

Kiresuk, Thomas J. 1973. "Goal Attainment Scaling at a County Mental Health Service." *Evaluation*. Special monograph. No. 1, pp. 12–18.

Kiresuk, Thomas J. and Sander H. Lund. 1977. "Goal Attainment Scaling." In Attkisson et al., eds., *Evaluation of Human Service Programs*, q.v.

Kiresuk, Thomas J. and Robert E. Sherman. 1968. "Goal Attainment Scaling: A General Method for Evaluating Comprehensive Mental Health Programs." *Community Mental Health Journal* 4:443–453.

—— 1977. "A Reply to the Critique of Goal Attainment Scaling." *Social Work Research and Abstracts* 13(2):10–11.

Kirk, R. E. 1968. *Experimental Design: Procedures for the Behavioral Sciences*. Belmont, Calif.: Brooks/Cole.

Kirk, Stuart A. and Aaron Rosenblatt. 1980. "Women's Contributions to Social Work Journals." *Social Work* 25:204–209.

Kish, Leslie, 1965. *Survey Sampling*. New York: Wiley.

Kogan, Leonard S. 1975. "Principles of Measurement." In Norman A. Polansky, ed., *Social Work Research*, q.v.

Kohler, Heinz. 1985. *Statistics for Business and Economics*. Glenview, Ill.: Scott, Foresman.

Kolotkin, Ronette L. and Marilyn Johnson. 1983. "Crisis Intervention and Measurement of Treatment Outcome." In Lambert, Christensen, and DeJulio, eds., *The Assessment of Psychotherapy Outcome*, q.v.

Kopp, Judy and William Butterfield. 1985. "Change in Graduate Student's Use of Interviewing Skills from the Cassroom to the Field." *Journal of Social Service Research* 9:65–88.

Krassner, M. 1986. "Effective Features of Therapy from the Healer's Perspective: A Study of Curanderismo." *Smith College of Studies in Social Work* 56:157–83.

Krathwohl, David R. 1985. *Social and Behavioral Science and Research*. San Francisco: Jossey-Bass.

Kratochwill, Thomas R. 1978. "Foundations of a Time-Series Research." In Kratochwill, ed., *Single Subject Research: Strategies for Evaluating Change*, q.v.

Kratochwill, Thomas R. ed. 1978. *Single Subject Research: Strategies for Evaluating Change*. New York: Academic Press.

Krippendorf, Klaus. 1980. *Content Analysis: An Introduction to Its Methodology*. Beverly Hills, Calif.: Sage Publications.

Kutchins, Herb and Stuart A. Kirk. 1986. "The Reliability of DSM III: A Critical Review." *Social Work Research and Abstracts* 22:3–12.

Kyte, Nancy S. 1980. "A Study of Intersource Consensus and Outcome Evaluation." Manuscript.

Lambert, Michael J. 1983. "Introduction to Assessment of Psychotherapy Outcome: Historical Perspective and Current Issues." In Lambert, Christensen, and DeJulio, eds., *The Assessment of Psychotherapy Outcome*, q.v. Wiley.

Lambert, Michael J., Erwin R. Christensen, and Steven S. DeJulio, eds. 1983. *The Assessment of Psychotherapy Outcome*. New York: Wiley.

Lambert, Michael J., David A. Shapiro, and Allen E. Bergin. 1986. "The Effectiveness of Psychotherapy." In Garfield and Bergin, eds., *Handbook of Psychotherapy and Behavior Change*, q.v.

Landon, Pamela S. and M. Fiet. 1987. *The Realities of Generalist Practice*. St. Paul, Minn.: West.

Lantz, James E. 1986. "Integrating Reflective and Task Oriented Techniques in Family Treatment." *Child Welfare* 65:261–70.

Larsen, JoAnn and Craig T. Mitchell. 1980. "Task-Centered, Strength-Oriented Group Work with Delinquents." *Social Casework* 61:154–163.

League of California Cities. 1975. *Assessing Human Needs*. Sacramento Prepared for the United States Department of Commerce. SHR-0000280.

Lebow, Jay L. 1983. Research Assessing Consumer Satisfaction with Mental Health Treatment: A Review of Findings." *Evaluation and Program Planning* 6:211–236.

LeCroy, Craig Winston. 1986. "Evaluation of Preventive Interventions for Enhancing Social Competence in Adolescents." *Social Work Research and Abstracts* 22: 8–16.

LeCroy, Craig Winston and Sheldon D. Rose. 1985. "Methodological Issues in the Evaluation of Social Work Practice." *Social Service Review* 59:345–357.

Lehman, Anthony F. and T. R. Zastowny. 1983. "Patient Satisfaction with Mental

Health Services: A Meta-Analysis to Establish Norms." *Evaluation and Program Planning* 6:265–274.

Levin, John R., Leonard A. Marasculio, and Lawrence Hubert Jr. 1978. "N = Nonparametric Randomization Tests." In Kratochwill, ed., *Single Subject Research: Strategies for Evaluating Change*, q.v.

Leviton, Laura D. and Edward F. Hughes. 1981. "Research on the Utilization of Evaluations, A Review and Synthesis." *Evaluation Review* 5:525–548.

Levitt, John L. and William J. Reid. 1981. "Rapid Assessment Instruments for Social Work Practice." *Social Work Research and Abstracts* 17:13–19.

Lewis, Oscar. 1959. *Five Families: Mexican Case Studies in the Culture of Poverty.* New York: Basic Books.

Lincoln, Yvonna S. and Egon G. Guba. 1985. *Naturalistic Inquiry.* Beverly Hills, Calif.: Sage Publications.

Locke, Harvey J. and Karl M. Wallace. 1959. "Short Marital-Adjustment and Prediction Tests: Their Reliability and Validity." *Marriage and Family Living* 21:251–255.

Loeb, Armin, Aaron T. Beck, and James Diggory. 1971. "Differential Effects of Success and Failure on Depressed and Nondepressed Patients." *Journal of Nervous and Mental Disorders* 152:106–114.

Lofland, John and Lyn H. Lofland. 1986. *A Guide to Qualitative Observation and Analysis.* 2d ed. Belmont, Calif.: Wadsworth.

Logan, Thomas H. 1977. *Use of Program Data in Continuing Needs Assessment.* Madison: University of Wisconsin, Department of Urban and Regional Planning. SHR-0001822.

Luborsky, Lester, Singer Barton, and Lise Luborsky. 1975. "Comparative Studies of Psychotherapy." *Archives of General Psychiatry* 32:995–1008.

Maas, Henry S., ed. 1966. *Five Fields of Social Service: Reviews of Research.* New York: National Association of Social Workers.

—— 1971. *Research in the Social Services: A Five Year Review.* New York: National Association of Social Workers.

—— 1979. *Social Service Research. Reviews of Studies.* New York: National Association of Social Workers.

McCabe, Alice et al. 1967. *The Pursuit of Promise.* New York: Community Service Society.

McFall, Robert M. and Craig Twentyman. 1973. "Four Experiments in the Relative Contribution of Rehearsal Modeling and Coaching to Assertion Training." *Journal of Abnormal Psychology* 81:199–218.

McKillup, Jack. 1987. "Need Analysis: Tools for the Human Services and Education." *Applied Social Research Methods Series* (10).

McNeece, C. Aaron., Diana M. DiNitto, and Peter J. Johnson. 1983. "The Utility of Evaluation Research for Administrative Decision Making."*Administration in Social Work* 7:77–87.

Mahrer, Alvin R. and W. P. Nadler. 1986. "Good Moments in Psychotherapy: A Preliminary Review, List, and Some Promising Research Avenues." *Journal of Consulting and Clinical Psychology* 54:10–15.

Maisto, Stephen A. and Christine A. Maisto. 1983. "Institutional Measures of

Marsh, Jeanne C. and Matsujiro Shibano, 1984. "Statistical Analysis of Time-Series Data." *Social Work Research and Abstracts,* 20:7–12.

Masters, Stanley, Irwin Garfinkel, and John Bishop. 1978. "Benefit-Cost Analysis in Program Evaluation." *Journal of Social Service Research* 2:79–93.

May, Edgar. 1964. *The Wasted Americans: Cost of our Welfare Dilemma.* New York: Harper and Row.

Mayer, John E. and Noel Timms. 1970. *The Client Speaks: Working Class Impressions of Casework.* New York: Atherton Press.

Mendelsohn, Henry N. 1987. *A Guide to Information Sources for Social Work and the Human Services.* New York: Onyx Press.

Mendenhall, William, Lyman Ott, and Richard H. Larson. 1974. *Statistics: A Tool for the Social Sciences.* North Scituate, Mass. Duxbury Press.

Merbaum, Michael and Michael R. Lowe. 1982. "Serendipity in Research in Clinical Psychology." In Kendall and Butcher, eds., *Handbook of Research Methods in Clinical Psychology,* q.v.

Meyer, Carol H. 1979. "What Directions for Direct Practice?" *Social Work* 24:267–272.

Miles, Mathew P. and A. Michael Huberman. 1984. *Qualitative Data Analysis.* Beverly Hills, Calif.: Sage Publications.

Miller, Donna. 1974. "The Influence of the Patient's Sex on Clinical Judgment." *Smith College Studies on Social Work* 44:89–100.

Miller, Roger R. 1958. "An Experimental Study of the Observational Process in Casework." *Social Work* 3:96–102.

Millman, Howard L. and Charles E. Schaefer. 1975. "Behavioral Change: Program Evaluation and Staff Feedback," *Child Welfare* 54:692–702.

Minahan, Anne and Allen Pincus. 1977. "Conceptual Framework for Social Work Practice." *Social Work* 55:347–352.

Minahan, Anne, ed. 1987. *Encyclopedia of Social Work* 18th ed. Silver Spring, Md.: National Association of Social Workers.

Mintz, Jim and Donald J. Kiesler. 1982. "Individualized Measures of Psychotherapy Outcome." In Kendall and Butcher, eds., *Handbook of Research Methods in Clinical Psychology,* q.v.

Mishler, Elliot G. 1986. *Reserach Interviewing: Context and Narrative.* Cambridge, Mass.: Harvard University Press.

Morgan, James N., Katherine Dickinson, Jonathan Dickinson, Jacob Benus, and Greg Duncan. 1974. *Five Thousand American Families: Patterns of Economic Progress.* Vols. 1 and 2. Ann Arbor: Institute for Social Studies, University of Michigan.

Mullen, Edward J. 1983. "Personal Practice Models." In Sharon Rosenblatt and Diana Waldfogel, eds., *Handbook of Clinical Social Work.* San Francisco: Jossey-Bass.

Mullen, Edward J., Robert Chazin, and David Feldstein. 1972. "Services for the Newly Dependent: An Assessment." *Social Service Review* 46:309–322.

Mullen, Edward J., James R. Dumpson, and Associates. 1972. *Evaluation of Social Intervention.* San Francisco: Jossey-Bass.

Murphy, Gerald J., Walter Hudson, and Paul P. L. Cheung. 1980. "Marital and Sexual Discord among Older Couples." *Social Work Research and Abstracts* 16(1):11–16.

Mustian, R. David and Joel S. See. 1973. "Indicators of Mental Health Needs An Empirical and Pragmatic Evaluation." *Journal of Health and Social Behavior* 14:23–27.

Mutschler, Elizabeth and Ram A. Cnaan. 1985. "Success and Failure of Computerized Information Systems Service Agencies." *Administration in Social Work* 9:67–79.

Nelsen, Judith C. 1978. "Use of Communication Theory in Single-Subject Research." *Social Work Research and Abstracts* 14(4):12–19.

—— 1984. "Intermediate Treatment Goals as Variables in Single Case Research." *Social Work Research and Abstracts* 20:3–10.

Nguyen, Tuan D., C. Clifford Attkisson, and Marilyn J. Bottino. 1976. "Definition and Identification of Human Service Need in a Community Context." In Bell et al., eds., *Need Assessment in Health and Human Services*, q.v.

Nuenring, Elane, Harvey Abrams, David Fike, and Ellen Fritsche Ostrowsky. 1983. "Evaluating the Impact of Prevention Programs Aimed at Children." *Social Work Research and Abstracts* 19:3–10.

Nugent, William. 1987. "Use and Evaluation of Theories." *Social Work Research and Abstracts* 23:14–10.

O'Connor, Richard and William J. Reid. 1986. "Dissatisfaction with Brief Treatment." *Social Service Review* 60:526–537.

Orlinsky, David E. and Kenneth I. Howard. 1986. "Process Outcome in Psychotherapy." In Garfield and Bergin, eds., *Handbook of Psychotherapy and Behavior Change*, q.v.

Orme, John G. and Terri Combs-Orme. 1986. "Statistical Power and Type II Errors in Social Work Research." *Social Work Research and Abstracts* 22:3–10.

Orme, John G. and Richard M. Tolman. 1986. "The Statistical Power of A Decade of Social Work Education Research." *Social Service Review* 60:619–632.

Owan, Tom C. 1978. "Improving Productivity in the Public Sector through Bilingual-Bicultural Staff." *Social Work Research and Abstracts* 14(1)10–18.

Pagano, Robert R. 1986. "Understanding Statistics on the Behavioral Sciences." 2d ed. St. Paul, Minn.: West.

Parihar, Bageshwari. 1984. *Task-Centered Management in Human Services*. Springfield, Ill.: Charles C. Thomas.

Patti, Rino. 1985. "In Search of Purpose for Social Welfare Administration." *Administration in Social Work* 9:1–14.

Patton, Michael Q. 1978. *Focused Evaluation*. Beverly Hills, Calif.: Sage Publications.

Pauley, P. Ann and Stan Cohen. 1984. "Facilitating Data-Based Decision-Making Managers' Use of Data in a Community Mental Health Center." *Evaluation Review* 8:205–224.

Perlman, Helen Harris. 1957. "Social Casework: A Problem-Solving Process. Chicago: University of Chicago Press.

—— 1963. "Some Notes on the Waiting List." *Social Casework* 44:200–205.

Pharis, David B. 1976. "The Use of Needs Assessment Techniques in Mental Health Planning." *Community Mental Health Review* 1:1, 5–11.

Phillips, Bernard. 1985. *Sociological Research Methods: An Introduction.*" Homewood, Ill: Dorsey Press.

Phillips, John L. Jr. 1971. *Statistical Thinking.* San Francisco: W. H. Freeman.

Pincus, Allen and Anne Minahan. 1973. *Social Work Practice: Model and Method.* Itasca, Ill.: F. E. Peacock.

Pinkston, Elsie M. and Emily W. Herbert-Jackson. 1975. "Modification of Irrelevant and Bizarre Verbal Behavior Using Parents as Therapists." *Social Service Review* 49:46–63.

Pinsof, William M. 1986. "The Process of Family Therapy: The Development of the Family Therapist Coding System." In Greenberg and Pinsoff eds., *The Psychotherapeutic Process,* q.v.

Poertner, John and Charles A. Rapp. 1986. "Purchase of Service and Accountability: Will They Ever Meet?" *Administration in Social Work* 9:57–66.

Polansky, Norman. 1975. *Social Work Research: Methods for the Helping Professions.* Chicago: University of Chicago Press.

Rankin, Eric D. and Jeanne C. Marsh. 1985. "Effects of Missing Data on the Statistical Analysis of Clinical Time Series." *Social Work Research and Abstracts* 21:13–16.

Rapp, Charles A. 1984. "Information, Performance, and the Human Service Manager of the 1980s: Beyond 'Housekeeping.'" *Administration in Social Work* 8:69–80.

Regier, D. A., J. K. Meyers, M. Kramer, L. N. Robins, D. G. Blazer, R. L. Hough, W. W. Eaton, and B. A. Locke. 1984. "The MIMH Epidemiologic Catchment Area Program." *Archives of General Psychiatry* 41:934–941.

Reid, William J. 1967. "A Study of Caseworkers' Use of Insight-Oriented Techniques." *Social Casework* 48:1–7.

Reid, William J. 1974. "Developments in the Use of Organized Data." *Social Work* 19:585–593.

—— 1975a. "A Test of a Task-Centered Approach." *Social Work* 20:3–9.

—— 1975b. "Applications of Computer Technology." In Norman Polansky, ed., *Social Work Research,* q.v.

—— 1977. "Social Work for Social Problems." *Social Work* 22:374–381.

—— 1978. *The Task-Centered System.* New York: Columbia University Press.

—— 1979a. "Evaluation Research in Social Work." *Evaluation and Program Planning* 2:209–217.

—— 1979b. "The Model Development Dissertation." *Journal of Social Service Research* 3:215–225.

—— 1980. "Research Strategies for Improving Individualized Services." In David Fanshel, ed., *Future of Social Work Research,* q.v.

—— 1984. "Treatment of Choice or Choice of Treatments: An Essay Review." *Social Work Research and Abstracts* 20:33–37.

—— 1985. *Family Problem Solving.* New York: Columbia University Press.

—— 1987. "Research in Social Work." In Anne Minahan, ed. *Encyclopedia of Social Work*, q.v.

—— 1988. "The Metamodel, Research and Empirical Practice." In Eleanor Reardon Tolson, ed. *The Metamodel and Clinical Social Work*. New York: Columbia University Press.

Reid, William and Inger P. Davis. 1987. "Qualitative Methods in Single Case Research." In Naomi Gotelieb, ed., *Proceedings of Conference on Practitioners as Evaluators of Direct Practice*. School of Social Work, University of Washington, Seattle.

Reid, William J. and Laura Epstein, eds. 1972. *Task-Centered Casework*. New York: Columbia University Press.

Reid, William J. and Laura Epstein, eds., 1977. *Task-Centered Practice*. New York: Columbia University Press.

Reid, William J. and Patricia Hanrahan. 1982. "Recent Evaluations of Social Work: Grounds for Optimism." *Social Work* 27:328–340.

Reid, William J., Richard M. Kagan, Alison Kaminsky, and Katherine Helmer. 1987. "Adoption of Older Institutionalized Youth." *Social Casework: A Journal of Contemporary Social Work* 68:140–149.

Reid, William J. and Barbara L. Shapiro. 1969. "Client Reaction to Advice." *Social Service Review* 43:165-173.

Reid, William J. and Ann Shyne. 1969, *Brief and Extended Casework*. New York: Columbia University Press.

Reid, William J. and Audrey D. Smith. 1981. *Research in Social Work*. New York: Columbia University Press.

Reid, William J. and Pamela Strother. (In press.) "Super Problem Solvers: A Case Study." *Social Service Review*.

Rein, Martin and Lisa Peattie. 1981. "Knowledge for Policy." *Social Service Review* 55:525–543.

Rein, Martin, and Sheldon H. White. 1981. "Knowledge for Practice." *Social Service Review* 55:1–41.

Rice, Laura N. and Leslie S. Greenberg, eds. 1984. *Patterns of Change: Intensive Analysis of Psychotherapy Process*. New York: Guilford Press.

Rice, Roger E. and Gloria Fowler, 1973. *Relationship of Mental Health Admission Rates and Other Selected Social Characteristics Among Twenty-five Geographical Areas*. Los Angeles: County Department of Health Services. SHR-0001592.

Rich, Robert F. 1977. "Uses of Social Science Information by Federal Bureaucrats: Knowledge for Action Versus Knowledge for Understanding." In C. H. Weiss, ed., *Using Social Research in Public Policy Making*. Lexington, Mass.: Lexington Books.

Richey, Cheryl A., Betty J. Blythe, and Sharon B. Berlin. 1987. "Do Social Workers Evaluate Their Practice?" *Social Work Research and Abstracts* 23:14–20.

Richmond, Mary. 1917. *Social Diagnosis*. New York: Russell Sage Foundation.

Ripple, Lillian. 1960. "Problem Identification and Formulation." In Norman A. Polansky, ed., *Social Work Research*, q.v.

—— 1964. *Motivation, Capacity, and Opportunity: Studies in Casework Therapy and Practice*. Chicago: School of Social Service Administration, University of Chicago.

—— 1971. "Family Interaction Scales." In Winter and Ferreira, eds., *Research in Family Interaction*, q.v.

Rogers, Carl R., Gene T. Gendlin, Donald V. Kiesler, and Charles B. Truax. 1967. "The Therapeutic Conditions Antecedent to Change: A Theoretical View." In Carl R. Rogers, Gene T. Gendlin, Donald V. Kiesler, and Charles B. Truax, eds. *The Therapeutic Relationship and Its Impact: A Study of Psychotherapy with Schizophrenics*. Madison: University of Wisconsin Press.

Rooney, Ronald H. 1978. "Prolonged Foster Care: Toward a Problem-Oriented Task-Centered Practice Model." Ph.D. dissertation, University of Chicago.

—— 1981. "A Task-Centered Reunification Model for Foster Care." In A. Mallucio and P. Sinanoglu, eds., *The Challenge of Partnership: Working with Parents of Children in Foster Care*. New York: Child Welfare League of America.

—— 1985. "Does In Service Training Make a Difference? Results of a Pilot Study of Task-Centered Dissemination in a Public Social Service Setting." *Journal of Social Service Research* 8:33–50.

Rose, Sheldon D. 1975. "In Pursuit of Social Competence." *Social Work*. 20:33–39.

Rosen, Aaron and Enola A. Proctor. 1978. "Specifying the Treatment Process: The Basis for Effectiveness." *Journal of Social Service Research* 24:25–41.

Rosen, Sidney and Normal A. Polansky. 1975. "Observation of Social Interaction." In Polansky, ed., *Social Work Research*, q.v.

Rosenberg. Morris. 1968. *The Logic of Survey Analysis*. New York: Basic Books.

Rosenthal, Robert. 1966. *Experimenter Effects in Behavioral Research*. New York: Appleton-Century Crofts.

Roskin, M. 1982. "Coping with Life Changes: A Preventive Social Work Approach." *American Journal of Community Psychology* 10:331–339.

Rossi, Peter and Howard Freeman. 1985. *Evaluation: A Systematic Approach*, 3d ed. Beverly Hills, Calif.: Sage Publications.

Rothman, Jack. 1980. *Social R & D Research and Development in the Human Services*. Englewood Cliffs, N.J.: Prentice-Hall.

Rubin, Allen. 1985. "Practice Effectiveness: More Grounds for Optimism." *Journal of the National Association of Social Workers* 30:469–476.

Rubin, Allen and Patricia Conway. 1985. "Standards for Determining the Magnitude of Relationships in Social Work Research." *Social Work Research and Abstracts* 21:34–39.

Rubin, Herbert J. 1983. *Applied Social Research*. Columbus, Ohio: Charles E. Merrill.

Ruckdeschell, Roy. 1985. "Qualitative Research as a Perspective." *Social Work Research and Abstracts* 21:17–21.

Ruckdeschell, Roy A. and Bufard, E. Farris. 1981. "Assessing Practice: A Critical Look at the Single-Case Design." *Social Casework: A Journal of Contemporary Social Work* 62:413–419.

Sarri, Rosemary. 1982. "Management Trends in the Human Services." *Administration in Social Work* 6:19–30.

Scheff, Janet. 1976. "The Use of Client Utilization Data to Determine Social Planning Needs." In Roger A. Bell et al., eds., *Need Assessment in Health and Human Services*, q.v.

Schinke, Steven P., Lewayne D. Gilchrist, Thomas E. Smith, and Steven E. Wong. 1978. "Improving Teenage Mothers' Ability to Compete for Jobs." *Social Work Research and Abstracts* 14(3):25–29.

Schlesinger, Benjamin. 1963. *The Multi-Problem Family: A Review and Annotated Bibliography*. Toronto, Canada: University of Toronto Press.

Schneider, Mark. 1975. "The Quality of Life in Large American Cities: Objective and Subjective Social indicators." *Social Indicators Research* 1:495–509.

Schoech, Dick. 1987. "Information Systems: Agency." In Anne Minahan, ed., *Encyclopedia of Social Work*, q.v.

Schuerman, John R. 1982. "The Obsolete Scientific Imperative in Social Work Research." *Social Service Review* 56:144–148.

—— 1983. *"Multivariate Analysis in the Human Services*. Boston: Kluwer-Nijhoff.

—— 1987. "Passion, Analysis, and Technology: The Social Service Review Lecture." *Social Service Review* 61:3–18.

Schwartz, Edward E. 1966. "Strategies of Research in Public Welfare Administration: The Field Experiment." In *Trends in Social Work Practice and Knowledge: NASW Tenth Anniversary Symposium*, pp. 164–178. New York: National Association of Social Workers.

Schwartz, Edward E. and William C. Sample. 1972. *The Midway Office*. New York: National Association of Social Workers.

Scriven, Michael. 1969. "Logical Positivism and the Behavioral Sciences." In Peter Achinstein and Stephen Barker, eds., *The Legacy of Logical Positivism*. Baltimore: Johns Hopkins University Press.

Seaberg, James R. 1965. "Case Recording by Code." *Social Work* 10:92–98.

—— 1970. "Systematized Recording: A Follow-Up." *Social Work* 15:32–41.

Seaberg, James R. and David F. Gillespie. 1977. "Goal Attainment Scaling: A Critique." *Social Work Research and Abstracts* 13(2):4–9.

Seaberg, James and Eve Tolley. 1986. "Predictors of the Length of Stay in Foster Care." *Social Work Research* 22:11–17.

Selltiz, Claire, Lawrence Wrightsman, and Stuart W. Cook, eds. 1976. *Research Methods in Social Relations*. 3d ed. New York: Holt, Rinehart and Winston.

Shapiro, Arthur K. and Louis A. Morris. 1978. "The Placebo Effect in Medical and Psychological Therapies." In Garfield and Bergin, eds., *Handbook of Psychotherapy and Behavior Change*, q.v.

Shapiro, Arthur K. 1984. "Opening Comments: 'What Works With What?' Psychotherapy Efficacy for Specific Disorders: An Overview of the Research." In Janet B. W. Williams and Robert L. Spitzer, eds., *Psychotherapy Research: Where are We and Where Should We Go?* New York: Guilford Press.

Sheafor, Bradford W., and Pamela S. Landon. 1987. "General and Emergency Assistance." In Anne Minahan, ed., *Encyclopedia of Social Work*, q.v.

Sherman, Edward and Katherine Skinner. (In press.) "Client Language and Clinical Process: A Cognitive Semantic Snslysis." *Clinical Social Work Journal*.

Sherwood, Clarence D., John W. Morris, and Sylvia Sherwood. 1975. "A Multivariate, Nonrandomized Matching Technique for Studying the Impact of Social Interventions." In Elmer L. Struening and Marcia Guttentag, eds., *Handbook of Evaluation Research,* q.v.

Shewart, W. A. 1931. *Economic Control of Quality of Manufactured Product.* New York: Van Nostrand Reinhold.

Shyne, Ann W. 1975. "Exploiting Available Information." In Norman A. Polansky, ed., *Social Work Research,* q.v.

—— 1980. "Who Are the Children? A National Overview of Services." *Social Work Research and Abstracts* 16(1):26–33.

Shyne, Ann W., ed. 1959. *Social Worker Judgments as Data.* New York: National Association of Social Workers.

Sidman, Murray. 1960. *Tactics of Scientific Research.* New York: Basic Books.

Siegel, Larry M., C. Clifford Attkisson, and Linda G. Carson. 1978. "Need Identification and Program Planning in the Community Context." In Attkinsson et al., eds., *Evaluation of Human Service Programs,* q.v.

Siegel, Larry M., C. Clifford Attkisson, and Anne H. Cohn. 1977. "Mental Health Needs Assessments: Strategies and Techniques." In William A. Hargreaves, James E. Sorenson, and C. Clifford Attkisson, eds., *Resource Materials for Community Mental Health Program Evaluation,* q.v.

Siegel, Sidney. 1956. *Nonparametric Statistics for the Behavioral Sciences.* New York: McGraw-Hill.

Simons, Ronald L. and Stephen M. Aigner. 1985. *Practice Principles: A Problem Solving Approach to Social Work.* New York: Macmillan.

Sloane, R. Bruce, Fred R. Staples, Allan H. Cristol, Neil J. Yorkston, and Katherine Whipple. 1975. *Psychotherapy versus Behavior Therapy.* Cambridge, Mass.: Harvard University Press.

Smith, Audrey D. and Gregory M. St. L. O'Brien. 1978, "The Carrot and the Stick." In Charles D. Garvin, Audrey D. Smith, and William J. Reid, eds. *The Work Incentive Experience,* q.v.

Smith, Audrey D. and William J. Reid. 1986. *Role-Sharing Marriage.* New York: Columbia University Press,

Spanier, Graham B. 1976. "Measuring Dyadic Adjustment: New Scales for Assessing the Quality of Marriage and Similar Dyads." *Journal of Marriage and the Family* 38:15–28.

Spitzer, Robert L., Jean Endicott, Joseph Heiss, and Jacob Cohen, 1970. "The Psychiatric Status Schedule: A Technique for Evaluating Psychopathology and Impairment in Role Functioning." *Archives of General Psychiatry* 23:41–55.

Sprinthall, Richard C. 1987. *Basic Statistical Analysis.* 2d ed. Englewood Cliffs, N.J.: Prentice-Hall.

Stein, Theodore J. and Eileen D. Gambrill. 1976. *Decision-Making in Foster Care: A Training Manual.* Berkeley: University of California Press.

Stein, Theodore J. and Eileen D. Gambrill. 1977. "Facilitating Decision Making in Foster Care: The Alameda Project." *Social Service Review* 51:502–513.

Stein, Theodore J., Eileen D. Gambrill, and Kermit T. Wiltse. 1978. *Children in Foster Homes.* New York: Praeger.

Stevens, S. 1951. "Mathematics, Measurement, and Psychophysics." In S. Stevens, ed., *Handbook of Experimental Psychology*. New York: Wiley.

Stewart, Richard. 1979. "The Nature of Needs Assessment in Community Mental Health." *Community Mental Health Journal* 15:287–295.

Stewart, Richard and Larry Poaster. 1975. "Methods of Assessing Mental and Physical Health Needs from Social Statistics." *Evaluation* 2:67–70.

Stollack, Gary E. 1967. "Weight Loss Obtained under Different Experimental Procedures." *Psychotherapy: Theory, Research and Practice* 4:61–64.

Struening, Elmer L. 1975. "Social Area Analysis as a Method of Evaluation." In Struening and Guttentag, eds., *Handbook of Evaluation Research*, q.v.

—— 1975. "Social Area Analysis as a Method of Evaluation." In Struening and Guttentag, eds., *Handbook of Evaluation Research*, q.v.

Struening, Elmer and Marcia Guttentag, eds. 1975. *Handbook of Evaluation Research*. 2 vols. Beverly Hills, Calif.: Sage Publications.

Strupp, Hans H. 1958. "The Psychotherapist's Contribution to the Treatment Process. *Behavioral Science* 3:34–67.

Strupp, Hans H. and S. W. Hadley. 1977. A tripartite Model of Mental Health and Therapeutic Outcomes: with Special Reference to Negative Effects in Psychotherapy." *American Psychologist* 32:187–196.

Stuart, Richard B. and Tony Tripodi, 1973. "Experimental Evaluation of Three Time-Constrained Behavioral Treatments for Pre-delinquents and Delinquents." In Richard D. Rubin, J. Paul Brady, and John D. Henderson, eds., *Advances in Behavior Therapy*. New York: Academic Press.

Sudman, Seymour. 1976. *Applied Sampling*. New York: Academic Press.

Taylor, D. W., P. C. Berry, and C. H. Block, 1958. "Does Group Participation When Using Brainstorming Facilitate or Inhibit Creative Thinking?" *Administrative Science Quarterly* 3:23–47.

Teare, Robert J. 1979. "A Task Analysis of Public Welfare Practice and Educational Implications." In Clark, Arkava, and Associates, eds., *The Pursuit of Competence in Social Work*, q.v.

Thomas, Edwin J. 1962. "Experimental Analogs of the Casework Interview." *Social Work* 7:24–30.

—— 1977. *Marital-Communication and Decision-Making: Analysis, Assessment and Change*. New York: Free Press.

—— 1978. "Mousetraps, Developmental Research, and Social Work Education." *Social Service Review* 52:468–483.

—— *Designing Interventions for the Helping Professions*. Beverly Hills, Calif.: Sage Publications.

—— 1987. "Assessing Procedural Descriptiveness: Rationale and Illustrative Study." *Behavioral Assessment* 9:43–56.

Thomas, Edwin J., Roland Etcheverry, and Robert Keller. 1975. "Repertoires of Behavioral and Nonbehavioral Treatment Methods Used in Social Work." *Social Service Review* 49:107–114.

Thomas, Edwin J. and Donna L. McLeod. 1960. *In-Service Training and Reduced Workloads—Experiments in a State Department of Welfare*. New York: Russell Sage Foundation.

Thompson, Victor A. and D. W. Smithburg. 1968. "A Proposal for the Study of Innovation in Organization." Huntsville, University of Alabama. Manuscript.

Tolson, Eleanor, 1977. "Alleviating Marital Communications Problems." In William J. Reid and Laura Epstein, eds., *Task-Centered Practice.* q.v.

Toseland, Ronald W. and William J. Reid. 1985. "Using Rapid Assessment Instruments in a Family Service Agency." *Social Casework* 66:547–555.

Toseland, Ronald W. and Sheldon D. Rose. 1978. "Evaluating Social Skills Training for Older Adults in Groups." *Social Work Research and Abstracts* 14(1): 25–33.

Toseland, Ronald W., Edmund Sherman, and S. Bliven. 1981. "The Comparative Effectiveness of Two Group Work Approaches for the Development of Mutual Support Groups Among the Elderly." *Social Work with Groups* 4:137–153.

Tripodi, Tony and Irwin Epstein. 1980. *Research Techniques for Clinical Social Workers.* New York: Columbia University Press.

Tripodi, Tony and Janice Harrington. 1979. "Use of Time-Series Designs for Formative Program Evaluation." *Journal of Social Service Research* 3:67–78.

Tripodi, Tony, Phillip Fellin, and Henry Meyer. 1983. *The Assessment of the Social Research.* 2d ed. Itasca, Ill.: Peacock.

—— 1969. *The Assessment of Social Research: Guidelines for the Use of Research in Social Work and Social Science.* Itasca, Ill.: Peacock.

Truax, Charles B. 1967. "A Scale for the Rating of Accurate Empathy." In Rogers et al., eds. *The Therapeutic Relationship and Its Impact,* q.v.

Turkat, Ira D. 1986. "The Behavioral Interview." In Cimeron, Calhoun, and Adams, eds., *Handbook of Behavioral Assessment,* q.v.

Vaillant, George E. and Eva S. Milofsky. 1982. "Natural History of Male Alcoholism: Paths to Recovery." *Archives of General Psychiatry* 39:127–133.

Van de Ven, Andrew H. and Andre L. Delbecq. 1974. "The Effectiveness of Nominal, Delphi, and Interacting Group Decision-Making Processes." *Academy of Management Journal* 17:605–621.

Videka-Sherman, Lynn and Harriet M. Bartlett. 1985. "Practice Effectiveness Project: Final Report to NASW Board of Directors."

Videka-Sherman, Lynn and William J. Reid. 1982. "The Structured Clinical Record: A Clinical Education Tool." *The Clinical Supervisor* 3:45–62.

Vogel, Lynn Harold. 1985. "Decision Support Systems in the Human Services: Discovering Limits to a Promising Technology." *Computers in Human Services* 1:67–80.

Wallace, David. 1967. "The Chemung County Evaluation of Casework Service to Dependent Multi-Problem Families: Another Problem Outcome." *Social Service Review* 41:379–389.

Warheit, George, Roger A. Bell, and John J. Schwab. 1977. *Needs Assessment Approaches: Concepts and Methods.* Department of Health, Education, and Welfare. NIMH Publication ADM 77-472.

Warheit, George J., Joanne M. Buhl, and Roger A. Bell. 1978. "A Critique of Social Indicators Analysis and Key Informants Survey as Needs Assessment Methods." *Evaluation and Program Planning* 1:239–247.

Waskow, Irene E. and Morris B. Parloff, eds. 1975. *Psychotherapy Change Measures.* DHEW Pub. No. (ADM) 74-120. Rockville, Md.: National Institute of Mental Health.

Watzlawick, Paul, Janet Helmick Beavin, and Don D. Jackson. 1967. *Pragmatics of Human Communication.* New York: Norton.

Weed, Lawrence l. 1969. *Medical Records, Medical Education; and Patient Care: The Problem-Oriented Record as a Basic Tool.* Cleveland: Case Western Reserve University Press.

Weinstein, Abbott S. 1975. "Evaluation through Medical Records and Related Information Systems." In Elmer Struening and Marcia Guttentag, eds., *Handbook of Evaluation Research,* q.v.

Weiss, Audrey Teren. 1975. "The Consumer Model of Assessing Community Mental Health Needs." *Evaluation* 2:71–73.

Weiss, Carol H. 1972. *Evaluation Research: Methods of Assessing Program Effectiveness.* Englewood Cliffs, N.J.: Prentice-Hall.

—— 1975. "Interviewing in Evaluation Research." In Elmer Struening and Marcia Guttentag, eds., *Handbook of Evaluation Research,* q.v.

Weiss, Carol H. and Michael J. Bucuvalas. 1980. *Social Science Research and Decision-Making.* New York: Columbia University Press.

Weissman, Myrna, G. L. Klerman, B. Prusoff, and B. Hanson. 1974. "Treatment Effects on the Social Adjustment of Depressed Patients." *Archives of General Psychiatry* 30:771–778.

Weissman, Myrna, E. Paykel, R. Seigel, and G. Klerman. 1971. "The Social Role Performance of Depressed Women: A Comparison with a Normal Sample." *American Journal of Orthopsychiatry* 41:390–405.

Wells, Richard A., Jeanne A. Figurel, and Patrick McNamee. 1977. "Communication Training vs. Conjoint Marital Therapy." *Social Work Research and Abstracts* 13(2):31–39.

Weissman, Myrna, D. Sholomskas, & John K. The Assessment of Social Adjustment. *Archives of General Psychiatry,* 38:1250–1258.

White, O. R. 1972. "A Manual for the Calculation and Use of the Median Slope-A Technique of Progress Estimation and Prediction in the Single Case." Regional Resource Center for Handicapped Children, Eugene, University of Oregon.

—— 1974. "'The Split-Middle'—A Quickie Method of Trend Estimation." Experimental Education Unit, Child Development and Mental Retardation Center, University of Washington.

Whyte, William F. 1981. *Street Corner Society.* 3d ed. Chicago: University of Chicago Press.

Wiehe, Vernon. 1984. "Self-Esteem, Attitude Toward Parents and Focus of Control in Children of Divorced, and Non-Divorced Families." *Journal of Social Service Research* 8:17–28.

Windle, Charles et al. 1975. "A Demographic System for Comparative Assessment of Needs for Mental Health Services." *Evaluation* 2:73–76.

Wood, Katherine M. 1978. "Casework Effectiveness: A New Look at the Research Evidence." *Social Work* 23:437–458.

Yalom, Irving D. 1985. *The Theory and Practice of Group Psychotherapy.* 3d ed. New York: Basic Books.

Zastrow, Charles and Ralph Navarre. 1979. "Using Videotaped Role Play to Develop and Assess Competence." In Clark, Arkava, and Associates, eds., *The Pursuit of Competence in Social Work*, q.v.

Zimbalist, Sidney. 1955. "Major Trends in Social Work Research: An Analysis of the Nature of Development of Research in Social Work, as seen in the Periodical Literature, 1900–1950." Ph.D. dissertation, Washington University, St. Louis.

AUTHOR INDEX

SUBJECT INDEX

Goal, definition of, 311
Goal Attainment Scaling (GAS), 296-98
Graphs, 249-50
Group experiments, 137-74; uncontrolled single, 137-43; exploratory, 138-42; "classical," 143-52; equivalent, 143-63; partial crossover, 152-53; micro, 154-55; comparative, 155-63; factorial, 159-63; nonequivalent, 163-68; time-series, 168-69; the experimental intervention, 169-71; generalization from, 171-72; analog studies, 172-74
Groups: homogeneous 79-80; in sampling, 79-83; multiple, 80-81; heterogeneous, 81-83
Group time-series design, 168-69
Guttman (cumulative) scaling, 220

Halo effect, 234
Hawthorne effect, 132
Heisenberg principle, 132
Heterogeneous group study, 81-83
Historical perspective, 36-40; scientific philanthropy, 37; survey movement, 39-40
History, as source of extraneous variance, 106
Hollis casework treatment classification scheme, 70
Homogeneity, aspect of reliability, 204-5
Homogeneous group study, 79-82, 96-97
Human-as-instrument, 88
Hypotheses: and inquiry, 43-44; and theory, 44-49; causal, 46-47, 49-50; definition, 49; formulating, 49-57; relational, 50; criteria for evaluating, 52-54; vs. questions, 56-57; research and null, in statistical testing, 261-62; rival, *see* Alternative explanations

Ideographic instruments, 334-35
Independent variable(s), 61-62
Indicators: of program outcomes, 315-16; of concepts, *see* Operational definitions
Inferential statistics, 259-69
Initial differences, *see* Selection
Inquiry: in social work practice and research, 43-44; role of theory in, 48-49; hypotheses and questions in, 49-57
Instability, of outcome measures, 109, 116
Instrumentation, as a source of extraneous variance, 107

Instrument construction, in interviews and questionnaires, 221-23
Instruments: standardized, 329-32; particularized, 332-33; ideographic, 334-35; decisions about, 335-36
Interaction among variables, 78-79, 162, 272-73, 277-78
Interaction Process Analysis, (IPA) system, 235
Internal measurement (scales), 197
Internal validity: threats to, 106-10; in single case experiments, 110-29; in classical (group) experiments, 150-52; *see also* Alternative explanations
Interobserver reliability, 203-4
Interpretation of research data, defined, 244
Intervening variables, 61-62, 271
Intervention characteristics, study of, 339-55; practitioner report data, 340-43; clients' impressions, 343-44; electronic observation and content analysis, 343-44; direct observation, 345-46; intervention analogs, 348-54; participant observation, 354-55
Intervention in social work: defined, 7; program and case, 10; knowledge, 12-13; manipulating in experiments, 60; problems in determining effectiveness of, 104-10; difficulty in defining, 107-8; placebo effects, 108; specificity of, 112; experimental, 169-71; analog studies of effects of, 172-74; *see also* Single case experiments; Group experiments
Interviews and questionnaires, 211-26; comparison of methods, 212-14; degree of structure, 214-15; type of questions, 215-18; use of scales in, 218-20; instrument construction, 221-23; in small-scale studies, 225-26; in study of intervention characteristics, 342-43
Interviews, types of: in-person, 213; telephone, 213-14; structured, 213-14; standardized, 214-15; unstructured, non-directive, clinical, 214-15; semi-structured, 215

Key informant studies, 307-9
Knowledge and technology: research-based, 17-20; terms differentiated, 20
Knowledge-building functions of research: exploratory, 68; measurement, 69-70; description, 70-71; explanation, 71-79